DUTY, HONOR, VIETNAM

TWELVE MEN OF WEST POINT TELL THEIR STORIES

IVAN PRASHKER

WARNER BOOKS

A Warner Communications Company

THE CRITICS SALUTE

"Prashker is a superb storyteller, creating vivid, memorable images of these men and their times."
—*Richmond News Leader*

* * *

"Written with clarity and understanding... winning and original... extraordinary.... Every serious student or reader of the Vietnam conflict should add this outstanding book to his or her library."
—*Charlotte Observer*

* * *

"Vivid... recommended."

—*Library Journal*

* * *

"Testifies to the high caliber of today's Army... a fact worth celebrating."

—*Washington Post Book World*

* * *

"The real pleasure in Prashker's volume comes from meeting 12 men from varied backgrounds who went through the greater stress of West Point—to survive the greater stress of combat in Vietnam."
—Lieutenant Colonel Bruce Bell, Directorate of Academy Relations, USMA (from a review in *Assembly*, the West Point alumni magazine

FOR CREDE,
AND IN MEMORY OF
ANNE AND ROMAN PRASHKER
AND MORRIS EINHORN

Contents

Prologue

"Imagine that you are creating a fabric of human destiny with the object of making men happy in the end, giving them peace and rest at last, but that it was essential and inevitable to torture to death only one tiny creature . . . and to found that edifice on its unavenged tears, would you consent to be the architect of these conditions?" Dostoyevski writes in *The Brothers Karamazov*. Of course, the answer is no, and it's the child's utter innocence that makes the question so terrifying.

But equally terrifying is the more modern tapestry showing children, ten years old, or perhaps twelve, tossing grenades into bunkers and concealing in their clothing and illustrated school-books highly secret maps or booby-trap parts later to be used by their fathers or older brothers. When children are compelled to kill, the phrase "robbed of their childhood" becomes an absurdity. Yet, of the many terrible things that occurred during the Vietnam War, innumerable small children masquerading as angels of death seems among the most terrible.

Meanwhile, on the other side of the world, cadets at West Point were still being told they were soon to become members of a professional fraternity, one not dissimilar to those of doctors and priests. And because they'd face countless life-and-death situations during the course of their careers, as do doctors and priests, they were offered an honor code that provided a standard of behavior they'd find not merely helpful but one, they were told, was absolutely necessary.

In point of fact, America adopted its conception of military honor from the British, Morris Janowitz notes in *The Professional Soldier* (1960), and it had four components: Officers were gentlemen, members of a self-regulative brotherhood, fought for glory, and offered personal fealty to their commander.

It was during World War I that the notion of an officer as a kind of international sportsman periodically engaged in a violent struggle suffered a grievous loss. How could it not once the trenches resembled not so much battlefields as abattoirs? The phenomenon of mass war, in short, made the very idea of combatant sportsmanship a mockery.

Nevertheless, West Point persists to this day in maintaining an honor code embodying a kind of rarefied sportsmanship as its institutional spine. At the Academy, cadets are taught to embrace an image of themselves essential to their existence. In sustaining that image, a definition of how an officer should act, young men presumably doom themselves to nobility.

Which explains, in part, why American society still finds itself fascinated by West Point and continues to lavish enormous sums upon its upkeep and upon the programs the institution insists it must foster. It's as if a society in thrall to success as measured by the accumulation of vast amounts of money still feels the fugitive, touching need at least to remind itself of the possibility of something as precious and gossamer as honor.

In order to perpetuate that possibility, the nation constructed a stony monastery on a bluff overlooking the Hudson Valley, surrounding it with overarching trees and sequestering it in bosky isolation. Yet the river traffic below, if not the splendid river itself, serves to remind those temporarily quartered within the monastery that beyond and not too far distant lies the wider world where even acolytes, nurtured on the bread and wine of honor for four years, must still retain the ability to function in the context of peculiarly terrible wars.

But given the intense pressures generated by a Vietnam, can those running the monastery continue regarding themselves as a purposeful governing body ruling a blessed fortress of stability in a dangerously unstable universe? Or are they forced to reevaluate their reason for being, making changes they find themselves compelled to administer if they wish to survive as a living entity? And what of the young monks they rush forth to foreign shores, proclaiming the virtues of not lying, not cheating, not stealing? In that world so brutalized where even children are taught to kill, can their monks' green coat of honor possibly avoid becoming a tattered rag of shame?

"It must be borne in mind that my design is not to create histories, but lives," Plutarch writes in *The Lives of the Noble Grecians and Romans*, and that will be the design here as well. Yet, clearly, without certain minimal historical facts, even the lives of "noble" men would soon appear untethered and insubstantial.

It is useful to note, then, that during the second week of January 1964, twenty-seven American helicopters flew onto an island in the Mekong River sixty miles south of Saigon, carrying fifteen hundred South Vietnamese soldiers. Together with an armada of junks ferrying another thousand soldiers, they destroyed a guerrilla training camp and supply depot defended by a Viet Cong battalion. Four Americans were killed and fifteen helicopters were hit. Gen. Paul Harkins, commander of the U.S. military forces in South Vietnam, had observed the operation.

The previous week, Lt. Gen. William Westmoreland had been called to the Pentagon, where he'd been told by Army chief of staff Earle Wheeler that he was being sent to Saigon as Harkins' deputy. Because Harkins had been closely identified with President Ngo Dinh Diem, who'd been assassinated less than three months before by the military now running the country, it was plain that Harkins had outlived his political usefulness and would eventually be replaced. In effect, Westmoreland would soon become commander of the U.S. military forces in South Vietnam.

His name had been one of four presented to President Johnson. But more than any of the other candidates, Westmoreland looked and sounded like a general. He had a jutting jaw and always seemed to walk twice as fast as men half his age. His personal bible was *The Power of Positive Thinking*, which fit with his burning ambition to command, take charge, provide men less courageous and decisive than himself with inspirational and energetic leadership.

Pushing particularly hard for the Westmoreland appointment had been Gen. Maxwell Taylor, chairman of the Joint Chiefs of Staff, who'd known Westmoreland since World War II, when they'd both served in the 82nd Airborne Division under Gen. Matthew Ridgway. Their paths had crossed a number of times after. It was Taylor who had appointed Westmoreland secretary to the General Staff, a little-known but bureaucratically powerful position, when he was Army chief of staff in the mid-1950s. Impressed by Westmoreland's devoted and skillful performance in that job, Taylor next offered him command of the illustrious and recently reactivated 101st Airborne Division. And it was Taylor again, two years later, who recommended Westmoreland's appointment as superintendent at West Point. By then, Secretary of Defense Robert McNamara and President Lyndon Johnson had been equally impressed.

Westmoreland had taken an advanced management course at the Harvard Business School in 1954, fitting in so seamlessly among the business executives who were his classmates that one of them later said, ''He might have been a vice president of a corporation.'' Throughout his career, Westmoreland indicated a passion for efficiency and a fondness for percentages. That meant he and McNamara, who'd not only once taught at Harvard but also emphasized charts and statistics when he was president of Ford, had many of the same instincts and spoke the same language.

According to Westmoreland's biographer, Ernest B. Furgurson, what appealed to Lyndon Johnson was the general's lingering southern accent, which the president first heard when, as Westmoreland's West Point guest, he'd addressed the graduating class of 1961. Johnson also thought that Westmoreland's recent exposure to teaching methods in a student environment would help when it came to improving the training of the Vietnamese Army. Finally, Johnson seemed most comfortable appointing obviously ambitious men to powerful jobs, as long as there were further promotions he could offer or withhold.

Even as a boy growing up in Pacolet Mills, South Carolina, twelve miles southeast of Spartanburg, Westmoreland liked to dress up in uniform and issue orders. His father managed a textile plant, later founding a savings bank that turned out, in his wife's words, ''to be a gold mine.'' The family lived in a shingle house of two stories that had a front porch, offering a pleasant view of oak and maple trees. Behind the house was a cabin for the black couple who served the Westmorelands, and down the hill flowed the muddy Pacolet River, where the brick mills were located. The mill nurse remembered there were still no sidewalks or paved streets in 1916, when Westmoreland was two, and she used a horse for transportation around the slippery red hills.

As soon as Westmoreland was old enough, he joined the Boy Scouts. When he earned merit badges, he insisted that his mother sew them perfectly spaced and aligned on his uniform. In 1929, as an Eagle Scout, he attended a World Jamboree in Birkenhead, England, along with fifty thousand other scouts from seventy-four countries. It was during this trip, when he was fifteen, that Westmoreland came in contact with a group of midshipmen from Annapolis and first seriously thought of attending a military academy.

Westmoreland liked West Point. The values of duty, honor, and country appealed to him, and he did so well there he was eventually appointed first captain of the Corps, the highest honor West Point bestows on a cadet. He looked splendidly impressive in uniform and appeared, wearing a plumed shako, on the cover of *Cosmopolitan* magazine beside the perennial Anita Colby.

Even in those days, Westmoreland not only looked but also sounded good. The story goes that during the summer of 1934, or between his yearling (sophomore) and second classman (junior) years, Westmoreland, as a counselor at a summer camp, would paddle a canoe through a remote neck of a nearby lake, shouting parade-ground commands while a friend listened carefully before offering advice and criticism. Thirty-odd years later, Pentagon janitors were astonished early one morning to discover the general practicing over a loudspeaker a speech he was scheduled to deliver before Congress that day. The janitors couldn't recall how many times Westmoreland recited his speech; they did remember, though, it wasn't once or twice.

Westmoreland was hardly, then, the kind of detached man who'd pinch himself, marveling with a bemused grin at the distance he'd covered from Pacolet Mills to Washington D.C. He was far too single-minded—twin, perhaps, to the fictional eight-year-old hero whose mother is constantly asked by the youth's jostling, visiting friends, "Can General come out and play with us?"

It was while Westmoreland was stationed in Japan in 1952, commanding a theater reserve unit that could be quickly transported to Korea, that he received his first star. When the Chinese Communists began their summer offensive the following year, Westmoreland's unit, the 187th Regimental Combat Team, was rushed to an area astride Route Three, which led down to Seoul. Here they were assigned a flanking position next to a South Korean unit, and Westmoreland told his officers and senior NCO's that an imminent attack was expected. Drawing a line in the ground with his shoe, he said, "You're here. If the enemy comes, you can go here, but no farther." He drew another line, about two feet from the first. "Here you will stand, and here you will die if need be." If it sounded vintage John Wayne, the enemy hardly performed according to script, because only minimal contact was ever established.

Following Korea, Westmoreland served in the Pentagon as deputy assistant chief of staff for manpower control. Then it was on to the Harvard Business School, after which he landed the choice assignment as Taylor's secretary to the General Staff, a second star, divisional command of the 101st, the West Point superintendency, followed by yet another plum—commanding officer of the XVIII Airborne Corps, which was the striking arm of the Strategic Army Corps, STRAC. It was here that Westmoreland received this third star, and less than six months later he was summoned to Washington, prior to being sent to Vietnam.

For the next ten days Westmoreland attended a series of Pentagon briefings. The talk then was of counterinsurgency, of winning hearts and minds, and of being aware that officers under stress often tell you what they think you want to hear rather than the truth, which is what you badly need to hear.

Before leaving for Vietnam, Westmoreland decided to go back to West Point. He wanted to talk to the Class of '64, his class, or those who'd arrived at the Academy the same year he became superintendent.

Among his predecessors as superintendent had been Robert E. Lee, Maxwell Taylor, Gar Davidson, and, probably most important to Westmoreland, Douglas MacArthur. It was MacArthur, Army chief of staff at the time, who'd journeyed to West Point in the spring of 1933, where he made the commencement address when Westmoreland had just completed his plebe (freshman) year. The same MacArthur who, at thirty-eight, had been the youngest superintendent in West Point history.

Given MacArthur's commanding presence and ability to inspire soldiers, it was hardly a surprise that on his eighty-second birthday Westmoreland dispatched a group of cadets to the Waldorf-Astoria, where the old soldier was living, to wish him well. That May, MacArthur reciprocated by coming back to the Academy, where he received the Sylvanus Thayer Award, named for the officer who, as superintendent from 1817 to 1833, was responsible more than any other for making West Point a prominent national institution.

There MacArthur reviewed the Corps of Cadets, standing in a jeep alongside Westmoreland and the cadet brigade commander. Then MacArthur entered cavernous Washington Hall, where the cadets ate, and Westmoreland introduced him "as one of America's most illustrious soldiers."

In the forty-minute speech that followed, MacArthur told the cadets that though the world might be changing, the soldier's mission of winning wars remained inviolate, a beacon, a fixed point in his life. "Everything else in your professional career is but a corollary to this vital dedication," MacArthur stated. "All other public purposes, all other public needs, great or small, will find others for their accomplishment; but you are the ones trained to fight; yours is the profession of arms—the will to win, the sure knowledge that in war there is no substitute for victory; that if you lose, then the nation will be destroyed; that the very obsession of your public service must be duty, honor, country."

Twenty years later, cadets who heard that speech still remembered it, and neither Kennedy's princely inaugural address nor Martin Luther King's "I have a dream" *cri de coeur* came close to having the same lasting effect for them. When MacArthur concluded that "today marks my final roll call with you," more than a few were moved to tears.

That was May 1962, and now it was not quite two years later, January 18, 1964, a Saturday, and this time it was Westmoreland, standing tall and straight before his "classmates," those who'd arrived in the summer of 1960. And this, too, was a kind of sentimental journey. And if it wasn't exactly a farewell address uttered by a brittle man in his wintry eighties, who could say with certainty what fate awaited a patriotic and ambitious general in the steamy jungles and exposed rice paddies of Southeast Asia?

Not only was he leaving for Vietnam with a sense of mission, Westmoreland told his audience, but also he thought all West Pointers were a special breed, men who "bore a sacred trust to provide the dedicated leadership and service to our nation, which is so essential to our national security." A noble cause, Westmoreland pronounced it, as well as a West Point tradition.

But living beyond the gates of the Academy, which they would be leaving in June, were other Americans, some of whom were dishonest and apparently bereft of any sense of duty toward country. "I feel that West Pointers must be different, and that is why as a group they have been universally and uniquely successful throughout history." Although satisfactions men derive from serving the country are real, Westmoreland cautioned, they require commitment. "It's been my observation over the years that the unhappy and discontented man is that man who is undecided and who's undedicated. He's the man who's restless. He's the man who's looking across the hill to contemplate greener pastures."

Even with commitment, though, life is difficult and some problems intractable. Still, Westmoreland added, "in my view the positive approach is still the key to success . . . and it's the one that has a strong influence over people."

Then Westmoreland offered a profile of man as someone frightened, lacking the will to cope with life and therefore requiring the guidance and strength provided by powerful leaders—men more energetic and braver than himself.

"Men welcome leadership," Westmoreland said. "They like action and they relish accomplishment. . . . Speculation, knowledge is not the chief aim of man—it's action. . . . All mankind find themselves weak, beset with infirmities, and surrounded by dangers. They want above all things a leader with boldness, decision, and energy that with shame, they do not find in themselves."

A cadet sitting there, who'd recently read *The Federalist Papers*, concluded that Westmoreland was talking about citizens of another country and wished he'd had the guts to stand up and say so.

But unchallenged, Westmoreland continued, warning his listeners to "beware of snow jobs" and concentrate on whatever task was at hand. "Give it your full energy and your best effort. The first principle of war is that of the objective. This is a good personal philosophy."

Westmoreland concluded by saying that he agreed with Rudyard Kipling's philosophy, which he considered profound, and he proceeded to quote lines prep school students and Boy Scouts around the world commit to passionate memory:

If you can walk with crowds and keep your virtue,
Or walk with Kings—nor lose the common touch,
If neither foes nor living friends can hurt you,
If all men count with you, but none too much;
If you can fill the unforgiving minute
With sixty seconds' worth of distance run,

Yours is the Earth and everything that's in it,
And—which is more, you'll be a Man, my son!

Leaving West Point, Westmoreland traveled down to New York City, where he visited General MacArthur. Age had hosted the usual indignities, and the older man was considerably weaker now than when he'd addressed the Corps in 1962. "I am sure you realize that your new assignment is filled with opportunities," MacArthur blessed the younger general, "and saturated with hazards."

At about the same time Westmoreland and MacArthur shook hands in farewell, Tina Gowen, a student at Dunbarton College in Washington, D.C., received a letter from Howie Boone. They'd been engaged since December. A member of the Class of '64, Boone cheerfully noted that the first semester of his senior (first classman) year was complete and he was happy to report that all of his charges had passed their courses. Boone, with brains to spare, was his company's academic rep.

"They couldn't have thought of a more fitting end for the term than a lecture by ex-Sup now Lt. General Westmoreland," Boone continued his letter. "He didn't have too much earthshaking to say, but it was an interesting philosophical insight on the Army, West Pointers, and Second Lieutenants. 'Westy' is on his way to be deputy commander of the forces in Vietnam and everyone here figures him for a fourth star soon. If he keeps his nose clean, he'll be chief of staff before anyone knows it."

Because Westmoreland soon got his fourth star and later wound up chief of staff, you'd have to say Boone had it more than half right, at least. . . .

BOONE, Howard E (Howie)
COL CE 460-66-9644
BORN: 21 Sept 40, Centralia, IL

When in the fall of 1985 I mentioned Westmoreland's going-away speech to the Class of '64, Col. Howard Boone instantly said he remembered it. But what he remembered turned out not to be the January 18 address Westmoreland had delivered just before leaving for Vietnam. To pinpoint that one, Boone had to refresh his memory by going through a stack of West Point correspondence his wife had saved.

"Westmoreland's other speech" was how Boone now amusingly referred to the one he'd immediately recalled, and it was an entirely different matter. He clearly remembered its delivery to the Class of '64 on a June morning in 1963, a day or two before Westmoreland left West Point to take over XVIII Airborne Corps at Fort Bragg.

"June Week was over and we were now first classmen [seniors]," Boone recalled. "We were waiting around for the next formation and doing a bunch of *macht nichts* kind of things, and Westmoreland was coming from the tennis courts over in front of the library. Some of the guys were lying down on a bench, and when Westmoreland walked by, nobody called us to attention to salute."

Boone cleared his throat for the third time, making a kind of "ech" sound. It seemed a nervous tic.

"Anyway," he said, picking up the story, "next morning we were all called together, the entire class, not just the guys who were on the bench, and marched into the Academic Hall, where Westmoreland chewed us out, his point being, you can't relax at any time. He left that day, or the following morning, and that's my final memory of Westmoreland-and-the-Class-of-'64."

While Westmoreland identified with Boone's class because he'd assumed the superintendency during the same month the class entered the Academy, Boone always thought the general had fostered mixed feelings toward it. When, for example, the time came for the class to pick its motto, it chose "Stars in Store for '64," and Boone remembered Westmoreland's reaction that such a choice was presumptuous.

Boone weighs about 210 and stands between six-one and six-two, although he doesn't seem that tall. The frames of his glasses are small and dark. He's almost completely bald and has blue eyes. Also a large lower lip, and when he gets excited, his upper lip seems to thin out, compressed to no more than a line on a page. There's a discernible tire encircling his gut. In other words, he looks like a soldier the way Omar Bradley, who resembled a kindly schoolteacher, looked like a soldier.

Yet there was something else different about Boone, an additional distinction hard to define. I'd already begun interviewing other officers who'd attended West Point in the 1960s and served in Vietnam, so I'd had a basis of comparison.

When Boone began drinking from a can of Diet Pepsi, I heard a click and glanced at his other hand, thinking, "Of course, the ring! No ring!" Unlike the others, I realized, he didn't wear a West Point ring.

"I wear it once a year normally, and that's on Founder's Day." Boone was referring to March 16, which commemorates the founding of West Point in 1802. "There are a couple of reasons," he explained. "Number one, I don't particularly care for jewelry. I'm certainly not ashamed of being a West Pointer by any stretch of the imagination, and getting the ring was exciting. But I don't like people taking preconceived notions of me as a function of seeing the ring. If you ask me, I don't mind telling you I'm a West Pointer. I accepted the challenge of going there, and I'm proud of what I accomplished. But I don't want you or anyone else to preconceive on that basis.''

Throughout his career, Boone will make a number of interesting and unusual choices. Of undaunted intelligence, he quickly grasps what takes most considerable time and effort. It's during those intervals when others are trying to catch up that Boone will occasionally get in a jam by rubbing people the wrong way. It's a mistake when he does that, Boone thinks, but not a cardinal sin. For Boone, the cardinal sin is to allow oneself to become bored, or to bore others, and he has an almost physical aversion to the predictable, which he equates with boredom.

Given this particular frame of mind, it hardly comes as a surprise that Boone harbored ambivalent feelings toward West Point almost from the beginning, and certainly dating from the first semester of his second year. As a plebe, he'd been a spectacular success, standing a luminous eighteenth in a class that began with more than eight hundred cadets. Yet less than a year later, Boone found himself questioning the system and institution so intensely that he thought seriously about resigning.

This pattern of succeeding spectacularly, followed by a period of disillusionment, appears like a leitmotiv throughout Boone's career. One reason is that while he has a mathematician's elegance of mind, he is by temperament a confirmed romantic. Another reason is that what most people find difficult, Boone finds easy, and vice versa. He's like the teenager who gets 100 in those miserable advanced algebra exams everyone else fails—a perfect score he'd gladly forfeit if only he were an all-state halfback pinned to the school's prettiest cheerleader. As a result, some of his peers refer to Boone as a flake, and he echoes that characterization. In truth, Boone understands, if the others do not, that he is more complicated than bizarre; and if his mind and temperament are often at odds, that's never prevented him from functioning at an extremely high level in a pressure-cooker atmosphere, and he has the glowing efficiency reports to prove it.

"Plebe (freshman) year was probably the second best year I had at West Point," Boone said. "The reason being, plebe year was totally reactive. I never had time to think where I was, who I was, or what I was. We were so regimented, so drilled, and you just worked so hard to stay up with the system, what else could a plebe do at night but study?"

The diet of math, math, and more math force-fed plebes six days a week is a greater weeder at West Point. And even those who finally achieve passing grades through sheer nerve-racking effort, retain powerful and humiliating memories of standing before a blackboard, reciting in a hollow voice, "Gentlemen, I was required to prove..."

But math came particularly easy for Boone. His challenge was to pass the phys ed requirements, which most cadets found a cinch. Also to avoid coming on too strong or knowing when confronted by upperclassmen. "I learned very early, yes, do it right the first time," Boone recalled. "But the one thing you don't want to do is stand out in that kind of environment." Boone remembered bringing attention to himself early during his first year by performing once in a marching formation too well. The result was that eight or ten upperclassmen came down on him, "staying with me for about forty-eight hours."

Still, Boone completed that first year with a feeling of intense satisfaction. "I said, 'My God, I've accomplished something.' And that was one of the problems. Because when I got to the end of plebe year, I was 140th in phys ed but eighteenth overall, yet what did I have to look forward to?"

What happened his second year was that with more time to himself, Boone began asking questions like, What am I doing at West Point? What am I learning? And how am I going to get through the next three years if what I'm learning is as inconsequential as I think it is? "Plebe year, yeah, there's a reason for underlining in red chalk and using yellow chalk for something else, because the Academy was challenging the individual in every way. But if you're going to try to train someone academically, you ought to let him be a student."

Boone remembered reading a poem by T.S. Eliot, after which an English instructor insisted on an A-1, B-1 answer in explaining what Eliot was intimating. "I thought that was a bunch of crap and said so."

Cadets, Boone felt, were neither encouraged nor allowed to swim in any kind of intellectual depth; worse, you couldn't love a subject. Write an eight-hundred-word footnote and you had an instructor throwing mental elbows amid a fanfaronade along the lines, "What's the big idea? Trying to show me up? That kind of footnote is the gesture of a wise guy, uncalled for, an act of rebellion." And maybe it was. But they were hardly challenging him intellectually, Boone thought. What did they expect? He was a growing boy in a college setting.

Denied the opportunity and satisfaction of immersing himself in subjects that captured his imagination, Boone decided to get even by beating the system that was enforcing the denial. For Boone it meant seeing how little he needed to study while still attaining good grades. True, he slipped from eighteenth to thirty-second by the end of his second year, but that hardly placed him in academic jeopardy, even if he still felt that what he was learning was less than sustaining.

The reason Boone finally decided to stick it out at the Academy was that for him West Point had never been an end in itself. It was rather a means of obtaining a Regular Army commission; and if you wanted an Army commission, the best to obtain, in terms of maintenance, was one offered a West Point graduate.

Boone's father had acquired an Army commission after going through OCS in 1947. But he'd been compelled to give it up in 1953, when the military experienced a reduction in forces. Although he later rejoined the Army as an NCO, went to Missile School, and became a warrant officer, losing that commission had been a humbling experience.

"Say to me there's something I can't do, and I'll show you how wrong you are. Tell me," said Boone, "I can't run up and down a basketball court at age forty-five, and you'll get the best possible game out of me." What better way to show the Army it was dead wrong in humiliating his father than by not only becoming an officer after passing through the hallowed, gray Gothic buildings of West Point, but, though he's hardly a physically gifted man, performing each task he's assigned so well he's promoted to colonel years before most of his classmates?

Boone was born in Centralia, Illinois, in 1940. His father was from East Texas; his mother, Illinois. They met while his father was working the oil fields in central Illinois one summer and married when he was nineteen, two years older than his bride. Boone's father, drafted toward the end of World War II, was training to participate in the invasion of Japan when the war ended shortly after two atomic bombs had been dropped in August 1945.

Boone spent three years in Japan when his father was stationed there and vividly remembered visiting ground zero in Nagasaki where the second of these atomic bombs had been detonated. A big, tall, four-sided wooden marker with Japanese characters on it pinpointed the location. "I've a picture at home of my dad, mom, me, and my younger brother, showing us standing at the base of the monument." At the time, Japan hadn't really begun to be restored, and Boone remembered walking along a beach that was still littered with trenches, strands of wire, and blockhouses. When Boone's father was sent to Korea with the 24th Division, one of the first American units to be deployed there during the early weeks of the Korean War, Boone, his mother, and his brother returned to the States.

For a number of years after rejoining the Army as an enlisted man, Boone's father was stationed at Fort Bliss, and Boone was fortunate to attend the same high school in El Paso for four years. There he committed the usual mischief that kids in skittish border towns find amusing, though he did graduate thirtieth in a class of 310.

Boone lived in a middle-class neighborhood, on the edge of what was the old Fort Bliss post. Although he considered himself a loner, he was one of a group of four or five who became reasonably close during his last two years of high school. Every couple of months, they'd go across the border. Boone remembered they'd pile out of an old car, leaving it in a large parking lot near the bridge connecting Texas to Mexico. "You had to pay a penny to walk across the bridge and two cents to return. It was a kind of lark. You could go into a bar and order a drink in Mexico, and nobody asked what your age was. I used to joke that I was nineteen before I ever had a date with a white woman and twenty before I ever knew that Mexican Americans were a minority."

In 1957, Boone began to ponder what he was going to do with his life. "I guess all along I carried a weird, emotional attachment to the Army." At about that time, he'd seen Tyrone Power in the movie *The Long Gray Line*. It not only stimulated his romantic curiosity but also got him to read a number of books about West Point. Soon after, Boone applied for a congressional appointment based on a competitive exam, which he won. "All I had to do now was meet the minimum physical requirements, and I'd enter West Point in the summer of 1958."

To his shocked disgust, Boone failed the strength events in the PT test. Dismayed about not going to West Point, he had the self-possession to apply to Texas A&M, which at the time was still an all-military school. Accepted, he received a letter to report for orientation in August.

But earlier that summer, Fate intervened when Boone, looking for a summer job in downtown El Paso, saw a sign that said, "Join the Army and Get Your Station of Choice in the United States." Because he was still smarting over West Point's rejection and wasn't really sure what else he wanted to do, he went into the recruiting station and signed along the dotted line. "I chose Detroit because I was madly in love at the time and my girlfriend had moved up to Detroit that summer." New York was his second choice.

The Army being the Army, he was sent to Nike installation two miles south of Summit, New Jersey, which is about an hour's bus ride from New York. Boone remembered spending a restless year there. "It was definitely a chicken outfit." The troops kept two lockers. One was next to Boone's bed, containing uniforms he never wore but would display for inspections conducted with white gloves.

Despite the discipline, Boone knew he was drifting, and because the urge to go to West Point hadn't died completely and he'd been told he was unacceptable, he decided one day to apply for a Regular Army appointment. That meant he'd have to attend a military prep school, whose sole purpose was to prepare people to pass the entrance exam to West Point. Coming from a spit-and-polish Nike installation, Boone found the more casual prep school atmosphere delightful. "While most of the other guys got in shape with the books, I got in shape with the exercise."

Any lingering doubt about entering West Point was utterly obliterated at a counseling session a captain at the prep school held with him, when the officer said he thought Boone had "an attitude problem" that would prevent his doing well at the Academy. Not only did this abrasive statement solidify Boone's resolve, it also specifically helped him pass the hated PT test, and he entered West Point in July 1960.

And it was there, during his second, difficult year, that Boone, along with the rest of the Corps and Westmoreland, heard MacArthur's "Duty, Honor, Country" speech in Washington Hall. "It was kind of funny, because I'd remembered seeing MacArthur when I was nine or ten years old," Boone recounted. In Japan, Boone and thousands of other Cub Scouts had gathered in a huge gym or exposition hall, and MacArthur, who was practically a Japanese icon those days, had come out on to a balcony high above the gym floor and stood silently watching, in a kind of benediction. "And now, twelve years later, I'm sitting there in the mess hall, hearing MacArthur giving this fervent speech, and my mind immediately connected the two events."

What made West Point's academic rigidity bearable in his third year was being able to fill his spare time usefully. When Boone got involved in the school's bridge club, he became its secretary, had all the administrative work dumped on him, and ran an eighty-team tournament. He also became his company's academic rep and was responsible for maintaining an audit of all cadets in his company who were having academic problems. Perhaps most helpful of all was simply the passage of time, and Boone, halfway there, realized that facing him was no longer a forbidding mountain; or, if it was still a mountain, he was definitely beginning to descend along what had been the more distant slope.

During Boone's fourth cadet summer he spent thirty days as a third lieutenant with a divisional engineering battalion in West Germany. This experience reinforced an earlier inclination to join the Corps of Engineers. Not that engineering particularly turned him on. "Sitting down, drawing trusses on a piece of paper wasn't my idea of what to look forward to in life." But he chose the engineers because of the role models he saw around West Point. Though he loved running through the woods in a T-shirt and beating his chest as a cadet, he wasn't sure he'd love it when he got to be forty or forty-five. Which meant he wasn't sure he'd want to choose, say, the infantry branch, because infantry officers were required to run through the woods at forty-five, beating their chests. "So I said, 'Hey, I'm going to be smart. I'm going into the Corps of Engineers.' Number one, certain engineering officers, those with combat units, do run through the woods beating their chests. At the same time, engineers get to go to graduate school earlier, so I'll achieve some kind of career orientation that is immediately transferable to the civilian world if I don't stay with the Army."

Yet there were no lingering doubts during Boone's final year that he wanted to graduate, and he found he was most concerned now about completing those things necessary in order to enter the Army fully prepared. He particularly wanted his personal life in order.

That November, on the Friday before Thanksgiving, John Kennedy was shot. Boone's girlfriend, Tina Gowen, was preparing to come up from Washington for the weekend; but hearing of Kennedy's assassination on her car radio, she got involved in a minor accident. They spoke that night by phone and decided to go ahead with their plans, despite Kennedy's death and the car mishap. "So she came up to West Point," Boone recounted. "It was a period when I think we reacted much as the rest of the world; we spent a quiet time together. Although I do seem to recall vaguely that this was also around Navy-game time, and there was a hassle about whether they were going to have the game or postpone it.

"Anyway, I think it was about that point in time we probably started getting very serious about what our personal plans were as a function of—not because it directly impacted, but as a function of—Kennedy's assassination happening to the population as a whole." As a result, from December on everything focused for Boone on marrying Tina at West Point that June. And they were wed less than two hours after he'd graduated, forty-second in a class of 565, the second couple to be married in the West Point chapel that year.

Ask a complicated man like Boone, who's put more than twenty years of distance between himself and West Point, what he thinks the value of the institution is, and he answers, "West Point turns out a very dedicated product, but the difficulty is that he's not only seen little of the world, but he's so controlled that he's emotionally and socially insecure."

Boone believes that what you choose as a basis for measuring West Point is key to deciding on the effectiveness of the institution. If you choose the proportion of generals based on the declining number of generals who have West Point degrees, then obviously West Point is failing. But if you choose the length and degree of commitment, which includes not only four years at West Point but also a five-year service obligation, then West Point has proven eminently successful. "What you lose in the process is what I mentioned before—the cadet's growth in terms of flexibility," Boone said. "You don't get to make conscious decisions at West Point as you're maturing. Your one decision is: Do I remain committed to the path I've set out on, or do I uncommit?"

Not surprisingly, the honor code, which says, "No cadet will lie, cheat, or steal, or tolerate anyone who does," particularly appealed to Boone's sense of chivalry. "I'm still romantic enough to think there has to be a certain number of idealists in every profession. You lose the last honest man, that profession is gone, or it's as good as worthless. And for that reason, I've always thought the honor code was and is a great thing. And where else do you find the one they have at West Point?''

If that's the plus side, the converse, Boone insisted, was that ''West Point ain't here for learning.'' And, that being the case, he suggested the Army develop a system whereby people are trained for a year to become officers. ''We just give them an honor code and unbridled hell for a year and make them officers.'' Boone would probably include airborne and Ranger training during those twelve months, though officers graduating from West Point take such training only after entering the Regular Army.

Boone, for example, graduated from the Academy in June 1964, and went on a sixty-day leave with his wife. During the last thirty days, they stayed in El Paso, and Boone got in shape for Airborne School by running through the desert with his brother. ''I made sure I could run forever,'' he remembered. ''Not fast, but forever.''

He found Airborne School, which he took at Fort Benning, an interesting experience, one reason being, ''I'll never know why I volunteered for it.'' But then, in practically the next breath, ''I know why I did it. I didn't want anyone telling me later I never did it.''

At Airborne School, Boone was harassed because of his old problem of not being able to lift himself. But it was a challenge, a kind of repeat of the PT test he'd failed the first time he'd applied for West Point. And he did then what he always attempted when something physical, which most of his peers accomplished with relative ease, seemed beyond his capacity: He locked everything else out of his mind, lived from minute to minute, and somehow managed to muscle his way through. He even stopped smoking, although the week he actually began jumping out of a plane, he reached for a cigarette again. He remembered the reason wasn't so much anxiety about jumping as it was anxiety concerning the pilots from the Pennsylvania Air National Guard, who were flying the C-119's taking him over the drop zones. Not only were they out of practice, but they'd also spent a lot of time boozing at night, and Boone always exited their wobbly planes with a sense of enormous relief.

During one jump, his rifle bent when he landed, a rather sobering experience. But it was his fifth and last jump that was easily the most memorable. The troops spent an inordinate amount of time waiting to board the plane, and that increased everyone's natural anxiety. Boone recalled that the man jumping immediately behind him was a wiry Hungarian from Special Forces. When Boone exited the plane, he started counting, "One thousand one, one thousand two," and, looking up, saw his chute opening. At the same time his chute opened, he saw the Hungarian hurtling past him and heard himself instinctively shouting, "Oh, my God, no!" He followed the man's horrifying descent perhaps another 150 feet, when the Hungarian's chute suddenly blossomed. The poor bastard had had a delayed opening, and Boone remembered marveling, "That's the best reaction I've ever gotten to a prayer in my life."

If Airborne School tested your capacity to withstand a youthful coronary, Ranger School tested your capacity to withstand almost total exhaustion. You eat maybe once a day and average two to three hours' sleep. You train in mountains, desert, jungle, and swamp. Hours of instruction that would normally be spaced out over six months are crammed into two months, during which you average nineteen hours of operations each day. If you *don't* lose twenty to thirty pounds, something's wrong with your metabolism. The idea is to simulate the most realistic combat situations possible by creating the most stressful of conditions, yet to get you to function despite that stress and those conditions.

What Boone hated about Ranger training was not the lack of food or sleep but the insistence that you run fast in the mornings. "I could run and run and run, and still be running when other guys fell down," he said. "But running fast was a real struggle for me."

In Ranger School, you're constantly on patrol. It might be during a simulated ambush, reconnaissance, or a combat mission. Boone recalled being a patrol leader one night after they'd been on the go for a day or two, and he was punchy. It was about three in the morning. The Ranger instructor told him to turn the patrol over to another lieutenant. Boone briefed the new patrol leader and then walked over to the side of the road. He could plainly see other members of the patrol, all of whom were kneeling, and he couldn't understand why. He decided to go over and talk to one. It took no more than a sentence or two before he realized he was talking to a tree. In fact, each of those kneeling men circling him was either a tree or a bush. Boone had been hallucinating, and without his having quite realized it, the patrol had gotten up and walked away. Experiencing a spasm of panic, he started racing in a circle, then cleverly widened the circle, until his arcing strides finally landed him back in the heart of the silent, well-spaced band of hollow-eyed troops.

Another time, it was midnight and the patrol consisted of twenty-five guys. They had to traverse a highway, and cars were zipping back and forth. They were on a side of a hill, crouched down in the shadows, and waiting to cross. Suddenly a car pulled up, stopped beside the road, and flicked off its lights. Boone remembered lying there, so close to the car he could reach out and touch a front wheel. Soon the two couples in the car began shedding their clothes, and distinctly sexual murmuring could be heard. The patrol got to their feet, all twenty-five of them, and started walking toward the car, bees drawn to honey. When the fumbling people in the car looked up and saw those blackened faces and extended carbines coming toward them, they went absolutely bananas.

"Ranger training was easily the most rigorous I ever took," Boone remembered. "Nothing, before or since, remotely comes close." But when he completed it, he'd again achieved that unmistakably gritty feeling of intense satisfaction. "I'd accepted the challenge and done what was necessary in order to get through. I'm not sure I was afraid not to do it. But I was afraid to fail."

Interestingly enough, it was neither at Airborne School nor at Ranger School that Boone heard mention made of Vietnam. But he did recall that during his senior year at West Point, at about the same time he heard Westmoreland's speech in January, someone else, another officer, mounted the stage in one of the auditoriums and told Boone's class that within five years they'd all be going to Vietnam. "Look to the right and left of you," the speaker said. "Some of those you see now won't be coming back." Prophetic words, considering that one of Boone's roommates was killed in Vietnam in 1966.

"I don't remember who it was who predicted we'd all be going to Vietnam," Boone said, "and I don't remember the occasion. But we had people around—and I heard one of them—who believed it was going to happen and went on record saying so."

Despite such fleeting intimations, when Boone was sent on his first permanent assignment, to Munich in December 1964, to be a platoon leader in an engineering battalion that was part of the 24th Infantry Division—the same division his father had gone to Korea with in 1950—Vietnam was not a country, and fighting there certainly not a way of life, Boone thought much about. It wasn't until a year later, when his unit started losing officers who weren't replaced, that he first really became aware of the possibility that he might be going to Vietnam himself. Troops were being pulled out of European-based units and sent back to the States, where they were then assigned to earmarked units in the process of filling empty slots before shipping off to Vietnam.

When Boone received his orders, he was one of the first inter-theater transfers—that is, he went directly from Europe to Vietnam. This was in June 1966, and knowing he was heading toward the sound of the guns excited him—it was, after all, what he'd been trained for. His wife, six months pregnant with their second child, considered Boone's rendezvous with violence somewhat less than enthralling. While Boone had misgivings about leaving her, he was curious how he'd perform when the bullets were for real.

The trouble was, when Boone got to Saigon, no unit seemed to want or need a young lieutenant with his experience and time in grade. The letdown was painful, especially when he thought about his pregnant wife, by now in Arlington, Virginia, and taking care of their older child alone. Soon his distress soured, turning to guilt, and hanging around Saigon, Boone found himself frustrated and angry. When the personnel officer handling his records asked an inane question about his career pattern, Boone found himself saying, "How far north can you send me? Because I want to be as far north from this stupid Saigon as I can go." The man at personnel mentioned the remote possibility of shipping Boone up to Qui Nhon, where the 1st Cav and units attached to it had been seeing considerable action. Boone's reaction was instantaneous: "Send me!" He was assigned to the 19th Engineering Battalion.

When Boone arrived at the 19th, he'd hoped to be made a company commander—that's what he'd been preparing himself for in Germany. But there were no vacant slots for company commanders, and he was assigned as an operations officer. In an engineering battalion that meant he did a lot of design work, and he particularly remembered designing an aboveground pipeline that extended from the coastal city of Qui Nhon through An Khe, the 1st Cav's base, and into Pleiku. The pipeline transported fuel that was used by the 1st Cav's helicopters. The fuel would be brought in on ships, then stored in tanks, before being siphoned into the pipeline. Occasionally thieves tapped the line, and parts would have to be replaced.

In the fall of '66, when the 1st Cav chose a new firebase, their divisional engineers, who in the German Army perform what are called "pioneer tasks," were rappeled into the area, which they cut and cleared. Then the cav troops were deployed in large numbers, securing the base. Boone's unit, a corps combat battalion, swept in behind the cav troops, building a road to the firebase. They did all the major earthworks, put up the berms, and helped construct the airfields. Boone remembered logging twenty- and twenty-two-hour workdays for three months, during which the troops coped with wet matériel that did not compact. Considerable time was consumed getting heavy equipment unstuck. "You always wanted to hire a guy who know how to get a 'dozer unstuck," Boone said. "I've seen bulldozers stuck in a rice paddy up to their exhaust stack. You get it out by winching, using logs and cables, employing a pulley system."

In December, Boone finally became a company commander, in charge of 150 men. His company was pulled back to Qui Nhon, and he was given the task of building a new logistics depot on the side of a hill crowned with dense overgrowth. They had to clear the overgrowth and do landfill operations before anything else. Boone received the first two Rome plows that were deployed in Vietnam. Tractors twice the size of tanks, the plows weren't terribly useful when it came to clearing thickets that had no trees, because the wet overgrowth simply slid off the steel 'dozer blades intact.

The depot was to consist of road networks and more than fifty storage buildings of perhaps sixty by 180 feet each. The spaces between would be of macadam surface. Though the design was someone else's, sixty acres of the depot as good as belonged to Boone. They were his baby, his project; he was answerable for them. He had 150 warm bodies, cranes, 'dozers, graders, concrete mixers, a bunch of dump trucks, and was told, "Perform, do your stuff." From a neighboring construction battalion he was able to borrow heavier equipment—tractor pans and big earthmovers. A certain percentage of the sixty acres had to be completed within a specified time frame. "I don't think I've ever been more personally challenged, in an organizational sense, than to have had what was required against what I had to work with." But as long as the tasks were challenges Boone respected, and even when they weren't, his energy level was always slightly astonishing. His wife, for one, considers him a confirmed workaholic.

The troops would pour concrete at night because of the intense heat, and even then the concrete would percolate. An occasional enemy mortar round would come whistling in, but the area was kept secure by South Korean troops, who had a fierce reputation, and neither the VC nor the North Vietnamese wanted to mess with the Koreans too much.

If the heat was terrible, the rain was unbelievable. Eleven inches once spilled from the sky in twenty-four hours. It was impossible to stay dry, and Boone had written home for a rain suit. "Off to the side of the road you've got four or five inches of rain falling; it's like you're filling a bathtub. You have to design, anticipating that kind of downfall. You have to make sure your culverts are big enough and your bridges long enough so that you've got space for whatever amount of water builds up behind."

Qui Nhon was being overrun by supplies, which encouraged pilfering, and the powers-that-be were anxious to move as much surplus as possible out of the city. Boone was visited periodically by a general who wanted to see how the work was progressing. Nothing like putting more pressure on a man afraid to fail. Yet Boone remembered enjoying the task. "My whole focus in Vietnam at that time was mission accomplishment—nose-to-the-grindstone kind of thing." That was his first tour.

By the time Boone was ordered back to Vietnam, in October 1970, America had turned against the war. Tet occurred early 1968, and Lyndon Johnson had been as good as driven from office. Nixon assumed the presidency in 1969, and the blood senselessly drawn at Kent State the following spring seemed to blot the national landscape. Because the country no longer supported the war, Boone was not looking forward to returning to Southeast Asia. "But when you take it to the bottom line," he said, "you're a soldier, you don't make policy. And that's part of the commitment business I mentioned earlier. Unless you violate my personal integrity, my signing the bottom line required I go back a second time."

Boone had hoped he'd be assigned to an American unit as a battalion exec or operations officer. But because of the Vietnamization program, he was slotted to be an adviser to a South Vietnamese engineering battalion stationed at Lai Khe. The assignment turned out to be a waste of time professionally, because Boone accomplished little and had relatively no influence. On the other hand, it deepened his understanding of how others live and survive amid pervasive tragedy.

Advisers usually resided in an American compound, where they socialized and drank at night, forming a clique. But Boone insisted on living with the ARVN 5th Engineering Battalion. "That's the way it was when I got there, and I refused to move back into the American compound. What it meant," Boone said, "was that my sergeant and I were the only round-eyes along with about five hundred Vietnamese living in the same area." Unfortunately, he'd had absolutely no training to be an adviser. Nor did he have any language background, although his sergeant had attended Language School and spoke a smattering of Vietnamese.

As adviser, Boone had a personal staff of three Vietnamese: a cook-orderly, a jeep driver, and an interpreter. The driver and cook-orderly were Cholon Chinese, and the interpreter was South Vietnamese. The battalion, proud possessor of a long history, had been formed by the French. It came from an area that was inhabited by the Ming Chinese, and there were still about fifty Ming Chinese among the troops, including the sergeant major, who, at six-one, was almost as tall as Boone. The key officers, Buddhist Catholics, were originally from North Vietnam, part of the surge that had swept south when the partition occurred in 1954. There was also a sprinkling of Cambodians, "and the Cambodians were the 'niggers' in that battalion," Boone said. "I only learned the differences between them over time, and only because I was living with them."

There were certain things Boone's interpreter would not do in concert with his driver and cook-orderly because they were Chinese. "In the U.S. Army," Boone said, "no one looks at the color of a guy's skin in the foxhole, although back in R&R they do. But the Vietnamese—they're making distinctions during an operation that I don't see, much less know exist."

Boone first came to perceive that differences between the troops were important when his counterpart, the South Vietnamese battalion commander, would make certain decisions that didn't make much sense in terms of producing efficient results. When Boone asked why that decision and not this other more logical one, the battalion commander would simply smile, shake his head, and go on about his business. That was one of the reasons Boone felt so useless. "But the point is, the reason he'd do it a certain way was because of the social differences, which I sensed after a while but never really grasped.''

The battalion commander was a Buddhist Catholic who went to Mass on Christmas but didn't attend church during Easter, and Boone wondered why. He also wondered how his Catholic background and training melded with his Buddhist background and training. ''I tried to figure out what he thought, what he felt, and why he did certain things but not others.''

Boone did not confine his contacts to the officers. He'd make a point of eating with and talking to Vietnamese E-3's, or the equivalent of American privates. Some Vietnamese officers frowned when they saw Boone fraternizing with their troops. His reason, Boone acknowledged, was more practical than democratic—it helped pass the time. ''Because what was I going to do with my nights?'' he asked. ''Getting drunk each night gets old after a while. You only have so many good things to read, and the TV set only worked occasionally. You had to figure out how to fill your days, and one of my choices was to try to learn as much as I could.''

He said that most advisers, let alone most American soldiers, never really made a serious attempt at understanding the Vietnamese, and the reason wasn't hard to grasp. ''Look how we acted toward them and how we talked about them,'' Boone said. ''A gook was a gook was a gook. I had a boss who used to ask me every day, as a measure of our effectiveness, 'How many gooks did you kill this morning?' No, 'dinks' was the word he used.''

And were our fathers and grandfathers much better? Boone wondered aloud. Didn't they call their enemies ''Nips'' and ''Huns''? Guys on the other side were always objects of derision; and where we had the added difficulty of determining between good and bad Vietnamese, seeing any of them as less than human was almost inevitable. ''The reality was, we didn't trust even the South Vietnamese, and that's the reason we brought over more and more American units,'' Boone said. It's hardly a surprise, given our attitude toward the Vietnamese in general and because of the nature of the war in particular, that Boone believed a massacre like My Lai ''to be virtually inevitable.''

Though he spent most of his time with the South Vietnamese unit to which he'd been assigned, Boone would occasionally visit a nearby American cav unit and a combat construction company attached to the cavalry troops. Boone got to know the construction company's commander, who was an engineer, and they'd trade shop talk.

Once, Boone visited when they'd brought in a band and a stripper. Big night, and there was a lot of drinking. Boone went back with the company commander to the man's hooch, which was a kind of trailer affair. He was sitting, propped against the wall, drinking a beer, when suddenly about eight M-16 rounds slammed through the trailer. "I was so stunned, I just sat there," Boone said. Evidently one of the construction troops was trying to knock off his commanding officer. Luckily someone grabbed the guy before he could do any real damage.

But morale in the American Army generally was "dirt poor" then, and attempted fraggings like the one Boone had witnessed were not uncommon. Discipline was a joke. Not only was the Army in terrible shape, but also the honchos were reluctant to do anything about it because they were afraid of the media. "And you still hear it today, when officers sit around and talk about the media," Boone said, clearing his throat as if a particle of food had gotten stuck there. "There's still that hate, that fear. Because of Vietnam, it's never gone away."

Boone began to pinch the lower right side of his face near his jawbone, grasping an oblong of flesh between his thumb and forefinger. "Actually, the media did an exceptional job," he continued, "of giving a one-sided story. See? See that fear and that hate?" His particular *bêtes noires* were TV reporters.

One night in Lai Khe, a nearby American unit was hit by a sapper team, which had infiltrated their perimeter and blown up several helicopters. Since Boone's ARVN 5th Engineers were putting in new wire and posts the next morning, he went over to see the troop commander whose unit had been hit. Boone arrived about the same time a TV reporter was asking the company commander, a captain, a series of questions. When the captain gave an answer the reporter did not like, the question was rephrased in such a way as to make the company commander imply that his unit ought to have been withdrawn because the Vietnamese couldn't protect him. "It was so damn obvious," Boone said. "There wasn't even an attempt at subtlety."

Boone finally thought the questions so misleading, he found he couldn't restrain himself. "I told this guy from CBS that what he was asking was horseshit. He gave me a big smile under his brown bush of a mustache. I can remember the incident like it was yesterday. I said to him, 'What kind of message are you trying to get across to people? Are you trying to report what happened here? Have you gone around to look at the security measures that had been taken? Or are you trying to get this officer to simply tell you what you want to hear?''

Boone pinched the side of his face again. Since he'd begun talking about the media, he couldn't seem to keep his hand away from his jaw, and his upper lip was no more than a thin pink line.

He was convinced he'd done in his military career and was sure he was going to get a call from higher headquarters informing him he'd been relieved. He could also visualize his wife seeing him cursing the reporter out on the tube. Because of the time difference, it was not uncommon for folks back home to see eighteen hours later what had happened in Vietnam that morning.

The press, Boone continued angrily, had had an obligation to report everything they knew to be true. But that CBS reporter had a specific message he'd wanted to get out, and he couldn't have cared less about anything else. But then, TV was never really interested in dealing with complexities, only in presenting dramatic vignettes that looked good in living color.

"If officers still feel such intense dislike for the media, why are you talking to me now?" I'd never written for a newspaper nor worked for a TV network, but, given what Boone had just said, it seemed the most natural of questions to ask. "And why have five other officers already begun allowing me to interview them?"

Approximately twenty-five officers attending the Army's senior instructional institution, the Army War College at Carlisle Barracks, Pennsylvania, in the fall of 1985 were either cadets from the '64 to '68 classes, or had taught at the Military Academy then or during the early 1970s, and could have chosen to discuss West Point, their Vietnam experiences, and subsequent assignments. Yet only six did. Boone was the last of the six who'd finally come forward after having expressed an initial interest, and, for that reason, seemingly the most reluctant. Did his antipathy toward the news media, an antipathy he could not help articulating, explain his ambivalence? I thought so at the time.

Boone said that in writing a book I'd be judged on the merits of how well I went about doing it in terms of truthfulness and fairness. But didn't I see that wasn't the case with the guy from CBS? The way he was judged was whether someone was watching him or not, or whether more people were watching him than were watching his counterparts on NBC or ABC. And the easiest way to get more people to watch him rather than the others was to be sensational rather than truthful. "Let me tell you, if those other five guys you interviewed were here with us now, they'd still be talking about the media as I've just talked about the media."

And rather than back off, Boone went on to insist that TV journalists blamed the military for an inability to do its job—a conclusion also predicated on a biased presentation. As a result, the officer corps withdrew for six or seven years, licking its wounds. "Yet I always tried to do the best job I could, based on the guidance of my superiors," Boone said. "And you heard me before, I make no excuses for the My Lais. I make no excuses for the body counts. Some people had to compromise their integrity for things like that to have happened. I hope I'll never have to do that. But I was not Medina or Calley, or even any of the infantry officers who had to produce body counts in order to get efficiency reports. I don't know what I would have done. I do know I wouldn't steal from U.S. forces for the Vietnamese. A lot of advisers did that, but I considered it stealing, and I didn't do it."

Before his tour concluded in the fall of '71, Boone remembered South Vietnamese officers telling him they knew they weren't going to win, because they didn't have the firepower or logistical backup that would enable them to accomplish what needed to be done. "We were pulling out, and as far as they were concerned, that was drawing it off the face of the earth," Boone said. "They couldn't support the technological war we'd brought them, and they knew it."

Boone himself was more sanguine at the time. Although anxious about the South Vietnamese, especially when the ARVN 5th Engineers went into Cambodia and got badly chopped up, he still thought their Army could retain control of South Vietnam from within. He certainly didn't envision the North Vietnamese invading the South and overwhelming it, which is what happened less than four years later.

In a letter to his wife summarizing how he felt toward the end of his second tour, Boone wrote that he thought he was probably a better person, because living as an alien among other aliens, he saw in concrete examples multiplied a hundredfold how different people have to think and act differently to survive in their own society. Life was no longer, he now knew, if it ever was, "a set of multicolored balloons."

As support for the war dwindled back home, America's political leaders felt increased pressure to pull the military out. Yet withdrawal left officers like Boone, who'd been ordered to advise the South Vietnamese, feeling as if they'd been placed out on a moral limb. Because how do you advise without gaining trust? And how do you gain trust without extending a measure of friendship or putting yourself at risk, the way Boone did when he chose to live with the South Vietnamese rather than move into the American compound? Yet who finally leaves a friend or someone one lives with when that person is in deep trouble? "I've thought about it a number of years, and from a military standpoint I'm not sure we could have done anything but be dishonorable," Boone said. "But, yes, our leaving *was* dishonorable, and I felt shame."

Despite that shame, Boone believed the real fault resided in what got us involved in Vietnam in the first place, although he did not confine his criticism to America's political leaders. Senior military officers, those generals and colonels who'd made key decisions in the mid-1960s, had bequeathed the Army "a sticky wicket it would take us years to overcome." Boone remembered that when such officers visited the Command and General Staff College at Leavenworth and started talking about the Army and ethics, majors would stand up and say, "And just who are you to talk to us about ethics? Look at the Army's fragmented shape because of Vietnam and the moral dilemma you placed us in." The generals naturally responded, "Hey, we don't have to defend ourselves to you people." There was, in effect, an obvious division between senior and midlevel officers.

"We'd asked for duty, honor, country," Boone said, "and what we got in return were politics, horseshit, and no support. And so we had to fight our own wars internally."

Sandwiched between Boone's two Vietnam tours was a three-year period, during which, 1968-70, he attended the Naval Postgraduate School in Monterey, California. There he studied operations research, systems, and analysis. He'd wanted to go to MIT to study international relations, having developed an interest in history and wishing, no doubt, to understand better what was happening in Vietnam. But the Corps of Engineers wasn't about to sponsor that kind of liberal arts choice. Operations research represented a compromise; while it wasn't international relations, neither was Boone fated to bore himself to death, drawing trusses until he saw them chasing each other in his dreams.

"An operations research guy is a mathematical modeler," Boone said. "The idea is to study a process and achieve, deduce, evolve a quantitative measure for that process."

Secretary of Defense Robert McNamara had decided back in 1961 that what had worked so well for him when he ran Ford Motor Company—quantitative analysis—would work equally well for the military during his stewardship at the Pentagon. At Ford, McNamara was able to control a large organization by converting an abundance of facts and figures into meaningful data, data he was able to apply to industrial production. Using statistics to break down expenses and using computers to get a handle on customers' buying patterns, McNamara seemed able to perform the miracle of raising quality without raising costs. It was hardly an accident that he was known at Ford from his earliest days as a "whiz kid."

In the Pentagon, he surrounded himself with young civilian whiz kids, whom he'd enticed away from various think tanks. Nor did it take the Army long to figure out that it was at least prudent to have some of their own grasp what McNamara and his whiz kids were saying, even if it meant having to send men in uniform to graduate schools where they'd learn relatively arcane subjects like operations research.

At Monterey, Boone found himself quickly and demandingly immersed in the world of statistics, probability, and programming. The ultimate aim was to be able to handle data fast and to understand what all the numbers, each number, the blizzard of numbers, really meant. Boone learned to program a computer, and in subsequent assignments to write his own computer programs. He had always loved math and found the purely mathematical aspects of the curriculum at Monterey particularly appealing. Unlike West Point, where he couldn't embrace a subject, at Monterey he could sink his teeth in as far as they'd go.

Meanwhile, beyond the gates of the school, the country was convulsing, and the coffee break talk between classes was, "What's happening in Watts?" "What's going on in Berkeley?" "Who's rioting today?"

What the Army gives, the Army takes back, and Boone repaid the military for sending him to Monterey by becoming in 1971 the equivalent of one of its uniformed whiz kids. He was to be a senior analyst for two and a half years in a Washington-based studies group, really a think tank-type of organization that developed analyses for the general commanding the Corps of Engineers. Then he repaid them a second time when he worked in the plans and program directorate in the Pentagon, 1977-80. The later assign-ment probably represented the nadir of his Army career, and he came to hate not only what he believed was useless about the job but also what it did to his relationship with his children.

In the fall of 1977 he was a major close to making lieutenant colonel, and he'd hoped, as a lieutenant colonel, to be picked to command a battalion. It was a dream Boone had nurtured for more than fifteen years, or since he'd served that month in West Germany as a third lieutenant with an engineering battalion. "My only desire in the Army was to command a divisional engineering battalion. It was to me the measure of my success."

Battalion command meant he'd be responsible for from five hundred to a thousand troops, all of whom were answerable to him. He would set the tone, tell them right from wrong, and teach them, as an experienced, professional officer, what a soldier's duty really meant. If they performed well, he'd be proud; if they bled, he'd hurt. He'd be their commander, the old man, the main man, *the leader*. It is the single job most professional Army officers who reach the grade of lieutenant colonel and achieve command look back on with the greatest pride and gratification.

When Boone learned, instead, that the Pentagon wanted him for one of its vaunted directorates, he tried to fight it, believing he'd already paid his dues in the engineering strategic studies group during the early 1970s. But he soon began receiving intimations that if he rejected the Pentagon, it would go down as a black mark—one that meant he'd never get to command a battalion. "So I prostituted myself," Boone said, clearing his throat again, as if that errant particle of food still hadn't gotten down, "and I accepted the assignment, because I didn't want to screw up my getting a battalion."

For the first four or five months in the Pentagon, Boone was assigned to a research and development budgeting team that dealt with equipment procurement. A previous member of the team had suffered a nervous breakdown; another had managed to get himself transferred just before Boone arrived; a third, a woman civilian, had recently spent thirty-five days in the hospital. The place was obviously in a shambles, and Boone studiously managed to main-tain a low profile.

Then it was March or April, and the 1979 command list came out with Boone's name on it. He thought that meant nothing less than deliverance. Now if he could just keep out of trouble till the end of the year, his dream of battalion command would come true. Jesus, he could practically taste it! The list had come out on a Friday, and there wasn't a happier man in the D.C. area that weekend. "I felt like a pig rolling in the proverbial stuff."

On Monday, black Monday, the two-star general Boone answered to called him in and said he was being moved to a program coordinating team. This was a more prestigious assignment than Boone's equipment procurement budgeting stint. On blacker Tuesday, the two-star coolly informed Boone he was being deferred— that is, he would not get to command a battalion in 1979 after all, but would remain in the Pentagon an additional year, or until 1980.

Boone explained that some generals get very proprietary, very possessive, and just won't let your warm bod go. Of course, the rationale they offer is, "Hey, I'm expressing the needs of the Army, and those come first. You're going to get to command. No problem, no sweat. We just need you to spend a little extra time here." Instead of leaving the Pentagon in February 1979, Boone's going to wind up leaving in June 1980; and instead of taking command early in 1979, he won't get a command until December 1980. Merry Christmas, Howie.

But first Boone sank into one of those thankless, miserable long-hour jobs in the Pentagon that officers who yearn to command troops never stop hating. Surprisingly, Boone found the job exciting in the beginning, because he got to make contact with the rest of the Department of the Army staff. He prepared briefings and sat in on meetings conducted at the highest levels; and he even got to brief congressional staffers up on the Hill.

"One year, I was coordinator of the R Deck," Boone said. That was the research and developmental acquisition committee, to whom experts from various parts of the Army would submit requests for a certain number of, say, tanks and trucks. Boone and other members of the coordinating team would put the requests together, formulating what they believed made a sensible proposal. Then they'd set up a meeting involving colonels and brigadier generals, who examined their proposal, offering suggestions and changes. Next would be a two-star meeting during which major generals would pass on whether the team had, in fact, coordinated a program the Army really wanted to submit. After further refinements, the modified proposal had to be merged with the rest of the Army's programs, through a next-level committee called, at the time, the program budget committee. Finally it went to the select committee, which is chaired by the vice chief of staff of the Army and consists of four-star generals and high Defense Department civilians.

"I was really at the center of the show, handling the whole picture," Boone said. "I was one of the iron lieutenant colonels who made the decisions in the middle of the night—'We're going to do this and we're not going to do that'—because those committees really come to nondecisions. And when they get through messing things up, someone still has to straighten everything out and say yes or no, and I wound up doing that as a lieutenant colonel. I never should have. But that's the way it worked."

Two words Boone learned to loathe those days were "game" and "player." It drove him up the wall when somebody referred to him as a "player" or called sitting at his desk wrestling with five or six billion dollars at midnight a "game." Because of the constant demand for changes and the conflicting input from the various committees, not only did the money eventually become unreal, but satisfying the system was like trying to also feed a cave full of hydra-headed monsters.

Boone found the only way to retain sanity and still function was to become arrogant. Astonishingly, the more arrogant he became, the more his superiors liked having him around. One day, the colonel above Boone made up a chart he called "Analytical Arrogance." He was referring to the analyst who makes decisions rather than illuminating them. The colonel sent the chart to his boss, a one-star, who returned it with a note, saying, "Please have Howard post this within vicinity of his desk and initial as a sign he's read it daily."

Two of Boone's children were young teenagers then, and there were periods, ten days at a time, when he never saw any of his kids awake. He'd get home at midnight and leave to go to work at five next morning. At least he got to sleep in his own bed those nights. Other times he'd go to work one morning and only return home twenty-four hours later to shower and shave. "That's when I lost my older daughter," Boone said, clearing his throat. "She was in the ninth grade and began developing poor school habits, getting into mischief, and finally into real trouble."

As a soldier, Boone wanted to believe he could justify his absence from home and his children in the name of duty. "But it just didn't add up," he said, "because, finally, I couldn't see what I accomplished and felt I'd wasted thirty months of my life. Things didn't change as a result of what I did; they still haven't changed there. And I certainly didn't leave any footprints in stone." Yet Boone got all the strokes—great efficiency reports, medals, the Legion of Merit, visibility, the whole enchilada, none of which prevented his hating the place in the end.

If Boone's Pentagon assignment was the equivalent of his second year at West Point, his tenure as battalion commander of a divisional engineering battalion at Fort Hood was the equivalent of his enjoyable plebe year. The job simply fulfilled the greatest of his expectations. As head man of the 8th Engineering Battalion, 1st Cavalry Division for thirty-one months, he was in charge of approximately nine hundred soldiers and got to do all the things he'd wanted to do, and for the most part he led them his way.

When Boone assumed command, the commanding general at Hood was in the habit of recommending certain procedures to his battalion commanders. But Boone didn't always act upon the general's recommendations. Once, when the general confronted him, Boone said it simply was a recommendation he didn't agree with. The general answered, "You're right, I didn't order it, it was just my recommendation." When Boone continued doing it his way, the general again expressed his displeasure, and Boone took some knocks in the short run; but he survived, in part, no doubt, because his own procedures turned out perfectly fine.

Boone had acted exactly the same way in Vietnam as a company commander. Only then it wasn't a general he'd had to win over but his first sergeant. He'd told the man he didn't want any papers mounting in his in-box; if a missive required his signature or attention, just place it on his desk. You could get snowed under dealing with paperwork if you weren't careful, and in-boxes were notorious repositories of useless matter you were always tempted to read. But the disbelieving first sergeant kept piling papers in Boone's in-box, and every morning Boone would tip the box over and watch the papers sliding, like sheets of snow dropping off a mountain, into his wastebasket. It took about a week to ten days before the startled first sergeant realized Boone was serious. "Of the stuff I threw away, maybe 6 percent came back to haunt us," Boone remembered. "But it was worth it. I needed to operate in a certain way, and I didn't want needless paperwork tying me down.

I needed to be free to move among the troops, find out what was going on and what was necessary to solidify the unit.''

No on was ever sure where Boone, as battalion commander, might turn up. Some found him wandering through the barracks, others the motor pool or a job site—that was his itinerant style. ''I didn't want people to know, because I didn't know,'' Boone said with a laugh. ''At nine o'clock, I'd say, 'What am I going to do today?' I insisted, you see, that my calendar would always be free from 0900 to 1500. Those hours were mine.''

He'd prepared for the job by spending two years as a battalion operations officer and exec. Executive officers usually wind up performing as a kind of left hand to their commanders. Boone's, for example, wanted him to be a stickler, hard on details, the bad guy. ''That's not my comfortable role, but I'm perfectly capable of doing it if it's necessary,'' Boone said. And, as if to confirm his success, a wife of one of the officers who'd reported to Boone drew a banner for him just prior to his leaving for the Pentagon. The banner read, ''Only Robinson Crusoe could have everything done by Friday.'' Each time Boone had ordered some task accomplished, it seems he's said, ''I want this, and I want it done by Friday.''

In general, officers were again flexing their muscles at about this time, the mid-1970s, because the Army was beginning to catch its second wind. Battalion commanders were reasserting their power, training time was more available, and the sense of a mission-oriented Army began to become pervasive again.

''As battalion commander I was lucky, I had some good people and you have to give them credit,'' Boone said. ''Some good majors, some good company commanders. I also had three or four bad officers, whom I ultimately had to fire. For the most part, the troops were good, too. I had a lot of young E-5's. We were promoting people fast, because we were trying to rebuild the Army. What problems I had with some troops were the same kind I saw in '64, or before Vietnam, when I was a lieutenant in a good unit. But they were problems I could do something about because I had the authority and because the 1st Cav was the kind of division in which a battalion commander could operate.''

Sprawling posts like Fort Hood become particularly valuable when armies are rebuilding, because commanders are able to move their troops around without worrying about tripping over people from other units. When Boone was running his show as a battalion commander, for example, he had his nine-hundred-odd people often out in the field. His priority was mounting a battalion that was cohesive and combat-ready; and building latrines and firing ranges, the principal occupation of his predecessor, took second place.

To support his priorities, Boone would design missions specifically requiring ingenuity and independence. "I had a bridge company that twice road-marched without any external support 450 miles to a training area in the United States, and that's something that's almost never done," Boone said. "They trained for a month on a river, then road-marched back. I went for anything that was innovative. Anything that would build cohesive units. That's the reason I went away from construction. I said, 'Hey, we're a combat battalion.' "

The Corps of Engineers basically consists of three types of battalions: construction battalions, which build the more complex projects; corps combat battalions, which perform less complicated construction but can fight as infantry when required; and divisional battalions, which are organic to a division, as Boone's 8th Engineers were organic to the 1st Cav Division. Divisional battalions accomplish forward area construction jobs that will get combat troops, like the 1st Cavalry, across rudimentary obstacles and help keep them driving on. Operating alongside forward units, they'll frequently be required, certainly more than other engineering battalions, to perform as combat troops.

"I told my division commander, 'We don't want to do any of the construction.' He said, 'I know where you're coming from, Howard. But I want you to compromise. There are certain things you may need to do for the 1st Cav.' I said, 'Those kinds of things I can handle, I can plan for. What I don't want is for just anybody from Fort Hood telling me I've got to build ranges or latrines, that kind of thing.' "

Although certain battalion commanders in the Corps of Engineers derive genuine satisfaction from seeing their units executing useful construction tasks, what Boone sought was to recapture for his battalion the spirit of the Army he'd known in 1964 when, as a young platoon leader, he'd found himself surrounded by experienced officers and NCO's, some of whom had seen combat in Korea and most of whom were technically proficient. The unit's morale was high, and its impressive cohesion typified the can-do Army that had existed before it was bloodied by Vietnam.

In placing great emphasis on cohesion and combat-readiness, Boone believed he was preparing his people to perform tomorrow in a war. That appealed to his intelligence and satisfied his sense of anticipation. What appealed to his romantic temperament was that Boone knew in his soul that he was, having finally been given the opportunity, the leader of troops who *were* combat-ready—warriors who just happened to belong to Corps of Engineers. Any wonder that he found battalion command, during which time his intelligence performed in harmony with his temperament, a rich, fulfilling experience. And believing that after two and a half years he had, in fact, fashioned a tough, ready, and accomplished battalion, Boone found it difficult leaving Hood, although his next assignment was also choice—attending the Army War College.

By this time Boone had had more than twenty years of service and had made contacts in the Dallas-Fort Worth area, where he learned he was eminently employable in the private sector.

It was his wife who said he'd regret till the day he died not taking advantage of the opportunity to attend the War College. She knew, as well as Boone, that only by so doing would he have a crack at a colonel's command. And if commanding troops in a battalion as a lieutenant colonel had been the high point of his career, how could he possibly leave the Army and forgo the War College, passing up the chance of commanding even more troops as a colonel, calling the shots for a brigade?

Thus in the summer of 1983, Boone and his family arrived at Carlisle. More than eight thousand students have graduated from the Army War College, and about a third of them later became generals. With the War College assignment comes the built-in bonus of providing still deeply ambitious officers in their early forties with a year-long opportunity to reacquaint themselves with their families. For Boone it amounted to a last chance to reestablish his bruised relationship with his elder daughter.

The bulk of Boone's academic year covered what the War College calls "The Common Overview." Seven courses are taught during a thirty-four-week period, in seminars attended by fifteen students: "What Makes a Professional Leader," "Strategy," "Operations Planning," "Leadership and Management of Army Systems," "Regional Appraisals" of places like the Middle East and the Soviet Union, "Applications of Power," and "America's Global Military Strategy." This is followed by a nine-week period during which the student has the opportunity to select courses that are extensions of the subjects introduced during "The Common Overview." The final week of the term is a seminar in which major national security issues facing the Army and the country are discussed with a number of guests representing current American leadership. In effect, the school is a kind of intellectual boot camp for those aspiring to become generals.

"At the same time, Carlisle is dedicated to doing pretty much what you want to do," Boone noted. "Mostly, is gave me time to get back to my family and catch up on all the reading I'd put aside while I was working in the Pentagon. On the other hand, I know of one guy who, during his year at Carlisle, played golf 180 times."

The Pentagon! Boone definitely did not want to return there. Unfortunately, the military personnel people informed him less than six months after he'd arrived at Carlisle that he'd done so well during his previous Pentagon stint that a research and development general had requested him, and his name stood high on the projected list of 1984 War College graduates slotted for Pentagon reassignment. Boone didn't say how he felt hearing the news; he didn't have to.

The gods, however, must have known and taken mercy on him, because not long after the new Pentagon assignment looked inevitable, two Carlisle honchos inquired if he'd consider joining them as a War College faculty member the following year. "It took me all of three microseconds to make my mind up based on what I knew the alternative was," Boone said. But because he also knew there was a complication at home, he didn't give an immediate answer. Instead, he talked to his family.

The problem was that Boone's younger son had hated leaving Fort Hood and, a sophomore now, he thought Carlisle High School was for the birds. When Boone said, "I can't make the decision to stay here with your current attitude and the way you're performing in school," his son didn't reply. Of course, in the back of Boone's mind was his daughter's rebellion when he was working twenty hours a day at the Pentagon.

Yet if both children had a rebellious streak, Boone knew very well how they came by it. "My older daughter and my younger long-haired son, who plays the guitar and wears an earring, have the same personality I do. That's not true of my older son, the straight-A, football-playing one." Boone didn't mention his younger daughter, who was a late child and only four.

His wife, Boone said, completing the family portrait, is an

introvert like he is, only she's a lot more organized. "I don't like maintaining calendars, and I didn't wear a watch for the first fifteen years I was in the Army, although I always managed to be at the right place at the right time." He was wearing a digital one with a black band now.

"My son didn't reply to me when I presented the alternatives," Boone repeated. "Instead, he went to Mama. 'If those are the only choices,' he said, 'I kind of like having Dad around. I think we'll stay here and I can live with Carlisle High School.'"

Once his son spoke his piece, Boone went back and told the Carlisle people, yes, he very much wanted to stay. Then he called the general at the Pentagon who was so hot to have him back. "For family reasons and the fact I've been on a treadmill for eight and a half years, I want to stay at Carlisle; I'm not ready to come back to Pentagon." The following week, Boone received orders assigning him as an instructor at the Army War College, commencing in August 1984.

He taught two courses in the Leadership and Management Department. The first, "The Requirements of the Professional Leader," was designed to propel the student into the world of making decision general officers are required to make. "The course," Boone explained, "is supposed to try to get them to coalesce as groups, by first getting them to know themselves and each other better." It proceeds to pinpoint exactly what a general has to do in terms of dealing with individuals and organizations that together, say, add up to the size of an Army division.

The second course revolved around current Army systems— what they are, how they connect, and how generals manage and utilize them. Teaching the course were experts in logistics, personnel, resources. Boone, the force integration guy, was expert in explaining how the systems come together and finally mesh.

He'd never taught before, but found he liked it so much he also began teaching an introductory management course at a nearby Penn State campus. There his students ranged from nineteen-year-olds just out of high school to grandmothers in their midfifties, all of whom were trying to earn two-year degrees. He'd sought the extra teaching to determine whether it might be a fulfilling possibility once he retired from the Army.

On three different occasions Boone has seriously considered leaving the military. The first was when he came back from Vietnam in 1968; his wife, he felt, had suffered real injury when she was pregnant and he'd left to go off to war. The second time was during his depressing and frustrating stint at the Pentagon, when the only thing that kept him going was knowing how close he was to attaining his heart's desire—battalion command. Finally, when he was completing battalion command, he was genuinely tempted to enter the private sector, possibly earning big bucks, instead of coming to the War College. The temptation to leave has, therefore, sporadically underlined Boone's entire military career, especially if you include his second year at West Point.

During this more than twenty-five-year period, Boone believes, he and the Army have undergone a number of major changes. Consider when he first became a second lieutenant, joining the post-Korea, NATO-oriented Army, which was characterized by less units and fewer divisions than now but manned by mostly competent people. "It was," said Boone, "a technically efficient peacetime Army, and I saw it briefly."

In the 1965-66 period, the Pentagon began building the mission-oriented Army for Vietnam, and Boone believes that some of the units sent there—the 1st Cav, the 11th ACR, the 101st Airborne—were excellent and that, generally, America had fielded a superb fighting machine. But because the reserves weren't mobilized, the Army stationed in Europe had all the competence bled out of it in order to build up the Army dispatched to Asia.

Then in the 1969-70 period, the Army that was left in Vietnam also began falling apart, largely because the country no longer supported the war. From 1971 to 1975 there was an Army devoid of real capability. "In that Army, a duty officer had to take a loaded weapon with him when he entered the billets at night," Boone said. "To me, it was absolutely criminal we'd ever let anything like that happen. There were race riots in the mess halls, and the *bandidos* were running the unit areas; and because we did not need any other publicity, we chose not to do much about it."

During the late 1970s, the Army, composed now of volunteers, began its orientation back toward competence. Officers, NCO's, and units received solid training. At the least, it was an Army in which a hard-driving executive officer could again insist everything had to be done by Friday.

"The fifth Army is the one we started constructing in 1980, and that's the technological Army we have now—the one with the new equipment," Boone said. It's the Army he's chosen to remain in.

Because Boone has his own way of seeing things and because he's refused to satisfy other people's expectations when they didn't comport with his own, his career has been shaded by a number of unusual markings. Certainly, neither first sergeants inundating him with paperwork nor generals offering recommendations he considered less than compelling have been able to modify his particular operating style. Clearly, Boone's made a point throughout his life of thinking for himself even in such specifics as living with ARVN troops and wearing his class ring only once a year. And if one doesn't always agree with his conclusions, his insistence on arriving at them seems both admirable and engaging. Not only has this independence kept him from becoming bored and predictable, but also anything less, one suspects, would have tarnished his sense of worthiness.

Boone's latest assignment, beginning in July 1986, took him to Korea as a district engineer, which meant he had approximately seven hundred people working under him. Of the seven hundred, about fifty were American soldiers, 250 American civilians, and the remainder Koreans. Any American military construction done above two hundred thousand dollars in Korea was his responsibility. "You might call a district a kind of contracting firm," Boone explained. "Congress gives me the money, and using my staff, I subcontract the actual construction."

As he set out, he would have preferred a normal troop command, a brigade or what's called a "group" in the Corps of Engineers. There were seven engineering and four troop command slots open; but because he'd commanded troops as a lieutenant colonel, he was chosen to be a district engineer.

No question, not getting to command troops again was a disappointment, but going to Korea as a district engineer was hardly a comedown, and Boone looked forward to it. His wife and two youngest children accompanied him.

All his children's names begin with the letter "C." Boone said, "That's because my wife's name, Christine, begins with 'C.'"

His younger daughter has the interesting but unusual name of Cassandra. Boone cleared his throat and began crushing an empty Diet Pepsi can between his hands. "It's the goddess of discord, right?"

Actually, Cassandra, the daughter of Priam, was endowed with the gift of prophecy, but it was her fate never to be believed, and the word has come to mean someone who predicts misfortune.

"Cassie was the illegitimate child of my older daughter," Boone said. "Only we adopted Cassie at birth, and the birth certificate is written in the name of my wife and me. But we let our older daughter, Cynthia, choose the name for her."

Boone went on to explain that he and his wife had elected to adopt Cassandra because they believed Cynthia was immature at the time. "I did everything in the world at that point because of her age to prevent a marriage, and Cynthia held that against me for a long time," Boone said. "We're father and daughter again, but it took a while to happen. We're also Roman Catholic, and one of the doctrines we have is the right to life, and Cynthia held to that doctrine; she didn't want an abortion. We said, 'Because you can't take the child because you're not ready to, we still have a responsibility, so therefore the child becomes ours.' And as I mentioned, the birth certificate is issued in our names. So it's just as if we had the child on the day she was born." Putting the crushed soda can down, Boone smiled. "I was too old to be a father and too young to be a grandfather. But she's the light of my life. She's a doll. She keeps us young."

Boone was wearing glasses with dark lenses today, dark as the inside of a church. Bifocals shaped like crescents were incised in the glass and suspended near the bottom half of the frames. His head was turned, almost in profile.

"Why'd you agree to talk to me, Howie?" I asked.

When he answered, his upper lip was relaxed and his right hand rested placidly on the table between us. "It would give me a chance to reconsider, maybe restructure my thinking," he said. "It's something I've wanted to do for a long time." The words came out one after another, without interruption, like beads on a string.

PASCHALL, Jim R. (Rod)
COL INF 457-50-3927
BORN: 1 Sept 35, San Antonio, TX

The question posed was, "What, if any, changes occurred at West Point as a result of Vietnam?"

"Oh, West Point experienced many dramatic changes," Rod

Paschall said, "as a result of Korea." He was wearing an open green shirt and a black sweater padded with a colonel's epaulets. A West Point graduate like Boone, like Boone he wore no class ring. Had he also confused Korea with Vietnam?

"Korea?"

"Korea," Paschall said with a nod. "If you take the longer view, and not within your own lifetime, but the view of West Point from its beginning, starting in 1802, and you compare the differences and changes that occurred in the 1960s and 1970s, that period in West Point's history represents dramatic change in comparison to what had gone on before. Before, West Point had remained virtually unchanged—certainly from the time Thayer became superintendent in 1817, through the nineteenth century, and until the 1950s. That's when the changes really begin, and they begin then because there was a perception of failure in the Korean War. The U.S. Army was no longer regarded as a successful institution but one that needed change in order to improve its efficiency. And that need for change was so great, it even extended to the most traditional of American institutions, West Point."

Before then, Paschall said, there was no reason to change. Consider the perception of success the Union Army experienced after the Civil War. No reason for change. Take into account the victory parades resonating in America's cities and small towns following World War I. No reason for change. Recall the Army's breakout into Europe after the Normandy invasion during World War II. No reason for change. But after the debacle of Korea, anyone who said we needed to do things a little differently in the Army and at West Point got a rather welcome hearing, because the Army as an institution was in deep trouble—deep trouble because we did not succeed against the Chinese in Korea.

"Can you imagine officers in the U.S. Army who'd served in China—and there were still many in the Army at the time—realizing that an army consisting of Chinese, whom they'd regarded as an inferior people, a race without military capability, martial prowess, actually defeated a U.S. Army in the field? Can you imagine the shock that was? That was the biggest defeat an American army had experienced in the field abroad since operations in Corregidor and the Bataan Peninsula."

The other great change affecting the Army that will also affect

West Point is the civil rights movement. *Brown v. Board of Education* and the conclusion of the Korean War occurred during the Eisenhower administration, and incidentally, that's really where you date U.S. military involvement in Vietnam as well, Paschall added. In April 1953, to be specific. That's when Eisenhower decided to employ civil air transport pilots with U.S. Air Force aircraft and maintenance crews. It was a move in opposition to Giap's attempt to take over Laos, and it occurred a year before Dien Bien Phu. "That was logistical transport, and they moved up seven battalions very quickly," Paschall said. "And if you want to check the April 1953 date, you ought to read William Leary, *History of Civil Air Transport*, 1984, University of Alabama Press." (The actual title is *Perilous Missions: Civil Air Transport and CIA Covert Operations in Asia*.)

It was also Eisenhower, Paschall continued, who decided to employ federal troops to enforce the Brown decision in Little Rock in 1957. When other presidents disagreed with court decisions, they found ways not to enforce them. What was it President Jackson said to Chief Justice Taney when he disagreed with a Supreme Court decision—"You made the law, you enforce it?"

Needing to back up, I broke in, "You're saying because of our defeat in Korea and because of the civil rights movement, history caught up to West Point and compelled changes there, and that it's a mistake to think Vietnam was the driving force?"

"I'm saying an entry point is very important when you make historical judgments," Paschall responded, "and the entry point you're reaching for is the 1950s. What Vietnam did was to emphasize further the need for changes. It reinforced everything about Korea. But it's doubtful if many of the changes that occurred at West Point in the fifties would have seen follow-through had it not been for the Tet attack and the resulting perception of military failure again. The minute that happened, women would be at West Point. And the minute that happened, there would be a change in the curriculum, so that a relatively narrow engineering focus was going to be changed to a multidiscipline approach. That had been initiated by Gar Davidson, superintendent in the late fifties, but it was by no means being implemented in the late sixties."

If Paschall kept sounding more and more like a practicing historian, that was hardly fortuitous. He'd earned an M.A. in American history from Duke in 1971, and his current job is director of the U.S. Army Military History Institute at Carlisle

Barracks. The institute is the Army's official repository of historical source material and includes the personal papers of many of America's leading generals.

We were talking in Paschall's office, which used to be the office of the commandant of the Army War College, who moved when the War College completed its new complex across the street. It would be difficult, though, to imagine the commandant working out of a larger office than Paschall's, which is shaped like a football field and looked about thirty to forty feet long.

As you enter the office, there's an extended screen blocking your view of Paschall's desk, down at the nether end of the long room. But if you look carefully, taking your time, you can make out Paschall's desk through the folds in the screen. Behind Paschall's desk, off to one side, is an American flag; on the other, an Army flag. Also behind the desk is a bookcase filled with dark green-covered Army manuals.

Immediately behind the screen and facing Paschall's desk is a red leather couch. To the left of the couch is a rectangular table with six chairs behind it, and that's where Paschall and I were talking. Nearby must be twenty to twenty-five figurines, some in bell jars, depicting military men in various uniforms through the ages; a number are obviously American, others Russian, a few are dressed in uniforms of the Indian Army. The figurines go about a foot high and were fashioned for the Army by a woman in the 1950s, Paschall says. There's a sheathed sword encased in glass not too far away and another hanging against a bright yellow board.

Paschall himself has blue eyes, is slender, and looks about five-eight. His hair is starting to turn gray and he has a high forehead. Although he wore no West Point ring, there's an ID bracelet circling his right wrist. A pipe, pouch of Amphora Tobacco, and an ashtray make up the trio of objects placed before him, though I can't recall Paschall lighting up.

He believes that just as it's a mistake to consider the civil rights movement and Korea separately, it's also a mistake to consider the civil rights movement and Vietnam separately. The Army was deeply involved in both. It was certainly the lead institution in the Vietnam War; and because it began to be integrated under Truman soon after World War II, it was a major influence then as well. "I think the Korean War reinforced the point of integration, that all men are equal," Paschall explained. "By God, if you had it in the depths of your heart, or if you needed any reinforcement, all you had to do was look at what the Chinese Army did to the American Army."

Paschall's father, a dentist, had served in the Army Air Force during World War II and was recalled when the Korean War broke out. He'd been sent to Walter Reed Hospital in Washington, and Paschall remembered his father coming home to Texas and telling the family about walking through a segregated ward seeing a large number of black amputees. "From that moment on, Dad became, not an overtly announced but very hard worker for integration of our local high school," Paschall recalled. His father said we just can't segregate anymore. We just can't ask men to do what we ask them to do and still treat them separately.

Another reason the Army was so involved in integration, Paschall believes, was that in the mid-1950s America was preparing itself for a nuclear confrontation with the Soviet Union. People were educating themselves in the use of shelters, school children were instructed to crouch beneath their desks and cover their eyes in bomb drills. "Society had a perception of a monumental forthcoming event," Paschall said, "and if we had a weakness, segregation, we better cure that weakness before getting on to the main event."

To the right of where I was sitting, facing Paschall's desk, was a portrait of Ulysses Grant. Because of the hump created by his shoulder, Grant's three stars form a crescent. His beard is neatly trimmed, and his expression is introspective but relaxed. Gone is that haunted look you often see in daguerreotypes taken of him during the Civil War.

Paschall said he was very fond of Grant. As a captain, Grant was, if not an alcoholic, well on his way toward becoming one. Yet he emerged from that, as well as from the ignominy of clerking in his father's leathergoods store in Galena after leaving the Army. And while he'd experienced good fortune in the early Henry and Donelson campaigns after having rejoined the Army, Shiloh was a disaster, and Grant spent a night sitting in the rain under a tree, while surgeons nearby were amputating, throwing arms and legs on mounting piles. Paschall surmises that Grant was close to going under that night. "Sherman did go under, he temporarily lost his marbles, and they had to call his wife to carry him off. But Grant hung tough. So did Lincoln—best general the Union Army had. He was, he was," Paschall said with a smile. "Lincoln looked at the profession objectively. Didn't accept what a general would tell him because he'd got bitten bad a couple of times. That was A. B, he'd read the Constitution and knew he was the commander in chief. The president bears that responsibility. He's the senior guy in our way of life. He's our first general, really. Presidents have to understand that.''

Directly across the room, I see what looks to be a brown ink sketch of an Army officer drawn on wove paper. The man, in khaki uniform, wears a tie and collar pin; a belt swings down across his chest, hooking on to a second belt circling his waist. He's partially bald, his face tapering and arrestingly sensitive, an aesthete's face. His eyes are reflective, and he seems to be pondering a mystery, some inward puzzle he hasn't resolved. I haven't the slightest idea who it is, and Paschall says with a smile, ''George Patton, as a colonel, circa 1932. He was a well-read officer, who studied his profession, and had a great knowledge of ancient warfare. He'd know, for example, that both Greece and Rome had a beginning, middle, and end, and that the value of ancient history is you have a complete story of society—its birth and death, how it rose and how it fell.''

Paschall pointed to a spot above my head. ''You might be interested in the third picture in this room.''

It was a painting that, unlike the other two, I thought, utterly lacked distinction. It seemed less a painting and more an illustration, of the kind that used to appear in men's adventure magazines like *Male* and *Stag* in the 1960s. It showed Gen. Matthew Ridgway in battle uniform, two strands of grenades worn like an uncompleted necklace down both sides of his chest, studying a map with a South Korean corps commander. Paschall said the picture suggested two things to him. When Ridgway commanded in Korea—the same Korea Paschall believes was a watershed event—Ridgway also commanded the South Korean Army; and whenever the president sought his advice during the Vietnam War, Ridgway always wondered aloud why Westmoreland didn't command the South Vietnamese Army as well as the American Army. The second point Paschall made was that when Ridgway took over from MacArthur in Korea, he'd assumed command of an army that had been sent reeling southward. It was Ridgway who'd stopped the rout, turned it around, and even gained some ground on the Chinese. While we couldn't conquer North Korea, neither could the Chinese drive us into the sea.

It was pleasant and stimulating listening to Paschall ranging with an historian's assured civility among ancient Greece and Rome, geopolitical Asia, and American society. Would the tone have been more refined and the distinctions more subtle had I been sitting in an Ivy League faculty lounge? The only touch Paschall lacked, I thought, was a tutorial offer of sherry, very dry. He certainly seemed as stimulating and poised as any Harvard or Yale luminary.

On the other hand, although a number of CIA alumni graduated from Harvard and Yale, what faculty member there now once also planned assassination operations against rival North Vietnamese officers in Darlac Province as a Special Forces officer in the fall of 1962? And who on the combined faculties of Harvard and Yale once also attempted, as an American military attaché in Laos in 1964, to involve a Laotian neutralist army in combat on the Plateau des Bolovens, and thus, by indirection, compel increased American presence there, contrary to stated American policy? Finally, who among the current deities in Cambridge or New Haven once also served as a member of a military equipment delivery team in Cambodia in 1975, flying out of Phnom Penh as its airport is being shelled a scant day or two before the Khmer Rouge entered the capital, wondering with a sinking feeling not if there's going to be a bloodbath, but who of the Cambodians he'd gotten to know well would be summarily slaughtered? How many?

Paschall, in short, was not merely a scholar who'd arrived at dispassionate historical judgments but also a professional soldier, yet one who'd often performed as a kind of soldier of fortune. The mix is, to say the least, unusual. But equally unusual is the impression Paschall conveys, which is that of someone possessing enormous reserves, a man who's absorbed large, dramatic areas of experience yet is still able, because of those reserves, to present himself perfectly rounded, all of a piece. Do I exaggerate when I suggest that Paschall incarnates the intellectual poise and virile proportions of a hero other worldly men can admire?

Special Forces, when Paschall joined it in the summer of 1961, was still involved in sending so-called White Star training teams into Laos. The teams consisted of covert Special Forces troops whose mission was to help train Royal Laotian soldiers who were fighting the Communist Pathet Lao. Paschall was barely aware of what he'd gotten into when he joined Special Forces; but he gradually learned the score the usual way—over a bar, talking to veteran officers who'd returned from Laos. Another indication that the unit was unusual and its mission serious was that even before he'd reported to Special Forces headquarters at Fort Bragg, he was first sent to Language School in Monterey, California, to study French for six months.

When he finally reported to Bragg in the winter of 1962, the Kennedy administration was in the process of negotiating the neutrality of Laos with the Russians, which meant, among other things, the withdrawal of U.S. advisers there. Kennedy, though, was still in love with the concept of counterinsurgency, and his administration was planning to send Special Forces teams into emerging Third World African countries.

In any case, after Paschall checked in at Bragg, he went to school for sixty days. School at the Special Warfare Center meant a lot of reading and book reports. "You read Mao, you read Giap, you read French counterrevolutionary doctrine and theory, you read Sir Robert Thompson, the British counterinsurgency specialist who fought the Communists in Malaya in the late fifties," Paschall recalled. Extensive field training commenced soon after Paschall was appointed to command a twelve-man Special Forces detachment. The detachment was sent off to the boondocks, where its members got to work among themselves as an independent, self-sufficient unit. It consisted of two officers and specialists in communications, weapons, engineering, and medicine. The men were all cross-trained in at least one other field, and many could speak a second language.

"Most people don't understand Special Forces business is that you take indigenous troops and you're the teacher, adviser, trainer, and, yes, on occasion you must lead," Paschall said. "But that means you not only have to know how to lead, you also have to know how to teach how to lead, which is a different thing, requiring a more sophisticated level of military expertise."

Two weeks before Paschall's detachment was scheduled to leave for Africa, they were told, "Switch continents, you're going to South Vietnam." New orders were cut. Their distribution was again limited because the detachment would still be operating under CIA authority. They were to travel in civilian clothes, and their cover was that they were American embassy personnel.

"We took off in the old crowd-crusher, the Skymaster," Paschall said. "No, it wasn't the Skymaster. It was that bulbous thing that opened in front, C-124. Two decks on it, huge plane, cavernous thing. But, shit, it wouldn't fly faster than twenty miles an hour."

When they finally arrived in Saigon, they were told by the tower not to open their doors, to sit tight, they'd be contacted. Paschall remembered it was brutally hot in the plane. But not to worry, because he could see in the distance a man being wheeled on a throne of portable stairs, with about fifteen Vietnamese pushing and propelling him about. The man, an American major, was going to different aircraft, opening a door, then slamming it shut. Naturally, Paschall guessed he was seeking out the clandestine Special Forces detachment. But when the major opened their door and looked inside, he said with disgust, "This is not the 88th Transportation Company." Bang! He slammed the door shut and they waited another sweltering hour.

Finally, someone remembered to come get them, and Paschall and his group were driven to a nondescript movie theater in downtown Saigon. More confusion, more uncertainty, before one of the embassy people, who was really CIA, mounted the stage and said, "Okay, we didn't know y'all were coming. But don't despair, we got plenty of work."

"Plenty of work" referred to the Montagnard program, which the CIA had organized, involving ethnic minorities living in the high plateau region of Darlac Province. The North Vietnamese were trying very hard to recruit tribes there, because the region held great strategic importance to them. North Vietnamese lieutenants and captains were, in fact, already circuiting the area, making their pitch. "Our scheme was to go in there and recruit the Montagnards before the North Vietnamese recruited them," Paschall explained. A big U.S. advantage was that the Montagnards had a great affinity for the Caucasian French and disliked the Vietnamese, both North and South.

"Unfortunately we've still got a little confusion where we're going to ultimately send you," said the CIA man. "But we've got you sequestered in a villa. Now you guys just relax on the town."

"Wrong goddamn thing to have said!" Paschall interposed. "You don't go into some new place and relax on the town. Shit! You lose control of your people in no time. Hell, they'll start drinking, screwing around, and saying things they shouldn't be saying."

As soon as CIA left the stage, Paschall made a beeline for him, asking what was the first mission coming up. When the man mentioned a new tribe they were thinking of trying to recruit,

Paschall said, "That's me. Paschall. P-a-s-c-h-a-l-l. I want that mission."

The place was disorganized, Paschall said, and the thing to do when you're thrown into something chaotic is take charge. " 'Roger that,' the embassy guy said, and within forty-eight hours we're on our way north, but not before I'd gotten into deep trouble."

What had happened was Paschall did not want to go north without any food. The CIA people had given him a brown paper sack with Vietnamese funny money and were prepared to send him on his way. Of course, that satisfied them, but it had placed Paschall in a position of dependency upon the civilian economy, perhaps forcing him to check into a Darlac hotel for food, something he didn't want to do because he didn't want to advertise his presence. What he wanted was to have the capacity of unloading himself and his detachment immediately into the jungle. To do that he needed C rations, as many as he could get his hands on. "So we went out and stole them," Paschall said. "You'd think they'd give you C rations if they're sending you into that kind of possibly dicey situation. But the Army, government agencies, don't think that way."

The general in charge of logistics in the U.S. Army, Vietnam support command was a one-star named Joe Stilwell, son of the famous Vinegar Joe Stilwell. Stilwell found out about the stolen C rations, and just before Paschall and his detachment were about to take off on an Air American flight headed north, Paschall was suddenly and unceremoniously escorted out of the airport and taken to Stilwell's office.

"You stole my C rations, you son of a bitch, you ought to be court-martialed, and I think I'm going to do it!" Stilwell greeted Paschall, who remembered thinking, "My God, it's my second day in Vietnam, and it's all over but the ball and chain." Stilwell read him the riot act. Who the hell did Paschall think he was? And who the hell did Paschall think he was dealing with? A woman? A child? His mother? Or maybe a goddamn girlfriend? On and on he ranted, and about the same time that Paschall saw himself irremediably disgraced, Stilwell stood up. "All right, Paschall, you son of a bitch!" the general said. "You take those goddamn C rations, you get your ass upcountry, and you kill those fucking Communists!"

Paschall laughed, remembering the scene. "You had to know Joe Stilwell," he said. "He wanted me to know that I may have gotten one over on him, and maybe even that was okay. But I just better remember Joe Stilwell, and I certainly do.''

So upcountry they went, in civilian clothes, clutching their precious C rations. They were met at Boony Nah by a captain, Ron Shackelton, who'd started the Special Forces program in Darlac Province. He'd been expecting them, and he gave Paschall a briefing. Shackelton, who'd written a how-to book about counterinsurgency that Paschall had read back at Bragg, had a truck and jeep ready outside and told Paschall the village picked for him was about twenty miles away. He would have to drive there down a road known as "Ambush Alley." The first couple of nights would probably be risky, but if Paschall took the proper precautions and his luck held, he'd probably be okay. He was given an interpreter, also a South Vietnamese Special Forces representative who, in reality, worked for Diem's brother, Nhu, who was suspicious of the Montagnard program. Paschall left that night, arriving the following day, September 23, 1962, a Sunday, at ten in the morning.

The date and time are precise, Paschall said, because they're cited in a log kept by a fellow officer, Capt. Terry Cordell, a log Paschall now retrieved from his desk at the other end of the room.

The log, which resembles a ledger, has a black cover and is about eighteen inches long. Its pages are of graph paper and have printed numerals at the top right-hand corner. On page 63, dated Sunday, September 23, the following entry appears: "1000: Lt. Pascall arrived with half team (remainder to follow) for assignment at Buon Dang BAK in LAC THIEN sector." Cordell kept missing the "h" in Paschall's name. There's a second entry on the same page: "2300—Lt. Pascall has several ambush sites I'm interested in. Will discuss his G-2 and coordinate."

Paschall flipped to page 107 in the log, to an entry dated October 15, 1962. The entry isn't scrawled but printed: "Cordell went down with Capt Booth, Sfc Foxx at approx 1530 hrs this date, L-28 crash vic . . ."

Cordell was killed that day, Paschall nodded, during a big operation for that time, involving seven hundred men and five helicopters. Its code name was TIGER, and Cordell had planned it. He'd been a transportation officer drafted into Special Forces because of their sudden expansion during the early 1960s.

"Anyway, when I got to Buon Dang," Paschall said, "I was given a slip of paper written in English or French by a VC officer, telling me to get the hell out of there within a number of hours, or my men and I would be killed. That's why we did a lot of work that first night, putting out those ambush sites Terry mentions in the log.'' One ambush netted two VC killed, another log entry records, and a third VC taken prisoner.

During the following months, Paschall found he had no trouble enlisting Montagnards: They were standing in line because they wanted weapons to protect themselves from the North Vietnamese and Viet Cong, both of whom were operating in Darlac Province. In those days, the bad guys worked at agitprop. Their technique was to enter a village that had no weapons. They'd walk in armed, perhaps four or five of them, and tell the village chief to gather the villagers. Then they'd propagandize. Talk down South Vietnam. Talk down Diem and his family and say how they were going to overthrow them all. Say what a glorious thing North Vietnam was. And if one of Diem's district chiefs made a mistake, they were smart enough to highlight it, striking a resonant chord. Finally, they'd require a rice tax, occasionally a money tax.

Paschall's mission was to defeat the agitprop teams by providing volunteer villagers with a civil defense organization within the village. The object was to force the agitprop teams to have to fight their way in. Paschall and his detachment would conduct ten-day training programs, teaching volunteer villagers how to fire weapons. Basic medication techniques were also taught. Radios weren't available, but there were other ways of getting help. Paschall particularly remembered a rudimentary method of raising air power. ''We'd have a large arrow that had gasoline pots on it, or burnable material that could be lit at night and would point in the direction from which they were receiving fire. If we could get an aircraft from Saigon, which admittedly took getting, to come in, then air power could be used to help them. In all, twenty to thirty villages in that area signed aboard.''

The terrain was extremely rough—marshes, lakes, rapid rivers, hardwood trees of immense size. Paschall recalled seeing black bears, wild elephants, and monkeys. Monkeys! ''If you're in the area, and you hear distant monkey chatter—monkeys in triple-canopy jungle will follow a patrol until they get bored, so if you pick them up and they start raising hell with you—the best thing to do is freeze and wait,'' Paschall said. ''They'll lose interest and leave, and then you can proceed. If you hear it elsewhere, you know somebody else is coming along. You don't know if it's a person or an animal, but monkey chatter in a jungle is something you can't afford to ignore.''

Paschall usually wore jeans and a Western-style bush hat. His detachment had been given German Schmeissers, 9mm submachine guns, which were beautifully balanced but misfired constantly because of their defective nine-cent magazines. They were also given Thompson submachine guns, which were too heavy. Paschall preferred a U.S. carbine, folding stock, which was a good weapon to use close in, or an AR-15, which was the forerunner to the M-16.

"We had talked to an outlying village, but they'd decided not to accept weapons," Paschall said, describing a typical contact he'd later managed with an agitprop team. "I'd gone in and made a little pitch, saying if you accept weapons you have to put up a defense perimeter and take some training. But this village chief didn't want to do that because, he said, it would create problems for him. Okay, he doesn't want to do it, fine, it's up to him, so I'm on my way out of the village with my patrol.

"Then a guy who doesn't buy the village chief stops me and says, 'Hey, this guy is under the gun because we have an agitprop team coming in. They know of your presence here, and they'll be here tonight.'

"I said, 'Okay. If I come up tonight, will you show us where the agitprop team is and give me some degree of assurance we're not walking into an ambush?' He nodded, and we agreed to meet by a tree. He was paying taxes and the VC were recruiting his sons, and that's why he agreed. The village chief had decided our base was too distant from his village, so he was going to have to live with the VC. Probably a lot more perceptive than this second fellow.

"So I head off back into the jungle and just cool it, wait for the sun to come down. Sun comes down. I waited an hour, and then came up and made my contact. There was probably one other American and five Montagnards with me. Wait, that's a little light for this. We put in an ambush over on the other side of the village, so I must have had a couple more.

" 'Okay,' he said, 'they're in the village and in this particular house. They have weapons.'

"We began having this whispered discussion in French about how we're going to do this head agitprop guy in. The scheme was, we'd just break in the goddamn door and shoot the son of a bitch, rather than play around. There was a regional force company in the area, and I had the sense, the feeling, that if we did it now and got out, we'd probably survive it fairly well. I also knew there'd be great consternation among the villagers, because of the village chief and his position against us. So it was in the nature of a raid—we'd go in, do the bad guy in, and then make it. But I was going to make it taking the opposite direction from which I'd come—actually heading toward enemy country. I figured they'd never suspect that. I'd find some place quiet and lie doggo until the sun came up, and then maneuver my way back.

"And it worked that way. We shot the son of a bitch in the mouth. One of my NCO's was the trigger guy. Rest of us provided security. I was out, supervising the whole thing. Collected everybody at the rallying point, not too far from the house. We killed, I think, three of that team. We'd put a little ambush on the other side, but the two guys coming out chose to go in the other direction. Big consternation in the village as we took off and hit the jungle."

Paschall estimated he was involved in similar contacts with the VC about every ten days, and while a number of his people were wounded, he never had a friendly killed, neither American nor Montagnard. " 'Make the other son of a bitch die,' " he quoted his watchwords, " 'but you be careful.' "

He did this for six months, practically operating on his own, almost as a free-lancer, before the Army began gaining control of the system. All the while, Paschall was writing reports in triplicate, fashioning them in such a way that each of the three men addressed thought he was commanding Paschall. "I had a Special Forces colonel in Nha Trang who was getting a report, and at the bottom line I'd write I need X, Y, and Z. I had a U.S. military adviser in the province headquarters who thought he was running me. And the guy who really had the authority was sitting down in the embassy, two hundred miles away. But they'd all come across with the radio batteries I needed, the weapons, the ammunition, the funds, and beyond a shadow of a doubt, we succeeded. Cleaned Charles H. Kong's clock in Darlac Province, hands down."

After the six months were up, Paschall went to Nha Trang, where he was debriefed by a lady who'd come up from the embassy. "Old Nan, I've forgotten her last name," Paschall said. Nan, a character, smoked cigars, and Paschall found it slightly disconcerting to report to her.

"I assume she was CIA?"

"Well, let's say the embassy." (Later, it occurs to me Paschall's reluctance ever to mention the CIA by name probably explains why he hadn't given the William Leary book about civil air transport its actual title.)

"Were you in uniform then?" I asked.

"No. Yes, and that's another interesting story." Paschall grinned, and because by this time I knew he knew how to tell a story, and knew which ones were particularly good, I sat back and relaxed.

It seems that a Captain Hussong, from the 1st Special Forces Group off Okinawa, was down in III Corps, below where Paschall had been operating, and this Captain Hussong was to be honored by a visit from Gen. Paul Harkins, Westmoreland's predecessor. Harkins had a U.S. senator in tow, showing him the glorious work that was being done in the Republic of South Vietnam. At the time, Harkins didn't really know a lot about how Special Forces operated, because it wasn't in the military chain of command, though it was starting to filter through because of Operation SWITCHBACK, which divested the CIA of its paramilitary operations. Anyway, when Harkins got out of his Caribou, Captain Hussong went out to greet him. Hussong was attired in his usual shower clogs and black pajamas, and he had a myna bird perched on his shoulder. Give Hussong credit enough to know the required military decorum, and he saluted the great man, whose four stars gleamed in the sunlight. The senator, however, sensed something rotten in Denmark and managed a hesitant backward step. Legend has it that Harkins, taking one long, disbelieving look at Hussong's tatterdemalion finery, turned crimson at the Adam's apple, though the red streak probably started at his toes. When it finally reached his head, Harkins exploded, chewing Hussong's ass from here back to Okinawa. The problem was that this got the myna bird excited. Intelligent enough to perceive that Harkins was a threat to everybody's casual existence, the myna bird decided to brazen it out by cawing louder and longer than the general was capable of shouting. Harkins, no fool, realized he'd met his match and, turning on his heel, loaded his shocked and bewildered guest back on the Caribou, and off they flew to Saigon.

Back in Saigon, the shit really hit the fan, and that night frantic, coded messages went out to remote, isolate jungle Special Forces camps: "Everybody in uniform! Not only that, but commanding officers, get your ass down to Saigon by any means available immediately!''

Paschall remembered sitting in Vietnam airliner the following day, next to an old lady chewing betel nuts and toting a live chicken. God knows the fate of the chicken, but it couldn't have been much worse than what befell the Special Forces officers now assembled in that same sorry movie theater Paschall had been taken to the day he'd arrived in-country. There, our perplexed coterie of warriors was brutally told, ''This is the Army. Who the hell do you people think you are? Get rid of all pets. Shoot them, strangle them, eat them if need be. Anyone found with a pet or out of uniform beginning at 0600 tomorrow will be drawn and quartered,'' or other hyperbole to that effect.

That afternoon, before returning to Buon Dang, Paschall retreated to a rooftop bar in the Rex Hotel. ''I was crying in my beer,'' he said. ''Jesus, fucking Army, get your goddamn priorities straight.'' He was the only one sitting at the bar until two lieutenant colonels wearing khakis came stumbling in. From the waist down their uniforms were splattered with mud.

Paschall had been looking off in the distance, toward the Mekong Delta, where a spectacular firefight had been going on this particular day, featuring flares, gunships buzzing in and out like a swarm of hornets, and clouds of billowing smoke. The two light colonels start talking, and because their conversation was interesting, Paschall joined in.

It turned out that the firefight they were all watching was being directed by Lt. Col. John Paul Vann, who later left the Army because he, too, didn't agree with Harkins' policies and directives; and the battle was at a place called Ap Bac, from where the two mud-spattered officers had just returned. Before that, they'd been advisers to a South Vietnamese division farther south, where they'd evidently taken up some of the local customs, specifically the female customs with some friends down there. When Harkins' deputy found out about this terrible breach of military decorum, he summoned them to Saigon to kick them out of the country. On their way up, they'd run into Vann and the Battle of Ap Bac, and Vann had stopped them, given them rifles, and forced them to go into an assault line. Although they knew their military careers were as good as over, into the assault line they'd gone, to fight this last miserable battle, and they were still sputtering with disbelief and rage at Vann's sheer nerve and lack of fraternal consideration.

"Whenever I have a bad day," Paschall mused, "I think about those two guys, because I know things could always be worse. Can you imagine their indignation at the Rex? It's one of the glorious memories I have of Vietnam."

During the time Paschall was operating in the Vietnamese jungle, he ran, among other things, a leper colony for two months and went north, looking to do in a VC general by the name of Amka, who rode a white horse. To find Amka, Paschall was obliged to organize an elephant convoy, which was necessary to transport rice for his Montagnards. Then he had to negotiate a settlement with the Montagnards when they disarmed his officers because the tribesmen were frightened to operate outside their native province. Little wonder that during those six months it seemed to Paschall he'd lived six lifetimes, and the experience was so heady, so high, and so unusual that he was not quite ready to reenter the Regular U.S. Army, finding it next to impossible to communicate with officers who hadn't had similar experiences. He felt out of touch to the extent that when he returned to the United States and that other government agency, which Paschall never mentioned by name, approached him about working for them, he took a lie detector test and submitted to a series of interviews over a four-day period, after which they offered him a job that would have sent him back overseas. But getting out of the Army was a big step, and he asked for some time to consider what to do.

"I did a smart thing then," Paschall said. "Got in my Corvette and went down home to Texas on a thirty-day leave." If he joined the CIA and it didn't work out, he knew he'd probably return to Texas, so he looked up his old high school friends. "What I found out · was they were bored. They also led rather dull existences compared to what I'd experienced. A lot of them were working on their second wives." When he reported back to the Army, he thought he'd give the CIA a crack, anyway. But then a number of senior Special Forces officers took a special interest in him at Bragg, kept repeating he didn't have time to resign, and otherwise convinced him to remain in the military.

Approximately a year later, in May 1964, Paschall was happy he'd retained his commission, because he was back in Southeast Asia, only then it was as an assistant Army attaché to the American embassy in Laos.

It happened that Kong Le, a Laotian general who'd fought for the Communist Pathet Lao, had switched sides and was now head of the neutralist army, and the Pentagon wanted a Special Forces officer who spoke French and had had experience in neighboring Vietnam to go to Laos and report on what was happening to Kong Le's forces.

Paschall, in civilian clothing again, flew to Laos carrying a diplomatic passport. He reported to Bill Law, an American officer who'd served with the OSS in Asia during World War II and who, consequently, was extremely knowledgeable about that part of the world.

Every Monday, Paschall would fly up to Kong Le's headquarters on the Plain of Jars. There he'd nose around, talk to Kong Le's people, and observe combat operations.

Laos, Paschall recalled, has no mountain chain; it's a jumbled mass populated by strange animals. "A bumble bee damn near the size of your first. I had one light on me and couldn't see where the bee ended and my hand began. We're talking animals here." Paschall also recalled the krait, a black cobra with yellow bands and a small, triangular head. One bite and you're gone.

On Fridays he'd fly back, writing his reports on the plane taking him to Vientiane, Laos's capital. He was able to work this civilized five-day week because, incredibly enough at the time, the opposing forces were each gentlemanly enough to knock off for the weekend.

Paschall had an additional assignment to perform once a month. When he'd arrive back in Vientiane on certain Friday afternoons, Colonel Law would meet him at the airfield and say, "I have a helicopter ready for you; go to point X." At point X would be a Royal Laotian battalion that had recently captured a new Chinese weapon—say, an AK-47. Paschall had been given some trading material to use in acquisition of the weapon. Cases of Salem cigarettes were particularly popular with the Laotians, who liked the menthol. Also popular were cases of Haig and Haig Scotch and Courvoisier brandy.

"Colonel So-and-so, glad to meet you," Paschall would say. "I understand you have such-and-such."

"Oh, yes, we have that," his Laotian counterpart would respond. "Come in and take a look."

"Oh, it's just beautiful," Paschall would say, looking the merchandise over. "We'd really love to have it. And, by the way, what would you ask for it?"

After some vigorous bargaining, a deal would be struck. the

worst part of these *mise en scènes*, Paschall recalled, was that you were considered an old stick-in-the-mud if you didn't take a drink after consummating the deal. It was maybe 110 degrees, Paschall hadn't eaten much of anything the previous five days, and there he was, standing out in the hot sun, drinking Courvoisier straight. Then back he'd get on the helicopter, off to the next stop, the next item, and the next drink. The rules of the game required you imbibe each time, and by the end of the trip you almost always came back more than a little potted.

Once all the matériel was firmly in U.S. hands, Paschall would fly with it to Bangkok, Thailand, where a complicated ballet of the blind between American and Thai authorities took place. The United States didn't want to embarrass either itself or Thailand by being discovered running what might be called contraband goods. Thus another American plane would be on the runway, cleared for takeoff. As the first plane pulled in, it would stop on the runway, quickly transfer the cargo, and the second aircraft would then immediately take off. When the arriving plane finally parked, there was no longer anything aboard to declare, except perhaps a maintenance emergency. The Air America pilot would crawl out and say, "This damn plane won't fly. We're going to have to spend the rest of the weekend in Bangkok getting it fixed." Paschall would add on cue, "Oh, shit, not again." Then he'd get some ground transportation and head over to the Oriental Hotel.

"There was nothing like the Oriental in those days," Paschall recalled. "Potted palms, rotating fans, first-class food, delightful people. You're looking out on the Chao Phraya River, and you expect to see Sydney Greenstreet wearing a white linen suit approaching your table."

During this memorable Lao tour Paschall had his closest call. It was in the summer of '64, when he participated in an action designed to seize the intersection of two Laotian highways the Communists had held since 1960. The arm of the attack Paschall was assigned to accompany was to approach from the west, about 50 kilometers from the intersection. To get there, the column had to traverse jungle terrain. They'd miscalculated and hadn't brought enough food, and Paschall remembered subsisting for a day or two on bamboo shoots, which are cellulose and have no food value, though they do occupy your stomach for a few hours. Water was also a problem. "But the Laotian colonel leading the column had a marvelous leadership technique," Paschall recalled. "When we'd reach a little stream, the column would keep walking, but the colonel, who'd been striding at the head of the column, would stand by the stream and collect his soldiers' canteens, which he'd fill. Then he'd race along giving each soldier his filled canteen, before taking a drink himself and regaining the head of the column.''

Despite the lack of food and the difficult terrain, the column reached its designated promontory at the specified time. They could see the intersection in the distance and witnessed a deception attack, which went off at zero hour. The idea was to induce the North Vietnamese guarding the intersection to move away from it, in order to repel the deception attack. Then the column Paschall was with would slip in behind them, seizing their base and the intersection.

It worked like a charm. Paschall remembered seeing the dust and the artillery miles away as the North Vietnamese left their base to repel the attack. The column Paschall was with started running through the jungle, toward the objective. Arriving at the now relatively unguarded intersection, Paschall stood there panting, out of breath, when somebody took a shot at him with a 57mm recoilless rifle. Paschall recognized the unmistakable whoosh sound. The damn thing couldn't have missed by more than six inches, and just the wind of it almost flattened him. It turned out, there was an additional attacking column, but it hadn't been coordinated with the others, and he'd almost been done in by a friendly. Lucky Paschall.

He wasn't quite so fortunate when Ambassador Leonard Younger got wind of a scheme he and another officer had cooked up to involve Kong Le in operations taking place near the Ho Chi Minh Trail. American policy was still geared toward maintaining the neutrality of Laos. But both Paschall and the other officer, whose name was Chuck Elliot, thought the policy was a farce, because they believed the Kennedy administration had given away half of Laos when America signed the Geneva Accords of 1962. It was unwritten, but there was an understanding, Paschall stated, that Laos would be longitudinally partitioned, and what had been given away included the Ho Chi Minh Trail, which was being used to great advantage by the North Vietnamese and the Viet Cong.

"I don't remember whose idea it was, Chuck's or mine, but it doesn't make any difference, because we were of the same mind,'' Paschall said. Their idea was to suggest to Kong Le that he put a portion of his army down south, which would get them involved with what was coming down the Ho Chi Minh Trail. Get part of his army off the Plain of Jars and put a platoon south, on the Plateau des Bolovens. If part of Kong Le's neutralist army was threatened, the United States would back that neutralist army.

"The minute we suggested it to Kong Le, he said, 'You're damn right. I've been thinking of that for a long time. The neutralist army should be represented down south, and we're only up on the Plain of Jars. Besides, I can recruit a lot better down there than up here. So how do we do it?'"

Easy, they told him. Get an Air America aircraft, a C-46 or C-47, take a platoon aboard it, and put it down there. Once it gets shot at, U.S. reinforcements would come pouring in.

"The trouble was Chuck Elliot and I got caught before we could pull it off," Paschall said. "Both of us were called in, got our ass chewed for making great moves, and then we're told that that evening there'd be a farewell cocktail party for us in the ambassador's residence. And then Unger laughed about it. But he threw us out of the country, although I still think it was a good idea. If we could get the war where it was supposed to be, the policy in Laos would tie in with the policy in South Vietnam. Instead, the policies were separate all during the Vietnam War, and they shouldn't have been. But next day I was out of it, on a plane going home."

Flash forward ten years. It's June 1974, and Paschall, now a lieutenant colonel, is on orders to command an infantry battalion in Panama, when he's suddenly handed a new set of orders, assigning him back to Southeast Asia. This time it's to Cambodia, and this time he didn't want to go because, convinced the Khmer Rouge insurgent forces had pretty much beaten the American-supported Lon Nol government army, he didn't particularly wish to attend a deathwatch. But the Pentagon insisted that an ex-Special Forces officer with Vietnam experience who spoke French go there as a member of a military equipment delivery team, and Paschall was chosen: "You will go."

His job was to look at the five-year defense plan for Cambodia and determine what, say, would be the number of mechanized vehicles they would need for 1979. "But I looked around and realized the very idea of such long-range projections was dumb, because there ain't going to be a 1979 for these guys," Paschall said. At the time, the American general in Cambodia was William

Palmer, and he needed to know what was happening in the field. Paschall wrote his own job description, which was he'd be an infantry inspector. This would enable him to nose around, because in the military assistance law was a clause that said every major item—and a truck could be considered a major item—had to be inspected once a year. No such inspection had ever been conducted in Cambodia. Henceforth, the law was going to be complied with.

So Paschall went about inspecting for the infantry as well as for Special Forces and psy war. Another officer did the same for the artillery, and a third covered the cavalry. They became field analysts, inspecting regiments, then wrote memos for General Palmer: "Here's what they told me. But here's what I saw. Here's what they needed yesterday And here's what they need tomorrow." Paschall said the Cambodian military was deeply corrupt, which made the future appear even more ominous.

"Cambodia was a terribly emotional thing for me," he recalled. "I'd invested so much time in Southeast Asia, and I knew I was going to witness the downfall of at least Cambodia. And then in March 1975, when the Communists took Ban Me Thuot, I knew Vietnam was going to fall, too. What particularly made everything happening over there then so emotional was that nobody gave a damn in America. We were there watching it happen, but it was of no concern back in the States."

Perhaps worst of all, he suspected a bloodbath would ensue when the Americans finally left Cambodia. Not in the magnitude it occurred—with an estimated two million, or a quarter of the population, systematically exterminated—but a bloodbath nonetheless. "I thought about all those Cambodians I knew—where were they going to wind up, and what was going to happen to them? They'd relied on us; the United States was their friend and ally. But we were selling them out. Yet when I was on those inspection tours, I was the United States to them, and I didn't feel very good about my role. Didn't feel very honest."

"What could you have done?"

Paschall shrugged. "Commiserate. 'Just hang in there,' I'd tell them. 'Do the best you can. How much do you need? I'll try to get it for you.'" Paschall looked away. "Jesus, the backwash of war is a wretched thing."

He said he'd begun closing himself off emotionally years before. "I could become a very unwarm person, particularly to someone I'd had a fondness for who didn't happen to be an American and to whom I might have to say, 'We're not going to do it the way you've requested.' You had to protect yourself. At the same time, it was a tremendous emotional drain.''

The people Paschall worked with knew to the day Phnom Penh was going to fall, because Congress had refused to authorize funds for further aid, and the Cambodians were running out of ammunition. Paschall left the country a day or two before April 17, when the Khmer Rouge entered the capital.

The crew who flew out the group Paschall was with were contract fliers, ex-Air Force pilots recruited in a San Francisco store-front. They wore cut-off jeans, shower clogs, and T-shirts. ''Bird Aviation was the outfit that did it,'' Paschall said. ''Bird needed the work because they'd finished with the Alaska pipeline. They were flying C-130's and DC-8's, big ones, that we could get into Phnom Penh if you really shot them in. When the planes began to land, the Khmer Rouge would start firing. They used the tower as the marking point. They could see the plane coming down, and they'd obliterate everything around the tower. But we were using a ramp on the other side. The scheme was to get the rice and ammunition off on the other side as soon as possible, and kick the plane in the ass to go. It was dramatic, because all that unloading would be going on with rounds hitting.''

The day Paschall's group left, they went out to the airport, turned over their keys to the Americans left there with the cars, and ran for a 130. ''The fire around the airport was such, the plane had to corkscrew coming in and corkscrew going out.''

The plane flew them to an American base off the Gulf of Thailand, and they were quartered in a BOQ fashioned in the form of an American motel. The beach was beautiful and there was an Olympic-size swimming pool. But neither then nor for a number of years could Paschall get Southeast Asia out of his system.

''Why was that? Because you'd been out there five years, put yourself on the line, had more of a stake in what happened there than most Americans?''

Paschall shook his head. ''Not only that, but *all* the friends who'd died—''

''That was an insensitive question,'' I said quickly. ''Dumb, insensitive question.''

''—both Asian and American.''

What seemed finally to have helped Paschall was an assignment he'd managed to finesse to the Language School in Monterey beginning the summer of 1978. To this point he'd never had a staff job at the Pentagon and didn't particularly want one. He'd spent part of 1977 and 1978 at the Army War College, where a number of fellow students worked the phones, hustling interesting Pentagon assignments. But because Paschall didn't want one, he made no phone calls that winter, hoping that by the time he felt he'd have to call, in March, all the Pentagon jobs would be taken. And they were.

"Rod, you're an operator," I said with a laugh, grateful for the opportunity to kid him so soon after having posed a dumb question. "A fox."

When they asked him what he wanted instead of the Pentagon, he mentioned studying Mandarin Chinese out at Monterey. He had a couple of reasons. First, it would help keep him clear of the Pentagon if some late opening popped up. Second, he'd determined he was not going to make general, because he'd been labeled a Special Forces officer, and those people weren't given stars—too much cloak-and-dagger about their Vietnam backgrounds to make them all-American choices. Consequently he'd decided to specialize the remainder of his career in Asia, trying to find interesting assignments over there, for which Mandarin Chinese certainly figured to come in handy.

It took a bit of maneuvering, but he finally managed to get a ticket punched out to Monterey. There were about eight people in each class, and the instructors were Chinese. Paschall believed he had a facility for languages, though, curiously, Russian was one of his toughest subjects at West Point. In any case, learning Mandarin Chinese at age forty-four turned out to be much more difficult than he'd anticipated. The difficulty meant he'd have to study hard, alone, and it provided a thick layer of isolation. His classmates were in their late twenties and early thirties—a second layer of isolation. His wife and children were living in Washington, D.C., which made for a third, deeper layer of isolation. Paschall thus knew from the beginning that the year was going to be tough. What it really sounds like, though, is that almost from the beginning he'd *wanted* it to be tough, as if he'd sought a kind of reclusion for himself within the Army.

"I turned it into a good year by adopting an almost monklike existence," Paschall remembered. He'd get up before six and run on the beach or in the mountains behind Monterey. Then he'd come down, shower, and eat in the troop mess. He'd go to classes in the morning, study at noontime, then eat a slight snack. Classes again the afternoon. Then he'd find the gym and go through a heavy workout schedule. He'd study at night.

On weekends he'd compete in ten-kilometer races in nearby California towns. He had to do all that to keep sanity because, although the best thing for being-sad is to learn something, Mandarin Chinese is extremely difficult. Of course, what Paschall really did, in simultaneously learning a foreign language and running marathons, was immerse himself in a kind of annealing solution. "But, by God, I just sort of rejuvenated my whole damn life, because when I came out of there, at forty-four, I was in better shape than I'd ever been." Paschall nodded more to himself than to me. "Hard work, physical and mental. But boy, I'll tell you, after Monterey, I was ready to go."

Paschall was, however, better conditioned than most who'd had similar experiences in Southeast Asia almost from the beginning, and certainly from his early teens, when he'd worked as a ranch hand and found himself riding a horse for long days in the bush country of northwestern Texas. He was born in San Antonio in 1935, worked on ranches summers and during the Christmas break from school, and hoped one day to run his own ranch.

"It's a tough existence," he remembered. "Four-thirty in the morning you're out, and it's the kind of bush country where you have to use a horse. If, as a kid, you had any affection for the animal, you lose it pretty damn quick, because a horse is a dumb animal that requires a lot of care, and it soon becomes only a means of transportation."

Ranching had appealed to Paschall because it was a way of life he'd have been able to call his own. "There's a romantic association with that. It's a very manly, *macho* kind of thing, and that struck my fancy as a kid." The problem was that a severe drought had occurred in Texas in the mid-1950s, and ranches began failing and going broke. "I knew enough to know that even the big ranches of those days wouldn't make it, so I had to change my plans."

He'd put himself through Southwest Texas State College in San Marcos for a year, selling his textbooks in March to make it the final couple of months. Money was tougher than ever to come by, and his father, a Democratic county chairman, suggested Paschall consider going to West Point. Not only was it free, but also West Point had the reputation of being a very good engineering school, and Paschall thought he had a facility for engineering. In addition, he thought he might like military life.

He remembers flying from San Antonio to New York City during the summer of 1955 in a Lockheed Constellation. He landed at Idlewild (now Kennedy) International Airport and, following instructions, took a cab to the Port Authority Terminal in New York. There he caught a bus up to Highland Falls, the small town at the gates of imposing West Point. Paschall stayed for the night in a hotel that was more like a boardinghouse. He thought that because he'd had a year of college and was an athlete of sorts he'd have it made.

The next morning, carrying his suitcase and wearing a suit, he entered the narrow gates, and Beast Barracks started. Beast is still called a "rite of passage," although old-timers say that since 1973 it's considerably less rigorous. But try telling that to the folks who've survived it since then.

In Paschall's time, it was a rough eight weeks, which began the first day. "In Beast Barracks we went into the central area, the sally port, and bang!" he remembered. "The first classmen got hold of you, put you into line by size, told you what a miserable animal you were, how shoddy you looked, and the necessity to change your posture. My God, the immediate degradation was just unbelievable. It was very hot, July, but they put you in wool uniforms right away. The opportunity to get water was difficult, and guys were passing out. They got your attention right away. I don't know if all that is necessary, but that's the way they conducted business and had for years."

The first classmen who ran Beast demanded compliance and performance in minute detail, and Paschall considered leaving a number of times. What made him stick around despite the constant harassment, what really intrigued him, was that he realized he was with a group of people who had talent he'd never seen before. "You could tell right away that a lot of these folks were educated in high school at a level that exceeded that of, I'd say, two years of college down in Texas. Well, I wanted to be with those folks, and I wanted to compete with them."

Because he'd taken a year of Spanish in college in Texas, West Point in its wisdom thought it might be useful for him to study Russian. The language almost did him in. "The course was taught by a Lieutenant Colonel Denezovich," Paschall said. "That rhymes with son of a bitch. The guy was the reincarnation of the tsar." At

West Point, fail a course, and you were gone; and Russian, Paschall remembered, had the highest number of failures in terms of percentages. During the term, Colonel Denezovich said, "From here down, we turn out." He swept his hand, and the motion, like a knife paring a loaf of bread, sliced away half of the class. Denezovich meant that in his teaching experience, half the people in the class would fail and be gone. Half did, and half were.

Paschall found he had to devote himself to Russian so totally, he could not afford to spend much time with other subjects. Harassment he learned to handle with humor. "We'd give the upperclassmen derogatory nicknames, and there'd be little snide remarks back and forth, to see what you could get away with when the other fellow wasn't watching. And that humor would pick up on their side as well. So what was building was a sense of camaraderie."

Although there was considerably less upperclassmen harassment the second year, Russian didn't go away. "Same clown was teaching the course. Jesus," Paschall said, offering an involuntary shudder. It was at about this time, too, that he first became interested in what was happening in Southeast Asia. "I was always keen on current events and there were some interesting problems occurring in that part of the world then."

That summer, the Class of 1959 went on the trip to several Army bases, where they were wooed by the different branches. Part of the wooing included dances, for which officers would make the supreme sacrifice by trundling out their petrified but eager daughters. "You'd have blind dates from one post to another," Paschall recalled. This was organized by hop, or dance, managers. The hop manager would wear a red sash around his tight uniform. "Okay, Paschall, your date is Chrissie Jones," he'd say.

"Well, what does Chrissie Jones look like?" Paschall wondered.

"Have no idea. But she's counting on it, and the last time somebody walked out on his date, somebody got a letter on it, and the word is if it happens again, the guy who walks is dead."

In the mid-1950s, America was having a difficult time getting missiles to fire properly. Nevertheless, one of the trips Paschall's class took that summer landed then at the White Sands Missile Range, where the artillery branch was preparing to impress them by firing a Corporal missile. First, though, the cadets had to hear a three-hour lecture on the glories of missiles. It was about 120 degrees, and about half the class began dozing after fifteen minutes. The lecture was classified, and from where Paschall was sitting he could see the man on the podium consulting material stamped "secret." In the background, Paschall noted a little desert whirlwind. It would drift here, it would drift there. But generally it was drifting toward the podium, and the cadets were beginning to nudge each other, indicating the approaching whirlwind. Was it real or a mirage? And if real, would it reach where they hoped it would reach, doing what they hoped it would do? When, to the infinite delight of the assembled, it finally entered the sanctified area around the podium, classified notes, like snow in a swirling blizzard, blew in every direction, and there wasn't a cadet face that wasn't masked by a shit-eating grin. Secret stuff flying all over the place! Scrambling, red-faced officers! It certainly seemed to wake everyone up, and people began paying serious attention to the upcoming main event—firing the missile.

In those days the Corporal was so ineffective that when you fired one, you had two ready, because one almost invariably got screwed up. In fact, you had two countdowns going on simultaneously. "Watch the missile on the right," said the man at the podium, barely recovered from the embarrassment of having to chase down his secret papers. Wham! The missile on the left went up!

Paschall's third year, no Russian, no reincarnation of the tsar, what a blessed relief! He was getting good grades and worked his way into the first half of the class, although he'd learned a valuable lesson when he took an advanced course in differential equations. He'd done well in algebra and calculus, but differential equations constituted a level of math he simply could not penetrate. "I was sort of devastated for a while," he said. "It's a prideful thing, you know. But then, I think I realized it was valuable to know that that was not going to be my forte."

That summer, as a first classman, he was selected to be a member of the Beast Barracks detail. The man running it was classmate Peter M. Dawkins. Dawkins—all-American halfback, tenth in a class of 499, subject of a *Time* magazine cover story, later a Rhodes scholar—a golden boy, a golden man, a golden everything. Yet Paschall remembered that Dawkins had entered West Point with a touch of polio.

Dawkins had wanted to get as much of the authority for running Beast into the hands of himself and his fellow cadets as possible. His real purpose was to make their Beast the best ever, but to extract a price, which was that the senior class would get to use their cars earlier, with more long weekends in New York. So

Paschall and the other cadets in charge of Beast that summer worked especially hard to make sure everything ran more than smoothly.

At the same time Dawkins was running Beast, he was getting himself ready for his last football season. "I would see him down in the sinks, in the basement area where you had the showers, as late as two in the morning, working with weights," Paschall recalled. "A lot of people don't understand where Dawkins came from. But he had some physical deficiencies when he walked into West Point, but by working at them, he achieved everything. I don't think Pete ever failed in any objective he ever set for himself."

Longer weekends in New York meant a lot to Paschall during his last year at West Point. The Hotel Piccadilly near Times Square gave cadets good breaks on rooms. Management also took a somewhat blasé attitude toward some fairly riotous conditions on Saturday nights. Cadets would bring their dates to the Piccadilly and all pile into a single room. If you didn't have a date when you arrived in New York, no sweat either. You could dial the Nursing School at Columbia Presbyterian, with whom the cadets maintained a kind of social compact. "You could call a number there and you could get a date right away," Paschall said. "And you didn't have to limit yourself to one. You could get five. 'Give us five.'

"We'd usually go with our dates over to Yorkville first, where the bars had polka dancing. It was dirt-cheap. You could eat brown bread, salami, drink beer, and then listen to some oompah band." Then they'd head down to the Piccadilly. "You have all these gals in a hotel room. The lights were out, so that people would get mixed up with other people. It was mostly fondling, but I often think about what we actually looked like—all those bodies strewn on the beds and around the floor."

After graduating from West Point, his first permanent assignment was at Fort Campbell, Kentucky, as a platoon leader with the 101st Airborne, commanded by William C. Westmoreland. Paschall, who was to serve in three divisions, believes Westmoreland was the best division commander he ever had. "It's unfortunate, I think, Westmoreland doesn't have the luster, either inside the Army or out of it, because people don't know. Possibly he'd been promoted beyond his abilities, but in troop command, in his element, he was a superb leader of men."

Westy relished addressing the troops, Paschall recalled. In the

101st you were in the field all the time, so you'd particularly look forward to getting off weekends. Paschall was going with a girl from Vanderbilt that year, and Fridays he'd come in from the field, clean up, and get ready to shove off for Nashville, maybe even that night. But then Westmoreland would show up in his jeep. A formation was called. The purported idea behind the formation was for Westmoreland to convey to the troops what a great job they'd just done in the field. Westmoreland would get out of his jeep and tell the troops to break ranks and gather around their commander. The officers would stand in the background. Then Westmoreland would say, "God, you guys did a great job. It was superb. I can remember seeing old Jackson here." Jackson was a pfc and his name tag wasn't visible, but Westmoreland had remembered his name. "I saw old Jackson humping that damn machine gun out there. You looked good, Jackson," and smiles would break out among the troops. Seeing those smiles, Westy would segue to his punch line: "Now, I know you fellows were scheduled for garrison duty this coming week, but there are a few things we still need to work on. Because if any damn crisis occurs, the first unit to go is going to be the 101st, and we can afford no mistakes. So men, we're going to have to go back into the field Monday."

Which meant that eager young officers wouldn't be driving to Nashville to meet pretty young Vanderbilt coeds that weekend, because if the troops were going into the field, said eager officers would have to work Saturday and Sunday getting everything ready for the operation Monday. But the troops, they're cheering their heads off, and Paschall, his heart sunk down near about his ankles, would be standing there, thinking, "You goddamn clowns know what you're cheering about? Do you? Do you?"

That Monday morning, Paschall stood in the doorway of a plane heading to a drop zone colder than a well digger's ass. The clay ground below looked hard as a rock. He was toting a load weighing 250 pounds, because to survive five days in the woods you needed a shitload of something or other.

It was, everything considered, a little rougher Army then, Paschall mused. The troops drank too much and got themselves killed on the road Saturday nights. One guy in his company held up a supermarket. "You know the phrase 'I don't know what they do to the enemy, but they sure scare hell out of me'?"

Paschall was with the 101st for about a year and a half when he ran into a slight problem at Campbell. There was a hoary tradition in those days that required every new airborne officer, regardless of rank, to go through an initiation ritual known as prop-blasting. The way it worked was you were dressed ready to jump, when a so-called doctor approached with a horse syringe containing raw alcohol, which he proceeded to squirt down your throat. Then you had to knock off a prescribed number of push-ups and squat jumps. After which they'd make you stand on a board that had been placed on a table. The board and table represented the inside of a aircraft. Near the side of the table was a second board, which was supposed to represent the door of the aircraft. Below the table was a raft filled with water.

You would shuffle to the board representing the door and grab hold of it. Attached to the board was an electrical device that would shock you to your toes. The jumpmaster wouldn't let you off the table until you'd taken the prescribed dosage. Then you leaped off the table. If you did the PLF, your parachute landing fall properly, you were henceforth a member of the outfit in good standing and you'd get a card certifying you'd been prop-blasted— an extremely important receipt, because it meant you wouldn't have to go through this miserable rite of passage again.

Anyway, when a new battle group commander joined, he was duly put through the ritual. The man was a colonel, full bird. Paschall was assigned to escort him home. Although the colonel seemed very drunk, in truth he'd fallen into an alcoholic coma, but nobody quite realized it. Paschall dutifully left the stricken colonel in the lovely hands of his young, brand-new wife, and departed. The brand-new wife was shocked at seeing her colonel in an almost comatose state. Soon shock turned to alarm, and she had him rushed to the base hospital. The brand-new wife, furious now, remembered Paschall's name and rank. Naturally, considerable finger-pointing erupted, and an official investigation commenced.

A day or two later, Paschall got a call from a classmate who was a personnel officer at Campbell. The classmate said, "This damn investigation is going on, but I can get you out of this unit now. I know you're not responsible, but if things really go sour, you'll get a bad efficiency report and screw up your career. You've been here a year and a half, and you'd be leaving in six months anyway. I advise you to leave now, go early." It took Paschall all of ten seconds to respond, "Roger, let's do it." Said the classmate, "The unit looking for people is Special Services. Come on up for a PT test this afternoon." Paschall thought Special Services had something to do with movies and wondered why a PT test, but his not to reason why. So up he went to personnel, did his mile run, squat jumps, and push-ups. "Okay," said the classmate, "you're now a member of the 77th Special Services."

Christ knows, the classmate's heart was in the right place and he had all the words right, too, save the last. It wasn't Special *Services* Paschall had just joined but Special *Forces*—the fabled Green Berets. "I literally didn't know what I was getting into," Paschall said, although little more than a year later there he was, wearing jeans and a bush hat and carrying a U.S. carbine, folding stock, in the steamy Vietnamese jungle.

During the next six years, Paschall got to play a variety of roles on the Asian continent. He not only performed practically as a free-lancer in Vietnam and attempted to become a policymaker before getting kicked out of Laos, but he also commanded a company in Korea, then one with the 27th Infantry Division back in Vietnam before becoming an aide to Gen. Fred Weyand when Weyand commanded first the 25th Infantry Division, then corps-level II Field Force Vietnam.

"Weyand was a first-class infantryman as well as a smooth politician, a combination you don't often see in the Army," Paschall noted. "He'd fire a guy in a minute, but do it in such a way the guy never knew he was really being crucified, his career damaged just enough so that he couldn't screw up troops again." Although Weyand looked like a gangly hail-fellow-well-met, in truth, Paschall said, he was a very private person, an excellent judge of character, and had a feeling for Asia most American officers of that time lacked. "A great guy," Paschall said, "and I enjoyed working for him."

Concluding that second long Vietnam tour, Paschall was savvy enough to prepare himself psychologically before returning to the States. He remembers holding an earnest conversation during a quiet moment with a friend, Bob Foley, about serving together back in the United States. Both were bachelors, and they agreed that wherever they wound up, the place would have to satisfy three requirements: women, a decent party life, and a regular eight-to-five job. One of the tenderloin posts, they further agreed, was Fort Belvoir, which is outside Washington. Neither wanted the Pentagon, with its miserable work schedules, although Paschall later served there for a year, beginning in mid-1979.

Foley left Vietnam first and managed to get himself assigned to

Belvoir; Paschall followed soon after. They shared an apartment on the sixteenth floor of the Southern Towers, a complex overlooking Washington. Parties were held there almost every weekend, and the great Sunday morning sport was to go out and see where people had parked their cars Saturday night. Paschall lowered his voice when he said, "But both of us fell." Pronounced *sotto voce*, it sounded as if someone had died, and I was about to say "Sorry to hear that" when he explained, "Both of us were married." Paschall met his wife, Pat, at one of those parties. She was a Vietnam widow and had a young daughter. "Pat's third-generation—long Army family-type thing."

At Belvoir, Paschall worked out of a research and development office and did a lot of traveling to factories that were manufacturing mechanized infantry vehicles. He was, in effect, a matériel officer and a briefer. It sounded pretty tame after getting off the roller coaster in Southeast Asia.

But at the time, the late 1960s, the Military Academy was looking for Army officers to teach military history at West Point. And because of an interest in history and the fact that he'd done well in the subject as a cadet, he got picked up for the program. It required his going to graduate school and earning a master's degree.

In the fall of 1970 he attended Duke University, where he wrote a thesis on U.S. Aid to China, 1932–40, and witnessed a number of student protests. Paschall's sense was that the country had swung against the war during or shortly after Tet. Despite that awareness, the campus protests had a hollow ring and rubbed him wrong, one reason being that those protesting "were obviously upper-middle-class students wearing peasant clothing."

At the same time, Paschall believed that the protests did suggest several levels of comprehension. The first was that the war had been going on too long, it didn't look like we were winning, so it was time to get out. Paschall thought he understood and even felt some of that himself. America should have been doing better by then.

"Another level of protest proclaimed that only American blacks were dying in Vietnam, and that was bullshit," Paschall said. "We now know that draft-age black males in this country constituted 13.5 percent of the population at that time and they absorbed 12.3 percent of the casualties. But for years people thought the blacks carried an inequitable burden. That's simply not true. Quite frankly, I didn't know it at the time, but I know it now.

"There was another element I did know at the time, and it really disturbed me. And that was the sense of guilt in upper-middle-class students who'd avoided the war. They knew somebody else was doing their dying for them, and their reaction was to get rid of the war, get rid of the guilt."

What perhaps bothered Paschall most about the war's critics was what he took to be their total lack of concern for the Vietnamese people. "As a Special Forces officer, I'd lived in a South Vietnam village. To the protesters, the people in those villages were superfluous; it was only Americans they were concerned about. They couldn't understand a Vietnamese who'd lay down his life against the Communists, and I'd seen that. They didn't have the depth of knowledge the Vietnamese had of what would happen if the North won."

This isn't to suggest American policy didn't indulge at least two important miscalculations about Vietnam, Paschall said. From the beginning, we'd misunderstood the fractious relationship between China and North Vietnam. China probably would have entered the war had the United States invaded North Vietnam, but Paschall doubts they would have employed ground troops had American forces operated in southern Laos. China never wanted the North Vietnamese to gain suzerainty over all of Vietnam, Cambodia, and Laos. Their centuries-long rivalry precluded that, and we never properly gauged their mutual antipathy. "Had we gone into southern Laos, we would have cut off the Ho Chi Minh Trail, which meant the North Vietnamese would have had to run them through Thailand. It would have been impossible. That was, by the way, one of the reasons to get Kong Le off the Plain of Jars and on to the Plateau des Bolovens."

The other big miscalculation the American government made was that it had grossly underestimated the resolve of the North Vietnamese. For us to have won militarily in Vietnam, Paschall believes, we would have needed considerably more than the five hundred thousand troops we once had there. "If somebody told me the North Vietnamese were going to put twenty divisions into South Vietnam in 1975, I'd have said, 'You're loony. They won't push that much.' Well, they did. We didn't know the price they were willing to pay. When I came back in '68, I thought the war was looking up, because we damn near killed them. Dumb! Dumb!

Didn't know the depth of their resolve. And didn't do some basic mathematics. The rule of thumb on a society is that you can put 10 percent of the population in uniform; if you go over 10 percent, you're cutting into the ability of that society to function. You can also spend 50 percent of the GNP to conduct a war, and for fairly extended periods of time—four or five years—without killing your economy. Well, they never got close to either figure.''

His year at Duke not only seemed to have given Paschall added perspective about Vietnam but also prepared him intellectually for teaching at West Point just as the Academy itself prepared him methodologically. Instructors at West Point have to go through a summer program before they're permitted to start teaching in the fall. During these summer sessions, the new instructor is obliged to present many of his lectures before a senior faculty member. The emphasis is on how to teach, using the most effective teaching methods, and the presentations are videotaped. The tape is played back, and criticisms are offered. Nor does it end after the summer. Often, during the academic year, the chairman of the department, or his deputy, will sit in during a class. After the session, he offers suggestions. The point is always how to do it better, and improvement is expected.

Unfortunately, Paschall found the cadets considerably less interested in the subject than he'd remembered his classmates were, and that was true the entire three years he taught there, 1971–74.

Part of the explanation was certainly Vietnam. During this period, too, you had Watergate and Agnew's resignation. There was a general lack of belief in authority throughout the country, and it had seeped into West Point as well. "I'd describe it as a kind of subliminal insolence in the minds of cadets toward those in authority," Paschall said. It certainly wasn't an attitude that had existed when he was a cadet. "The early seventies *were* different. Generally, in military terms, you could say that morale was not very high."

Teaching military history got him to wondering if he could write it, and when he retires from the Army that is what he has his heart set on doing. At the Army War College, he'd completed a manuscript titled "Defense of the West," in which he defined the West in geographical, religious, and racial terms. Then he analyzed every war fought in or by the West, determining what was a successful defense and what wasn't.

More recently, he was written a number of published articles about counterinsurgency, and he was planning to write one on terrorism. (From 1980 to 1982 he was commander of America's DELTA Force, trained to rescue hostages, but that was the one assignment of which he said, "There's not too much I can tell you.") In any case, the articles would form the basis of a book on low-intensity conflict, and that's the area he hopes to specialize in.

But it was Southeast Asia we circled back to near the end. That part of the world had played so crucial a role in Paschall's life, it was difficult letting go without giving him an encore or two.

"The effect it's had on the American people is certainly significant," Paschall said about the Vietnam Memorial, "not only because of the memorial, but because of its replica, which has been going around the country, only I'm not certain why. Mixed in it, I suppose, is that sense of guilt I mentioned before on the part of those who didn't serve. Another element is that bizarre phenomenon of the Vietnam vets wearing their camouflage fatigues, talking about having to kill babies and not sleeping at night as a result." Paschall shook his head. "I put no credence in that whatsoever. Somebody killed a baby, that son of a bitch ought to be in jail right now. Calley got everything he deserved, and, unfortunately, his battalion commander was later killed in combat. But he should have been in jail, too. You don't do that as a soldier, and you don't permit that as an officer. But there is a perception of those horrid events and of good men being distorted and scarred for life. Bullshit! There was a higher percentage of becoming a combat fatality in Korea than there was in Vietnam. Almost twice. Data on that is in Thomas Thayer's *War Without Fronts*. I haven't heard of Korean vets killing babies and being scarred for life, have you?" When he gestured with both hands, it rang a bell for me, and I couldn't recall if I'd asked why he, like Boone, wasn't wearing a West Point ring.

"That's a funny story," he said, my cue to lean back.

When he reported to Special Forces, after leaving Campbell following the prop-blast imbroglio and taking six months of French at Monterey, he was interviewed by a captain who'd asked where he got his commission. When Paschall said "West Point," the captain looked at him kindly and said, "I advise you, son, to take off that goddamn ring, because the guy you're about to report to is Col. Garbage Gut Riggs, and he hates West Pointers with a passion. Just hope he doesn't bring the subject up."

A word to the wise, and Paschall removed the ring, slipping it in his pocket. Then he knocked on the colonel's door. Riggs glanced at his record and happened to note that Paschall was born in San Antonio. Riggs was a fellow Texan. "Aggie?" he asked. "Gig-em!" replied Paschall, and he never had a single problem with the man.

But he never put the ring back on, either. Not then, nor during any subsequent assignments with Special Forces or with any other unit. By keeping the ring off, Paschall, in a sense, acknowledged the stamp others applied to him—Special Forces. Unfortunately for Paschall, a number of senior officers still believe that if you promote one of those guys to general, you might be opening a can of worms.

"On the other hand, that's a good cry-in-your-beer story on Saturday nights, and I plan to do a lot of that when I retire," Paschall said with a grin. "Hell, if they made me a brigadier general, that would screw up all those good Saturday nights."

"Sure," I thought.

TAYLOR, Wesley B., Jr. (Wes)
COL INF 068-36-8728
BORN: 5 Jun 44, Covington, KY

"My son's a freshman in high school and hasn't decided what he wants to do yet," said Col. Wes Taylor, a courtly man whose voice is spun with mountainy cadences. "But my daughter's a premed student in college and carries forward many of my charac-teristics and values except one: She's a very good student. But what I mean for a parallel—she's driven, and the prospect of failure upsets her a great deal. She establishes her goals and then manages herself through the steps necessary to realize them."

At six-two and 212, Taylor offers a tight end's intimidating presence. Mostly bald, he has brown eyes, a thick neck, and surprisingly small feet. He wears what appears to be a Porsche design watch; at any rate, it has an imposing face, lined with five or six hands, and is spangled by at least four different sets of numbers. The large watch looks good on Taylor—appropriate, certainly not overwhelming.

Taylor was the youngest cadet of the Class of '65, barely a month older than seventeen when he first walked through the Academy's gates. He was accepted for West Point as a high school junior, though he hadn't taken trig, solid geometry, and physics. Although West Point has a vaunted selective process, it appears someone there blew it, because Taylor was plainly admitted a year too soon. And if he hadn't been absolutely driven, even as a kid, made utterly miserable by the prospect of flunking out, there's no possible way he could have graduated. Frequently he thought he wasn't going to. "As a result, I didn't have time to be homesick or anything else," Taylor remembered. "I was so concerned with academic survival, I was so wrapped up with just living day to day, survival became an end in itself, almost a consuming passion." Delete the "almost" and you'll have it exactly right.

It was as a tall seventeen-year-old, quite independent and alone, that he employed a relay of Greyhound buses from northeastern Tennessee up to New York City. Considering the trip an adventure, it was only when he arrived in New York, boarding the last bus, which would take him to West Point, that the realization sunk in that he was out on his own. That night he got a room in the Thayer Hotel, had a pleasant meal, and found he couldn't sleep, wondering if some of the terrible stories he'd heard only that evening about what was to hit him the next day could possibly be true. Up bright and early the following morning, he was probably one of the first to report in.

The admitting process those days began in the gym, and Taylor remembered it as rather orderly, with a plethora of signs and arrows indicating where to go next. It was when he stepped out at the other end of the building and reported to a uniformed cadet, who promptly marched him over to his barracks area, that the real excitement, the real trepidation, the real trauma set in. Suddenly Taylor wasn't politely asked to do this or that. He was told, and the voices doing the telling were sharp and abrupt. Within minutes he found himself lower than the lowest, suddenly someone who not only could do nothing right but also knew even less than that. His sense of confusion and dislocation was total and frightening. "The first day was like being thrown into a cold shower," Taylor recalled. "I remember it graphically. Your values, your sense of proportion, everything seemed to be uprooted. And the noise, the chaos, the activities of the day were so intense, you didn't find time to analyze. You were constantly reacting.''

Because he'd done a lot of traveling with his parents as a boy, Taylor believed he was probably more adaptable than most of his classmates to Beast Barracks. Still, he was never given credit for knowing or doing anything correctly, and nothing was taken for granted. ''You leaned quickly that, in the Pavlovian sense, proper performance and proper conduct were rewarded by the absence of punishment or abuse, and poor performance was correspondingly dealt with severely.'' West Point, Taylor noted, was absorbing a civilian product, and within a short time changing his outlook on how he approached performance. That, basically, was the bottom line: how responsive the man was in the performance of a particular task.

It certainly wasn't a pleasant eight weeks, but Taylor found Beast child's play compared to what followed: West Point's academic regimen. While he'd been a good student in high school, skipping his senior year meant he'd immediately have to decipher mathematical subjects that seemed to be written not in the X's and Y's of difficult but ultimately comprehensible English, but in sinister-looking characters vaguely resembling what—cuneiform? ''It threw me immediately, because I looked to my left and right, and my classmates appeared to be adjusting readily,'' Taylor said. ''Yet in many cases, I simply couldn't understand what I was reading. It was traumatic, because I wanted very much to be at West Point, but saw early on the potential for me to lose the Academy.''

Trying to catch up, he seemed to study harder than anyone else. In those days, lights out were at eleven. But Taylor often found himself in the hall or latrine, trying to make sense of what he was reading until two, three in the morning. Not only was he losing sleep, but also he wasn't eating right, and he grew thin. What saved him, especially in that first year, were other cadets in his company, who proved effective coaches.

Though athletic, Taylor could not afford the extra time varsity sports required because of his poor academic standing, and his social life hardly fared much better. ''If it hadn't been for a roommate's parents kind of semi-adopting me and meeting a roommate's sister, I'd have had no social life at all, because I spent my weekends and every spare moment I had studying. It was only at my roommate's insistence to get out and take a break that I met his folks. And I found that change of pace, that relaxation, helped release the tension. While it helped, I wasn't smart enough to recognize the value of that early enough. And left to my own devices, I'd go right back to pouring it on in the books, trying to catch up or get ahead, so I'd be ready for next week.''

Harassment didn't bother Taylor all that much. The only time it really got to him was when an upperclassman, aware of his poor academic standing, used it as a tool to badger him. ''That probably hurt worse than anything else. But then, learning to deal with that probably steeled me for a lot tougher things to come.''

Taylor concluded his plebe year with a huge sigh of relief, figuring, only when he couldn't help thinking about it, that his second year just had to be better.

But that September, he quickly discovered he was compelled to take still other tough math courses as well as physics. ''At that point I guess it hit me it wasn't ever going to get much better.''

Taylor approached his third year with guarded optimism, finding he did a little better, but not much. Academics still required an enormous effort. ''I was always concerned day by day. To me, just getting a passing grade was difficult, and I could never relax.''

It was after being released from an English class during the first semester of his third year, Taylor recalled, that there was more commotion than usual in the hallway. A cadet, bracketed by a crowd of his peers, was pressing a portable radio against his ear. ''President Kennedy had been shot in Dallas minutes earlier that Friday afternoon, and you could see jaws dropping all around you.''

Monday, Taylor was part of the West Point contingent that marched in the president's funeral, and he remembered that the train ride to Washington wasn't marked by the usual kidding around. ''Life goes on, especially at that age,'' Taylor said, ''but the open joking and rowdiness were on a far more reduced scale.'' The Corps of Cadets is always the lead parade unit when it marches, and during the final preparations in the marshaling area before the first cadet stepped out, cadet officers kept repeating, ''Make an extra effort, look sharp, demonstrate pride.''

Taylor had been a fan of Kennedy's since at least his last year in high school, when he was a member of a debating team supporting the notion that Kennedy, the first Catholic president, would be dominated by the pope. Because he'd admired Kennedy, Taylor found debating on the side against him difficult. "Besides, I'd been raised that race and creed didn't really have a place in deciding whether to vote for a man, as long as he wasn't a Communist. And the more I read Kennedy's speeches and learned about him, the more I got excited about his exuberance, apparent zest for life, and vision for the country."

When Taylor completed the first half of his senior year, he began to tell himself, "I'm only a semester away from graduating. *Nothing* is going to stand in my way now!" He knew he was a proven survivor. He'd learned not to wait until troubles started and then try to dig his way out on his own. At the first indication of academic problems, he requested help. He felt he'd trained himself within the system to use the system as much as possible. At the same time, he never felt tempted to violate it. "There was nothing to be gained by my doing that. Everybody knew I was a dummy, so to speak, academically; so my focus was purely on getting through academically. I got the help I needed. My professors were concerned about my status, and I felt as long as I demonstrated interest and concern about surviving, they'd be supportive." He was particularly fortunate his senior year in that one of his classmates, Pete Cahill, had all the gifts and know-how for doing well in science, and it was Cahill who'd helped Taylor understand the engineering courses he remembered were his last major academic hurdles.

"Graduating from West Point was the biggest day of my life until that point," Taylor remembered. "I'd shown myself I could do anything I basically put my mind to, and I was very proud of just having made it academically."

Ask Taylor how he came by the furious tenacity that seems to impel him, and he'll respond with a shrug. "I'm certainly a product of my parents." Times were tough, and Taylor, the eldest child, had three sisters. "The things I never wanted for, I felt, were love and affection," he said. "But the material things, my father taught me, were up to me. I had to earn them."

As a boy, Taylor worked four summers and during a number of Christmas vacations for an uncle who was a dairy and tobacco farmer in Bowie, a small Kentucky town of about 150, fifty miles northeast of Lexington. While his uncle wasn't a pauper, neither did he have tremendous riches to throw away. Work and survival came first. The rewards, like Taylor's learning how to fish and hunt, which he came to love, were offered only after all the chores were done. "I think my uncle and my dad had the most impact as far as establishing my value system."

As for his mother, she was very determined for Taylor. "When I was a Boy Scout, she was continuously on me to get this requirement done or meet the next objective. And if I slacked off or forgot about it, she was the one who got me back on the stick. And that kind of coalesced with the masculine values my father and uncle passed on. The rest of it was produced in the pressure cooker of West Point. There, survival was really up to me." His parents weren't around. Neither were his sisters nor his high school friends. But they all knew he was attending West Point, and attending it early. "That said, I certainly didn't want to be placed in the position of having to go home, hanging my head and admitting defeat or anything else. I guess I recognized it was up to the good Lord and me to get me through, and He was going to be the biggest part of that equation. I think that helped reinforce my Christian faith a little bit; well, not a little bit, a great deal."

Taylor was born in Covington, Kentucky, which is south of the Ohio River and across from Cincinnati. His father was a reserve officer called to active duty during World War II. After leaving the Army in 1946, his father continued to work for the government as a civilian engineer. Then he was recalled to active duty after the Korean War broke out, and the family joined him when he was stationed in Japan. The following year, Taylor contracted malaria, compelling the family's return to the States. Subsequently, his father, now an engineering staff officer, was sent to Iran, and Taylor lived in Teheran for two years. His father's responsibility was constructing border camps along the Soviet frontier, and Taylor remembered how exciting it was visiting there, with bristling Cold War Russia just across the way. About this time he caught, not malaria again, but the travel bug. "Here I was, in my early teens, and I'd already been around the world in two different directions." His father's next assignment took him back to the States, where he was an adviser to National Guard units in southwestern Virginia. The family lived just across the border, in Tennessee.

It was there that Taylor first thought of attending West Point. Many of his father's friends were officers who'd been commissioned at West Point, and he found himself attracted to them. Taylor also remembered seeing *The West Point Story* on television, and the weekly program further excited his interest. When he talked to some of his father's friends about the Academy's admissions process, one of them suggested he take the test in his junior year to gain the experience. To Taylor's considerable surprise, he was accepted for admission that summer; and though he hadn't quite earned a high school diploma, the Academy waived the requirement, saying his schooling overseas had placed him on the same educational level of would-be peers entering the Class of 1965. Whichever officer decided that could not have been more wrong even if, four years later, as a result of Taylor's courage, he'd possibly deluded himself into thinking he'd been right all along. On second thought, perhaps he *had* been right all along. Perhaps he'd administered a little-known, still top-secret test that measures sheer guts, and Taylor chalked up an almost perfect score. In any case, Taylor later said, "I felt very prepared to handle anything the Army might put in front of me after graduation. I figured that that was what I was there for, and I'd had some pretty tough experiences already."

Taylor knew from the beginning he wanted to deal with people, not machines, and he wanted to have an impact on other men's lives—to lead, to influence, and to train them. And because he believed the infantry was the cornerstone of the combined arms team, he chose that branch. "I wanted, most of all, to be on the cutting edge."

At West Point he'd been aware there were American troops over in Vietnam, but it wasn't until after he'd graduated that the real buildup picked up steam. By that time, Taylor had already been assigned as a platoon leader with the 101st Airborne at Fort Campbell.

It was at Campbell that Taylor met his wife, Linda Aylor. She'd been dating another lieutenant; but Taylor, attracted to her, asked for a date at the first opportunity. They hit if off and saw each other for the better part of a year. "Linda was an 'Army brat,' and her father had retired at Campbell," Taylor said. They became engaged before Taylor was scheduled to depart for Vietnam. Then they had a change of heart and were married three days before he shipped out. "There's a real case of making a decision, a commitment, and running out the back door."

Arriving in Vietnam in June 1967, Taylor wasn't assigned to a specific unit. But because of his parachute training and background with the 101st, he was interviewed as a possible adviser to South Vietnam's Airborne Division, considered by most Americans that country's best. Anointed, Taylor's duty assignment was assistant battalion adviser to the 3rd Battalion. He was one of three Americans serving with the battalion. Of the other two, one was an officer senior to Taylor, the second was an NCO. They wore the same uniform as the Vietnamese—standard jungle-type camouflage and the international maroon beret of parachute forces.

The mission of the Vietnamese Airborne Division was to respond quickly to hot spots throughout the country. The advisers' job was to make sure that artillery and close tactical air support were properly coordinated and appropriate headquarters informed of the Vietnamese mission and presence in the area. Thus the job was one more of liaison than advice.

The senior American adviser, a captain, circulated with the battalion commander and his staff. The American NCO, a sergeant first class, accompanied the flank company. Taylor was usually up with the lead rifle company. Because their mission was to go wherever the action flared, they were battle-tested; and almost immediately after Taylor arrived, the battalion was part of a task force sent up to western II Corps in the Dak To region. They were responding to a North Vietnamese regiment that had infiltrated through Cambodia and overrun two Special Forces camps twenty-five miles north of Dak To. The specific mission was to rescue a brother Vietnamese airborne battalion that had been badly bloodied. As it turned out, the enemy was unwilling to engage the reinforced South Vietnamese.

Once up there, Taylor's battalion remained in the area a number of months, and his first real combat occurred in November, in the Tou Morong Valley, which ran east, out of the mountains, and toward the more populated regions of the Central Highlands. In that fight Taylor's battalion encountered an opposing regiment of particularly dedicated troops.

"Initially it was very close-in, infantry fighting, and since I was with the lead company I was right near my Vietnamese counterpart when he was wounded in the opening minutes of the fight," Taylor remembered. He saw a number of other South Vietnamese soldiers go down, but his immediate concern was getting information back to his boss, the American captain, so that appropriate artillery support could be brought in. It was then Taylor's responsibility to adjust the artillery fire the way a forward observer would, moving it from sector to sector with dexterity.

Although he'd heard other, more experienced officers say that contact with the enemy was usually of short duration, in this case the struggle lasted three days. It was give-and-take, nose-to-nose, with each side jabbing, trying to find a weak spot before moving in for the kill. "But they were well entrenched, well supported, and very determined to hold on."

Taylor believes there's no way of being prepared for your first battle, in the sense of being able to anticipate how it actually unfolds. In fact, he found each combat experience—and he'd probably notched about a dozen during that first tour—a separate and unique event. "The most prominent common characteristic, though, is this very knotty, sickening sensation in the pit of your stomach."

If you survive the initial burst, training tells you to take cover and return the fire. What Taylor found helpful when he'd report back to the American captain was just hearing another American voice over the radio. Also, there were questions the captain would ask. That meant Taylor had to concentrate on specific matters, minimizing the temptation of being caught up in the swirl of panicked soldiers crying out amid the staccato and concussive sounds of a well-planned ambush.

During the evening of the second night, Taylor's battalion was making little headway; they'd already lost fifty to sixty soldiers. The battalion commander gave orders to the lead company commander to make a night attack. This was an operation very few Vietnamese units would attempt.

They were on the side of a ridge, and they waited an hour after dark before moving out. The idea was to bypass the main pocket of resistance and come in from the flank. But as they were moving into position, the point man dislodged a rock, which rolled down the side of the mountain. Against this otherwise silent drum, the rock made an eerily syncopated sound, and they were immediately pinned down. Because they'd been discovered, forfeiting the element of surprise, it was fruitless to attempt to continue the maneuver; and they couldn't move to a safer position until many hours later anyway. A pity, because before they'd been discovered they were no more than fifteen meters from the enemy.

The morning of the third day, there was considerable mortar and artillery fire, and Taylor's company moved in behind the barrage. Then the artillery lifted, and when it began again, it rained down just beyond the objective, attempting to seal it off, as Taylor's company made a final frontal assault.

"Not only was it scary, but it was dangerous and risky," Taylor said. He remembered seeing a flanking position taken out not twenty meters away, one he hadn't even realized was there. An NVA had popped up firing wildly, following a second enemy soldier also firing. But two South Vietnamese paratroopers returned fire, killing them instantly.

"Something starts to build up as you experience success in close-in fighting," Taylor said. "You see you're achieving success, and you realize you can't stop—you're out in the open, you have to keep going. If there's such a thing as what people call a lust for blood, this momentum is perhaps as close as I can come to describing it. It's not something I could have hoped to anticipate. It was more something I was exposed to, saw happening around me, and it carried me along."

Once they were on top of the enemy objective and the shooting stopped, the feeling was one of great accomplishment and great exhilaration. "There's this natural high, a euphoria that sweeps over you," Taylor said. "You know you've met your fellow man, that the stakes were high, but you overcame him, you were able to prevail. I can remember that on this particular occasion, since I was with the lead elements, among the first through to the objective, there was a kind of big reunion on the spot as the other two Americans came up with their units. A lot of laughing and back-slapping." But it's at this point you're most vulnerable, Taylor cautioned. Training tells you there are other things you need to be doing; for example, you ought to be pushing on through the objective to get your security out.

During those three days, Taylor found that food wasn't particularly important, nor did hunger really catch up to him until the fight was over. Sleep was infinitely more precious because he wanted to be utterly alert when he had to be, so he'd catnap. "But all the time the adrenaline is pumping you're scared, and you're concerned about what you need to do. I don't think any of the time I was in Vietnam I was ever really comfortable. There was always that knot resting in the pit of my stomach, and I think it kept me on edge the whole time I was there."

In this particular battle, three NVA soldiers were captured. They'd remained in their fighting positions when the artillery had been brought in, and they were badly wounded and stunned. The South Vietnamese troops were not calmly disposed toward them, and if the officers hadn't stepped in, they would have been shot.

But the leaders understood the need at least to get intelligence. And, as it turned out, one NVA did provide some good information later; the other two subsequently died of their wounds.

But Taylor was aware of occasions when the officers didn't or couldn't step in quickly enough. Although the actions hadn't occurred in his presence, he knew there'd been enemy survivors because he'd heard the reports over the radio. Then, after the fighting stopped, before the prisoners could be interrogated, Taylor would hear shots, and the explanation invariably was that they'd tried to escape.

"Sure, it's not the way we're trained to deal with those situations," Taylor said. "But this is not the ethic of everyone else in the world. Emotions take over, and retribution comes swift. You can disagree with that. You can do all the talking about it, all the philosophizing. But unless the troops are predisposed toward taking prisoners, it's not going to have much effect, especially when the action is intense and close-in."

That initial combat experience was doubly memorable for Taylor, because on that same day—November 23, 1967, Thanksgiving Day—his daughter was born. She was a premature baby, weighing only three pounds, and because there was some question whether she'd survive, Taylor was granted an emergency leave and returned to the States. "It was touch-and-go for quite a while," he recalled. "But she did survive, the good Lord was with us, and after about three weeks' leave, I returned to my unit." Taylor found them back in the Saigon area, which was their headquarters, preparing to leave for the Van Kiep Naval Training Center, in southern II Corps, along the coast.

Their annual training, however, was cut short by reports that opposing NVA forces were moving against the nearby port city of Vung Tau. Taylor's unit was informed that, along with two other battalions, they'd be participating in a spoiling attack: Two battalions would make a combat parachute jump; the third was being brought down from the north by truck to block the presumed escape route of the North Vietnamese. For Taylor this parachute assault would be another first.

The idea was to jump not directly on the enemy's position but immediately adjacent to it. Once on the ground, the South Vietnamese forces were to close in quickly. Presumably sandwiched between the jumpers and the blocking battalion, the enemy would be squeezed, crushed, destroyed.

It was a fairly large jump, involving between seven hundred and eight hundred paratroopers, and they were landing on two relatively close drop zones, about a mile apart. They jumped at a mere six hundred feet, half the customary training height, both to reduce exposure time and to keep the force as tightly concentrated as possible.

Although there was some sporadic firing about a kilometer from where Taylor's unit landed, they came across only small enemy elements; evidence suggested, however, that a battalion-size force had been in the area. The jump was made January 19, 1968, eleven days before the outbreak of Tet, and possibly the NVA had been positioning themselves to strike at the Naval Training Center or Vung Tau.

The same knottiness Taylor experiences in combat accompanies him each time he jumps, and he's make hundreds of them. It stems, of course, from an apprehension that something could go wrong, although the more jumps he's made the more confident Taylor's become of being able to handle any emergency that might arise.

"With the T-10, the chute we use, the opening shock is really a gentle tug," he said. "You feel a definite sensation, because the harness you're in catches the tug at your shoulders. It pulls back. What you hear is a flag flapping in the breeze, a kind of rolling cloth sound. It's comforting to hear. What isn't is the firing as you're coming down. You always have the sensation they're all firing up at you. And though the ride down can be short—in this case, six hundred feet—you wish it was even shorter."

When you land, Taylor said, you receive about the same jolt as if you've jumped off a ten-foot wall. It's a definite, hard impact, some of which you absorb on the balls of your feet. Then you quickly collapse. Paratroopers are trained to cushion the shock, absorbing as much impact as possible on the meatier parts of the body—the buttocks, side of the hip, and push-up muscle.

About a week after the jump, Taylor's unit was moved back up to Saigon. It was their turn to patrol what was referred to as the capital military defense sector—a ring of South Vietnamese forces encircling Saigon. In one sense, it was a kind of R&R, because soldiers' leaves were liberally authorized when their units were thus deployed. Which perhaps explains why the unit was in a less than totally alert posture on January 30, when Tet occurred.

"Some contact was expected," Taylor remembered, "but we obviously did not do a very good job of reading the indicators."

Viet Cong and NVA forces struck throughout South Vietnam. As for Saigon, they'd moved into the city from the west and south of Taylor's unit, which had been posted to the north of the capital. A large contingent of NVA forces attacked the Chinese, or Cholon, section of the city, and that was where Taylor's battalion was rushed in response. There, for the first time, he encountered the type of nasty, house-to-house fighting more commonly experienced in Europe during World War II.

Although fighting in a jungle is different from fighting in a city, Taylor quickly learned that in both you always want to gain the high ground. In cities that means buildings, upper windows, rooftops. Your avenues of approach are alleys and streets, and if the enemy has the high ground, those thoroughfares can be death traps.

When Taylor and four South Vietnamese soldiers rounded a corner in Cholon, a sniper from a second-story window opened up, not at them but at another group who'd also rounded the corner. "But here you are, in the midst of the street, it's wide open, no cover, no protection. First thing you do by instinct is get down. But then you realize you're still out in the open. So you scramble behind a couple of light posts, and then you make for the nearest doorway," Taylor recalled. Four or five soldiers—a *mucho* big American and four tiny Vietnamese—stuffed together in a very narrow doorway must have looked like a pastiche spliced from a Mack Sennett silent movie comedy routine. The space was about four feet, maybe a foot deep. Twisting themselves into position, they began firing, trying to pin down the sniper. At the same time, they notified another platoon leader by radio, who was able to get some of his people into the building from which the sniper was firing.

Knowing there's a sniper on the second floor and going into a building you're unfamiliar with can be nerve-racking. While you're aware he's on the second floor, you don't know how he got there. Where's the stairway? The enemy covering it? And what about corners, if any, near the stairway or elsewhere? If wisdom is the handmaiden of survival, you proceed very slowly until you get to where you have to go. Taylor found that house-to-house, alley-by-alley fighting—and Cholon lasted days—was difficult to sort out. It was often a problem determining where the enemy was, much less how to go about getting at him. Air strikes, if they're available and you're willing to use them, can be extremely useful in such circumstances.

Taylor came closest to, in his words, "meeting my demise" when the South Vietnamese Airborne Division was lifted into Khe Sanh in April. Their mission, along with that of America's 1st Cav, was to reinforce the battered U.S. Marines holding Khe Sanh and reclaim a Special Forces camp at Lang Veh that had been overrun by the North Vietnamese. As the helicopter Taylor got out of took off, a shell came in, fragmenting a shard of runway matting and throwing it high in the air. When the metal came down, it slammed across the top of Taylor's helmet and back of his knapsack, pounding him to the ground, where he tore up his right knee on a second fragment. Suddenly he was nowhere—out on Queer Street, as boxers sometimes say—and he was able to get to his feet only with the assistance of a couple of Vietnamese soldiers, who helped him stumble to cover.

"The force of that big piece of metal coming down felt like being hit by a hammer," Taylor recalled. "It drove the helmet into my head, and I was in a kind of fog. I'm not sure if I was unconscious or merely stunned. But after the fogginess wore off and reality came back, I had this tremendous headache. I got hit in the back of the head, but the headache was up here, right in front." Taylor pointed to his sinuses. "It lasted the better part of that day, and I had to get some aspirins." His head still hurt the next day and he had a deep laceration stretching across his kneecap, but he moved out with other members of the battalion when the helicopters came to take them to an area of high ground overlooking Lang Veh. Taylor remembered that what made both Lang Veh and Khe Sanh terrible places to defend was that they were on a plateau ringed by mountainous ridges from which the enemy could shell them at will.

When his tour concluded that June, Taylor knew he'd be going back to Vietnam in 1969, but for now it was a relief leaving for a year. He found the America of 1968 he returned to confused and frustrated by the Vietnam War. "I think the big thing that probably affected the American public more than anything else was the tremendous loss of life associated with the Tet offensive," Taylor said. "If you use the measures of military success on the battlefield, we won all the fights—recaptured everything they attempted to capture or did capture. But what Americans were asking then was, one, was it worth it, especially considering the losses? And number two, we keep hearing the end is near; yet if that's true, how'd they manage to mount their nationwide Tet offensive?''

The Army sent Taylor to the Advanced Infantry School at Fort Benning, although it's hard to believe the instructors there could have taught him much he hadn't already picked up in a year of combat. At night he'd watch the news programs, which seemed almost exclusively devoted to the Vietnam War. If a big fight occurred earlier that day, he anticipated that most of the half hour—twenty minutes, anyway—would be devoted to color shots of that particular battle. He found he was disappointed in the coverage, because he could tell where there were logic gaps in, say, whom they were interviewing. "As an example, a reporter would be asking a pfc or a spec four about why a certain operation was being conducted and what he thought about it. Certainly it's appropriate to ask what he thought about it. But a private soldier perhaps knows what his squad task is, maybe even what his company's mission is. But to ask a private why the mission was conducted makes no sense because he's in no position to know. Then, sometimes because of his frustration, the soldier would say something foolish, and viewers tended to interpret that as factual. The result was I don't think people back in the States were getting a balanced picture, and that may have hurt support more than anything else.''

Although it was impossible not to realize that America had turned against the war, Taylor still felt obliged to return to Vietnam the following year. For one thing, he knew that the South Vietnamese soldiers he'd served with wanted no part of North Vietnam or communism. For another, Taylor was a professional soldier with a strong sense of duty. Third, he believed most Americans failed to appreciate that the American government was attempting to help a wounded and weak ally. "So, agreeing with the government's position, with my understanding of what duty required, and having served with the South Vietnamese, I was still committed and still felt we were doing the right thing.''

This time Taylor was assigned as a company commander with the 503rd Infantry, 173rd Airborne Brigade. He had about 120 soldiers under him. The company was operating in northern II Corps, not too far from the coast, and its mission in mid-1969 was one of pacification. There was no great evidence of main force units moving through the coastal regions. Fighting had shifted farther west. As a result, the strategy near the coast was to move back into the populated areas, establish a military presence, and provide an armed protective umbrella within which the Vietnamese could pursue their daily tasks, support the economy, and raise foodstuffs to conduct trade. The idea was to build confidence again in their ability to control their country and sustain day-to-day activities. To support this mission, units like the 173rd maintained relatively static positions over a fairly large area. Taylor's responsibility was to assist local forces in controlling a smaller, specified sector. His company conducted patrols ensuring that enemy elements were not infiltrating the area and provided low-level military training to local military forces.

The area was agricultural, a coastal lowland in Binh Dinh Province, studded with rice paddies. The primary means of moving across the paddies were dikes, paddy walls, and small roads, and the enemy's main effort at undermining American efforts was booby-trapping. They'd seed the traps at night, then withdraw. One way of countering this was checkerboarding the area with night ambushes and launching occasional forays up on the high ground.

Taylor saw combat about a half dozen times during his second Vietnam tour. That made for a total of about twenty for both tours. Although he had a number of good NCO's during this second tour, others were young and inexperienced, learning the ropes. "I tried to bring them along as much as I could," Taylor said. "But if I saw they weren't getting anywhere, for the good of the men I had to relieve a couple of them and send them to the rear. It's difficult, it's unpleasant to do. But it's very necessary. As company commander, I was responsible for all those soldiers. And in combat, you learn very quickly if you've got an indecisive or ineffective leader, and he's dangerous. The price in too many cases is the blood of your soldiers. So you've got to do it. You're fair about it. You explain early on what defects you see in the man's style, or in what he's attempting to do. You offer him suggestions on how he might improve. Then you turn him loose. And if he doesn't respond in a reasonable amount of time, then he should understand when you come back to him and say, 'Hey, you're going to have to go. You're not making the mark.' "

One of Taylor's troops lost a foot as a result of tripping an antipersonnel mine. Another detonated a trap that fizzled but, fortunately, it didn't explode. Because booby traps were a constant menace, soldiers were encouraged to get their feet wet—walk through the paddies and stay off the dikes. Other things to watch for were bottlenecks and strictures in the pathways. If the ground was swept smooth, soldiers were taught to look for tripwires, which were hard to detect because they were of thin wire or fishline. They'd usually be strung at ankle level. "We'd teach a man to get down, take off his watch and ring, and to feel very slowly," Taylor said. "The idea was to start high and work your way down. If something crossed his palm, he'd stop and we'd check both sides of the trail."

Taylor had a cross section in his company—blacks, Chicanos, farmboys, wise guys from the big cities. "I thought the world of my people," he said. "When we had a mission, they performed admirably." In combat units you were involved in survival on a daily basis. You therefore had something important to do every day, so the idleness that seemed so conducive to racial tensions and drugs had much less chance of occurring. "I was always more aware of malaise in the rear areas than when I was with a combat unit," Taylor said.

By the time he'd returned to the States at the conclusion of his second Vietnam tour, in June 1970, he'd been awarded many honors, including the Silver Star and a Combat Infantryman's Badge. But America had turned even more sharply against the war, and he found the seemingly endless barrage of criticism tough to take. Compounding his frustration was the fact that he'd been assigned to teach ROTC students at the University of California at Santa Barbara, where antiwar protests were practically an everyday occurrence.

"I can remember having things thrown at me when I came on campus in uniform." Taylor was also cursed and spat upon. He felt those giving him a hard time would have loved seeing him run down an offender and beating hell out of him. But as long as he experienced no personal harm and his person wasn't touched, he decided he'd just laugh it off and go on about his business. "Of course, I'm a pretty good-size guy, and they didn't want to carry it too far when I was by myself." To Taylor their actions represented a kind of fad—something that was popular on campus. "I can't recall any incidents when it was a case of one-on-one. It was always someone in a group, and I think it was done more to impress his or her friends and be one of the crowd, to demonstrate his commitment not to be committed."

Taylor made a point of involving himself in campus activities because he was trying to sell his profession to the few ROTC students then attending the school. He coached lacrosse as well as football, and he took some undergraduate courses. In part, he was trying to demonstrate he was no different from anyone else. "I had some talents to offer, and if people would just put aside some of their prejudices and preconceived notions of what I was, they'd see there was a little bit more there."

While he was teaching ROTC students, Taylor decided to see if he could survive an academic pursuit of his own choosing. He took courses that would lead to a masters degree in international relations. Advanced education had become part of an officer's career development. But because of Taylor's poor undergraduate standing, he knew he would not be selected by the Army to go to school. So he decided he'd do it on his own, using the GI Bill, which he'd earned in Vietnam. "I'm just as competitive professionally as anyone else around me," Taylor said. He told his boss, the professor of military science at Santa Barbara, that he would like to pursue graduate study, assuring him that such a pursuit would not interfere with his instructional duties. Because of his poor West Point record, California accepted him on probation only. Taylor had to prove himself by taking four undergraduate courses in history and government, and he wound up getting three A's and a B-plus.

In graduate school he concentrated on Europe and the Soviet Union. He felt that understanding how nation-states interact and what defines the national interest would complement his vocation as a military professional. Happily, Taylor's graduate course grades were as high as those he'd scored on probation. Then he had the option of taking an oral exam or writing a thesis to gain the degree, and he chose the former. "I felt confident of my ability to express concepts, articulate trends, and explicate theories in an oral format."

The oral exams were administered by three-man panels, one member of which Taylor could choose. He picked the professor he'd worked with most, and he crammed thoroughly. Entering the examining room with butterflies in his stomach, Taylor quickly got the gist of the questions. "The lead interviewer was the professor I'd picked, and I kind of played to him." The exam took about two hours, although it seemed a lot longer. Then the panel adjourned for fifteen minutes, telling Taylor to smoke a cigarette or get a drink of water. When he walked back into the room, they said, "Congratulations, Captain Taylor," shaking his hand. Does it get any better than this? Taylor, a former cadet who'd dangled by his thumbs for four anxious years at the Academy, had just been awarded an M.A. with honors.

When officers are majors, usually between their eleventh and thirteenth year of service, about 40 percent are selected to attend the Command and General Staff College at Leavenworth, where they are trained to assume duties of middle- and high-level command. The institution is the Army's senior tactical and operational school, and those who attend are chosen by a Department of the Army selection committee. Each CGSC class consists of about eight hundred officers, six hundred of whom are Army officers on active duty. It's pretty near impossible to get promoted to lieutenant colonel without having passed through Leavenworth.

Taylor was already assigned there when Cambodia fell to the Khmer Rouge and North Vietnamese troops entered Saigon. "I didn't feel a great sensation of personal defeat," he said. "But the pullout, the final fall of the country, was kind of like someone switching on a light for me. I guess my first sensation was of tremendous disappointment, feeling we'd failed as an Army and as a country. It was, I believe, a shared failure of political ends not being clearly defined and military objectives that were defined equally unclearly."

Much of the time, discussions at Leavenworth would focus on Vietnam in terms of what kind of ethical climate it had left the Army and what changes were needed. "Certainly the problems of drugs, fraggings, and malaise were now fully upon us, and the Army was concerned how to make things better from within," Taylor said.

Given that backdrop, he sought as his next assignment a staff position with a Ranger unit. Among the best light infantry in the world, the Rangers had been reactivated in January 1974 and consist of handpicked volunteers. "As I understood the purpose of these units, not only did we bring them back on the books to perform a vital mission, but they were also to serve as a beacon for the rest of the Army—to show that we *could* pull ourselves out of that malaise of the post-Vietnam era, that we *could* be as good as we wanted if only we put our minds to it and applied the necessary resources. As I say, the pullout in Vietnam and our apparent loss of professional face there disappointed me greatly. But I guess in some sense I'm the eternal optimist, because I tried to leave that experience behind me and see what I could do and where I could be involved in turning things around. My hope and commitment were to convince others that this profession was an honorable one, and being assigned to a Ranger unit was a vehicle for doing that."

Because there were no appropriate Ranger openings as Taylor was completing his one-year tour at Leavenworth, he did the next best thing: managed to get himself assigned to Fort Stewart, Georgia, as an operations officer with the 24th Infantry Division—the same Fort Stewart where Ranger units were headquartered and where it would be easier to seek interviews if and when an appropriate opening occurred. It took eight months before Taylor was able to finesse an assignment as an operations officer to the 1st Battalion of the 75th Ranger Regiment. "It was," he said of this assignment, "a kind of professional shot in the arm, an injection of adrenaline at that point in my career. Those guys were and are the very best we have in our Army."

The Ranger mission, often involving deep penetration into enemy territory, is one of total combat, and infantry fighting skills are taught to the exclusion of everything else—unlike, say, Special Forces troops, whose training includes the acquisition of a variety of skills, such as first aid, communications, and often a foreign language, their basic mission being to train indigenous personnel to defend themselves and fight their own fight.

Even after troops volunteer for Rangers units and are considered serious candidates, they have to go through a rigorous screening and indoctrination program that's specifically designed to cull the weak of heart and the weak of mind. This is accomplished at the Ranger School at Fort Benning by exposing Ranger candidates to a number of trying circumstances against a background of constant stress, punctuated by little food and less sleep. "Can we load him down with a heavy pack on a road march and give him a time constraint to finish by?" Taylor said. "And will he take the task and challenge, and translate it into a personal goal? Or will he, because of the pain and effort, say, 'This isn't for me'?"

Rangers are trained in hand-to-hand combat, taught escape and evasion techniques, night infiltration behind enemy lines, hit-and-run operations, and survival in difficult terrain including desert, jungle, and mountain. They trace their history back to the years when England recruited crack shots and expert woodsmen in the French and Indian Wars. The danger and hardships such missions entailed gained these irregular troops recognition in the form of higher pay and distinctive uniforms. Special and different in 1763,

Rangers are still special and different two hundred-odd years later. And Taylor found serving with them so heady and fulfilling an experience that he promised himself to somehow return to a Ranger unit if the opportunity even remotely presented itself. Nor did he particularly want to leave after less than a year and a half, especially when he learned that the Army was going to send him back to, of all places, West Point, as a tactical officer. West Point? Taylor?

But in 1976, the Military Academy had been rocked by a serious scandal, when a large number of cadets were suspected of cheating. The scandal broke in May, before final exams, and involved the Class of 1977. That summer, panels consisting of three officers interviewed those thought to be tainted to determine whether charges against them should be dropped or whether further investigation was warranted. Many cadets left the Academy as a result.

Part of the problem, it was decided, part of what had caused the scandal or made its occurrence almost inevitable, was that many of the instructors had themselves become cynical, no doubt as a consequence of Vietnam and Watergate. It was as if monks in their cells had, after passing quite by chance through the city's expanding red light district, suddenly taken to women and wine, performing less than holy acts back in their hallowed hilltop monastery. The officer corps at West Point, the belief went, had, at the least, turned a blind eye, or not been aggressive enough in taking action to curb the widespread problems that arose with the honor system and the whole manner of dealing with the Corps of Cadets. In response, the Academy decided it now needed more senior captains or junior majors, officers with recent troop experience, and people who'd so far proved successful. "I fit the categories and was told I was being sent from the field and reassigned to West Point because it was a mission requirement," Taylor recalled. "They said that as a tactical officer I'd be filling a position that potentially would make a contribution to the future of the Army."

Taylor makes little of it, but he'd be less than human if he hadn't derived a certain satisfaction that the Army, in its wisdom, had decided it wanted him back at West Point—the same West Point whose rejection when he was a cadet seemed imminent for four years and would have absolutely humiliated him.

That aside, one of the reasons he'd never asked for a West Point assignment as a tac was that he considered the Academy as a kind of railroad siding, a microcosm off by itself, a college campus—an unusual college campus, to be sure, but certainly nothing like the virile headquarters of a Ranger battalion. At this point, too, Taylor felt he was well integrated again into his profession and had certain career goals he wanted to accomplish. But, all that said, his orders read West Point, and he really had no choice.

A tactical officer has more interface and impact on the life of a cadet than anyone else at the Academy. "He's a counselor, mentor, disciplinarian, coach—in every aspect he's the commander and/or parent of about a hundred cadets," Taylor said. "In effect, I was their company commander." Besides managing a company, Taylor trained the upperclass chain of command. He also gave classes on honor. Taylor had long felt the honor code was a natural and basic part of the profession, and when he returned to West Point thought he could interpret and explain the system, using concrete examples based on things he knew happened in Vietnam.

A major concern cadets have, he suggested, was how they'd be perceived by their peers. But he'd remind them that when they left the Academy, they wouldn't be surrounded by their peers; they'd be out in the Army by themselves, interpreting and analyzing situations requiring them to take or not take an action, as they saw fit, but based, hopefully, on an adherence to the honor code.

One example he remembered offering occurred during his second tour in Vietnam, when he was a company commander. Ubiquitous booby traps meant some units did not perform when it came to conducting ambush patrols. In a neighboring sector, Taylor learned, another company commander had recommended a platoon leader for court-martial. When this platoon leader had been given a night ambush mission, he'd merely moved his people down the road, to a distance out of sight of his commanding officer, but he'd go no farther. Keeping his platoon in a tight perimeter, he'd radioed back false reports. Not only had he lied, Taylor said, but he'd also placed the tactical integrity of the company in peril, rendering his commander as good as deaf, dumb, and blind.

"You can tell people not to do things, but unless they really understand what the impact or price will be, they may not absorb it quickly or completely," Taylor said. "But I felt very confident of my ability to use what I'd learned as a role model for cadets."

After a three-year stint at West Point, Taylor spent an unhappy year as a staff officer in the Pentagon, working in an operations directorate. Too often it seemed Taylor was running from one piece of paper to another, and it was difficult if not impossible to achieve any sense of fulfillment or accomplishment. To a man who lived to be on the cutting edge, a Pentagon assignment back-to-back with one at West Point must have seemed like two bisecting circles of purgatory.

Thus it's no wonder that Taylor vividly remembered being in the basement of the Pentagon, involved in a big war-game exercise and up to his neck in problems and pressure, when another officer said that the general commanding his directorate wanted to see Taylor in his office. There the general told him his name appeared on a just-released command list, which meant he'd probably be leaving the Pentagon within months. In short, deliverance was at hand.

"I guess I lost my composure," Taylor said sheepishly. "I jumped up."

It was amusing to think of Taylor, who can be formal and even stern, actually bouncing out of his chair, all six-two of him. "You didn't kiss the guy, did you, Wes?"

Taylor looked startled before smiling. "No, I retained that much composure."

Of course, as a lieutenant colonel soon to command a battalion, Taylor wanted that battalion to be a Ranger one. But again, none was available at the time, so he was assigned to command a battalion of light infantry of the 193rd Brigade based at Fort Kobbe, Panama, in charge of about 750 soldiers.

"I think the best way to describe battalion command is you're somewhat your own boss," Taylor said. "You're top dog, so to speak, within the organization. They're looking to you for leadership, for direction, for focus, and so on and so forth. You're fully in command of a relatively large organization, given the opportunity by the Army to put into practice all the things you learned at school and all the things you've been experimenting with or developing during past assignments. While you're always working for a higher command, within your unit you're running the show, you're the one making things happen, you're the decision maker. It's fulfilling and it's challenging."

Although he'd enjoyed commanding American troops patrolling the Panama Canal, Taylor's heart was set on getting back with Rangers, and after about a year he heard of a command opening in the Ranger battalion with which he'd served as an operations officer. "Those of us who've served in Ranger battalions kind of keep an eye peeled for who's there, how long they've served, and so on and so forth." In this case, "so on and so forth" meant when the dude's time was up and he was scheduled to move on. At any rate, the possibility of actually leading a battalion of men thought to be among the best light infantry in the world excited Taylor, and he asked to be considered.

He was subsequently called from Panama up to Fort Stewart for an interview in January 1983 and told he was one of several semifinalists. He would be interviewed by the division commander at Fort Stewart.

"It was going to be a tough interview, from the standpoint I didn't know what he was going to be interested in or what he was going to be asking." But Taylor felt confident, both about his professional background and his record.

The interviewer, Gen. John Galvin, seemed, in Taylor's words, "to want to get into my head as to what my philosophy of command was, and he'd pose questions that would require me to diagnose a situation and tell him how I'd handle it." A particular question Taylor remembered was one Galvin had asked about the off-duty conduct of Rangers.

"Whenever you're dealing with soldiers specially selected and treated differently, there's a perception that these guys have a prima donna complex, and in many cases it's true," Taylor explained.

Keeping that in mind, Taylor responded to the general's question, citing the charter Gen. Creighton Abrams, Army chief of staff at the time, had given to the Rangers when he activated them in 1974. Abrams had stated they were to be the best light infantry in the world, but if they ever became a fraternity of brigands and hoodlums, he'd disband them. Homing in on that particular phrase, Taylor said, "It would be my charter to ensure that hooliganism and machoism would be severely dealt with, and I'd be ruthless in separating out those who couldn't maintain the proper standards."

The interview lasted about forty-five minutes, and when the general was done with his questions, he coolly thanked Taylor for coming up, said he was pleased with his responses, and wished him the best of luck. Taylor would be notified of his decision as soon as the general completed the interviewing process.

"Now he really had me guessing—how many guys, who they were, and so on and so forth," Taylor remembered. "So I left, went back to Panama, and I guess it was about three weeks later I found out I'd been recommended by Galvin and the nomination had been approved."

The Rangers were every bit as good, if not better, than Taylor had remembered. What was especially pleasing to him was that many of the junior NCO's, who'd been with the battalion when he was its operations officer four years before, were now back as senior NCO's. His top NCO, the battalion sergeant major, had been first sergeant of B Company, a soldier Taylor remembered respecting a great deal.

"I think there were a lot of expectations, because word got around very quickly Taylor's coming back," he said, referring to himself in the third person. Not that his predecessors hadn't been very good, Taylor added. Yet one of the things he'd specifically wanted to commit himself to was ensuring that the organization *was* the best light infantry in the world. From the beginning, Taylor placed great emphasis on the Ranger creed, which he described as, more or less, a prescription for living as a Ranger. "In one page, it lays out for this particular unit its bond of camaraderie, its purpose for being, and its direction. It's pretty much a codification for how we should live our lives as professional soldiers."

Although, generally speaking, the soldiers were exceptional, Taylor found he had some NCO's and officers who'd somehow wiggled through the screening process and were not of high caliber. Superficially they'd appeared to be, but they did not have the commitment of heart and the professional commitment to maintain the standards Taylor insisted upon. He started weeding them out, and he believes that maintained his credibility with the troops; they saw that, regardless of rank, every soldier in the battalion was expected to live up to the standard enunciated in the creed. And when they couldn't, they'd go.

"I relieved four officers, and we're talking lieutenant through major," Taylor said. "I was more disappointed than upset or mad. They'd let the organization, themselves, and the officer corps down by what they'd done. And in a couple of those cases, we're talking moral turpitude." But that's as far as Taylor would go.

He said it was the collective impact of those firings that made them, when he thought about the past, the hardest things he'd done in recent years. "It was tough, because you're really digging into the personal domain of the individual," he said. "But once their indiscretions became public knowledge, their effectiveness as leaders and example-setters became seriously impaired. And that's the point I made to them when I relieved them." On those occasions, the knot came back—the same he'd invariably experienced in combat and when he jumped. "I was concerned about the impact it would have on the lives of those people, and I lost sleep while I was deliberating. In fairness to them, I'd make a point of deciding between forty-eight and seventy-two hours. But I realized it was something that had to be done. They knew what the creed was, and they thought they didn't have to live up to it and could do differently. And I was the guy who held them up to the task." Taylor shook his head. "It probably ranks up there with a chancy decision in combat—sending people into a particular war situation where you know the odds aren't very good for success."

Combat for Taylor didn't end, as it so far has for most of his contemporaries, with Vietnam, because he jumped with the lead contingent of Rangers who parachuted into Grenada in 1983. Taylor said he'd first learned his services were required when he was awakened by an emergency phone call at 3:00 A.M. on Friday, October 21. The person on the other end, an officer calling from Fort Bragg, was serving on the staff of the joint special operations command. Because Taylor's home phone was an insecure one, the officer merely said, "Wes, something hot's brewing, and we'd like you up here as soon as possible." Given the command that had just alerted him and the fact he'd never gotten that kind of call at home before, Taylor realized it had to be something serious, and he felt as if he'd been jolted, snapped into his senses. He showered, shaved, got into his pickup, and was on the road a half hour later.

He arrived at Bragg before nine, where he was told a real world mission was in the works. The problem was occurring in a place called Grenada. At first, Taylor thought they'd meant a city in Spain, Granada, but that didn't make much sense, nor, he later realized, were the locales pronounced the same. "Grenada?" he'd said. They showed him a map of the place they had in mind—a tiny island in the Windward Islands of the southeastern Caribbean. Then they told him there'd been a recent coup involving a leftist, pro-Castro element, which had assumed control of the island, including numerous American civilians, most notably a group of five hundred medical students. The American government was concerned that the students might be harmed or taken hostage and used as political leverage.

That morning, Taylor began receiving intelligence briefings and was shown aerial photos of the island. His particular mission would involve seizing the uncompleted, ten-thousand-foot airstrip at the southwestern tip of the island, Point Salines, and he began analyzing how he might go about it. The word hadn't definitely come down that the mission was on, and as the day wore on it seemed less and less likely a possibility. By Friday evening it even appeared that intervention was not going to occur, and Taylor was told to return to Stewart but keep himself available in case the situation changed. So he drove back down to Georgia. There he spoke to his exec and operations officer, alerting them to stick around as well. At about this time he got another call to return to Bragg on Saturday, and momentum was picking up again. He asked if his key officers might accompany him.

Early next morning they rented a couple of vans and drove up to Bragg. A second Ranger battalion was called in after Taylor had arrived back at Bragg, and they were starting to receive an initial briefing involving a second objective. Momentum kept picking up all Saturday night. Those who could would catnap in corners of the planning room and on couches in offices that were available. But most of the time was spent in coming up with various courses of action.

On Sunday morning, the decision was made that they'd go. A two-star general of the special operations command called his commanders in, Taylor among them, and passed along the word. They were told to return to their headquarters and complete their detailed planning. Before they dispersed, coordination with the Air Force was initiated.

Taylor returned the Georgia early Sunday morning, somewhat punchy. His troops were alerted, and more planning proceeded the rest of Sunday.

The following day, about three in the afternoon, Taylor was in the process of clearing his final concept back to the general at Bragg, when he was notified of a delay in execution time. They were to have arrived in Grenada at two on Tuesday morning; the delay would be between two and three hours, shaving pretty close whatever cover of darkness they could hope to expect. Launch time for Taylor's unit from Hunter Air Force Base was set for nine-thirty.

Before boarding their aircraft, Taylor got up on a packing box and, using a PA, called his troops together in the hangar. He told them this was the real thing and said he felt confident of their ability to perform the mission because of their training. Now was the opportunity to put into practice all they'd learned. He repeated what their company commanders had already told them—that they'd be among the very first troops to go in, and they were about to make history. Then he said a prayer over them before announcing it was time to load up.

The flight took more than eight hours. If you flew direct, it would take considerably less; but because of the waiting time—the loitering period necessary to get other forces into their launch positions—the planes of Taylor's battalion had to fly in a holding pattern. He had 350 men aboard seven C-130's and modified C-130's. The hope was to land them on the airstrip under cover of partial darkness. But they were prepared for a worst-case scenario of having to jump. Because of the aircraft's crowded conditions, Taylor had decided to deploy from Hunter rigged for the worst case. That meant they'd be wearing their parachutes for the entire time they'd be in the C-130's. Hardly very comfortable, but Taylor felt he had no choice, because a timely in-flight rig would be difficult given the less-than-roomy aircraft. They kept their straps loose and tried to make themselves comfortable.

Taylor was aboard the number three plane, inside the cargo compartment but forward so he'd have access to the radio. Between three and four Tuesday morning he received word they were having problems getting a reconnaissance element in to determine the condition of the runway at Point Salines and whether they should land or jump. About an hour later, Taylor learned that an intelligence aircraft had determined the runway was blocked with obstacles. That meant they'd be jumping.

"We had two lead aircraft, and then a thirty minute separation in time, and trail five," Taylor said. It sounded like a jazzy football play.

Approximately forty minutes prior to drop time, Taylor got the word that the sophisticated navigational aids on board the lead plane had malfunctioned. "Terrific," Taylor thought, consulting the air mission commander, the senior Air Force guy aboard his aircraft. The solution they decided upon was to take the two lead aircraft and tuck them in around to the rear of the trail five. The reason for that was the number three plane, Taylor's, had similar backup navigational aids. Now instead of being number three, Taylor's plane was number one. But that meant an additional delay. Instead of the initial jump occurring at five, it would take place five-thirty, in broad daylight. "Terrific," Taylor thought again, only that's not really what he thought either time.

As the lead aircraft approached the landing threshold of the airfield, the jump doors were open, and the Rangers made their final preparations. Taylor could see a bright, sunshiny morning's light marked with deceptive, carnival-looking striations that were actually a barrage of spaghettilike tracers.

They were going to jump at relatively low level—five hundred feet. Taylor had decided on that back at Hunter. "Some reporters later made it seem I'd made the decision at the last minute and I was able to do that with some miraculous insight," Taylor noted. "If it was 'miraculous insight' to jump at five hundred rather than the more usual twelve hundred feet, it hit me earlier, before we even launched." Possibly he'd remembered the combat jump he'd made in Vietnam at six hundred feet. Also, the drop zone in Grenada was a narrow peninsula. "I'm afraid if we'd jumped from high altitudes, the trade winds would have blown us out to sea."

So in they went, as low as possible, but because of the intense ground fire only fifty paratroopers aboard the lead aircraft, including Taylor, were able to jump on their initial pass.

The familiar knot in his gut accompanied Taylor down. "It's got an element of fear and it's got an element of hype in it," he said. "But I've gotten used to its being there in difficult situations, and it's kind of like an old friend cautioning me to be exceptionally alert. The challenge is to keep it under control and keep yourself focused outwardly, on what's happening."

Meanwhile, the other planes had to divert and come back around what the Rangers call "a racetrack" to make successive passes. At the same time, those on the ground were busy calling in suppressive fire from an armed C-130, which was able to knock out a number of antiaircraft sites.

Taylor said his soldiers were trained to roll up, creating mass as they moved together. Because Taylor was the commander, his radio operator, fire support officer, and liaison officers began converging on his position. They could see barrels and barbed wire fences that had been thrown across the runway; and as Taylor began moving there, he started dragging one strand of wire to the other end. With covering fire provided by some of his soldiers, others also began trying to clear the runway of obstacles. But there were too many, and they were too few.

Helicopters had landed Marines at the Pearls Airport on the other end of the island at five that morning, and they'd encountered minimal resistance. Taylor, by contrast, was receiving unanticipated, concentrated fire from experienced Cuban military personnel.

It took another half hour before enough antiaircraft positions were knocked out so that the other six C-130's could pass safely enough over the drop zone, allowing the other Rangers to jump in. Then, shortly after Taylor's 350 troops were on the island and because resistance was still intense, Rangers from another battalion, consisting of an additional two hundred soldiers, quickly parachuted in. By about seven or seven-thirty there were some 550 Rangers operating at Point Salines. Many were completing the process of clearing the runway. "We even had guys hot-wire some bulldozers to sweep away some of the barrels blocking the runway," Taylor said. During that time, he lost one of his soldiers—shot in the head, no more than 50 yards from where Taylor had landed.

The fight was then through scrub bush; uphill; and among houses that had been barricaded and converted into fighting positions near the airfield. "Opposing troops had been in prepared positions, concealed and protected," Taylor said. "That gave them certain initial advantages. The problem was moving through dense vegetation and rooting them out. In some cases you were on them before you knew it. Your first recognition they were there was when they opened fire on you. That's where we took a lot of casualties. I had nine soldiers wounded and five killed in action. That was out of 350, so it was pretty nasty and intense throughout the first day."

That afternoon, the landing strip was cleared and securely in American hands as a thousand troops from the 82nd Airborne touched down and disembarked. It took more than a day for the Americans to find the five hundred medical students, who weren't on one campus, as the Army had been told, but on three, and evacuate them from the island. Part of the reason for the confusion was a series of well-publicized snafus, attributed to a lack of coordination among the different services participating in the action. In any case, five days after the first American troops landed, there were five thousand in Grenada, and all but small pockets of resistance had been brought under control.

Despite critics who later referred to Grenada as "Reagan's splendid little war," Taylor couldn't help feeling that, unlike Vietnam, the Army had done this one, Grenada, right. The scales were in no way comparable, but it was still immensely satisfying to have commanded a battalion in combat and been on the cutting edge of an American military operation that succeeded.

Because Taylor has served in the Army twenty-odd years and found himself in perhaps twenty combat situations, he knows that when soldiers shout and curse after the surprise of an initial contact, their cries are really whispers concealing panic and bewilderment. Taylor didn't acquire this knowledge from a book or from having heard others describe it in their cups. *He knows.* He's also aware of how, during a combat jump, it feels as if each weapon going off below seems directed your way alone. Most men would like to think they, too, know, and, given human nature, would like even more for their contemporaries to think they know. And isn't that really what Samuel Johnson meant when, coming at it from the other direction and speaking of war, he said, "Every man thinks meanly of himself for not having been a soldier or not having been at sea"?

Taylor said that after talking to a group of former cadets who'd graduated from West Point in the 1950s and 1960s and then served in Vietnam, a stranger would probably come away thinking he'd found "a commonality of the base case." That might be because the experience of West Point during the 1950s and 1960s was relatively uniform. The student body was still for the most part at the twenty-five-hundred level, there was a small-campus atmosphere, and the camaraderie was palpable. Now the Corps was almost twice as large, and some older West Point graduates believed as a result of that, of women now attending West Point, and of modifications in the curriculum, the Academy had eroded in value or quality.

But Taylor said he didn't agree. "I don't think you can change that place. I think its tradition is too rich and too strong. The point I'm trying to make is that whether you took a snapshot of the Academy in the 1960s, 1860, or 1980, what the Academy does for folks remains the same, constant. Is the constant. While the personalities are different, I think the values we brought to the Academy, and then the pressure-cooker process the Academy put us through, reinforcing and strengthening those values, is the similarity between us—all of us. We each have a strong concept of duty, of honor, and of what integrity means. And very specifically, how to distinguish the line between right and wrong."

Taylor went on to say that not only did he believe this was true of West Point graduates, but also of other members of the officer corps. "Attending the Army War College, the senior educational institution of the Army, are many more student officers who'd received their commissions through OCS and ROTC rather than at West Point. But because they share the same qualities and the same values, I conclude the service has done a good job of instilling those values in its leadership over time. You have to understand, the armed forces are very much a subculture within our society. We tend to be a conservative bastion for, I think, qualities most of us respect, qualities of human decency."

Then Taylor looked slightly troubled, vaguely dissatisfied, as if there were one last thing gnawing at him from the beginning that he hadn't so far addressed. "I think," he said, "there's a perception that exists in American society that products of the Academy, or products in the military in general, are marionettes or cookie-cutters."

I had to laugh. If there was anything I'd come away with after having talked to Boone, Paschall, and the others, I told Taylor, it was that such a perception was absolutely fallacious. Boone, a cookie-cutter? Paschall, a marionette? Jesus . . .

Taylor, too much the Christian gentleman to jump up and hug me, contented himself by nodding. "That's been my experience, too," he said.

TURNER, Robert A. (Tex)
COL INF 460-54-8840
BORN: 7 Feb 37, Williston, FL

It was a sunny January morning, cold but bright. The appointment with Col. Tex Turner, director of military instruction at West Point, was scheduled for ten o'clock.

Two cabs were parked outside the Peekskill railroad station. The one I decided on had a painted "TAXI" sign posted in its front right-hand window. The car was a dark station wagon from ten to fifteen years old, and its driver sported a peaked cap he wore at a jaunty angle. He was a slender black man, who appeared in his sixties, with tan-colored, parchmentlike skin and a thin mustache. There was a lethal-looking yellow flashlight hooked to his belt, like a cop's gun. A guy with his can-do mien would surely be able to get me to West Point on time. When I told him where I wanted to go, he looked me over carefully before saying, "It'll cost you twenty dollars." The train ride to Peekskill had totaled five bucks and change. "Fine," I said, and, elated we were almost ready to roll but depressed at the cost, got into the backseat.

The driver's name, I learned from various handpainted index cards splayed in the taxi, was C. Brown. "No Smokeing," read one card. Another said the local fare to Peekskill was two dollars. There was a plastic statue of Christ, the size of a man's fourth finger, Scotch-taped to the ledge above the dashboard, and the taxi smelled as if it had been sprayed with an amalgam of perfume and disinfectant. Immediately after we pulled away, the Hudson, flashing into view, sparkled with currents of coiled light.

Mr. Brown, I learned as we headed west, then swung north, was a longtime resident of Peekskill, whose wife once told him it was either quit driving trucks long distance for a living, or she was going to quit him. Subsequently he worked for Amtrak. A diabetic who'd had some trouble with his foot last year, he'd had the satisfaction of telling off the doctor who'd mistreated him at the local hospital.

During the half-hour drive to West Point I'd thus gotten to know Mr. Brown well enough, I thought, to inquire if it might be convenient for him to pick me up back at the Academy at, say, twelve-fifteen. Mr. Brown said with a grand smile, "Sure, twelve-fifteen." I gave him the twenty I owed him. Another twenty would make forty bucks, or four times what the train fare was costing me. No question, I was a live one, which undoubtedly explained Mr. B.'s grand smile.

My own appeared when I arrived at Colonel Turner's outer office ten minutes early, told his adjutant my name, and said I had an appointment with his boss. The adjutant, a captain, said Colonel Turner hadn't returned from a meeting and offered me some coffee. From where I sat I could see the door to the colonel's office, and shortly before ten I spotted a colonel with a bristling crew cut entering it. He was followed by a man in fatigues wearing a single star on his collar. "That's General Boylan, commandant of cadets," said the adjutant. We could hear the general and Colonel

Turner begin a conversation. Lowering his voice, the adjutant said the general came up from his office on the floor below once a week for a few minutes to talk to Colonel Turner. The colonel preceding Turner and the general hadn't gotten along, so the general almost never came up then; but Colonel Turner and the general got along just fine. Colonel Turner had been in the job since mid-July.

After about fifteen minutes, the adjutant nervously asked if I wanted him to remind Colonel Turner of my appointment. But because I'd spent two years in the Army twenty-five years ago, I knew that even anxious, well-meaning captains aren't supposed to remind colonels of previous appointments when generals are talking to them. "That's okay," I said. After another fifteen minutes, the adjutant said, "The general almost never stays this long." By this time, inconvenience had matured into annoyance, and it must have shown, because he added, "I'm not conning you."

Maybe, but it still wasn't until almost eleven before the great man finally left and Tex Turner came out to take me into his office. He looked about 185 and just under six feet, had blue eyes, a crew cut the like of which I hadn't seen since the early 1960s, and a pair of ears that, folding away from the sides of his head, made him appear vulnerable despite a chest that seemed to strain against his green shirt and black tie. "Lord Almighty, keep a guy waiting for almost an hour," he said, shaking his head.

His fifth-floor office faced out to a central area. We sat in two leather chairs opposite his desk, with a table positioned against the wall between us. One of the phones on Turner's desk, he said, was a hot line to General Boylan's office. "Don't ring, you son of a bitch," I thought.

Turner said a lot of folks—reporters, TV people, writers—come up to West Point but miss the essential thing about the place. West Point was interested in turning out combat leaders, he remarked, and the Academy went about it in a special way—a way that "hasn't changed since Caesar was a road guard." This was Turner's third tour at West Point, and he was obviously suggesting he ought to know. He'd been a cadet, graduating in 1959, served as a tactical officer during the early 1970s, and was now, as I'd been made aware by his chatty adjutant, director of MI since July 1985.

The essential thing about West Point, Turner continued, occurred to him one day when he was sitting in, of all places, a rice paddy in Vietnam in December 1965. "I was scared, I was lonely. I wanted to quit. Been in Vietnam in the field for about six months.

Been out in the woods and hadn't had a real bath for about forty days. Well, I'm sitting there, contemplating the stars, and I wanted to go back to the States and see my wife and kids.'' Turner has a son and daughter. ''I wanted to be cool again, because in Vietnam you were never cool. Tired of being shot at, of being sticky and dirty, and the fear of stepping on a mine. I was really down. And all of a sudden, something just occurred to me. I looked up at those old stars and I said, 'Wait a minute. I've already been through Beast Barracks, I survived plebe year. I survived three more years of very, very strenuous competition to graduate from West Point under a lot of stress.' And believe you me, four years at West Point is very stressful—time schedules, living under regulations and rules, doing everything right, making grades so you can pass, always in competition with the guy on your right and the guy on your left.'' Turner began unwrapping a Wolf Brothers' Rum Crook cigar. ''Competition every day on the football field and on the wrestling mat. Putting out and then getting hurt, and having to spend time in the hospital. Trying to build yourself back up, trying to make the team. The old saying, 'No pain, no gain.' Living under that edict for four years. And then going through the Ranger course—that was probably the hardest thing I ever had to do in my life.''

Turner didn't smoke, but he twisted and chewed the cigar as he talked. '' 'Well,' I said to myself, 'at least I'm getting chow every day here, and I'm not freezing to death, like I was in the Ranger course. The stresses and pressures are here, but I've learned how to deal with them. I get mail every other day.' I started counting all these things, and I realized how much better off I was. Because of West Point and the Ranger course, I'd decided that combat was actually a hell of a lot easier. It was simple, no big deal. So it occurred to me that I'd been trained to do what I was doing. And I'd been trained very well. And all I was doing was sitting feeling very sorry for myself, sniveling.

''Well, how was I prepared to do this?'' Turner said, jerking the cigar away from his mouth. He offered a multiple-folding postcard showing fourteen depictions of Ranger training. ''Check it out.''

Included were scenes of Rangers patrolling in swamps, with water up to their armpits, Rangers patrolling in a desert whose dust you could practically taste, Rangers jumping out of planes, climbing obstacle courses, practicing rappeling techniques, holding rattlesnakes. It's fairly common knowledge in the military that anyone wearing a Ranger tab has gotten through just about the toughest training the Army currently offers. Well, Turner had not only passed the Ranger course in 1959 but also was an instructor at Ranger School for two years in the late 1960s, then headed the school for three years prior to coming back to West Point. In fact, there was a gold and black Ranger tab hanging from the nameplate sitting in the middle of his desk now. And the more a visitor sat listening to Turner, the plainer it became that although Turner hadn't jumped when the Rangers performed their airborne assault in Grenada, he was as spiritually rigged as any other Ranger who'd ever experienced combat. If West Point had sifted Turner's impurities and refined the compound, it was the Rangers who'd added the finishing touches; and in learning more about them, one learned a lot more about Turner.

He distinctly remembered the day he concluded the Ranger course at Fort Benning in 1959—December 18. It had been, he said, the coldest fall in Georgia and Florida in years. That was tough enough. But the worst part of the two-month course was the cumulative physical and mental stress. Turner had averaged three hours' sleep and was fed one ration a day. "I think I was hungrier during the Ranger course than I'd ever been in my life. Actually, in a garrison environment, they feed you a ton, all you can eat. But once you're out on an operation, you get one meal a day, and you're more than burning it up."

For, say, a five-day operation, you're given five rations. How you divide the food is up to you. "I tried to kick it out so I'd eat about every twelve hours, when I got the chance," Turner said. He remembered thinking more about candy bars and banana splits than anything else. And when he completed the course, he purchased twenty-four Mars candy bars, ate them all, then found the nearest place to Benning that sold banana splits and ordered three. While Turner had hallucinated about chocolate and ice cream, he'd seen others trying to insert quarters into trees, believing they were soda machines.

It makes perfect sense once you grasp that in Ranger School the basic idea is to stress the soldier. You can't shoot at him in peacetime, nor can you give him the fear of stepping on a mine or being killed by the enemy. So the way to simulate war conditions, Turner said, is to put him under physical and mental stress. Then observe how he'll react when placed in a leadership position.

For instance, he's suddenly told to take over a patrol because the patrol leader has been killed. It's three in the morning, and the troops have been tramping in the mountains all night. He's been averaging three hours of sleep for the past week. He probably hasn't been following the map he'd been briefed about before the mission began; but it's his duty as a member of the patrol to have kept abreast of the situation. And now, suddenly, he's told it's his job to lead the group to the objective, accomplish the mission, and get them back alive. A Ranger instructor, an RI, is along, observing and grading the soldier, measuring how well he assumed command, whether he's functional and accomplished the task. He's asked to do all this precisely when he's physically tired and perhaps even emotionally disoriented. Turner has seen soldiers go running off into the woods like wild people in such situations. "You have to go out and tackle them, then bring them back. Some folks can't stand the pressure, and sometimes you even have to get them medically evacuated."

One of Turner's most cherished memories of going through the Ranger course occurred when the windchill factor felt like minus twenty. He was a member of a patrol walking along the side of Hawk Mountain, a height in the Ranger camp near Dahlonega, Georgia. It was so bitterly cold, word circulated that the troops could build a fire. They found an area in a draw, with rocks high on both sides. First they camped under ponchos and got their Sternos going, and it was just enough to knock the chill off. "Then we built this fire, and I remember looking up on this rock, about twenty feet above the fire," Turner said. "The light was flickering, and I could see this Ranger instructor had gotten up there and he was just sitting, leaning against a tree. Had his poncho wrapped about him, and he had one eye open—so help me. He was looking down, right at me. I'd just kind of glanced up."

Turner then must have dozed off for an hour or so. When he woke, his first thought was to check out the Ranger instructor. Where was the sucker, and what was he doing? So Turner looked up at that rock twenty feet above the fire. "And he was still looking at me with one eye open," Turner recalled. "He never went to sleep. He just kept looking at me. He was looking at all of us. He was"—and here Turner's voice turned hushed, almost reverent—"he was the shepherd." Turner wasn't kidding, or, if he was, it was hard to tell.

And perhaps it was even the vivid memory of that night on Hawk Mountain that had made Turner want to become a Ranger instructor himself. He'd certainly enjoyed being out in the woods, doing those daring things Rangers do—jumping out of planes and rappeling down cliffs.

"As for the Ranger instructor," Turner said, "it's amazing, but he's always there, he's always there. He's not telling you how to do it, but he's grading you. Although there may come a time he'll say, 'You did it wrong. Do it again!' " Turner said he's required Ranger students to do things four times. It took them all night, and they missed the helicopter that would have carried them back, and they had to walk. "I kid you not. There's a right way to do these things and a wrong way."

Turner said that Ranger instructors stay with a group during a planning session, rehearsal, and then actually walk with the group. "You're on for, say, twenty hours, then you get relieved. Of course, the Rangers have to keep going. But the new Ranger instructor would kind of appear out of the fog bank. Then I would disappear into the fog bank." Turner laughed. "That's the mystique. What you want was for the troopies not to know you were there."

Turner loved being an RI and for a number of years wanted to head the Ranger School. When he heard in 1982 the job would soon become available, he fought hard to get it. "You better betcha I did." The day he found out it was his, he was happy—more than happy, overcome. The attraction then was what it had always been—being around "sweaty, stinking Rangers, being outdoors, in the woods, doing dangerous, Ranger-type things."

The Ranger course starts out at Benning for nineteen days, after which the candidates go to the mountains for two weeks. Then the troops are loaded aboard a C-141 aircraft and flown to the Dugway Proving Grounds, Utah, a four-and-a-half-hour flight, during which they rig their chutes and jump into the desert, where they operate for a week. Then they reboard their C-141's and fly to Florida, do another in-flight rig, and jump into the swamp, operating there for three weeks. No rest in between. One phase immediately following the other. It is eight weeks plus of intensive training.

When Turner was running the show, there were fourteen classes per year, programmed on the basis of 150-man classes, although the classes usually started out with approximately 185 troops. Forty percent would not graduate with the class they entered. Each student would be evaluated during each phase—jungle, desert, swamp, and mountain—and if the man didn't meet the standards, he'd either be recycled or tossed out of the school. The attrition rate, taking into account recycling, shrunk down to 23 percent.

Some simply couldn't pass the required tasks; others were injured—broken arms, busted legs, torn ligaments. "Most of the injuries occur from the knee on down," Turner said. "The course'll just tear your body up. Your hands get mauled and cut. Your whole body suffers. The average Ranger will lose twenty pounds." Then Turner stated with a grin that the Ranger course today is even more difficult than it was when he was a student. "We've made it tougher," he said, his voice turning screechy with feigned horror.

Nor is the school restricted to the Army. A number of Marines have attended, as well as Navy Seals and Air Force personnel. Foreign officers are also welcome. Everyone removes rank, and officers are treated no better than enlisted men. Turner has seen certain majors pass through the course; a number did very well, he said, because they were intelligent enough to get in great shape before arriving, then knew how to pace themselves.

Turner also remembered a Sergeant Major Owens, of the Infantry School at Benning, doing extremely well. "Tough as nails," Turner said of Owens. "That guy just about maxed it. Went through the course like a dose of salts: Forty-five years old. His forty-fifth birthday was the day he graduated. That's very unusual. Owens, the guy looked like Joe Louis. Solid as a rock. Hard, smart. Knows how to handle troops. Can operate in a stressful environment. He'd done it all. But he went through the old Ranger course because, though he was an infantryman, he'd always wanted that Ranger tab."

Glancing at his watch, Turner said he'd have to stop now; he was scheduled to be somewhere else at one o'clock. We'd do it again next week, same time, okay?

When I left his office at twelve-fifty, I wondered if Mr. Brown was still waiting for me. I said I'd meet him by twelve-fifteen, because how could I possibly have figured on the general's pulling rank, whether he knew it or not, and on a civilian, for Christ's sake?

"I'm awfully sorry, Mr. Brown," I said, getting into the backseat. He'd given his chariot a fresh dose of perfume, and, between sneezing a few times, I explained what had caused the unconscionable delay.

"You don't seem like the kind of man who'd tell me one thing and do another," Mr. Brown said. His rebuke sounded impersonal.

Had his judgment of human nature gone awry? he seemed to be saying. Was it slipping? "I wondered if you'd forgotten the time you said. I didn't forget," Mr. Brown snapped.

Impersonal? Well, not exactly. In fact, he looked and sounded now as if he wanted to tattoo the side of my skull with that yellow flashlight, and can't say I really blamed him. His rebuke was, in short, personal all the way, and coming to my senses, I dug into my pocket. "You probably lost this much waiting for me, and I want to square things with you." I handed him another ten bucks. That left me with just enough cash for what he was charging to take me back to Peekskill, a train ticket, subway fare, and maybe one Mars candy bar.

When Mr. Brown drove me over to West Point the following week I told him to pick me up not at twelve-fifteen but an hour later. No point in taking any chances, and lucky for me I didn't. Don't you know that that goddamn general had Turner in his office on the floor below until almost eleven-thirty. Zapped by the same one-star twice! I couldn't believe it, but that's a true story. Ask Turner. It was almost as bad as sitting in a gastroenterologist's waiting room. If those guys keep you hanging around for less than two hours, they act as if they'd done you a reckless favor. This time the adjutant seemed too embarrassed even to attempt to make small talk, and Turner himself, when he finally turned up, just offered a kind of hopeless shrug.

He said he first became aware of Vietnam in 1962, when he began hearing all kinds of hairy tales from guys who'd served with Special Forces in Southeast Asia. Soon after, Turner volunteered for Special Forces and had passed the test, but at about that time he was made a company commander in Germany.

It seemed appropriate that Turner, who loved anything connected with Rangers, wound up being assigned as a battalion adviser to the 35th South Vietnamese Ranger Battalion. This was in July 1965. He wore a red beret, carried a carbine with a folding stock, and toted a lot of banana clips—precious things, because the Vietnamese loved those thirty-round banana clips.

As a captain, Turner headed a five-man advisory team consisting of three sergeants, himself, and a first lieutenant. Turner had a Vietnamese battalion interpreter always by his side, although the Vietnamese battalion commander and his exec both spoke fairly good English. Not only did the five-man team advise the Rangers how to fight, but they also were able to get them fire support, of which the Americans had a preponderance. Turner did this through radio contact he maintained with his own higher headquarters.

The battalion was operating in III Corps, just north of Bien Hoa, and the heat was unbearable. "Hot?" Turner remembered. "My God, the humidity was so bad, you could reach out and grab water with your hands. Total saturation." The terrain consisted of woods, rubber plantations, and rice paddies, which extended for miles and offered perfect fields of fire.

The ride paddies were made of piled-up dirt. Usually they were three or four feet high, maybe five feet wide. They reminded Turner of grid squares. When he tried to run across them under fire, his feet would get stuck in the mud. The safest place to be was in the water, which usually was knee-deep. A lull in the firing, and you dove over a paddy and plopped into the water, using the paddy for cover.

The battalion was under orders to seek out the enemy. Turner remembered one probe particularly. The battalion commander had been in the job for two months, and Turner had been agitating for more flank security. "'You're not moving across these wideopen spaces with enough security,' I kept telling him. When you're in open space, you spread out, or one round will get you all." Although Turner had been after his Vietnamese counterpart much of the day, the man kept resisting his advice.

Finally Turner got to the point where he told the guy, "Look, if you don't put out flank security, I'm pulling out, leaving." The commander didn't believe him. "Screw this," Turner thought, summoning his team and radioing for an American helicopter to come in and fly them out. Only when the helicopter actually began to pancake in did the battalion commander hurry over, saying, "Wait a minute. Time, time. You want them out there, I'll put them out there." Of course, it wasn't so much Turner's absence he feared losing as it was the artillery and gunship support only Turner could provide. Turner remembered going over to the American helicopter pilot and telling him thanks. "I explained what the situation was, and he said, 'Understand.' Then I asked if he had any extra C's."

About thirty minutes after the security had been put out, the right flank company uncovered a twenty-man VC force and maneuvered in behind them. Caught in a crossfire between the flank company and the battalion's main body, the VC were blown away, all twenty of them. "After that," Turner recalled, "I could do no wrong."

Yet something Turner could never quite do anything about were the battalion's camp followers—wives, children, parents, cousins. They'd ride buses, following the battalion into areas putatively controlled by the VC. Which probably meant they'd bribed their way past VC patrols. Sometimes Turner would be out checking a defense position, and he'd find a soldier sharing a foxhole with his wife. "It used to drive me up the wall." He'd go to the battalion commander and tell him of the necessity to get the wives out of there; but the battalion commander would say the soldiers needed their families, it was good for morale.

After six months, Turner became an operations officer with a brigade of the 101st Airborne and found it an immense relief to be back with American soldiers. "I was flat tired after being with the Vietnamese in the woods for six months, and I was a little tired of working with them, to be perfectly frank. I really wanted to get away from the Vietnamese. I wanted to be with my own soldiers. I was tired of batting my head against the wall and trying to get them to do things that were right. Frankly, I didn't like them. I've thought a lot about why, but I really don't know, I can't tell you."

Upon reflection, Turner thought perhaps the reason was they weren't dedicated to winning the war. They didn't he said, want to come to grips with killing the enemy. If they happened to run upon the VC, fine. But they weren't all that enraptured about going out and reacting to intelligence reports pinpointing the enemy's location. Not like the Americans, Turner said, who went where the intelligence reports indicated the enemy was operating. "You seek the enemy out. And then you suppress him with fire. And then you attack his flanks. And then you destroy him. And that's the name of that game."

But the Vietnamese, Turner continued, didn't think that way. Of course, they'd had to live with the war twenty-four hours a day, 365 days a year, and had been fighting for centuries. There was that historical perspective to take into account. "Yet why were the North Vietnamese so dedicated to winning the war?" Turner asked. "Hadn't they been fighting for centuries, too?"

As for the 101st, Turner considered them fine soldiers. "Absolutely squared-away troops, who went out to find the enemy and destroy him. Nor do I ever recall being involved in body-count problems and anybody lying about body counts," he added.

I hadn't brought the subject up.

"Jesus," Turner said. "I heard an awful lot about that. You read a lot of books about integrity, lack of integrity on the simple term of 'body counts.' "

"You ever encounter any of that?" It was impossible now not to ask.

"I saw a lot of bodies over there, but I never got bent out of shape, nor was I ever forced by any of my commanders, or felt any pressure to inflate a body-count report," he responded heatedly. "And I submitted a lot of body-count reports. You know, one body, two bodies, three bodies. 'What did you see out there?' 'Well, I went over and kicked this one body.' You know, it got to the point where if you couldn't go over and kick a body, you didn't count him. If you saw him lying on the ground out there, you didn't count him as a body count. You reported, 'I kicked this guy and he's dead'—that's a body count. It got so blown out of perspective, and so many people got on top of it, started saying the Army didn't have any integrity, because they were lying about body counts."

"I didn't say it, Tex. I didn't bring it up, and I didn't say it."

"I get a little incensed sometimes."

He sounded like Howie Boone discussing the media. Plainly, different subjects were still sore spots with different guys twenty years later. Or maybe they'd been looking for the opportunity since then to get what was bothering them off their chests, and this was simply it—the opportunity.

Turner began a second Vietnam tour in July 1969, a year and a half after Tet, and I asked if it was his feeling the country had turned against the war then and if that affected his going back a second time.

"I had that feeling," he acknowledged. "But I always said this: I don't care what the media says people feel about Vietnam. I don't care. I care about my family, my friends, my values, my Army, West Point, the things I've done—those are valuable to me. I cherish those things." Turner, in fact, believed that only a minority of the American people were against the war, and that minority specifically consisted of the young people eligible for the draft who'd remained in college. "But I didn't let that bother me. And it didn't."

At the same time, when he returned to Vietnam in 1969, things were different. There were more regulations and rules. For instance, no-fire lines—lines beyond which American forces could not fire. "If you fired anything in that area, you were going to get it," Turner said. "If something happened, and you even killed an enemy in that area, you were screwed. It was frustrating."

Turner was an operations officer, back again with the 101st, running a divisional tactical operations center or TOC, which was about ten feet underground so it wouldn't get blown away by an incoming rocket. Turner, however, often found himself out on the firebases. One, it was hot as hell in the TOC; and two, it was important for an operations officer to get a feel for what was happening where it was happening, and just sitting in the TOC, consulting maps and talking to troops on the radio was, Turner thought, doing the job only half right.

He would hit periods when he'd be working twenty hours a day, seven days a week, and it would take him a while to get used to the regimen. "Basically, you're the guy keeping things moving. The troops on the ground, of course, are the ones fighting the battles. But you're kind of controlling them, allocating helicopters, putting in air strikes. You know where everybody's going, and if you have to stop them, you get the word from the old man and say, 'The word is to stop where you are.' "

After six months Turner became a brigade operations officer based at Camp Evans, and this got him closer to the daily action, because he'd be out with the brigade commander each day as a necessary function of his job. They spent considerable time on the firebases, which they'd reach by helicopter.

The brigade commander was Col. Bill Bradley. "I loved him with a passion," Turner said. "Real warrior. Always wanted to fire in a no-fire zone, and I'd have to hold him up, hold him back. I had that no-fire map in my pocket. I'd sit there in that old command patrol helicopter, with maps in front of me, and we'd be popping along, and I'd be popping the secure set. He'd be sitting right there in the door of the helicopter, and we'd be flying in northern I Corps, where we were still heavily involved."

Turner was awarded the Silver Star after an encounter the 101st experienced toward the latter part of May 1970. Firebase Henderson, a battalion command post secured by a company, was getting zapped by mortar and rocket fire. When their helicopter landed, Colonel Bradley, Turner, the fire support coordinator, a captain by the name of Hopkins, and the brigade sergeant major got out of their chopper and headed up a hill, toward the command post. Just about the time they reached the bunker, a mortar round landed at their feet. Hopkins got riddled behind one leg, Turner was hit superficially in the neck and along the ridge of the nose, and they fell on top of each other, their momentum carrying them inside the bunker.

At first, with blood all over his eyes, Turner thought he was blind. He reached up, swiping the blood away, and his hand looked as if he'd just slipped on a shiny red glove. "My God, I've had it," he said to himself, rolling off Captain Hopkins, who was crying out in pain.

When Turner saw that the sergeant major, who'd also been knocked to the ground, was lying very still, he instinctively jumped on top of him and began pounding his chest. "It probably wasn't a very controlled reaction, but I was trying to get him to talk to me." But the sergeant major's eyes remained closed and he was lying flat on his back.

"He'd gone down as if he'd been hit right between the eyes, like when you shoot a cow," Turner recalled. "They just go down, whop!"

Turner had his hand behind the sergeant major's head. He was blowing in his mouth, yelling at him, and pounding on his chest. Mortar was still coming in, and people were running around. Colonel Bradley was in the bunker; he hadn't been scratched. When Turner moved his hand away, he noticed some blood on it. He thought it was from the blood that had gotten in his eyes. But then he put his hand back behind the sergeant's major's head again, and that's when he felt the neat little hole. It was right under the sergeant major's helmet. A small fragment of shrapnel from an 82 mm mortar round had torn loose, shot up, and slipped in just under the helmet.

"The round had gone pop!" Turner recalled. "Just like a firecracker. It wasn't a large, horrendous explosion. When these rounds land, they don't make fireballs, like what you see in the movies. It's brown or black smoke, and it's a kind of crack."

Suddenly the sergeant major did a kind of heave. It was a death rattle, and he died practically in Turner's arms.

Meanwhile, a medivac chopper arrived for Hopkins, whose leg was badly messed up. Turner threw him on his back and ran down the side of the hill to the chopper pad. As the helicopter came in, it flew directly over Turner's head. The landing pad was narrow, out on a ridgeline. Just as the chopper was about to set down, another mortar round came hurtling in, messing up the helicopter's stabilizer. Turner could see the pilot's eyes grow wide as the guy began pulling pitch full power to avoid crashing. As he pancaked in, Turner could practically feel the blades whipping around on top of his head. Finally the chopper did land, and Turner threw Hopkins aboard. Then he ran back and got the sergeant major, placing him aboard the chopper as well.

Back at the command post, it soon became apparent that the unit, suffering heavy casualties, was running out of medical supplies. While Colonel Bradley and the company commander were directing the defenses, Turner commandeered a second helicopter and took off in search of drugs and bandages. It took a while before he was able to find what was needed and fly the supplies in. Then Turner got them distributed and tried to take care of soldiers. Air strikes were called in, and that eventually chased away the enemy battalion. "It was an interesting day and night or two," Turner remembered. "We lost twenty-one soldiers. A big hit. They took us by surprise. That was probably the biggest welter of fire I've been in."

Turner said he'd always wondered how he'd react under fire, and found he developed a sense that death couldn't happen to him. A great calm descended, and he went about his business as purposefully as possible. "You're really scared to death, but this kind of defense mechanism seems to take over." Still, there were times Turner found himself saying over and over, "Control, control."

It occurred, of course, when he most feared losing control. The first time was when he'd been with the South Vietnamese Ranger Battalion for two days, and a VC fired an AK-47 at one of the Rangers. "Blew his arm off, and there was blood flying everywhere," Turner recalled. "One of the other Rangers grabbed him and popped a tourniquet on. I looked at that arm and felt this bile coming up in my throat. You get over that—the bile coming up. But you don't ever get over the horror of seeing someone getting blown away. You never get used to it, but you have to learn how to control it. Scared shitless, just scared shitless, but you have to overcome it. You can't show fear to your soldiers. You talk about it. You tell your soldiers after it's over, 'I was scared shitless out there, goddamn it.' You laugh about it. You kid about it. You also do that before the battle. You kid about the prospect of dying. Because it's the only way you can live with it. If you couldn't kid about it, it would be unbearable. You leave a hundred bucks at the base camp and tell everybody. 'Have a beer party on Tex if I don't come back.' ''

Turner was relieved to leave Vietnam after each tour. ''No, I was not like some, who really wanted to stay there. I know some people in Forces who, deep down and in their hearts, truly loved it, enjoyed it. They spent a lot of time in Laos, Cambodia, way back there.''

Did he mean Rod Paschall? Paschall and Turner had been West Point classmates and later became good friends.

''Rod might be able to tell you some different things,'' Turner said. ''He spent a lot of time in Forces over there, although I never heard Rod say he loved it. But Rod's a warrior. He likes to fight, I want to tell you.''

Then Turner repeated how relieved he was to be going home, because he never could get used to seeing guys get hit. ''After they're hit, they're still living, they're even smiling at you, and then suddenly they die of shock.''

Turner remembered coming back to the States and going with his wife to see *Alive*, the movie based on the book about survivors of an Andes airplane crash. One guy's guts were shown hanging out, another had his arm torn away. To stay live, some survivors ate the flesh of those who'd died. ''I just got up and walked out,'' Turner said. ''I couldn't take it. It was horrible and reminded me of Vietnam. The horror of war is something no good soldier likes. Every good soldier hates war. Especially if he's been in it. Just hates it. I don't know any warmongers in the Army. Maybe because we're the ones have to go over there and pay the ultimate sacrifice.''

If the death of comrades and the horror of war are among the worst things officers have to endure, among the best is being the leader, actually having a group of men look to you to make decisions. ''I always thought that once I left being a platoon leader, I'd never be able to be with troops again,'' he said. ''Company commander was just too high. Well, I got to be a company commander, and, Christ, it was just as great. It was even better. I had more people to be around, to train, to deal with, work with, and help. Then I said, 'That's it.' '' But when he got to be a battalion commander, he had about four times the number of people to lead that he'd been responsible for as a company commander, and that was better still. ''Christ, there I was, out in the foxholes, taking PT tests with them, walking forty-, eighty-kilometer raids with them, doing all that—which I'd set up, I'm sorry to say. Goddamn, it was beautiful."

The men he commanded were generally good troops, Turner said. "You know, a soldier is a soldier is a soldier." He meant they were as good as their leader. "It only takes one good man, and the unit will go out and operate. They'll accomplish a mission and do it as a team. It just take one good man to make it happen."

Every so often, Turner would come across a trooper who'd never make it as a soldier, a rotten apple. "You work with him for a while, until you determine he's beyond redemption. Then you get rid of him."

Because Wes Taylor had commanded a Ranger battalion during the same time Turner was head of the Ranger School, it figured they'd known each other, and I mentioned the time Taylor felt obliged to relieve a major.

"I know the major you're talking about, I'd given him to Wes." And, that being the case, Turner believed he had a responsibility to both men. "I felt that the major just stepped on his yang a little bit in the wrong direction, and Wes had to do something. Wes bit the bullet. The major is the finest guy you'll ever want to know. A soldier right down to the last nub. I'd trust him with my life. Just made a mistake. Bad judgment, if what happened was true, and I don't know about all that. But I backed that officer. Wrote letters and called everybody. Called the division commander. I don't know how I would have reacted in the same situation. Probably if I was in Wes's shoes, I'd have done the same thing. I don't know, though."

Turner never relieved a major but he vividly remembered relieving a first sergeant two days after he took over as a battalion commander. He was walking between his battalion's two mess halls on Thanksgiving Day when he found the first sergeant "in his green uniform, taking a leak against the mess hall wall, out in front of God and everybody." Turner stood watching him. When the first sergeant looked up, he didn't quite know what to do. "He had his hands full," Turner said. "Then he composed himself, got everything in order, and saluted." Turner told him to report to his office 0600 the following morning, at which time he busted him.

Another time, he relieved a captain whom he found inspecting a company when the troops were wearing low quarter shoes and shirts—not a one had on a jacket or coat though snow was on the ground, it was twenty degrees, and they'd been standing there for forty-five minutes. Turner told the captain to dismiss the company and report to his office in five minutes, at which time he asked for an explanation.

"Why didn't you put some clothes on those people or inspect them inside?" Although the barracks in Germany are commodious, the officer said the troops were tough and had to learn to withstand the elements.

"But, Captain," Turner said, "don't you understand what you did was stupid? It made no sense to them to have to stand out there in the cold—why put up with it? You have to have a reason for doing something like that. If there's a reason, and troops understand it, then you do it and it's okay, then it's acceptable. But you don't have to practice to be miserable. You got any other explanation?"

"No, sir," said the captain.

"Well, you're relieved. Report to the brigade commander."

He saw the man just last week, Turner remarked with a sigh. A sergeant these days, the man was currently assigned to the Army War College.

It was after one o'clock now, and it seemed an appropriate time to leave and find Mr. Brown. I didn't fancy him relieving me of an extra ten dollars again. Besides, talking about all the soldiers he'd seen wounded and killed in Vietnam had, I thought, gotten a little to Turner.

When I reached Mr. Brown's cab and glanced at my watch, I was still three or four minutes to the good, and I could see that Mr. Brown was a little disappointed.

Driving back to Peekskill, he told me he was seventy years old and his wife wanted him to retire, but what would he do with his time? On the other hand, he wanted to move to Virginia, but his wife wanted to remain in Peekskill so they'd be near their children. Was Mr. Brown as confiding to all his riders? or maybe it was SOP to throw in a colloquy for any fare twenty bucks and above.

The last time Mr. Brown drove me to see Tex Turner, the commandant wasn't in Turner's office, nor was he in the commandant's office, and I was slightly disappointed, the way Mr. Brown was disappointed when I wasn't late the second time he'd picked me up at West Point.

Turner had wanted to go to the Academy, he recalled, since the eighth grade. His father had been in the Army and traveled about, but Turner, who'd had relatives all over the South, had grown up living with his grandparents and various uncles and aunts in

Florida and Texas. He'd gone to high school in Killeen, Texas, which he considers his home and is the town next to Fort Hood. Before 1949, when they'd transformed Hood from a camp to a fort, Killeen was nothing more than a crossroad, Turner said, with a bank on one side of the road and a barbershop on the other.

When he was growing up, Red Blaik's West Point football teams seemed to beat all comers, and the Academy's halcyon teams, especially those featuring Doc Blanchard and Glenn Davis, had captured his imagination. Turner also remembered hearing in the school gym General MacArthur's moving address to Congress after President Truman had fired him, and it struck Turner that a soldier was a noble creature. One of his teachers was married to a West Point graduate, and Turner sought the man out, asking about the Academy. The former cadet advised him to get involved in the Boy Scouts, school politics, sports—in short, give evidence of leadership potential. And, for God's sake, take all the math and science courses you can. From that day on Turner prepared himself for admission to West Point and dreamed of playing in an Army-Navy game.

High school football is taken with deadly seriousness in Texas, and Turner devoted himself to making the team each year. "Texas coaches put you through some horrendous physical conditioning-type drills," he said, recalling practicing twice a day in 113-degree heat, with no water. "Coaches chewed you out constantly when you missed a tackle or a block." Though not particularly large, Turner played guard and tackle, and in those days kids went both ways, offense as well as defense. "Those coaches were absolutely relentless, drove you right to the end."

Although his parents had gotten in touch with the local congressman, when it came time to choose, the Honorable W. R. Poage had given his principal appointment to someone else. But that year Turner had made all-state, and the Quarterback Club got together and wrote a letter signed by a thousand members to Poage. "They wrote," Turner recalled, "that if you don't give Bobby Turner an appointment of some kind, then you're going to be in a strain." As luck would have it, the Honorable W. R. Poage subsequently thought to proffer a qualified alternate appointment, and Bobby Turner made it in right behind Poage's principal appointment.

In those days, West Point would send athletes to a prep school for six weeks at Cornwall-on-Hudson shortly before the July they were scheduled to enter the Academy. This would give the budding

Doc Blanchards some notion of the fun and games to expect. Turner remembered visiting West Point that spring, walking around the campus, and getting a chance to talk to some of the cadets. But having an idea what to expect and dealing with the real thing were two different matters, and Turner, like almost everyone else, found he had his share of problems from day one.

"They showed you how to march that very first day," Turner said. "You always stepped off on your left foot. Always. And I always stepped off on my right foot." He also recalled receiving instructions on how to make his first report to his first sergeant. The new cadet had to salute, stand tall, and spout off exactly right. "The report was, 'Sir, new cadet Turner reports to the first sergeant of the 4th New Cadet Company for the first time, sir.'" It took Turner five times to get it right, and each time he fouled up he'd had to go to the end of the line.

In Beast Barracks, you were given a minute to shower. But before showering, you had to show a puddle of sweat beneath you; couldn't get into the shower without that open sesame of a puddle. Turner said he could always sweat faster than the others by tensing all his muscles, although he might not want to swear today the puddle beneath him always consisted only of sweat. In the shower was an upperclassman, holding a watch and yelling at you. Then you had to make your report. "Sir, I have properly showered and dried. I do not have athlete's foot and I have had a bowel movement in the past twenty-four hours."

One night, Turner recalled, the guy in front of him spouted off, "Sir, I have properly showered and dried. I do not have athlete's foot and I have not had a bowel movement for the last five days." Turner did not recall how the sucker had snuck by the other nights, although his recollection was the guy had gone to the hospital for something, and this was his first night back. Of course, his report raised the roof, and the powers-that-be told him in no uncertain terms to go sit in the john and concentrate, making damn sure he came up with a bowel movement.

If Beast was a comic and cosmic misery for eight weeks, plebe year was a continuation of that, lasting to June, because, in those days, plebes didn't go home for Christmas.

"I had a habit of smirking as a plebe," Turner remembered. "A first classman would be hollering, screaming at me, and I'd be standing there with my chin well in, and for some reason he just looked funny to me doing all that hollering. So I'd start smirking, and that was something you just didn't do. *You did not smirk.* You had to brace back then, put your chin in as many notches as you could get. You call these little puckers along your throat and neck 'wrinkles.' Upperclassmen would always say, 'Grab a wrinkle!' So I'd be standing there with my chin pulled in, and I felt silly. Then I'd start smirking and get chewed out for it. We stopped bracing in 1970, I believe. Someone figured out it caused bursitis.''

Like innumerable other cadets, Turner hated with a passion the seemingly interminable math courses at the Academy. ''Math blew me away, and it almost got me thrown out of there,'' he said. He'd done well in math in high school, in part because he'd made it a point of religiously studying from Sunday through Thursday, beginning at eight o'clock each evening until late into the night. Friday night he reserved for football; Saturday night was left to raise other kinds of hell. But at West Point he simply found he didn't have enough free time to devote to subjects that were bedeviling him. And that first year he remembered passing math one tenth of a point to the good. It was a terrific relief, and so was being recognized by the upperclassmen.

Recognition occurs immediately after the graduation parade in June, when the entire underclass passes in review before the first class, all of whom are lined up along the entire length of the parade ground. ''It's the longest eyes right in the world,'' Turner said. After that, the plebes form in the area and the yearlings and second classmen (sophomores and juniors) approach them and shake their hands. Then the first class comes off the parade ground and does the same. ''Thereafter, henceforth and forevermore, you don't have to keep your chin back nineteen notches to the rear and you didn't have to walk double time,'' Turner said with a smile. ''It's the most tremendous relief in the world. You get great pleasure in walking out into the hallway of the barracks without your shirt on. Or even without your hat in your hand.''

Because of the lack of harassment, his second year was infinitely easier than his first, although math continued giving him fits. It was his third year, though, when he encountered engineering courses, which he found toughest of all. He studied electronics that year, fluids, thermodynamics, mechanics of fluids, and Turner grimaced just reciting the names. ''You got through that, you were good to go.''

Throughout his West Point career, Turner was playing second-, third-string, and B Team football. He was a pulling guard. Each year, it seemed, he wound up in the hospital with either a broken ankle, a busted knee, or a smashed bone in his hand. He would work his way up from the B Team to third-, then second-string, then get destroyed, go into the hospital, come out of the hospital, and have to start over at the end of the line. Consequently he wound up holding a lot of blocking dummies for Saturday's heroes. "Although I enjoyed it and it was a lot of fun," he later said, "the thing I'll take to my grave with me is that I never got to play in an Army-Navy game."

At the end of his third year, or his first-classman summer, Turner was appointed a platoon leader at Camp Buckner, where he'd gone two years before to learn the basic and advanced soldier skills West Point teaches third classmen during the summer. This time Turner was one of the honchos, working with younger cadets, inspiring them, developing them, getting them to do difficult tasks. Turner thought it was the best job he could have gotten, because it was there he learned how to be a platoon leader. "And that's what they're trying to develop at West Point—good platoon leaders, who have the potential to develop themselves and go on to make the Army a lifetime career."

He was looking forward to getting out of West Point his final year. While you're a cadet, he mused, the Academy is the worst place in the world and everybody hates it. "You hate it, but you love it, and everybody wants to get it over with. You want to see West Point in your rearview mirror—that's the happiest sight, and everybody feels the same way."

During his senior year, Turner was a company commander. It was a kind of continuation of leadership responsibility he'd experienced at Buckner. The job had status, and Turner got to wear a bunch of stripes. But it also had its complications. "I guess I always felt more gung ho than I should have been," Turner said. "If you're too gung ho, you turn into an asshole, and I think I probably had that problem, because I pissed off a lot of classmates." He was in the tricky and difficult position of giving orders to peers—people who felt that as first classmen they didn't want to hear any guff from one of their own, and certainly not after having paid their dues the prior three years. "I probably have enemies to this day among my classmates, and I probably handled a lot of things incorrectly here. But, thank God, I was able to bounce back," Turner reflected. "I might have done it incorrectly here, but when I got out into the real world, I knew how to handle it and never had the problem."

Turner got married at the West Point chapel the same week he graduated. He'd first met his wife in the winter of 1954, when he visited his father, who was stationed in Germany. Her name was Caroline Bell, and her dad was chief of staff of V Corps at the time. The family returned to the States, living in Cornwall-on-Hudson the same time Turner entered West Point, and the couple kept the relationship going on and off for the four years Turner was attending the Academy. "I graduated on the third of June, and we got married on the sixth. From the frying pan into the fire."

The reception was at Cornwall and included five hundred guests, 490-odd of whom Turner didn't know. Then the couple flew to Bermuda for a honeymoon. Turner had saved twelve hundred dollars. Half he had to spend on his uniforms. The rest he blew on the honeymoon. He guessed it probably would cost ten times that if he took his wife to Bermuda for a week now.

Turner next returned to West Point in an official capacity eleven years later as a tactical officer. He'd requested coming back while he was still in Vietnam the second time. A major then, he knew he couldn't get a command until he made lieutenant colonel. That meant a staff job somewhere, and he didn't want to go to the Pentagon then. Because he'd loved West Point, he wrote the director of physical education, asking to be considered as an instructor.

The story goes that when Turner was a plebe, an upperclassman renowned for doing push-ups challenged Turner to see who could do more. Turner knocked out something like 130 and jumped to his feet, while the upperclassman, his total considerably less than 130, lay panting in the dust. This probably helps explain why the director of phys ed wrote back words to the effect, "We'll take you, Tex. Drive on."

That fall, Turner was scheduled to attend the University of Wisconsin, where he'd earn a masters, a requirement for teaching phys ed at the Academy. But the next letter he received from West Point said that because of a recent budget constraint Turner would not be able to attend Wisconsin, after all. Would he consider returning to the Academy as a tactical officer, which, in those days, required no advanced degree? "I said, 'Heck, yes. Take me,'" Turner remembered.

He found that being a tac was almost like being a company

commander again. He was the legal commander of about 120 cadets. The idea was to mold and put them together, lead and guide them in the right direction. "You see them every day," Turner said. "You watch them when they march into the mess hall. You go down and look at their room. You counsel them each day. You're concerned with things like their military development, and you're trying to help them reach their full potential while they're attending the Academy."

When Turner was a cadet, he had three tactical officers, and it seemed to him all three did an effective job for their country and enjoyed what they were doing. Recalling their good influence was another reason he looked forward to returning to the Academy as a tac. Like them, Turner tried to keep his cadets fired up, motivated, and gave innumerable pep talks, guarding especially against their becoming cynical. "Cadets have a problem with being cynical. Got to be cool. That's bad."

It was easy for Turner to show he cared and worried about cadets, because his predisposition was to get close to them. "Besides, if you're unwilling to get down there and jump into the foxhole with them, they're not going to learn to do that with their people when their time comes."

Turner thought the cadets he got to know during the 1970s were no different from the cadets of his time. "They really don't change," he said. "They were the same in 1955 as they are today. They're smarter now, but the identical basic values are there—love of country, wanting to do what's right, a sense of honor." He concerned himself with developing each of his charges because he took at face value the mere fact they'd been admitted meant each had the potential to become an officer.

"I like to say about West Point that you have to love it, but you don't have to like it. Nobody likes pain, and living four years at West Point is very difficult. But when you leave, you look back and you say, 'Hey, that was a great experience. I owe everything to the Academy.' In your heart you love it, but you don't like it. At the same time, when you come back as an officer, it's different. At night, I go back to my wife; the cadets have to go to their rooms—'the little green cells,' we used to call them. Green, because that's what they were painted."

Turner was asked if he'd be interested in heading the Military Instruction Department about six months before he was due for reassignment, while he was still number one at the Ranger School.

MI appealed to him, he said, because teaching cadets about leadership wasn't that far removed from what he was doing appearing out of a fog bank, teaching Rangers the finer points of patrolling.

As head of the Military Instruction Department Turner has approximately forty people under him, and they come from all the combat and combat support branches. MI is responsible for the military education and training of the Corps. During the summer it offers new cadets training in the basic military skills and prepares them for entry into the Corps. It supervises the third classmen's training at Camp Buckner, emphasizing soldierly skills associated with combat and combat arms support. To the second class it offers specialty training in programs as varied as airborne, escape and flight. It supervises first classmen who serve either as cadre at Buckner or to the incoming class during the eight weeks of Beast Barracks. In addition, the department teaches courses during the academic year, including map reading, combined arms operations, and Army systems management.

It seemed that Turner, having attended the Academy before Vietnam as a cadet, then as a tac during the Vietnam War, and finally as head of MI ten years after American involvement in Vietnam, was in a unique position to comment about the changes he noted from the year he entered the Academy to the present time.

"I know what you want to hear," he said. "But the basic structure of West Point hasn't changed. Not in my time—the last thirty years."

While the introduction of women to West Point in the mid-1970s was a literal change, Turner said, he didn't believe their presence caused much of an impact on the system. As for the increased number of blacks now attending West Point compared to the time Turner was a cadet, he said, "Their presence hasn't changed the system either. The fact we've got more blacks doesn't mean a damn thing. It means that we have to drive on and do the same things we've always done. And that's to teach soldiers how to be good cadets and then good lieutenants."

It was hard to believe, but Turner said that even military training hadn't changed as a result of Vietnam, not at West Point and not in the Army. "Even in places like the Command and General Staff College and the Army War College we don't study jungle tactics anymore. I don't understand that; I disagree with that. But Vietnam hasn't caused us to change as far as training goes. We prepare for the big one. We throw in a little jungle operations. But our doctrine isn't keyed around limited war. Our doctrine is keyed to the big war, wherever it might be."

No one, Turner expanded, sat around at West Point and said now that Vietnam was over, what does the Corps need to do to fit into the great scheme of things? Changes like women's lib and the civil rights movement were absorbed into West Point, which Turner likened to a big sponge.

"The techniques change, but the structure remains the same," he said. "The basic philosophy—duty, honor, country—remains the same. It's immutable. It can't change. If you change it, you're wrong. You don't change your bottom line, which is to be a winner. We want cadets to be winners. If you don't train them to be winners, they're going to lose our wars, and we don't want that. We want them to win our wars, to preserve freedom. That's why we exist in the military, and that's why our leaders exist. To go out and beat the other guy. It's the name of the game. Beat the other son of a bitch! Whip his ass! And if you don't teach cadets to do that, you're escorting folly."

Turner doesn't expect to make general, which means he'll have to retire when he completes thirty years, in 1989. After he retires, he thought he might like to teach somewhere, perhaps coach high school football. Of course, what he'd really love is to remain in the military. "If they want to throw me out of this Army when I'm fifty-two, then they'll lose a good man. It's too bad, but that's what happens. You got to make room for the young guys. I'd stay in the Army forty years if they'd let me as a colonel. Would love it. Just do what I'm doing now. Move from here to another job that deals with soldiers. As long as it deals with troops and soldiers, I could love it. Just drive on and bring smoke."

Although Turner was relaxed and reflective while we were talking, even slouching in his chair, when we walked into the hall, he visibly knocked his shoulders back and down, sucked his nonexistent gut off the line, and popped his chest up in the air, standing tall.

"Everybody wants to be remembered," he said. "I'd like to be remembered as a good soldier. I hope that's the way I'll be remembered—as a good soldier. People say, 'Yup, I knew old Tex Turner, he was a good soldier.' That's enough for me, that's enough. If my peers say that about Tex Turner, I can rest. Go to my grave, go to my resting place, wherever that is." Not that he was in any particular hurry to get there. He'd be forty-nine Friday, Turner said, with a lot of living yet to do. He walked me to the elevator where we shook hands.

Outside, I was a couple of minutes early, but Mr. Brown and his chariot were waiting for me. The forecast was for snow that night, but the sky looked raw, angry enough to jump the gun.

On the drive to Peekskill, Mr. Brown said his foot was acting up, it always did when it was about to rain or snow. Then he asked what I did for a living, and why I kept coming back to West Point. He said he'd worked there for a couple of years during World War II. I started telling him about Turner—how much he loved the military and regretted never having played in an Army-Navy game. Then I told him how Turner remembered wounded soldiers smiling before they died and the sergeant major who'd practically died in his arms.

"Now he's in God's arms," Mr. Brown said. "Jesus won't forsake him."

It started to snow just as we arrived at the train station. Perhaps Mr. Brown guessed I had it in mind to mention him, because when we parted, he said with great courtliness, "Give my regards to your wife."

Wife? What wife? Who'd ever said I was married?

DEFRANCISCO, Joseph E. (Joe)
COL FA 069-34-7511
BORN: 9 Mar 42, Albany, NY

In February 1970, Joe DeFrancisco, now a colonel, then a captain, who'd won a Silver Star during his first tour in Vietnam, brought his wife home from the hospital after she'd given birth to their second child, a daughter. A few days later, he told her he'd definitely be going back to Vietnam that summer. He'd heard the news while she was in the hospital.

"I just said, 'I can't do it anymore, I can't go through it

again,'" Lynne DeFrancisco remembered. "I said, 'Get out. We just need to get out of the Army. I can't handle it anymore. You already went once. Why go again? You survived the first tour. Who's to say you'll survive the second?'"

DeFrancisco had left for Vietnam the first time in June 1967, when their son, Eric, was a week old, and Lynne felt she'd been more than supportive. But he'd already missed a year away from Eric, and now, if he went back a second time, Lynne could just see both children growing up without a father. "So I just said, 'Get out, get out!'" Lynne knew that many of their friends in the Army, her husband's contemporaries, hadn't, for one reason or another, served in Vietnam once. And she also knew that a number of DeFrancisco's other contemporaries had left the Army around 1970, because wives like Lynne didn't want their husbands going off to Vietnam a second time. DeFrancisco's father was another who'd thought it terrible that his grandchildren were growing up without their father. "Why are you living this way?" Lynne remembered him asking.

After returning from Vietnam the first time, in June 1968, DeFrancisco was assigned to take advanced artillery training for a year at Fort Sill, Oklahoma, and Lynne remembered they were at Sill for perhaps five months when the officers attending the course began filling out preference statements, listing their next assignment choices. DeFrancisco jotted down ten, and Lynne typed up the list. Not too long after, DeFrancisco learned that none of his choices would be forthcoming. Come the summer of 1970 he'd be returning to Vietnam, because two years was the turnaround time for artillery officers. He could go either to Germany for a year, he was told, or remain at Sill, before returning to Vietnam. But Germany for twelve months was too tough a move to make with two very small children, so DeFrancisco opted to remain at Sill, where he was assigned as a battery commander with the 14th Field Artillery.

It was at Sill, beginning the summer of 1968, or about six months after Tet, that DeFrancisco had first sensed America's turning against the Vietnam War. There he was exposed to the nightly news, the talk shows, the newspapers, and began to become aware of the protests. "At first I thought the protest marchers were not that pervasive, that they weren't a true reflection of the spirit of the country," he said. It was about that time he'd also first heard of guys ducking the draft by going to Canada, and he figured they were war criminals. "Most of the protesters were young, and it seemed to be centered on college campuses: Here were young guys, I thought, who were using a moral argument because they didn't want to face the music. I didn't pay a great deal of attention to them, because I felt they were in the vast minority. Then, of course, things continued. . . ."

He remembered being particularly shocked and upset seeing the Democratic National Convention in Chicago on the tube, when protesters outside the hall burned the American flag and waved the North Vietnamese one in its place. "All along, I thought there had been a purpose behind our effort in Vietnam, and all along I trusted that our government had used the military in a legally constituted fashion. And now I'm seeing candidates saying, 'Well, we shouldn't fight anymore.' And now I'm hearing all those other groups of people saying, 'Anymore? America was wrong to have gone over to Vietnam to fight the war in the first place.'"

The Nixon-Humphrey presidential campaign that fall affected DeFrancisco a great deal, because here weren't barely marginal candidates but the nominees of both major parties saying America was going to get out of Vietnam, and neither was talking of winning the war. "It was a real eye-opener, and I started thinking, 'If that's the case, good gosh, why don't we just leave?'" On reflection, DeFrancisco knew the country owed an obligation to the South Vietnamese, so, at the least, there'd be some kind of orderly transition.

At the same time that he was focusing on American society's changing attitudes toward the Vietnam War, DeFrancisco became aware of the changes taking place within the Army itself. As a battery commander, he faced innumerable disciplinary problems. Drugs were prevalent; so was on-post violence. Courts-martial were common, and soldiers were being tossed out of the Army at what seemed alarming rates.

Both DeFrancisco and his wife remembered being frightened at a unit party on post because of the way the soldiers looked and acted. "It was a buffet, cookout-type thing," Lynne recalled. "Picnic tables all around, and couples like ourselves were definitely in the minority." It was mostly soldiers, and they were dressed in civilian clothes. When the DeFranciscos stood up to go through the food line, they walked past groups of troops sitting at tables and listening to blaring music. Just below the insistent beat, they could hear soldiers talking unpleasantly about them. Some were leering openly. "Even with Joe there, I felt totally unsafe," Lynne said, "as if five or six of them could have just gotten up, come over, and done something to me or to us. I'd never experienced anything like that before."

DeFrancisco's recollection was that "the troops looked and acted like thugs." The whole tenor, the whole atmosphere was chilling, and he had the immediate sensation of the Army he cherished deteriorating among a checkerboard of picnic tables to the urgent howl of wordless rock music.

It was as if both society and the Army reflecting society had turned incredibly nasty and sour. These transformations stunned DeFrancisco, because his last contact with the outside world before returning to the States in the summer of '68 was the previous February, when he'd met his wife for R&R in Hawaii. "People were still treating the military like a king then," he remembered. "Free drinks, free food a lot of places you'd go, and everybody being nice to you."

A deeply honest man, DeFrancisco acknowledged he really didn't want to return to Vietnam the second time. "The first time, there was no way I wouldn't have gone to Vietnam, because I thought what I was doing was right," he said. I thought I was fulfilling my mission in life. But the second time, I wasn't so sure anymore. What were we doing in Vietnam? I didn't know anymore. We no longer seemed to have a goal. 'Peace with honor,' was Nixon's slogan, as I recall." DeFrancisco grimaced.

Lynne remembered sticking for all of a week to her demand that he leave the Army. Her problem with embracing it any longer was that she knew DeFrancisco loved the Army, and she finally did not wish to have it on her conscience that he'd given up something he loved because of her.

Besides, Lynne added, the Army had dangled a carrot. For a variety of reasons, DeFrancisco wanted to teach military history at West Point. In fact, the Academy had approached him before he graduated in 1965, saying he'd done so well in the subject, if he ever wanted to return to teach it they'd be pleased hearing from him. Now the Army was telling him that after his return from his second Vietnam tour they'd send him to graduate school, following which he was assured of a three-year teaching assignment at West Point. "I knew he wanted this desperately," Lynne said. "But if he didn't come back from Vietnam, that wouldn't materialize either. The first time he went to Vietnam, it was with the famous

1st Cav—ta-ta, and all that. The second time, you know, a year doesn't go that fast, and he knew full well what he was in for. The first time, he had no choice. This time, there really was, basically, a choice.

Yet, after a tense, angry, and bitter week, they started making plans for his returning to Vietnam that summer. "So here it is already February," Lynne recalled, "and you think, March, April, May, June . . . and you know it's coming. It seemed we spent the first five years Joe was in the Army always knowing. It was so constantly Vietnam, even when he wasn't there, he was there."

Between Vietnam tours, DeFrancisco seriously considered leaving the Army. But it would have broken his heart to resign, and he decided, finally, to stay in and go to Vietnam a second time, figuring guys before him had served in a lot more than two years of war; and though this one was particularly nasty and unpopular, the possibility of good things coming after was real enough. He also believed that after having gone through the advanced course at Sill, he still had a commitment. "I might have been able to finagle that," he said. "I probably could have gotten out of it, but it wasn't in my nature to do. So I just figured I'd go. But it was very, very hard going at that time. It's hard going anytime, but that time was much harder than the first, because I really didn't want to go. The motivation wasn't there. The patriotism, if you want to call it that, wasn't at all like the first time."

The first time, as Lynne recalled, DeFrancisco went knowing he was assigned to the 1st Cavalry Division, and the prospect excited him because the division was renowned for its esprit and had earned during its initial battles in Vietnam the nickname "The First Team." He joined the division's 1st Battalion of the 21st Field Artillery as a headquarters battery commander at Kontum in the Central Highlands. It was not a job he particularly wanted. He'd hoped to be assigned as an FO, or forward observer, which would have meant he'd be out with an infantry unit in the thick of the action. That's what young, ambitious artillery lieutenants sought, and DeFrancisco was no exception. But when he'd arrived at Kontum, the need was for the headquarters battery commander, because his predecessor had left two days before and the slot was still there to be filled.

DeFrancisco was in charge of a hundred soldiers. "As a headquarters battery commander you really take care of the headquarters and service elements that provide administration and support for the rest of the battalion. You're not out walking in the bush. You're in the base camp." DeFrancisco frowned.

Shortly after he'd arrived, the unit moved from Kontum to Bong Son. At Bong Son, DeFrancisco asked the battalion commander for another job. This was about two months after he'd arrived in Vietnam, and he was still itching to see action. The unit was ordered north, up the coast, past Chu Lai, to a place called Hill 63. DeFrancisco volunteered to do some aerial observation, and he experienced enemy fire for the first time.

The rainy season had started, and the troops lived in tents. DeFrancisco was still requesting a permanent assignment that would guarantee he'd see action on a daily basis. Finally, in December, the need arose for an LO, an artillery liaison officer with an infantry battalion. It was a very sought-after job at the time. What the LO did was accompany the infantry battalion commander and his S-3, or operations officer, wherever they went. He was their fire support coordinator and rode in their command helicopter, which housed a bank of radios. One belonged to the LO, who had a sergeant and another enlisted man on the ground on twenty-four-hour duty; and because DeFrancisco's ground contact had access to considerably more radios, they were the ones who passed along his instructions to the battalion's various artillery support units.

As battalion LO, DeFrancisco was also responsible for the forward observers assigned to the four infantry companies in the battalion. In practice they worked for the company commanders, but DeFrancisco was their immediate supervisor in terms of their artillery support function. When the battalion commander would fly in to brief his company commander, it was DeFrancisco who would seek out the FO, briefing him on what was going on and making sure he was providing the company with adequate support.

When Tet occurred, the 1st Cav's mission was to reinforce battered American and South Vietnamese units around Hue, South Vietnam's third-largest city, an ancient imperial capital. DeFrancisco remembered that the day they took off was very dreary, rainy, and cold, and they wore field jackets. All the other times it had been very hot. It was also the first time, as far as DeFrancisco knew, that the 1st Cav came together as a single force since they'd arrived in-country in 1965.

They were engaging stubborn remnants of North Vietnamese forces that had wreaked havoc on the once-beautiful walled city now reduced to corpse-strewn rubble, and DeFrancisco remembered running out of 105mm shells, requiring his unit to rely on offshore naval gunfire for its artillery support. At about this time DeFrancisco also remembered seeing the body bags lined up outside the mortuary tent at Camp Evans.

When you see a body bag, he said, there's no mistaking it for anything else. It looks like a rubberized sleeping bag, except it zips all the way up. "It's a kind of sobering thing to see, especially the first time and if the weather is terrible and dreary." The tent was overflowing; hence the piles of bags, stacked like cordwood, outside. "You look over, and there the bags are, with their tags, and you know they're being flown out soon. Or you hope so."

On April 1 the unit began its drive to help relieve the battered Marines at Khe Sanh, the westernmost anchor of a line of combat bases that ran west near Route Nine, paralleling the DMZ and within striking distance of the Ho Chi Minh trail. About five thousand Marines defended the base. By mid-January it was thought the base was surrounded by fifteen thousand to twenty thousand North Vietnamese soldiers, and the fear was that the Americans would be overrun in Dien Bien Phu fashion. Huge American air strikes and more than fourteen thousand tons of parachuted supplies aided the Marines in holding off the NVA. Then, at the Tet offensive began losing steam, General Westmoreland ordered the 1st Cav and the South Vietnamese Airborne Brigade to lift the siege of Khe Sanh.

DeFrancisco recalled that many 1st Cav troops carried handheld radios, and while they were aware the Marines had taken a pounding at Khe Sanh, they were utterly unaware that back in the States Tet was perceived as an American defeat. "As far as we knew, we'd done great in Tet," DeFrancisco said.

He wasn't particularly nervous or scared setting out for Khe Sanh, because the 1st Cav was a very positive, go-for-it unit. The jumping-off point was a place called Landing Zone Stud, which had been turned into a major airfield by the Seabees. Row upon row of helicopters—so many you couldn't count—lined the entire length of the airstrip. It was no longer than a football field, but narrower, a flat spot nestled among the mountains. "To me, being a young guy, moderately gung ho, it was very inspirational seeing all those helicopters."

They were mostly Hueys, with a crew consisting of a pilot, copilot, and two gunners in the back, one on each side. That left room for about seven or eight soldiers, and photos often showed their legs dangling over the sides. DeFrancisco was still flying in the battalion command helicopter. There the officers sat strapped in web seats. The doors were off. There was a lot of noise, but you could distinctly hear the flop sound the blades made as they circled, whipping above the aircraft. Inside, the officers conversed, using headsets.

DeFrancisco's outfit, the 2nd Battalion of the 7th Cav, 1st Cavalry Division, began taking off that afternoon, soaring into low-hanging clouds. He remembered flying above military bases he'd heard of because they were among the American Army's first that had fired into the DMZ. He saw jet fuselages ornamenting the valley, as the unit kept leapfrogging its way toward Khe Sanh. Before putting down, there was usually a fire preparation intended to discourage any enemy that might be lurking nearby and detonate booby traps.

The first night after taking off from Landing Zone Stud, they went to a place called Landing Zone Michael, where the unit dug slit trenches. It had gotten warmer, and they shed their field jackets. They were positioned along a series of steep slopes. The vegetation was lush. The unit wasn't meeting a great deal of resistance, although DeFrancisco did recall being involved in an artillery duel, his first, which was kind of scary. The shells made a whining sound coming in. For outgoing ones, you'd hear the bang before the whine. Luckily, they were on a ledge; you have to score a bull's-eye to hit a target on a ledge, and most of the enemy shells kept landing behind them. American artillery answered. Unfortunately, the North Vietnamese seemed to be firing twelve rounds for every six the Americans attempted. That was something new and not terribly pleasant, and DeFrancisco hunched down as far as he could get. Finally the Americans stopped shooting, and the NVA did the same.

On April 6th, the 2nd Battalion of the 7th Cav fought west along Route Nine in a day of continuous combat, and DeFrancisco was involved in an action for which he received the Silver Star. He was aboard the command helicopter that was so badly shot up the craft was forced to return to base and land. Almost immediately, the crew took off in a second chopper. The battalion commander had insisted on going back because he'd seen a number of casualties on the ground and wanted to bring out those he could.

The firefight was still going on when the chopper landed, and now much of the enemy fire seemed directed toward the helicopter. DeFrancisco remembered hearing branches cracking and the ping sound when enemy rounds hit nearby trees. He's an extremely modest man, who shies away from describing actions he took that others later consider worthy of merit. And the most he'd say now was that he and the battalion commander loaded some of the more severely wounded aboard their helicopter and got them back to a secure landing zone, where they were off-loaded by medical personnel. One of the soldiers died, either on the helicopter or immediately after being taken off it. The others were pretty badly shot up. The helicopter was so battered it couldn't fly again.

The battalion commander commandeered a third helicopter, and DeFrancisco went up with him again. This time they didn't land, but DeFrancisco helped call artillery fire in. "A lot of times the guy on the ground, the FO, doesn't know exactly where he is, and it's difficult for him to adjust artillery because he can't see through the jungle. So I'd start it off. I could bring it close enough to him so then he could adjust it. He certainly knew better where his guys on the ground were and what they needed than I did."

By the time the unit reached Khe Sanh, the NVA were no longer there. "We didn't have to fight our way in," DeFrancisco said, "and I don't want to portray it otherwise." But because of the large caches that were uncovered, it was fairly clear that large enemy units had made a hasty withdrawal into neighboring Laos.

The surrounding area was lush and green, but Khe Sanh itself looked like a moonscape, DeFrancisco said. It had been pounded, in a siege lasting seventy-seven days, during which more than 110,000 tons of bombs had been dropped and more than 142,000 rounds of artillery fired. The earth looked a brownish-red. "You could see the trenches," DeFrancisco said. "The Marines were still inside. You could smell the decaying bodies. It's a terrible smell."

DeFrancisco remembered that his unit was given responsibility for the base defense of Khe Sanh. "I had to arrange for the fire support around it—this unit has this sector, that unit has that sector. We took over a Marine bunker. When we got there, we found all sorts of canned fruit juices we hadn't had for a while." No doubt it was stuff that had been dropped in, because before the siege had been lifted no C-130 could land. The NVA had ringed the base with artillery and antiaircraft, and even managed to dig a trenchline across one end of the airfield. They'd come that close. So it was a big deal when the first C-130 landed—a sign of control being reestablished.

On Easter Sunday, April 14, the people in the headquarters bunker decided to pool their food and eat a big Easter brunch. Fighting had died down, there wasn't much going on. "So we got our C rations, sat on the floor, and cooked up a wild conglomeration."

Ironically, a number of 1st Cav troops thought that Khe Sanh was perhaps going to be the last big battle of the war. "Admittedly, we were very naïve and did not know the so-called big picture," DeFrancisco said. "But that was the talk and that was the sense of it. I'm sure it was different for other people in other places. And certainly different for me at other times."

A few days after Easter Sunday, DeFrancisco was reassigned and became an assistant S-3, a fire direction officer at battalion headquarters. His Vietnam tour would be over in two months, and, ready for something new, he rather welcomed the change. He was on night duty, from three in the afternoon till three in the morning for two days, when he was given a temporary assignment that genuinely frightened him.

Hoping to short-circuit any future attacks on the old, virtually devastated city of Hue, General Westmoreland decided to strike at the staging area the NVA had used to attack Hue. This was the rugged A Shau Valley.

The A Shau straddles Vietnam's western frontier. It is mountainous, remote, and inaccessible. Ranges on either side of the valley extend five thousand feet up and often are shrouded in mist. The valley is a mixture of elephant grass and tropical rain forest, and the 1st Cav was selected to go there to clean out any remaining NVA infantry.

Anyway, DeFrancisco was pulled away from his relatively safe staff job of two days and told he'd be needed to command temporarily a small firebase atop a mountain overlooking a sector of the A Shau where 1st Cav units would be seeking to engage enemy infantry. No landing zones were large enough to accommodate the firebase, so the weapons would have to be helicoptered in, lowered as gently as if they were twin babies. "I wasn't scared at all going into Khe Sanh, but I was frightened going into the A Shau," DeFrancisco said. He'd be accompanying two howitzers and their five-man crews. But there'd be no attached infantry to defend them if the NVA got ambitious, canny, and decided to trek up the mountain and overrun the base. Hence, DeFrancisco's anxiety.

True, the summit already accommodated a signal detachment, acting as a radio relay for the troops patrolling in the valley, and a couple of Lurps, long-range reconnaissance soldiers capable of infiltrating deep away from U.S. troops and observing enemy forces before reporting back. But, altogether, there'd be no more than thirty soldiers on the mountaintop.

After the howitzers and ammunition were sling-loaded, the choppers took off. Because the mountaintop kept playing hide-and-seek among the clouds, the pilots had a difficult time dropping in when they could clearly see where they wanted to land. Compounding their problem was the summit itself, which was so rocky choppers weren't able to put both skids down. A Lurp got his foot cut off at the ankle because one of the choppers suddenly tipped unexpectedly.

The weapons were 105's, which had a normal range of about 11.5 kilometers, but probably more here because the weapons were so high up. As soon as the weapons were set down, the troops broke out the ammo boxes. More ammo kept pouring in, and it reached the point where there simply was no room for any additional boxes. Later, they wound up using some of the still unemptied ammo boxes for shelters. It was like sleeping on a pillow of TNT, a crazy thing to do, but, given the limited space, they had little choice.

During the week to ten days DeFrancisco spent on the mountaintop, the weapons were fired often despite a late monsoon that inundated the valley. The weather was really vile, and it was impossible to keep dry. The fog was often dense, and they couldn't fire then, because they couldn't see their aiming stakes or collimators. "A collimator looks like a squat telescope," DeFrancisco said. "It sits on a tripod, and you flip it up. What you do is sight in on it with the sight on the howitzer. But you couldn't even see it when it was foggy, and the instrument was maybe five feet away."

The 1st Cav commander those days was Maj. Gen. John Tolson. He was a paratrooper who'd made a number of jumps in the Pacific during World War II, and the division seemed to reflect his blend of imagination and daring. DeFrancisco was amazed one day when Tolson flew in and scrambled out of his helicopter. "I'll never forget it. Here was a division commander, head of the 1st Cav, piloting his own chopper, landing on this difficult peak, and stepping out. There was no one up there for him to impress. I was the ranking officer, a captain, there was a lieutenant, and what did we have totally, thirty people? But he was checking to see how we were doing. It was probably no more than a five-minute visit, but I've always had a lot of respect for him since then."

A trio of important political events adumbrated the last months of DeFrancisco's first Vietnam tour. The first was President Johnson's decision not to seek reelection. Johnson made the announcement March 31, and DeFrancisco recalled hearing about it on his way into Khe Sanh. "The battalion S-3 came over and said, 'Hey, Johnson's not going to run.'" DeFrancisco remembered wondering why Johnson had decided to call it quits when everything was going so well in Vietnam. "We had no idea he'd lost the confidence of the country. To us, things were going great."

A few days later, Martin Luther King, Jr., was shot, and Robert Kennedy was killed the first week in June. Both, DeFrancisco thought, were tragic losses, but he remembered the King death more vividly, because his radio operator, a black soldier from L.A., had come over and told him about it, "Sir, some fool killed Martin Luther King." The soldier was terribly distraught, and DeFrancisco sat down and talked with him for a while. "It was a genuinely traumatic thing, and I'll never forget how really upset he was."

Probably these events should have alerted DeFrancisco that he'd be returning to a society reeling from what seemed a series of violent spasms. But he was too happy going home to have paused and made the relevant connections.

When DeFrancisco arrived back from Vietnam the first time, his wife remembered that, "being Italian, we had a big welcoming committee at the airport." DeFrancisco was wearing his uniform, and suddenly his middle brother, Jerry, turned to Lynne and pointed to his ribbons, saying, "I'll bet you didn't know about that." He meant DeFrancisco's Silver Star. "Huh?" Lynne said. She'd had no idea what Jerry was alluding to, because DeFrancisco hadn't mentioned the medal in any of his letters.

Lynne DeFrancisco is a petite, attractive woman, outgoing and bubbly. She has thick brown hair cut stylishly short. She'd worked as a dental hygenist and was a stewardess for American Airlines for two years. Lynne had met DeFrancisco when they were either in the sixth or the seventh grade—it's a running debate between them exactly when—and developed a crush on him. They were married in the fall of 1965, after DeFrancisco graduated from West Point and completed Ranger and Airborne schools.

Neither of them knew much about Vietnam, not when they got married nor when they left for Germany, DeFrancisco's first permanent assignment, although the first large troop commitments to Southeast Asia had been made by the Johnson administration months earlier. "Didn't even think about it at the time," Lynne said. "Our life was grand and marvelous, and we were on our way to Germany for three years, excited about going there." The first indication they might not remain in Germany to complete the tour was when they began hearing that other young officers were receiving orders returning them to bases in the States, prior, they were told, to embarking for Vietnam. "That's when we started getting nervous," Lynne said. "I mean, *I* was a nervous wreck. And then, six months after we'd gotten there, Joe was notified he was to come back, too. I cried for days."

DeFrancisco was sent to Fort Bragg, North Carolina, where, as a company training officer, he ushered recruits through basic training for nine months. Lynne remembered their time there "as one of the worst tours we ever had." They'd decided to have a baby. Lynne was pregnant the entire time she spent at Bragg, while they kept waiting for DeFrancisco's Vietnam orders to be cut. "I didn't know if I'd give birth before Joe left or not. And most of my next-door neighbors were in the same boat. We were all just waiting, and it was bad."

Lynne was not really prepared for Vietnam despite those nine months at Bragg, and despite attending a party two years before at West Point for engaged first classmen at which she inquired about a term she'd heard, "hardship tours," knowing it meant a separation. "I asked a couple of the wives of the married officers, and one said, 'Oh, don't worry about it. My husband has been in for fifteen years, and we've only had one.' Another echoed, 'My husband's been in for ten years, and we've only had one.' So I thought, once every ten or fifteen years, that's not so bad, that's to be expected. But I wasn't ready for it that fast."

They decided Lynne would return to their hometown of Albany, New York, and live with her parents while DeFrancisco served in Vietnam. She had no real roots at Bragg, and the decision seemed to make sense. Both sets of grandparents would be nearby. Besides, most of the wives married to young officers seemed to be doing the same thing.

Lynne moved back into her old bedroom. Because there were only two bedrooms in the house, they put the crib in Lynne's room; it made for tight quarters. Lynne tried to tell herself the year would fly, that she'd keep busy taking care of the baby. Both of her parents worked, so she had the house to herself during the day. On Saturdays she practiced dental hygiene and her mother baby-sat.

Despite having to care for an infant, working Saturdays, and living with her parents, Lynne remembered the year as "terrible, it was awful." She found herself constantly worrying about her husband. Two months after he'd left, she got a call from her former next-door neighbor at Bragg. The woman, a nurse, phoned to say that her husband had been shot in the spinal cord in Vietnam and was paralyzed. "It could have been Joe."

Perhaps even more shattering in the long run, though, was TV's coverage of the war. "It was there every night, in living color, what had happened that day or the day before," Lynne said. "And it wasn't news that was two weeks old. It was yesterday, today, and you'd see them carrying the mangled bodies and you'd see the helicopters shot down. Then I'd hear them say, '1st Cav,' and I knew that was Joe's unit. Two weeks later, I'd get a letter from him, saying he'd gone to Khe Sanh or wherever. But I'd already known he'd been there, from television. It just made everything much, much harder to take." Although TV's nightly news left her feeling miserable, she found it was like an addictive drug to which she could not help exposing herself.

While both families were close and supportive, there was no one nearby experiencing exactly what Lynne was going through, and she felt a gnawing sense of isolation. The country hadn't rallied around the Army, and the people she'd gone to high school with seemed to be leading lives utterly unaffected by Vietnam. They were having children and buying homes. Sometimes they were kind and invited her to lunch. "Bring Eric," they'd say. But at night, their husbands would return home, and Lynne found herself constantly wondering if her son would ever see his father again. Her existence struck her as strained and unreal. Yet the people she visited didn't seem really to know, much less care, that that unreality was the result of American soldiers dying in a forlorn corner of the world and tomorrow her husband might be one of them.

When she saw him in Hawaii the following February, it was plain he'd lost a lot of weight. Other than that, he wasn't particularly different. And that was another thing that bothered Lynne. "When you'd go to a movie about Vietnam those years, almost all of them showed Vietnam veterans as either half kookie before they left or totally deranged when they returned. But the vast majority who went were perfectly normal and came back as normal people," she said. "I mean, Joe doesn't break out into cold sweats and have those nightmares."

He didn't talk much about the war, neither during R&R in Hawaii nor in his letters. He'd write almost every day, Lynne said, but never about the fighting. "It was always more what he had to eat, or just asking me questions, or saying he missed us. Joe never wrote or talked about what he was actually involved in. He'd just say that he went somewhere for two weeks."

They had a wonderful time together in Hawaii, and, surprisingly, Lynne didn't find it tough returning to the States alone. She'd heard other wives say the plane ride home alone made everything worse, but her experience was that it didn't turn out as difficult as she'd been led to believe it might.

If Lynne found her husband's first Vietnam tour awful, the second was much worse. Yet when DeFrancisco left for Vietnam the second time, he'd decided it was, after all, only a one-year tour, and, resigned to going, he'd make the best of it. There weren't that many American units in-country anymore. Vietnamization was well under way, which meant the brunt of the fighting was being conducted by the South Vietnamese.

DeFrancisco was made a battery commander. It was not a job he'd have chosen, having just come from a battery command at Sill, during which the bulk of his time was consumed by courts-martial and disciplinary Article 15 procedures. This time, fortunately for DeFrancisco, Firebase Sandra was isolated, perhaps a hundred miles from battalion headquarters, which was near Phan Thiet, in southern II Corps. Because the base was isolated, he could exercise greater control. There was no road access to it, so everything had to be brought in by air. When new people arrived, they were searched as they got off the helicopter, while they were still on the pad. If liquor or drugs were found, they were confiscated. It was a precaution, as well as an initial signal to the new man that DeFrancisco was running a tight ship.

He had perhaps 105 troops, full battery strength. In addition, there were two radar detachments on the firebase, old World War II air defense guns, four .50-caliber machine guns, and a couple of

Dusters, which looked like little tanks but were track vehicles with turrets.

DeFrancisco spent perhaps 90 percent of his time walking from section to section—artillery batteries are organized in sections—talking to troops and keeping them informed. Sustaining morale was one of his chief priorities. He had troops build a full-length basketball court, a volleyball court, and a theater dug out and sandbagged with overhead beams. There were two showings of movies each night. Drills were conducted daily. The basic mission was to show the flag and survive. There were guard towers and a system of alerts. Ringing the base were claymore mines and other booby traps. Security was uppermost, not least because no one was around to help in case the base got attacked. What DeFrancisco developed, therefore, was a daily routine that involved certain set things done at certain set times, a laundry list of base improvements, and competitive athletic events emphasizing teamwork. All in all, it made for a fairly active day.

After six months he was reassigned and sent to Nha Trang, a beautiful resort coastal city, where he lived in a BOQ with a number of other captains. It was basically a corps headquarters, and he was a member of the corps artillery section. His official title was assistant S-3, 1st Field Force, artillery. As such, he instituted an inspection program for artillery units still active in the 1st Field Force, checking on their employment and making sure they followed standard artillery procedures. The focus was to cut down on American casualties. Certainly no one wanted an American firebase overrun at that late stage of the war.

In this job DeFrancisco, now away from his small, isolated firebase, was exposed to a wide range of soldiers and became aware of their generally deplorable morale. Discipline was terrible, even to the point of wholesale nonsaluting. Dapping was popular. Dapping, DeFrancisco explained, was an elaborate salute of sorts—one that black soldiers developed among themselves; it could go on anywhere from five seconds to five minutes. Fingers snapped, elbows touched. American soldiers, black and white, knew they were there just until it came their turn to go home. There was no intent or attempt to win the war. War? What war?

The lack of discipline was a disheartening thing to see if you were a military professional. But there seemed little an officer could do, because it was so pervasive and because people were literally getting away with murder. "I mean, there were fraggings and there *were* murders," DeFrancisco said. "About every third guy had a fragging story. Things were out of control, and the best you could do, about the only thing you could do, was control the people who worked for you. Your problem came if you tried to do that with another unit, another group of people who were under somebody else's chain of command. Because you didn't know what to expect."

DeFrancisco was relieved when his second tour was over. He really didn't know what he'd accomplished, except that no one who worked for him got killed or wounded. The promise was that after his second Vietnam tour the Army would fully fund his going to graduate school and then he'd have a three-year teaching assignment at West Point. He was looking forward to both. That, and being back with his family, who were waiting out his second Vietnam tour, as they had the first, in Albany.

Lynne, now the mother of two, had rented a duplex in the suburbs. The woman moving out was getting back with her husband, who'd just returned from Vietnam, and she'd warned Lynne, "Be very careful. You're a wife without a husband." An attractive woman, she knew that a number of wives in the neighborhood had considered her a threat and would similarly consider Lynne a danger. Still, Lynne was surprised when she actually received phone calls, and some of the men would say nasty things to her.

Before DeFrancisco left the second time, Lynne had thought about remaining at Sill, where she'd lived for two years, because this time a lot of young wives in the same situation had opted to reside on or near the post. There Lynne would have had access to the PX, the commissary, the hospital, and, most of all, people to talk to who, because they were in the same situation, presumably would have understood. But she'd finally decided to return to Albany, because she did not want to deprive either set of grandparents the opportunity to see their grandchildren. In hindsight, it probably was a mistake.

In the neighboring duplexes were mostly young couples with children. Most of the men had never served in the military. College deferments were common, and many of the men had married, either while they were still attending college or immediately upon graduation, thus circumventing the draft. The war by this time, July 1970, was thoroughly unpopular, and neighbors would question Lynne why her husband was over in Vietnam.

"Why," they'd ask, "is your husband fighting in a war like this?"

Lynne would answer, "It's his duty, his way of life. He's a soldier, and that's where he had to go at this particular time."

Lynne invariably felt beleaguered whenever they asked. Maybe the people questioning her didn't approve of the war, and maybe they didn't approve of the Army and what her husband was doing. But it seemed to Lynne that their lives were progressing unaffected by the war, while hers often felt as if it was unraveling, and that was tough enough, without being placed in the unenviable position of defending political and military decisions she neither made nor could possibly influence.

Lynne wondered what the young businessmen questioning her would have done had they been drafted. Collapse into a state of shock? Faint? Suffer a heart attack? She often found herself angry at them, and remembered being particularly hurt on Halloween when it seemed all the other neighborhood children were taken trick or treating, yet no one thought to ask her son to join them. Lynne couldn't accompany him; she was taking care of the baby. Nor was Halloween the only instance when she'd felt absolutely alone. All that winter she'd see the neighborhood children out sleigh riding, but not once did anyone ever ask to take Eric with them. Lynne understood that it wasn't a question of fairness. Her husband was a career officer and had chosen a way of life requiring him to go off to fight a war when the military was told by its civilian superiors that the national interest was threatened. Yet neighbors, fellow Americans untouched by the war, seemed chillingly incapable of understanding the anguish and isolation experienced by relatives of soldiers stationed in Vietnam.

"Nothing you read, nothing you see about Vietnam ever shows or tells what the wife felt like," Lynne said. "And I wasn't alone; there were many like me." Nor did Lynne exclude parents whose sons were in Southeast Asia. They, too, were exposed to the nightly news, which always seemed to focus on soldiers' mangled bodies. "It's different if you look at it in *Life* magazine," Lynne explained. "That's still pictures. You don't see people trying to run away, or stepping on a booby trap, wondering if it's your son or husband they're filming, wondering if it's Joe."

Joe DeFrancisco wears gold, metal-framed glasses and looks like an exceptionally compelling parish priest. He stands just under six feet and weighs about 185. He has brown eyes and short,

Brillo-like hair that's starting to turn gray on top. DeFrancisco had more than the usual reasons for wanting to return to West Point to teach military history. True, he'd loved the subject and, as someone who'd enjoyed working with people, thought he'd like teaching. But, as a West Point cadet, he'd also decided early on that he was to back off from everything else in order to survive academically. "In future years I translated that to mean I didn't do all I *could* do. So I wanted to go back and do more. Plus, growing up, I'd always had difficulty talking to people, and I figured the best way to overcome that was to be a teacher."

DeFrancisco first thought of becoming a cadet when he was a junior in high school. His father had been a B-29 bombardier, but World War II ended before he was deployed overseas. "He had some books about the Army lying around the house," DeFrancisco said. "And whenever he talked about the Army, he seemed to be happy and very proud of his experiences."

Growing up in Albany, sports had been a big part of DeFrancisco's life, and he remembered watching with special interest a number of Army-Navy games on television. He played American Legion ball, and was good enough to start on a team that were repeat winners of the New York State American Legion championship. The games were held at Cooperstown, site of The National Baseball Hall of Fame and Museum, which added to the excitement. DeFrancisco remembered being pretty good with the glove but had trouble hitting a curve.

He was the eldest of three brothers. The family went to Mass and received communion every week. Dinner on Friday was fish. During Lent they went to daily Mass. DeFrancisco attended Catholic schools, starting in kindergarten, all the way through high school. There he was an altar boy, which meant that if you didn't show up for Mass Sunday, you didn't play football.

At the time DeFrancisco applied for admission to West Point, the appointment was in no way competitive in Albany. Because the principal appointees made it the year DeFrancisco applied, there was no room for him, and he decided to go to Holy Cross, a Worcester, Massachusetts, university run by the Jesuits. It was almost a continuation of parochial school, because you had to attend Mass every morning, and religious courses were mandatory. DeFrancisco entered the school's Air Force ROTC program but wound up quitting because it seemed less than serious, a waste of time. While he was attending Holy Cross, DeFrancisco learned that due to his father's persistent efforts he'd be entering West Point the following summer after all.

He remembered his parents driving him from Albany down the Thruway early in July. It took about two hours. When they came to a West Point sign that read "No Parents Beyond This Point," DeFrancisco, nervous the whole way down, said good-bye to his folks and walked in.

The hard part, he found, was simply making the transition from civilian to military—just getting into a regimented routine and going without sleep. The days were long, and nights were consumed by studying rules, songs, and famous sayings, all of which new cadets were later quizzed on. Although the eight weeks of Beast Barracks added up to a traumatic blur, DeFrancisco never considered quitting. "I knew enough so that I understood it was a rite of passage, and I'd made up my mind I was going to do it. So it wasn't that hard."

In Beast, the new cadets outnumber the upperclassmen. But around Labor Day—or "Reorganization Week," as it's called at the Academy—all the upperclassmen return, and they outnumber the plebes, who now have more people watching them. Academics are also beginning then, and DeFrancisco was yet another plebe who struggled with calculus.

"Math was every day, every day being six days a week, and every session lasted eighty minutes," he said. By now the tune is familiar and so, alas, are the words. "It wasn't fun, it was very difficult. Just learning the whole system was difficult, and so was being graded almost every day in almost every subject. There was no escape from it. You're answering to people each day in class, and when you leave class to return to the barracks, you're answering to people there. And even meals, which you'd think would be a time to relax, was another time to perform. As a first-year man you can't talk until you're talked to. You have to ask permission to eat, as I recall, and you have to serve the food."

His roommate the second year was a cadet from the South named Don Appler, with whom he constantly argued about the Civil War. At ten minutes of six they'd be standing outside at reveille and Appler would be swearing, "Goddamn this Yankee weather." Anything wrong with New York was his roommate's fault, because DeFrancisco was from Albany. Appler, whose forebears had served in the Army, was very patriotic. When the Cuban missile crisis flared in the fall of 1962, he stormed about, grabbed his rifle out of the rifle rack, broke the weapon down, and started cleaning it. By God, if the Russians really wanted to play hardball, here was one cadet ready and more than willing.

DeFrancisco found that academics were tougher the second year than his first. "You just stepped up another notch, and it was a constant struggle to keep your head above water." During his first year, he'd made the plebe football squad as a halfback. But it was rough playing for the plebes. They had a lot of good ballplayers. In addition, practice was a big drain on time and physically demanding, and math was still driving him up the wall. That spring, in a physical aptitude test, he hurt his knee and it had to be placed in traction. He couldn't play spring ball and decided not to go back. To get any kind of decent grades, he gave up all thought of intense extracurricular activities. He was an acolyte in church and participated in intramurals, but mostly he hit the books.

At the end of his sophomore year, he chose to be a member of the Beast Barracks detail. A squad leader, he was handed eight kids. "I was on the first detail, which meant I got them off the street. You saw these young guys coming in just as you had two years before, all scared and nervous, and you knew what you had to do with them and how you had to help them. You teach them everything—how to walk, how to talk, how to wear their uniforms, how to polish their shoes. I had them four weeks, and they all got through. My parents have a picture of us together."

DeFrancisco went on leave after his Beast stint. He and two other cadets, Ron Floto and Tim Simmons, had studied Portuguese and decided to try to fly to Brazil using military hops. To get to Rio, they had to go via Charleston, South Carolina. There DeFrancisco saw his first civil rights protest march, a group of blacks chanting and carrying signs. It was tough finding a drink in South Carolina, and DeFrancisco remembered going to a speakeasy that had a front door with a sliding panel. Three other cadets had hooked up with them, but when it came time for the plane to Rio to take off, it turned out there weren't enough seats. So the group decided to head for Puerto Rico instead. "In San Juan we went to all the bad places," DeFrancisco announced sheepishly. "We had a great time, and did it on maybe fifty bucks apiece."

By the third year, DeFrancisco felt he knew the West Point system, by which he meant knowing "what you needed to do to survive. You know you've already gone through so much, there's not going to be anything they can give you you won't be able to deal with. You know you're going to make it." By this time he'd taken American and European history courses, which he'd loved, and in his junior year he took a course in Russian history. "You know why it was tough? The damn names. Who can remember Russian names? Names of cities, names of people. And if you can't remember the names, it was tough to relate the concepts."

That summer, the entire class was flown to Germany for what was called overseas training. They were going as third lieutenants and got to pick a branch; DeFrancisco chose armor. He was assigned a platoon of about twenty people, found he loved Germany and the spirit of the troops, but decided that armor, like math, wasn't for him. "I didn't feel very comfortable with tanks; they spent a lot of time in the motor pool. But I did learn I wanted to go to Germany on my first assignment."

That summer, too, DeFrancisco's class toured different posts in the States. This was to give them a taste of what each branch offered and was meant to help cadets when it came time to choose in which branch they wished to serve. "It was a pretty exciting summer with all that traveling—traveling around the United States and traveling in Europe. This for someone who at the time hadn't done a whole lot of traveling outside of New York." It's exaggerating only slightly to suggest that for a guy who'd grown up in a tightly run city, attending a high school whose principal was the parish priest, that that summer was a kind of breaking away; the world, DeFrancisco saw with appreciative eyes, was wider than he'd realized.

He found his senior year the most enjoyable of all. DeFrancisco remembered taking a lot of government and history courses. As a senior he had increased privileges and spent considerable time in New York City, where Lynne was living. He knew they'd be getting married soon after graduation and was looking forward to his first assignment as an artillery officer. The future seemed full of promise and excitement. "I vaguely knew Vietnam was going on, but I'd chosen Germany and fully expected to spend three years there. I didn't think Vietnam was going to be any big deal. But I should have expected something, because they'd made us go to Ranger School after graduation. They'd done that with the Class of '64, too. Somebody upstairs must have had an inkling."

DeFrancisco was very happy on graduation day, but he didn't remember thinking graduation was a great accomplishment. Perhaps he'd have felt that way if he'd ever doubted graduating. "But

I was never really scared I wasn't going to make it. So when the day came, it was great, but I was looking forward to—lunch. And as soon as I got out of the uniform, I was looking forward to—a party that night.

While attending the Academy, DeFrancisco admits to doing his share of bad-mouthing the place. Yet when he thinks about West Point, he finds himself ultimately admiring the institution. "I guess more what it stands for than what it is. And what it stands for are high ideals—ideals probably unattainable, like total devotion to duty, honor, country. But those are pretty heady things if you really mean them, and what they give you is a reason for being." At West Point, in short, DeFrancisco, a man predisposed to seeking an ideal, found the ones he wished to serve. Which was another reason he'd looked forward to returning to the Academy to teach there after his second Vietnam tour.

First, though, he'd have to earn a masters in history. He was given a choice of attending Michigan, Stanford, Rice, Duke, or Temple. He chose Rice, where his thesis was on British-American command relations during World War I. It won a prize.

As valuable to DeFrancisco as earning the degree was the chance, under relaxed circumstances at Rice for two years, to become reacquainted with his wife and children. He hadn't really known his children before. Fully funded by the Army, he was able to buy a house in Houston, Lynne didn't have to work, and the four of them found time to do family things together.

He began teaching at West Point in the fall of 1974. Military history was a six-day-a-week course, and he'd teach two eighty-minute classes each day. He taught them in blocks of four, or the same lesson four times. He was nervous when he started, but found the History Department very helpful. Its head was Thomas Griess, at the time a colonel, now a brigadier general, retired. The head of the military history section was Roy Flint, now the academic dean at West Point. "They both had a profound influence on me, because of the example they set as officers, historians, and men," DeFrancisco said. "They were willing to see you were somewhere they'd already been, and they were willing to help you as an individual to develop. They were at West Point for an important mission as they saw it, and that's the education of future Army officers and the development of officers on the faculty. And they were good enough to do both of those things simultaneously."

In May 1976, an electrical engineering instructor noticed something irregular in a number of take-home assignment papers by members of the Class of 1977. An investigation commenced, more irregularities were uncovered, and a full-fledged cheating scandal blossomed, involving more than 150 cadets. DeFrancisco was tapped to be a member of one of a number of three-man internal review panels.

"What we did was interview suspected cadets throughout the summer of 1976," DeFrancisco said. The questioning would take about an hour, and most of the cadets were extremely nervous. "Our panel interviewed perhaps fifty of them. We had their papers; we had the papers of others who'd been given the same assignment. Then we made a recommendation—whether charges should be dropped or a further investigation was warranted." It was pretty clear-cut in most instances, the panel was usually unanimous, and most of the time the recommendation was that the investigation should be continued.

DeFrancisco found the experience painful because it was obvious there'd been cheating on a massive scale. He thought the scandal was symptomatic of a general questioning of authority. "Plus you have to look at the society these kids were coming from. You had Kent State, you had the Christmas bombing business, you had Watergate, you had My Lai, you had General Koster, the superintendent of West Point in 1970 having to leave as a result of the Peers Commission, which investigated My Lai and concluded there'd been a cover-up in the Americal Division, which Koster had commanded."

But closest to the bone, as far as DeFrancisco was concerned, was the tone the officers on the staff and faculty had set. "They didn't set the correct tone, is what I'm saying. We went through a period where people who were damning the Army were getting out, and some in the Army and others at West Point looked upon those getting out as heroes. I didn't think that was healthy then, and I don't think that's healthy now." Additionally, too many officers were tampering with the ideals, heritage, and spirit behind West Point, DeFrancisco continued. They upset a delicate balance. "You always have cynics, and a certain amount of that is healthy. But when you erode the very basis of what you're doing, then, I think, you're getting into trouble. And I think that's what happened."

The cynicism was transmitted from the officers to the cadets, DeFrancisco said, and Vietnam was the trigger. The kids didn't start out cynics. "But I think they were allowed to miss the point, to miss the spirit and ideals of West Point." Perhaps for that reason, of the 152 cadets who were expelled for violating the honor code in this particular instance, 105 were offered readmission. Ninety-eight returned to the Academy with the Class of 1978, and ninety-one graduated.

From 1971 to 1978, or from the time DeFrancisco returned from Vietnam and entered Rice until the time he left West Point, he'd been away from troops, and now he was anxious to get back with them. He was a major then, and he dreamed of becoming a lieutenant colonel in command of a battalion. He felt fortunate when he was sent to Augsburg, Germany, becoming a battalion executive officer with the 18th Field Artillery, an assignment, he believed, that would help prepare him for battalion command.

Most of the troops he dealt with in Germany had never been to Vietnam, and all were volunteers because the draft no longer existed. He found the problems troops were experiencing overseas no longer appeared to stem from the backwater left in the wake of Vietnam. Rather, overseas assignments simply weren't what the travel brochures made them seem, and if homesick troops wanted to return to the States now it was because there they could get six or seven TV stations and there they could talk to girls in their own language. If any comfort was to be gained from this, it was that the Vietnam virus no longer circulated among the ranks.

As battalion XO, DeFrancisco's job was to run the battalion staff, making sure they were doing their jobs to support the battalion commander and the unit's mission. His other big job was readiness in terms of maintenance, the prime responsibility of the XO in most artillery units.

Lynne, too, enjoyed being back in Germany and living on a military post. She'd always found people on military posts friendly and supportive, unlike her civilian neighbors when her husband had served in Vietnam. "As soon as you see a moving van pull up on a post, you automatically go over and say, 'Hi, you need anything? Our phone's in, if you need to use the phone. The gas is on.' The quarters aren't always the best, but military people's concern for each other is something special."

She remembered once living near a woman whose husband was sent on a short tour to Thailand. The woman had three children in school and didn't want to take them out and move back near her parents. So she remained in her quarters on the post. "One of the men told her, 'If you have any problems with your car, let me know.' Another shoveled her sidewalk. And if we had a neighborhood party, she was always included. If we were all going shopping, same thing. She was just like anybody else. All the young couples looked out for each other.''

In June 1982, DeFrancisco was appointed commander of the 1st Battalion, 84th Field Artillery, 9th Infantry Division, at Fort Lewis, Washington. He was in charge of 560 soldiers for two and a half years, and he loved it. Characteristically, he hesitated talking about the assignment, because he didn't want to sound as if he were bragging, nor did he want to sound as if he were currying favor with officers he'd served under at Lewis who are still on active duty. The most he'd allow was that his unit was involved in a big force modernization, which meant his troops had learned how to fire new weapons. For instance, they were introduced to the M198 howitzer, a weapon that can shoot thirty kilometers, or almost three times the distance the weapon DeFrancisco had employed on the mountaintop overlooking the A Shau Valley. ''Anything new, of course, is great fun to play with, and you're rebuilding new teams to do different things.''

As battalion commander, he naturally wrote efficiency reports of officers who served under him. ''By no stretch of the imagination would I say that West Pointers were the best in my battalion. And I'd say the same thing for senior officers for whom I worked.'' In DeFrancisco's experience, West Pointers covered the spectrum, ranging from the very best to the very worst.

Perhaps one reason all West Pointers don't excel is that some never learn the *negative* lessons the Academy imparts. DeFrancisco thought the biggest was that at West Point you didn't have to do your best work to succeed. ''They purposely give you an overloaded academic schedule to see if you can handle stress and know how to prioritize. Well, that's good to a certain extent,'' DeFrancisco acknowledged. ''But the negative side of that—at least it was for me—was that it teaches that you can get by without doing your best. The better way of saying that is it makes you satisfied with completing a requirement by not accomplishing that requirement to the best of your ability. But you really can't get away with that in the Army and be a success.''

Nevertheless, cadets are constantly faced with the problem that if they do their best in one subject, because of the overload, the cost will be severe, they'll fall off in something else—and perhaps fall off so precipitously they'll risk failing and expulsion.

The second negative lesson DeFrancisco felt he'd taken away from the Academy was that it's a closed society, yet cadets can leave with the feeling that the rules and regulations there are the rules and regulations everywhere; and as long as you succeed by West Point's rules, the rest don't matter. "You get a certain ethic, and there's a certain ethos about the place. To give you an example that always comes to mind—I had a good friend who had a broken leg as a cadet. Well, this guy was looked down upon, and people were actually calling him 'a goldbrick' because he had a broken leg and couldn't do everything. I said, 'Wait a minute, the guy's got a broken leg.' They said, 'If he was really putting out, he could do this or that.' I said, 'Hey, the guy's on crutches.' I guess the way to put it is if it fits in with the system at West Point, it's okay, good, and if it doesn't, then it's not good. That bothered me a little at the time, and it bothered me a lot before I finally washed it out of my system."

Still, the whole time DeFrancisco was in Vietnam, he had an awareness that he was a link in the chain of American experience at war—a link he'd been made aware of at West Point. It was there he'd seen the monuments and the names plastered all over the place, and it was there he'd studied military history. Hardly any surprise, then, that when he'd served in Vietnam it was with the feeling, I know about those who've preceded me in the Argonne, at St. Lô, and on Cemetery Ridge. But now it's my turn.

"I was so excited about going to Vietnam the first time and stayed excited," he recalled. "You know, I wasn't anxious for it to get over with the first time. Not that I didn't want to come home; certainly I did. But I badly wanted to be in on what was happening over there."

DeFrancisco's more than content that he remained an Army officer and can't think of anything else he'd rather do. Ask Lynne if she's glad her husband is still in the military, and she'll answer, "Depends on the day you ask. Depends on whether we're moving soon." Then she laughs, a broad, generous laugh. "After his first five years, after Vietnam, each of his tours has been terrific in its own way."

An oddly ironic note crept into DeFrancisco's voice when he began talking about his children. He wasn't sure what his fifteen-year-old daughter, Laura, wanted to do with her life. But Eric, his eighteen-year-old son born a week before DeFrancisco had left for Vietnam the first time, was suffering, it turns out, from the usual travails experienced by most West Point plebes. DeFrancisco grinned. The news was a little surprise he'd saved for last.

DeFrancisco had ambivalent feelings when his son first mentioned trying out for West Point. He was pleased, but as one who'd previously walked through its narrow gates, he felt obliged to identify some of the rougher potholes. "I told him the truth about West Point," DeFrancisco said, grinning again. "But what can you tell a hotshot high school kid? Now he knows."

Eric was struggling with math and had just dropped competitive swimming—something he'd done since he was eight—because it was absorbing time he'd discovered he needed for worthier purposes, such as academic survival.

"Now he's doing it, and we'll see how it turns out." DeFrancisco sounded amused, apprehensive, paternal, and infinitely worldly-wise.

As for Lynne, she merely said, "Eric and West Point were made for each other."

FLINT, Roy K.
BG INF 383-22-6574
BORN: 22 Oct 28, Highland Park, MI

"One of the lieutenant generals on the search committee asked me what the reaction would be at West Point if I, a nongraduate, was chosen dean," Roy Flint remembered. "I said, 'First of all, I am a graduate. I'm a graduate of the University of Michigan.' General Scott, superintendent of West Point at the time and chairman of the committee, thought that was funny. But I think I also said, 'The question is probably irrelevant after I've spent thirty-five years in the service. The origin of my commission has probably been lost somewhere along the line in terms of its importance.'"

Roy Flint stands an even six feet and weighs 175 pounds. Although he's in his late fifties, there isn't the slightest pear-shaped hint of a paunch. Flint has hazel eyes, his hair is turning gray, and he wears bifocals. "The first thing that went were my eyes," he said with a laugh.

In 1984, West Point's seventh academic dean, Brig. Gen. Frederick Smith, Jr., announced his intention to retire the following year. Smith had been dean since 1974, and after his announcement a search committee was formed, its members appointed by the Army chief of staff, Gen. John Wickham. The committee consisted of three lieutenant generals and two major generals, and they proceeded to interview each West Point department head because, by law, only department heads are eligible to become dean. The committee would, after completing its interviews, make recommendations to the secretary of the Army. Flint, head of the History Department, was naturally one of those interviewed.

He had decided before the interview that he'd respond to questions as frankly as possible. "I went into this with the idea I am what I am. If I'm what they want as dean, then they're going to have to take me as I am." He'd taught military history at West Point for a year in the late 1960s, then returned to the Academy as a permanent associate professor in 1972, and has been teaching there ever since, heading the History Department for four years, beginning in 1981.

"I've probably been here longer than most graduates," Flint remembered thinking before the interview with the search committee. "I know more about the place than most graduates, and I probably love the place more than most graduates. So the fact I'm not a West Point graduate is something I'm not going to worry about, although I discreetly stand at the side during alumni exercises, just as other nongraduates, and cadets, are standing there watching the exercise up close, but not necessarily in the middle of the formation."

What was in the minds of the search committee when they considered recommending Flint to be dean? Why, for instance, would they be willing to break precedent by recommending a non-West Point graduate to assume one of the two or three most important jobs at the Academy?

Flint hardly strikes one as the classic outsider who has transformed himself, compelling acceptance as an insider by becoming more West Point than its graduates. Perhaps even more intriguing, then, is the question of how Flint, an outsider, wound up in a position from which he might be appointed dean at West Point. Was it by accident, design, or a combination of both? And regardless how it happened, what does it suggest about West Point as a social institution that prizes tradition, *that* it happened?

Roy Flint was born October 22, 1928, and grew up in Pleasant Ridge, a suburb of Detroit. His father, born in Canada, had served in the Canadian Army during World War I and was a civil engineer who lost his job as a result of the Depression, about which Flint had three distinct memories: The first was that his father was out of work; second, Flint remembered always having food; finally, the family never had to move out of their house.

Flint subsequently learned that the trauma attached to his father's unemployment was pretty strong. "But he was a very practical man, and after pounding the pavement looking for a job as an engineer, he came to the realization there was not much hope. So he decided, 'Well, hell, I'll just work close to home,' and he found a job bagging groceries." Flint and his mother used to walk to the grocery store and bring him his lunch, invariably no more than a sandwich, and then walk back home together. They had a car, but didn't drive it very much. "I remember the car so vividly because it was always in the back of my mind as times got better and my dad did get a good job—a good engineer's job. He was never wealthy. But you know, in those days if you made a hundred dollars a week, that was a major milestone. And I remembered when my dad came home and said, 'Well, I got a raise. I'm making a hundred ten a week,' and I thought, 'Oh, it's over.' I remember that so well. 'It's over—the uncertainty of the Depression.'"

Although Flint was never hungry, he believes that during the worst of the Depression his parents more than once were.

The house, he recalled, was two stories and bigger than they needed. As a little boy it had seemed enormous to Flint. When he went back years later, he remembered saying to himself, "My God, it's a dinky little place." Nevertheless, his parents didn't have to give it up because the man to whom Flint's father was paying off the mortgage was decent enough to reduce the payments, allowing Flint's father to meet them on schedule throughout the Depression.

Later, when his father bought the house, his engineering career revolved around constructing water and sewer lines because a lot of America then, including the wooded country of Michigan, was discarding the septic tank. His father worked those years for a Detroit engineering company but was never his own boss. "He was one of those men others rely on," Flint said. "He had an incredible knowledge of the geology of southern Michigan, and he built his expertise on knowing what was underground. He could tell you, for example, where quicksand was located. And in bidding wars, he was always able to trim his company's bid, and that little bit often meant the difference in landing the contract. So he was an incredible asset."

Although Flint was an only child, he never felt lonely because he had a number of very close friends, particularly three boys and seven girls whom he still considers close friends, a strong support group, though he doesn't see them all that often. While they were attending Lincoln High School in nearby Ferndale, the boys got involved in writing for a radio morning program at the local radio station. Flint thinks of it now as a kind of Bob and Ray Show. "It was fun," he said. "But the point of it, as so often's the case, is that what we did over the radio was incidental to preparing for it. Our friendships—and the pleasure we got from each other's company—came from the gag lines of the situations we tried to create."

After graduating from high school, Flint attended Albion College for two years before transferring to the University of Michigan. "I had a poor college experience, because I wasn't a very serious student. I didn't study. My talent in college was social." One time his father, worried about his grades, openly expressed concern. Flint said getting good grades wasn't that difficult, and he proceeded to notch four A's and a B during the second semester of his junior year. When his father said, "That's very good," Flint said, "I told you I could do it." But sinner that he was, he reverted to his old consuming social ways during his entire senior year.

Entering college, he'd thought about becoming a doctor. Quickly realizing that the practice of medicine was not one that Fate meant him to fulfill, he'd nonetheless remained a science major because biology interested him. He'd also begun taking a smattering of history courses and found he enjoyed them a great deal. Yet it was not very clear in his mind that that was what he should have been majoring in until much later.

Graduating with a degree in microbiology, Flint went through a terrible turmoil because he didn't really know what he wanted to do. He thought about wedding microbiology to a related field in agriculture, and went so far as to apply to Michigan State's Agricultural School, which accepted him. But a few days after graduating from Michigan, the Korean War broke out, and he decided to join the Army.

His father convinced him to become an officer, so when Flint entered the service that October, it was with the idea of going to OCS. Although Flint went through basic training at Fort Riley, Kansas, with a bunch of recruits from the Northwest who'd grown up with rifles in their hands, he turned out the best shot. They couldn't understand that and neither, in a sense, could Flint, who'd fished as a boy but didn't particularly like hunting. Completing basic, Flint and six or seven other recruits were called out of formation by the first sergeant, who told them they'd been selected for jobs with the Professional and Scientific Personnel Program. Because of his degree in microbiology, Flint was assigned to the Armed Forces Institute of Pathology at Seventh and Independence in Washington, D.C. In other words, he was being diverted from OCS.

Unfortunately, he found working as an histologist boring, nor did he get along with the sergeant running his section. They'd gotten into a heated discussion over the MacArthur-Truman controversy. "The sergeant took me aside and chewed me out, because you don't say critical things about Jesus Christ," Flint remembered. "I wasn't a student of the Korean War in those days, but I was sufficiently historical in my outlook to believe that MacArthur had to be wrong. 'Whether you agree with President Truman's policy or not,' I said to the sergeant, 'how can you argue that MacArthur's got the right to oppose the president?'"

Aside from not getting along with the sergeant and finding the work at the Pathology Institute deadly, Flint knew he'd done well in basic and that soldiering in general had captured his imagination. A complicating factor was that Flint's mother had been serious ill, and while he was in Washington, she died. In fact, one of the reasons he'd accepted diversion from OCS was his mother's illness. But now that she'd died, he felt less inhibited about trying to get back into OCS.

He approached the administrative chief of his department, a lieutenant colonel, and said he wanted to become an officer. "It's funny, but I had to be a little devious," Flint recalled. "I put down the Medical Services Corps as the branch I'd serve in as an officer, and that just made him all warm and friendly. Of course, once I got out to Riley and Leaders' School, which preceded OCS, I changed it to Infantry." Incidentally, Flint continued with a grin, the colonel later confided that the three previous people he'd agreed to send to OCS had all flunked out. Flint told him without blinking, "Well, you're going to be lucky with your fourth, because I'm going to make it."

In between Leaders' School and OCS, Flint got married. He'd known his wife, Joy Goldsworthy, all through college, and they dated soon after graduation. "She was there as I negotiated my way through this process of becoming an officer, although she claims I never discussed it with her. To give you her story: I came home and told her I took a Regular Army commission."

If soldiering had captured his imagination, it had truly begun his first days in the Army. He remembered being made a squad leader in basic training, shortly before the squad was handed an attack problem. "We're on a hill looking down," Flint said. "There were a couple of houses at the foot of the hill. The objective was to take the houses. As I sat watching, one rifle squad after another proceeded down the face of the hill, and then a machine gun opened up on them, and they were critiqued for doing badly. I kept wondering, 'Why are those guys all pouring down the face of the hill where anybody could shoot them?' So I said to my squad, 'We're not going to do that. We're going to go the back way, get in behind the two houses, and surprise them.' And that's what we did. Captured the platoon leader who'd commandeered one house and the people firing the machine gun in the second house. I don't want to overplay this, but that was a success experience. And after, people seemed to listen to what I said, and we had some more success experiences. Now, don't get me wrong—I'm not the hero type. We have people in the Army who by force of personality overwhelm their subordinates and maybe even the enemy. Well, I'm not that way. I have to outsmart them, trick them. And so I did that, and it seemed to start back in basic."

In any event, Flint did so well in OCS, which he took at Fort Benning, that he graduated with distinction and received his Regular Army commission. Then he got selected to stay at Benning as an OCS tactical officer, an even stronger indication that he'd been a distinguished graduate. Of course, these things tend to be incremental, but he seemed to be doing well at everything he was undertaking in the Army, and it was at about that point he decided to make the military a career. "Napoleon says men will do anything for a bauble," Flint noted, "and it's true. Another part of that equation is it's only eight inches between a pat on the back and a kick in the ass. And here I am, still trying to play the eight inches off."

Flint found that once he decided to make the military a career, it was a huge relief, because soldiering turned out to be not only something he was good at, but also a profession his father respected. "My dad thought it was great. In fact, he was always proud of me, and I'm only sorry he died before I got my last promotion."

Flint remembered the mood of his contemporaries during the Korean War as one of people upset they'd been drafted or recalled. "But the difference in those days from Vietnam was, although upset, they served when the nation was at war and there was no question of disobedience or demonstration. It was more, 'Hell, God, I just got going. My life was on track, and now I'm in the Army.' " Flint felt sorry for the reserves who'd been called back. As for those like himself, who'd been too young to serve during World War II, the belief that all young men should be conscripted into the armed forces because they're of no further value to their parents and haven't got a skill was one Flint modestly echoed. "That described me exactly. I was a hell of a good shot, and that was my sole accomplishment."

When he was sent to Korea in 1953, the fighting had just about stopped. Flint was assigned to the 23rd Infantry, and his battalion was positioned on the left flank of the 2nd Infantry Division, the pivot point of a divisional counterattack. That made it exciting. Additionally, though hostilities had ceased, contact patrols were going on constantly, so there was a kind of uneasy, residual tension, which kept everyone alert.

Flint loved his battalion commander, Hank Harmeling, and he learned a trick from Harmeling he later used when he commanded a battalion in Vietnam. Harmeling turned the clock around. His battalion would get up late, then work all night, through the night, and go to bed in the morning. The idea was to train the unit in darkness. "It's an incredible experience," Flint said. "What happens is that after a couple of nights, you're totally adaptable. Your eyesight gets better, and you develop senses you don't or can't develop in daytime."

Years later, Flint wrote his doctoral thesis on the Korean War, and he's currently three fourths of the way toward completing a book titled *Korea: An Entirely New War*. In a paper called "Delay and Withdrawal: The First Battle in Korea, July 1950," a chapter in a book analyzing America's first battles, Flint writes that the American Army that entered the Korean War was a "hollow shell." A dangerous reduction in support units, which are essential for sustained combat, had taken place after World War II and extended into 1950. Concomitantly, the American Army in those days resembled a "colonial army concerned with administrative duties rather than poised and ready for commitment to battle."

Prior to World War II it was an army, Flint expanded, that had existed largely overseas in the Pacific, with colonial origins—the China force in Tientsin, the Philippine Army, the Army in Hawaii. All of these assignments involved the Regular Army, which was a very hard outfit that trained and played like hell but was not necessarily mission-oriented. And, unfortunately, after World War II, that army reverted. Though it was serving in Japan on occupational duty and had units in Hawaii and Okinawa, it again bore all the characteristics of a colonial army. Saturday nights were set aside for cocktail parties, there were rounds of dinner parties during the week, and once a month officers and their wives dressed formally for a "regimental hail and farewell." Sports became a focal point of regimental life for enlisted men, and good athletes were recruited as seriously as pro football teams now recruit college seniors. Korea, as a consequence, was an important lesson in unreadiness.

In Korea, Flint had read a critical paper written by a battalion commander that began with a sentence he still recites: "There is a terrible sameness creeping into our training." Flint didn't have much chance in Korea to do anything about that sameness; but as a company commander in Hawaii, in a garrison situation, almost the first thing he did was seize the initiative and write his own training schedule. He took it to the battalion's operations officer, who said, "But you've got to do this on this date and that on that date," Flint said, "Fine, just mark them in there and tell me what you want me to do and when you want me to do it. But leave the rest blank and I'll fill it in." The S-3 said okay, and the battalion commander offered his total support. Then Flint set to work with his innovations.

"For instance, everybody charged into the Expert Infantry Badge competition," Flint said. "It's a combination of character, military skills, and high standards." Flint disqualified some in his company as not being good enough soldiers; but he set up classes for the rest, nightly classes, telling them, "I'll spend as much time as needed to help win that badge for you." He also said he'd take the test with the soldiers, and so did his officers.

So they began to hold nightly classes for those who wanted to attend, during which they simulated test conditions, and Flint remembered that thirty to forty of his soldiers showed up each night.

The day came when they went out to the firing range, which was a big weeder because everyone couldn't shoot well enough to qualify. Then they proceeded with the rest of the test. "We ended up with twenty-four badges," Flint recalled, "and that was more than the rest of the regiment combined."

Essentially, though, the Army in Hawaii was still not mission-oriented, and the difference between that army and the one Flint discovered during his next troop assignment, in 1960 with the 82nd Airborne at Fort Bragg, was enormous. The idea in 1960 was to be able to deploy in an hour. Rifle companies had their packs all laid out, read to go; trucks were earmarked to pick them up and speed them to neighboring airfields. A division ready force of a battle group was reinforced, and it was capable of quickly boarding a plane fully rigged. Nothing like that had existed before. The change began in the backwash of the Korean War and can probably be associated with Gen. Maxwell Taylor's reorganization of the Pentomic Division, a change that focused everyone's attention on being capable of actually fighting before tomorrow.

Flint had wanted an airborne assignment and became a battle group adjutant with the 501st Airborne Infantry. He found the pressures intense but interesting. First off, there was the sheer nerve-racking matter of jumping out of an airplane. "No matter how much you like jumping," he said, "there's a king of anxiety. I loved it. There's no greater feeling than being suspended at the end of a quiet parachute. Honest to God, you've never heard silence like that." But in those days, airborne troops used a parachute called a T-7. The canopy came out first, and you fell to the end of it. "My God, you felt it, you really got whipped around," Flint recalled. "I got knocked out once for an instant by a D ring that hit me on the helmet. Fortunately, it didn't hit me underneath the helmet, or I might have been killed."

Being an adjutant was not that thrilling to Flint, who considered himself more the operations type. The big plus of the job, however, was that he got to know intimately Col. Royal Taylor, who commanded the 501st. "Royal Taylor was one of the best soldiers I've ever known, and I really enjoyed working for him."

He was, Flint said, an outstanding trainer of troops and understood readiness and just about everything associated with operations. But he didn't worry about AWOL's and courts-martial. When Taylor left, the succeeding commander was appalled by the unit's courts-martial and AWOL rates. Flint tried to explain the reason there were so many was that Colonel Taylor trained the troops hard. And when they screwed up, he didn't reward them, he court-martialed them. Taylor's successor's viewpoint was that AWOL's and courts-martial reflected an inadequacy on the part of the commander.

"But ever since the time I served under Royal Taylor I've never worried about disciplining people," Flint remarked. "I don't want to say this in a loose way, but I've thrown three officers out of the Military Academy. I have no concern that the three officers were a disciplinary problem. Somebody else might say, 'You had three disciplinary problems.' But what has that to do with me? That's not me. I didn't do anything wrong. They were foolish enough to have transgressed in my outfit, and I punished them." The three officers had transgressed in the area of family relations to the point that it was impossible for Flint to continue tolerating them or their behavior. He knows not all marriages are made in heaven. "But that's not what I'm talking about. What I'm talking about is people acting like alley cats. I don't go along with that." Nor did his outlook regarding discipline come from Royal Taylor. He'd felt that way before. But Taylor, an older man, was the validation of his own ideas without his having had, at the time, the opportunity to test them.

Flint's second major assignment at Bragg was assistant to the chief of staff of the 82nd Airborne Division. The job was a kind of revelation, because it put Flint in the position of seeing how a division operates. Working for a brigadier general, Bud Mearns, Flint became an expert on what the division staff did, gaining a clearly focused picture of a specific man performing a specific function in operations, logistics, intelligence, and personnel.

In part, Flint's own job was interesting because the 82nd Division commander was Maj. Gen. Ted Conway, whom he found a constant challenge. "While I never really was a whiz at staff work, I developed a perception of what good staff work is, mainly by anticipating problems, and it was Conway who taught me to do that. He used to come to work and say, 'I want the DRF to rig up, ready to move.'" The DRF was the division ready force, units able to deploy on an hour's notice.

During the day, Flint would learn, Conway had read *The New York Times* and was tracking something going on, say, in Central America. Conway used to say, "There is no military excuse for Pearl Harbor. If it's in your capability to be ready, it's your duty to be ready." And that was the way he ran his outfit. "After Conway," Flint said, "I always blamed myself if I was surprised when something occurred that I should have been able to anticipate."

He considers himself unusually fortunate in having been exposed to the generals he worked for at Bragg. "Take Mearns," Flint said. "One time his door flew open and he stormed out of his office, obviously agitated. I was sitting outside his door. 'Which is worse?' he said. 'Which is worse?'—and I looked down. 'Which is worse—to be caught in a park in Houston stark naked screwing a girl, or stealing an exam out of the education center?' I said, 'Stealing the exam.' He said, 'You're damn right.' Then he turned around and went back in, slamming his office door." Flint grinned, tickled that the reminiscence still amused him even if it proved perhaps less than illuminating to a relative stranger.

The assistant division commander of the 82nd then was Bruce Palmer, who later became Westmoreland's deputy commander in Vietnam. Palmer, Flint noted, was very different from, say, Gen. Creighton Abrams, who, along with Westmoreland, was Palmer's 1936 West Point classmate and later succeeded Westmoreland as America's senior officer in Vietnam. Abrams, said Flint, was explosive. Palmer was pleasant. "If he was feeling badly about something, or mad, he really tried to spare you that personal turmoil. That didn't mean he didn't want to share it at the right time. He and I used to play tennis, usually toward evening; that was his way of unwinding, and it helped me stay in shape. After, we'd go back and have a beer before dinner. I worked for him in 1967 in Vietnam, and that beer before dinner was a private period when he got to ask me questions. He'd tell me things about what was going on in Vietnam that were bothering him. The vehicle was—and I remember he said, 'You know, you and I ought to write a book.' We'd written an article together. 'We really ought to write a book about this war. The American people need to see this war in its total breadth. Why, for example, it takes so long, what the problems are in overcoming the cultural differences with the

Vietnamese.' So the vehicle was this book, and later he went and wrote it alone, calling the book *The 25-Year War*, and I think it's the best one so far about Vietnam.''

Suddenly Flint squinted with displeasure. "I just noticed something," he said, standing up. He walked over to the handsome fireplace in his large, high-ceilinged office and pushed forward a small ashtray-crowned table, which had stood opposite the fireplace, moving it next to a chair facing his desk. "My secretary likes it near the fireplace, I prefer it near that chair." Flint shook his head, smiling. "I guess she thinks this is her office."

While Flint wasn't exactly a replica of Palmer, Mearns, Royal Taylor, or Conway, he said, regaining his seat, each had contributed a measure of influence on the way he viewed life.

An indication that he'd been an effective, talented officer at Bragg, someone on the way up, was that generals for whom he'd worked in the past requested he work for them when he arrived in Vietnam. For instance, Flint went to Southeast Asia assigned to 1st Field Force headquarters in Danang as chief of plans. But within hours of arriving at Long Bien, the port of entry, he got a call saying that a car was going to pick him up and take him to U. S. Army Headquarters, Vietnam, because a Brig. Gen. Robert Taber wanted to talk to him. Taber? Flint didn't know any Taber.

But Taber, chief of staff to General Palmer, who was now Westmoreland's deputy commander, said both he and Palmer were looking for an assistant, a kind of secretary to the General Staff, the same kind of job Flint had done back at Bragg; and because Palmer wanted him, Taber wanted him, and the general at 1st Field, who'd also requested Flint, was going to be overruled. When Flint protested, saying he wanted to work in plans up-country, General Taber replied, "Well, you might as well forget about it, because you're going to be the assistant to me and the assistant to General Palmer."

The chief, Taber, served the deputy, Palmer, very closely. Taber had an aide, Palmer had an aide and an administrative assistant. "It was a funny kind of SGS arrangement," Flint said. "There was also a secretary to the General Staff; but I didn't work for him; I worked for General Taber and General Palmer. As a result, I was in a position of really expediting staff actions between those two offices and among the staff." It almost sounds as if Flint had so impressed Palmer at Bragg, once Palmer learned Flint was arriving in-country, he created a unique job for him so that he could have Flint around.

Flint worked hard at trying to keep the staff informed about what Taber and Palmer were thinking, as well as advising the generals when it was timely to arrive at certain decisions. Part of Flint's job was also to get in early and compose a briefing book. It included what had occurred overnight, combat operations all over the theater, as well as the staff work—planning for future operations and management operations that were ongoing.

Not too surprisingly, things got done in the Army in Vietnam the way things get done everywhere else, Flint suggested with a shrug. By way of illustration, he told how he got a volleyball court built for the staff. He'd approached the officer who commanded the engineering group in Long Bien, Col. Richard Groves, son of Gen. Leslie Groves, who'd been in charge of the Manhattan Project during World War II, and asked if Groves could have his engineers build a lighted volleyball court. The staff living in the compound at Long Bien needed one, because guys on shift work weren't getting any exercise. Groves said he'd build the volleyball court, but in return there was a certain warrant officer with a particular MOS, possessor of certain skills, he needed who was arriving from San Francisco. Unfortunately, the man had been assigned elsewhere. Flint said, "I'll see what I can do." He went to the officer running personnel, saying, "I can get us a volleyball court if we can get Groves this warrant officer." The man at personnel said, "No problem." So the warrant officer for reasons to this day he probably can't fathom was diverted from somewhere up north and brought to Long Bien. Groves had his warrant officer, and the staff at Long Bien soon had a splendid lighted volleyball court.

During the six months Flint worked for Palmer, he often accompanied the general, who flew around the country daily, observing company operations. It was an interesting introduction to combat situations and helped him prepare for taking over the 3rd Battalion, 22nd Infantry, 25th Division. His division commander was General Mearns, who'd asked him back at Bragg, "Which is worse . . ."

Tet had erupted on January 30, and Flint had worked that day for Taber and Palmer. By the end of the day, Mearns had called Taber, asking if Flint, who was due for reassignment to the 25th Division, could be released immediately. Taber said yes, if Flint could find a replacement. Flint found the replacement and reported to the 25th Division that evening. By noon the next day he'd taken command of a battalion consisting of four rifle companies, three of which were in contact with the enemy.

Surprisingly, it was not that difficult assuming command of a battalion already engaged in battle. The outgoing battalion commander showed Flint a map indicating where each of the rifle companies were and described their objectives. Flint watched the battalion commander get out of the command helicopter and heard him say good luck. Then Flint boarded the chopper, map in hand. Lifting off, Flint was in command.

He flew over each company, asking for a situation report. The first, he recalled, was C Company, under the command of 1st Lt. Charlie Boyle. "This is Falcon Six," Flint said to Boyle, below him. "Falcon Charlie Six, I want a situation report." Boyle, hotly engaged, said Flint couldn't land. Flint said he didn't have to land then; he'd return later. Then Boyle gave him a fast rundown, although he was slightly circumspect because this was the first time he'd heard Flint's voice.

As the battalion CP, Flint kept reconstructing what was happening by listening to each of his company commanders issuing their orders that evening. He found he was quickly able to grasp the essentials, "because I'd spent my whole life getting ready for this." If anything surprised him, it was that he soon became almost totally oblivious to enemy fire, so complete was his absorption in what was happening to each of his companies.

That said, it was still a kind of comfort serving under Mearns again. They liked and respected each other. On the day of a victory following a nasty, two-week fight, Flint remembered standing on top of a bunker, feeling elated. General Mearns had called, saying, "This is Tropic Six. I understand you've finally beaten your foe."

"That's right," Flint said.

"Never despise your enemy," Mearns said.

"I'll never despise my enemy," Flint said. "But his ass has had it today."

Sometimes Mearns would visit Flint's headquarters, lay a map down, and say, "Here's what I think I'll do." Then they'd talk about it, almost like equals. Flint wasn't part of Mearns' staff; but Mearns was looking for an independent source to bounce ideas off, and Flint would tell him what he thought. "This is the adjutant complex," Flint explained. "Same relationship I'd had with Royal Taylor back in the 501st."

Flint loved being a battalion commander. Leading men in the

Army, he observed, commanders plot and scheme, trying to compel soldiers to improve; then they remeasure the troops' level of performance, still looking for new opportunities to reach further heights of excellence, from the smallest detail to, say, the general concept of a training program. Nor is it enough to make corrections on the ground. "What really challenges the commander is, having made an improvement, how he institutionalizes that improvement so the next time the situation or a comparable one arises, the unit reacts to the new situation in the improved way and without having to make a further correction." This frame of mind, Flint said, applies to both garrison and combat duty.

Which is one reason why, when young officers say, "God, I don't know how I'll behave in battle," Flint invariably thinks, "How do you behave in peacetime?" By which he means: What are the things that drive you then? What do you think about when you're in training situations? How intense are you then? And how carefully do you make corrections?

Flint wound up, he said, with four young but very good company commanders, although he'd had to relieve two officers before he settled on the four who satisfied him, not because two were incompetent so much as because he judged they did things that bore the fruit of disaster in the future.

Although the soldiers were a direct reflection of their leadership, Flint said, morale was a function of the enemy. In the post-Tet period, contact was almost daily, so no one could afford to grow lax. You expected to be shot at every day. Therefore, your senses were heightened. "But after periods of sustained quiet, and I'm talking about several days, the first shot will frequently cause a casualty, and then everybody's up again. Yet you pay a price."

When Flint, as battalion commander, learned that Martin Luther King, Jr., had been assassinated, he called in his sergeant major. The battalion had already begun the first day of a three-day stand-down. Flint asked the sergeant major, who was black, to join him in making separate rounds to inform the soldiers about King's death. Fortunately, there was no racial response in the battalion. "I suspect these guys were realistic enough to know they counted on each other for survival on a daily basis. That doesn't mean that later they didn't develop hard feelings, or what have you. But at the time, it wasn't there."

Flint's sergeant major wasn't really a sergeant major, nor even a first sergeant. Flint had brought him over from Headquarters

Company, and he was very effective. But his importation illustrated, Flint said, a real weakness in the Army, a lack of experienced NCO's. "You had a few very good experienced NCO's. Then you had some really inexperienced NCO's, and you had to give them responsibilities for which they were not prepared." Inexperienced noncommissioned officers inherited the unflattering sobriquet "shake 'n' bake NCO's," and their lack of experience was particularly noticeable when the unit operated at night, those hours when everybody was a little scared. "Being cool, being the father figure to a bunch of young people is very difficult if you're not cool, if you're not a father figure," Flint said. "Older guys really had an advantage then."

Soon after Tet, Flint's battalion was given the mission of stopping 122mm rocket attacks on Tan Son Nhut Airport. They were sent to Nhi Binh, a small village near Saigon. Nhi Binh was roughly fifteen square kilometers and interlaced by a network of rivers and deep canals. It was here Flint first ordered nighttime operations on an extensive scale—using the trick of turning the clock around that he'd picked up in Korea. Two rifle companies lay in ambush nightly, while the other two companies secured the defensive position and rested. The two operating companies hid near their ambush sites for thirty-six to forty-eight hours. Then they were relieved. By continuously rotating the companies, operations could be sustained over a fairly lengthy period. Specific targets were selected, such as canal crossings and junctions. In the end, the enemy lost more than a hundred soldiers, and his supply lines were closed down. Flint's battalion suffered two casualties.

His professional training had led him to believe that as battalion commander he would be surrounded by a staff who'd offer advice and recommendations, following which he could calmly make decisions before a perfectly positioned map. "In fact," Flint has written, "the battalion commander must 'calmly deliberate' while stuffed into the left front seat of a three-seat helicopter, clutching his windblown maps, and trying to juggle command frequencies of a woefully inadequate radio set. In the front right seat sits his artillery liaison officer who, from his equally cramped vantage point, controls a vast array of artillery and mortar fire. From this excellent observation platform—if inadequate operations center— the battalion commander directs his companies and their fire support. He judges difficult time-distance problems involving resupply, the replacement of committed units by fresh companies, as well as the tactical maneuvers of his units."

Flint's battalion fought almost daily through May and June. They operated in an area to the west and north of Saigon, up through Cu Chi, Trang Bang, Tay Ninh, and over to the Saigon River as it goes north. It was mostly flat country, a lot of jungle. Rather than cut a swath through the clotting vegetation, Flint developed a strategy consisting of assigning clusters of trails to interdict. The troops would advance up the trails, seeking out the enemy. At the same time, they'd control the edge of the jungle. Flint melded this strategy with his notion of dominating the night. He always wanted to be in the position to ambush, getting off the first shot, and calling the tune. His battalion would infiltrate the trail intersections, lie in wait, and strike when the enemy passed. Once his troops mastered the trails and the night, it meant they'd never commit the cardinal sin of "getting wrapped around the axle." In other words, they'd never get caught in a firefight, pinned down so they couldn't disengage and exercise freedom of action.

His tour as battalion commander lasted six months, and Flint not only considered it easily the best assignment he'd ever had but also thought it should have lasted longer, at least another year. "At the same time, I suppose, like everyone else I was subject to the idea of rotation. If anyone's honest, the thought of going home is an alluring prospect. And so I'm sure at the end of my tour, although we were not less active than we'd been before, I sometimes wondered if I did not portray as aggressive an air as I might have earlier. But I don't know; I'm not a very good judge of that."

Even before he'd left for Vietnam in 1967, Flint had been in touch with the chairman of the History Department at West Point, Col. Thomas Griess, about the possibility of teaching military history there. Griess had heard from a mutual friend and former department member, Lou Arnold, who'd recommended Flint. Arnold, a major at the time, and Flint had gotten to know each other in 1963, when they'd both attended the Command and General Staff College at Leavenworth. The reason Arnold had recommended Flint and suggested he ought to consider teaching at the Academy was that Flint kept thinking in historical terms at Leavenworth. "A lot of my solutions to tactical problems were derived from familiarity with the principles of war and their application—particularly the Civil War, which was of great interest to me," Flint said, "and Arnold knew that."

He'd become seriously interested in history in the mid-1950s. Flint found when he sat down with a history book then that he'd derive enormous pleasure from reading. "In fact, I made a kind of life pattern of playing with my kids or doing whatever the family wanted to do till they went to bed, and then I'd just sit down and read until, say, twelve." So when he was sent to teach ROTC students at the University of Alabama after completing his assignment at Hawaii, and the ROTC job left him with considerable time to kill, it seemed a natural short step, a progression of sorts, to utilize those unoccupied hours by earning an M.A. in history.

In Flint, then, Colonel Griess would be getting an instructor who'd not only earned a masters on his own, but also a man teaching military history who'd just completed a combat tour in Vietnam as a battalion commander. A sweet combination, from Griess's point of view.

Leaving Vietnam August 12, Flint arrived at West Point two weeks later, and began lecturing that September. He taught a course called "The U.S. Army" and another called "The History of Military Art," which the West Point syllabus describes this way: "Traces the evolution of the art of warfare from ancient Greece to the present by examining the development of generalship, strategy, tactics, theory, doctrine, professionalism, and logistics, and their interactions with social, political, economic, and technological factors." About the course Flint more succinctly says, "We try to teach cadets they're the inheritors of a long tradition, and there are certain aspects of that tradition that represent continuity."

Cadets, he found, were not only interested in his Vietnam experience, but having been there proved a big advantage in teaching military history. "For instance, there's an ambush Hannibal set up at the Battle of Lake Trasimene in 217 B.C., an L-shaped ambush along the shore of the lake," Flint said. "The Roman Army moved along the shore but was confronted by a part of Hannibal's force, which blocked them. Then the bulk of Hannibal's Carthaginians, swinging the L closed, trapped and killed the Romans by rolling them into the lake. Well, I'd seen an ambush in Vietnam of a lead company of an adjacent battalion that was done precisely that way. So I was able at the appropriate time—one, describe the ambush in Vietnam in terms of Lake Trasimene; and later, talking about an ambush set up in Vietnam, ask as a review question where they'd seen it before. And some picked it up, saying it was Lake Trasimene.''

Although Flint began teaching at West Point less than a year after Tet, when the vast majority of the country had turned against the war, he found cadets receptive and teaching there rewarding. Cadets in 1968 and '69 were young men who'd come to the Military Academy in spite of whatever ideas were loose in the community, Flint reflected. "The unpopularity of the war in Vietnam may have had the effect of filtering out the people who came to the Military Academy; yet during those years we had men of high quality. There may have been men of low quality who chose to come, yet I don't recall men of low quality. Our own screening process made sure they didn't enter the program." What happened, Flint thought, was that the pool got smaller but the standards were maintained. "That means, I guess, that those who were here had already internalized whatever reinforcements there were against the unpopularity of the war."

He thought the assignment to teach at West Point would last three years, but before even the first was up he received orders assigning him for a year to the Air War College the following August. Colonel Griess asked if he wanted West Point to try to get the orders deferred so he might continue teaching at the Academy to complete the three-year tour. But at that point, Flint was thinking in conventional, traditional terms as far as his professional life went, and he said, "No, somebody wants me to do something else, and I'll just follow my orders." So he did.

But on the night Griess held a farewell party for those in his department who'd be leaving, he approached Flint and asked if Flint had ever considered coming back to West Point permanently. Flint said he never had. Griess then said he had permission to select some permanent associate professors, and wondered if Flint would like to be considered. If he decided yes and was chosen, it meant Flint would be withdrawing from the mainstream of the Army. Griess didn't have to add that generals didn't teach at West Point. Flint, an ambitious man, already knew that. So it was obviously a big decision, and rather than decide quickly, Flint said he'd think about it and let Griess know before leaving the War College.

Flint thought about it for the next eight months. "I thought about it, thought about it, thought about it, thought about it," he remembered. "Analyzed it every which way, before finally deciding that that's the contribution I can make to the Army: I can teach. I can teach military history and make, in my opinion, a lasting contribution, as opposed to going from job to job. I'd already been in command in Vietnam, and to me that was the ultimate. I had no great aspirations other than just simple rank." At the same time, he would have wanted to command a brigade and a division. But he'd had that indelibly impressive command experience in Vietnam that would fuel his memories, and what better could he want than that? So commanding brigades and divisions wasn't that important to him. "There were all kinds of guys who could be battalion commanders," Flint reasoned. "But could there always be people who'd love to teach as much as I did? And particularly military history? I didn't think there were. So I decided, if I'm the one they want, I guess that's what I'll do, and I came back here for a shoot-out—an interview session." A number of officers wanted the job, but Flint won it. "Anyway, I came back on that basis, and interestingly enough, I've never really looked back. I've never really worried about what might have been. I just enjoyed doing it."

Flint doesn't say so, but the decision undoubtedly appealed to his imagination as well. It was something different, out of the ordinary, in the same way turning the night around in Vietnam was different and going the back way down the hill and surprising the platoon leader in basic training was out of the ordinary. What could be more different, out of the ordinary, particularly in those days, than for a non-West Point graduate to be appointed a permanent associate professor at West Point?

Flint said he'd discussed the West Point offer with his wife and she was happy with the prospective stability it would introduce into their lives; Flint had never served a full three-year tour before, let alone thought in terms of spending ten or fifteen years at the same post. But stability wasn't really why he'd decided on West Point. "My wife says, 'Well, you came back here for us.' I said, 'No, this is going to be very deflating to you, but I didn't come back here for you. I came back here for me, and it had to do with things I thought were important.' And that makes her mad when I tell her that. But that's true."

Before returning to West Point on a permanent basis, Flint attended Duke for two years, where he earned a Ph.D. His oldest daughter, Lisa, entered Duke as an undergraduate during Flint's second year, and he had a kind of odd relationship with her as a father and fellow student. Lisa's peers were tough on her because they knew Flint was an Army officer who'd fought in Vietnam; and when they posed difficult and painful questions, she'd sometimes ask Flint, "How do I answer them?" Consequently, they spent a lot of time talking about how to respond to charges that he was, among other things, a baby-killer.

"I felt some hostility that my daughter should be held to account for my life," Flint remembered. He also remembered seeing one large demonstration, a big crowd swelling the crosspoint in the cross outlining the Duke campus. A number of cops stood nearby. People were lying in front of the ROTC building, their clothes spattered with blood. "They looked silly," Flint thought. Others were carrying signs and picketing.

"But the thing that probably bothered me more than anything else, as I look back on it now, was a feeling of depression I developed over the racial aspect," he said. Flint took a couple of sociology courses and got to know a young black instructor who was teaching a course in social politics, which was a look at political science from a demographic standpoint—that is, who lives where and what effect this has on representation and reapportionment. Flint respected the instructor a great deal. "But one day, he was talking and I detected this tone of bitterness that in effect said, 'It doesn't matter who you are, if you're white, you're my enemy.' " Flint was so disturbed, he asked the instructor if that's how he really felt, and the man acknowledged it was. "You know, you really disappoint me," Flint said, "because I've spent my whole life trying to teach my kids that that's not the case. I hope you're being excessive in the heat of the discussion. I'd hate to think I've wasted my whole life with my kids." Flint said the man didn't back off. "I think I was probably more troubled by race relations and the seeming futility of the struggle than by any other aspect of the antiwar protest."

In 1968, the first year Flint taught at the Academy, there had been ambivalence toward Vietnam in the attitude of the civilians who lived near West Point. Some had undoubtedly expressed outright discontent with the war, but Flint remembered no specific incident, save one, he said with a mischievous expression: His Volkswagen bus was dappled with handpainted flowers, courtesy of his kids.

Flint is the father of four, and his family, he goes out of his way to say, has meant a lot to him. "Anyway, one day I discovered the flowers, the next I'm driving around West Point, in my first assignment at the Academy, in a Volkswagen covered with them. It didn't bother me; I'd been in Vietnam, I wasn't part of the movement. But my boss was sensitive to this. Colonel Griess didn't say anything, but he sort of harrumphed a couple of times when he saw my car. Eventually it broke down, and I bought a new one without flowers.''

When Flint returned to West Point in the fall of 1972 as a permanent associate professor, it was plain that the civilian antiwar movement had crystallized, and he recalled attending a Christmas Eve service in the chapel, after which he was confronted by demonstrators. The custom in those days was to attend the service in uniform, and the demonstrators extended coin boxes to the emerging officers, saying, "Will you give for Vietnam?" Flint recalled that his response was instantaneous. "I already have," he said, brushing past them.

He also remembered reporters from local newspapers and *Time* magazine coming up to West Point, asking how he and other officers felt as the Vietnam War kept unraveling. "We were constantly being asked to apologize for our role, and I never did that," Flint said. "First of all, as a soldier, knowing what I'd done, I knew I had nothing to apologize for. And secondly, as an historian, I knew that apologizing for world events was just a fool's errand. You don't apologize for the crucifixion of Christ. It's part of history. So was the Vietnam War. You may be introspective about your role, but my feeling was that I'd acted as an enlightened commander.''

As an historian, Flint sees the Vietnam War occurring at a time in America when a number of great issues were ripe to be resolved. The country had entered the world stage after the closing of the frontier, he said. And as America grew out of the cocoon of the nineteenth century, protected by distance, its frontiers, and British sea power, it suddenly found itself a force to reckon with; but it was an insecure power, one that was drawn into World War I, for example, in spite of its protestations. The same might be said of our involvement in World War II, but with this difference: After the conclusion of that war in 1945, America became the preeminent power, acknowledged leader of the free world, advocating a particular point of view, the avowed enemy of the communist world, and somewhat suspect to the growing Third World.

At the same time that it was clearly the world's leading international power, Flint continued, there was some catching up to do internally. One of the issues that unmistakably emerged from World War II was human rights, civil liberties. Women had worked in defense plants, blacks had moved all over the country and served overseas. Expectations had been created. World War II, in short, had had a tremendous socializing and mobilizing effect on American society, and the Korean War reinforced it, bringing into sharper focus the racial question, especially in light of President Truman's desegregating the Army.

Not too long after, we became involved in Vietnam, taking over from the French, at about the same time that Martin Luther King, Jr., began his crusade. Lyndon Johnson's Great Society was, in part, an attempt to meet the expectations created during World War II, Flint said. Yet Martin Luther King made a speech saying America's first concern is feeding its poor, but where is the bulk of the country's treasure being spent? It's being spent in Vietnam, and in a war most Americans don't support. There was, consequently, a feeling building in the late 1960s that America was working at cross-purposes. And as Vietnam War casualties started mounting over a protracted period of time, the resistance to the war intensified, which explains to a large extent why within the Army itself there began to be disaffection. As people entered and left the service, they were being replaced by others coming from what amounted to a fragmented background. National turbulence was thus stimulated and catalyzed by Vietnam, and it was Nixon who brought this turbulence to an exhausted end with Watergate, which finally caused people to say, "Jesus Christ, have we destroyed ourselves? What's happening to America?"

Since then, Flint continued, the country's been picking up the pieces. Many of the values debunked during the 1960s and 1970s were put back and are still being repositioned. But people have historically tended to pick out the best a revolution has to offer and reject the worst; the best is then merged with the best they've retained from the tradition. "The only thing we haven't controlled that we unleashed in the political sense during that time is selfishness and greed," Flint said. "There are few bastions of service, and I'm not even prepared to say we're one at West Point. I think some of our cadets come in with the idea they're going to get a free education, serve five years, and get out. And that's all right. They probably always come with those attitudes, to some extent. And why should I worry? I don't. But I guess I have to say, having noted all this, that this *is* the background, a very complicated social background, in which a cell of monks tries to take people from disparate backgrounds, bringing them here, and says, 'You must be honest.' To some, if they'd been honest all their lives, they'd probably be dead, they'd have had their throats cut. But suddenly we put them in an environment that says, 'You must relearn your whole life's experience....' ''

It was in this same monastery, also known as West Point, that the deputy head of the History Department retired in 1975, and a search committee, less star-coated but similar in outline to the one later seek a dean, was formed to recommend his successor. A number of History Department members competed for the job, and Flint was chosen. It was another major step in his life, because it meant that when Colonel Griess retired, Flint would head the History Department and become, in effect, one of the Academy's reigning cardinals. "As long as I was doing it," Flint said with a shrug, "it was sort of like anything else I've done: I'd want to do it at the highest level I could. There's a certain parallel to being a commander; I don't mean so much in the function as I do in the ambition."

When Griess retired in 1981 and Flint succeeded him, the transition didn't prove that great, because Griess had allowed Flint to have a hand in the biggest job the department head manages—selecting the faculty. The turnover is constant, because teaching at the Academy usually involves a three-year assignment. In addition, it takes a year to choose the people, then two years for them to go to graduate school and earn an M.A.

Flint said he'd looked for three things when he considered potential instructors. "First, the man had to want to come back to West Point." Approximately two thirds of the instructors are former cadets. "I never assigned anyone if he didn't want to come here. Second thing is he has to have a good field record; he had to be judged to be a good officer. And the third thing, you look not so much for what kind of student he was as for his potential intellectual growth."

As head of the History Department, Flint also now became a member of the Academic Board, a group of about twenty, consisting of the superintendent, the academic dean, the commandant, and the department heads. The board, to which the department heads and the dean are permanent members, has been likened to the Catholic Church's Curia, "except that the superintendent, unlike the pope, normally serves for only three years instead of for life.'' Nor does the superintendent appoint the department heads, as does the pope his cardinals, and it's the cardinals who run the Curia. Each member of the board has one vote, so the permanent members, the dean and department heads, can obviously outlast and outvote ambitious superintendents who outrank them. The board, in short, consists of a preponderance of colonels, and they just might be the most powerful colonels in the American Army.

Flint continued teaching while he was a board member and even after he became dean, and one of his courses in 1986 was called "Korea, Vietnam, and the American Experience." Cadets had hung their hats and coats on pegs outside the classroom, and the long, dull hallway seemed to brighten only when the shiny black of a cadet's peaked hat reflected the overhead lights.

"Let me try to lead us up to a discussion into post-Tet," Flint said, beginning an April class. He was dressed in a short-sleeved green shirt and wore his watch well above his left wrist, perhaps the better to see. The students were sitting in three or four horseshoe-shaped tiers, about thirty-five cadets. There was a black-board and a couple of TV screens behind and above Flint.

Flint told his students about the glowing year-end report General Westmoreland had submitted in 1967. A month or two later, Tet occurred, and the contrast between Westmoreland's unbridled optimism and the ferocity that characterized Tet couldn't have been more striking. Then Flint told about Gen. Earle Wheeler, chairman of the Joint Chiefs of Staff, saying Tet was a near thing as a function of trying to get more troops dispatched to Vietnam. But President Johnson, feeling the political walls closing in, was reluctant to expand the war in early 1968. Flint then brought up the discrepancy between Westmoreland's estimate of enemy troops and the CIA's. When one of the cadets mentioned Westmoreland's Vietnam memoirs, calling them self-serving, Flint said he thought that rather than being self-serving, Westmoreland was often frank to the point of writing unflattering things about himself. Yet when Flint was pressed by another cadet, he also said that in his opinion Westmoreland was probably too conventional a commanding general for the war he'd been dispatched to wage.

Flint himself was promoted to brigadier general upon being appointed dean. When word of that appointment had reached West Point, Flint couldn't be found, because he was up at Fort Drum, in northern New York State, evaluating a brigade. "As General Scott likes to say, 'It's appropriate that the dean was out of contact for a full twenty-four hours in the field when we were trying to tell him he'd been appointed dean.' "

Ask Flint what a dean actually does, and he bounces up, walking over to his desk. "Let me see if I have my notebook. I jot down things I want to remember—just things I want to make sure I won't forget." He thumbs through the book for an uncomfortable minute or two before he spots the appropriate entry. "Here we go," he says. "You ready?'

"I'm chief of the faculty. I try to develop a vision of the contribution of the faculty to the institution. In this regard, I'm encouraging research as a way for our faculty to become better teachers. On the one hand, I'm encouraging that which we're already good at; on the other, filling the gaps at research that we're not all that good at. I have this vision of contributing to the Army while making ourselves better teachers through the research that we do.

"I'm a subordinate of the superintendent. Therefore, I'm his adviser on academic matters.

"I'm chairman and head of a variety of committees and boards. I get involved in everything from the academic class committee, which determines who's going to stay or who's going to fail out of here, to the Installation Planning Board, which is sitting in judgment on construction projects.

"I'm the administrator of budgets, facilities, and resources.

"I'm the administrative commander of the departments. I write the efficiency reports of the chairmen of the departments.

"I'm the creator and protector of the curriculum. Mostly protector. If we're considering a curriculum change, it would start with my tasking a curriculum or ad hoc committee to look at the question. They'd come up with a study. The Academic Board has the final vote, and then it would go to Washington for approval.

"I'm the operator of the academic schedule, the assignment of classrooms, all that sort of thing.

"I'm the director of academic automation. Beginning with the Class of 1990, each cadet will have his own personal computer, and that's going to change the whole concept of teaching at the Academy.

"I represent the Military Academy publicly and professionally.

"I'm a classroom teacher.

"I do personal research.

"I lecture.

"I administer research grants for faculty members.

"I'm supervisor of the library, and that's about it."

Given this appropriately lengthy and impressive compendium, it was no surprise when Flint said the toughest problem he'd encountered his first year as dean was managing his time and learning to say, "No, I won't do this," without hurting anyone's feelings. "I didn't do very well at that last year, so I'm really going to be looking at that for the coming year."

The book he's writing about Korea sits on a table at home, three fourths finished, Flint said. One shelf supports sixteen completed chapters. He's got another five to go, about 150 pages. "It's very discouraging to me to be in this position, particularly because I see other people finishing their books."

Yet for someone uncertain of his future after having graduated from Michigan with a degree in microbiology, Flint is a man who's obviously found his way, from basic training on, in the military. "I don't know if I could have said that about civilian life."

In selecting Flint to be West Point's eighth academic dean, the Army, of course, chose a specific man—a child of the Depression, who grew up just outside Detroit, a natural when it came to soldiering, a student of military history who demonstrated a marked degree of intellectual growth, a talented officer who impressed a number of powerful generals relatively early in his career, and a commander who, grasping the peculiarities of the Vietnam War, imaginatively turned them to his battalion's tactical advantage.

The Army also chose a man of unfailing poise, an officer as much at ease in dealing with an NCO as he is in functioning as a constituent of a twenty-member board. Flint, up close, seems to possess the rare self-confidence of someone not out to prove things so much as a man who enjoys discovering those occasions during which he can express himself in effective and sophisticated ways.

But in selecting a non-West Pointer to be its eighth academic dean, the Army did something more than choosing this particular man. American society has changed enormously since World War II; and West Point, an institution slow to change for more than 150 years, also found itself compelled to move great distances, especially after the Vietnam War, perhaps even changing to the extent of graciously accepting a non-West Point graduate to be its new dean. It would have done so before the Vietnam War just as it would have accepted women and larger numbers of blacks before the Vietnam War. Which is a sneaky way of saying neither would have occurred.

During Vietnam, one unnamed senior American officer was quoted, "I'll be damned if I'll permit the United States Army, its institutions, its doctrine, and its traditions to be destroyed just to win this lousy war."

It's instructive to compare that statement with a view Flint expressed in 1971 in an article he published in *Military Review* magazine titled "Army Professionalism for the Future." Flint wrote that the military did not have a monopoly on dedication to America's national well-being and that it was dangerous to risk isolation of the military service from the mainstream of American thought. "Above all," he concluded, "we must guide our actions by the same dedication to the national well-being that motivates all rational Americans."

In the context of those contrasting statements, and given Flint's past resourcefulness, both he and his selection would seem to signify a shrewd choice by an Army increasingly aware that if it fails to reflect the country it serves, the country it serves might decide its services are no longer required in the same old, trusting ways.

RUDERMAN, Gill H.
LTC FA 246-68-7376
BORN: 28 Nov 43, Tel Aviv, Palestine

"It wasn't hard being a Jew at West Point," Lt. Col. Gill Ruderman said, although there were but eight or nine others in the Class of 1966 and maybe a total of twenty-five to thirty in the Corps, or roughly 1 to 2 percent of all cadets. Chapel was mandatory in those days, and Jews and Lutherans shared the same facility. Because both services were held on Sundays, two Jewish plebes used to march down before seven-thirty prior to the services, replacing the Lutheran artifacts with Hebrew cloths and prayer books. It was a long walk out along Washington Road, near the cemetery, and Ruderman remembered how marching to the chapel we used to curse the early-morning winds whipping off the river during the miserable Hudson Valley winters.

"But there were some benefits with it, too," he said. Every Jewish cadet, for instance, was a member of the Jewish choir, whether he could sing or not, and he got to go on several weekend trips, during which he'd sing Hebrew and West Point songs before various Jewish communities. Ruderman particularly remembered going to Minneapolis and Palm Beach. There the resplendently uniformed cadets were treated royally, getting not only to stay with the leading Jewish families but also meeting the local Jewish girls. "I have to be careful how this comes out," Ruderman said with a cautious smile. "Sure, we'd meet the girls, but the main thing were the services. The community would have a dinner for us, in conjunction with the services, at which we sang. Although, one night, the choir director did look at me and say, 'Gill, don't sing tonight, just mouth the words.'"

Acolytes of a sort, they usually began their religious pilgrimages Friday, got to where they were going before sundown and the inception of the Sabbath, and returned to West Point Sunday. It was, to be sure, a blessed break from the rigors insisted upon in the gray, Gothic monastery high on the hill, although the trips did understandably strike the other seminarians as a convenient occasion to let off some steam.

"I'll never forget once during my plebe year," Ruderman said. "I had a sophomore Jewish guy in my company. There were only three Jewish cadets in the company—this sophomore, a senior, and me. We were going on a trip one day, and we were leaving right about noon. We had to walk across the company formation at lunchtime, then in front of the battalion formation, in order to reach the bus. They all knew where we were going and began giving us catcalls. 'Oh, I wish I was Jewish!' they called out. 'Oh, I wish I could sing!' Of course, my classmates, who were plebes, couldn't say anything. But the yearlings, the sophomores, they were just riding this Jewish sophomore crazy. He was a real little guy, and as we kept walking toward the bus, he kept saying to me, 'Stand tall, Ruderman, stand tall. Every time you hear something, stand taller. You're Jewish, be proud of it! You're going on a trip, they're not, and be proud of that, too!'"

Ruderman is a rangy six-two and weighs about two hundred,

with brown hair and eyes. While he might not be able to carry a tune, speaking he sounds like Robert Mitchum. His nose has been broken nine times—once playing football, another time wrestling, once swimming, and God alone remembers how the other six times. It comes as no particular surprise to learn that Ruderman continues playing his favorite sport, rugby, though he's had two neck operations. "I try to play more carefully these days," he insisted.

He'd served in seven Vietnam battle campaigns, was wounded there, and awarded the Bronze Star for valor. Ruderman wears a Ranger patch plus a master parachutist's badge, and as a lieutenant colonel attending the Army War College it was likely he'd be promoted to full colonel. It gave me an extra charge, being Jewish, that a lieutenant colonel who'd graduated from West Point and fought in Vietnam was also Jewish.

Ruderman's father, an American, had, with other members of his family, lived in Israel, then called Palestine, from the mid-1930s and joined the American Army in the Middle East when World War II broke out. He'd married Ruderman's mother in 1942, and Ruderman was born in Tel Aviv the following year. His father likes to say, "Not a whole lot of West Pointers were born in Israel." At the war's conclusion, his father decided to remain in the Army and became a warrant officer. Ruderman, his younger brother, and his sister were thus "Army brats," and they lived in Pittsburgh, Maryland, Germany, and Fort Bragg during their father's military career, which lasted until 1962. When Ruderman mentioned Bragg, I made a point of telling him I'd been stationed there myself from 1958 to 1960, and who knows but that we might have passed like ships in the night in the town about ten miles outside of Bragg, Fayetteville, North Carolina.

Before graduating from Fayetteville High School, Ruderman applied to the Air Force Academy. But there were no vacancies, and he bided his time for a year attending East Carolina College. The following year, he applied to all three military academies. He wasn't sure he wanted a military career, but because of his father the military was all he knew, and he wasn't sure what else he wanted. So it was pretty easy to follow in his father's footsteps. Accepted by West Point, he traveled up to New York in the summer of 1962. Although he'd talked to some West Point graduates whom his father knew, he had little real idea what awaited him. "I figured it was pretty well regimented, but if I sat here and told anyone that even after a year in college I knew what to expect at West Point, I'd be lying.''

Although Beast Barracks proved the same shock to Ruderman it invariably does to all plebes, he looked around, saw other people surviving it, and told himself, ''Hey, if they can, I can, too.'' He was lucky in one respect: He'd taken Air Force ROTC at East Carolina and knew the rudiments of military drills and ceremony. ''As a result, I did not catch the shit some of the people around me did who had little or no experience. But if they find you do well in one area, they look for others where they can pick on you. I really can't describe Beast Barracks. Everybody should probably experience it once, and once is enough.''

Ruderman struggled with academics the four years he attended the Military Academy. Yet he seemed to have had a genius for just getting through each term. ''Everybody probably has stories about plebe math and plebe English, and they're probably all true; and as you get older, you probably think you're able to forget them. But I am able to isolate very clearly on the high points, meaning the low points.''

One English exam held on a Monday was especially memorable. It consisted of a single question, an essay. ''I'll never forget the question, words to the effect, By referring to six of the nine books we have allegedly read and mastered—and they listed the books in case we'd forgotten we'd mastered them—show how man transcends his lower nature by dedication to an ideal.''

Ruderman said it took him twenty minutes to look through his dictionary, which was the only reference he could use, to make sure he knew what all the words in the question meant. Chairs were spread out to prevent copying, as if anyone could read the next man's ungainly scrawl. But Ruderman was close enough to hear one guy muttering, ''Jesus Christ.'' Another said to himself, ''I don't remember reading this book.'' Ruderman did poorly, and about a third of the class bollixed the exam. ''I guess they realized they couldn't flunk a third of us, so there was a second exam later that week, which enabled many to recoup points we'd lost on the first.''

Every so often, classes would be resectioned, so people with high scores wound up in one section, folks with lower scores in another. Ruderman invariably found himself with the low-score guys each semester and got to know them very well. He said that after a while, cadets in the low sections would surprisingly take some courses very cavalierly, figuring if they couldn't learn the lesson the night before, crashing twenty minutes prior to class wasn't going to help. Guys in low sections, Ruderman recalled, would play games like baseball with a piece of chalk and slide rules before the class began. Foul lines would be drawn on the boards. Hit a particular board and it was a single; another, more distant board, a double. They'd miraculously come to order fifteen seconds before the instructor showed up.

Sometimes Ruderman even unscrewed an unsuspecting fellow student's slide rule, and the middle piece would go bouncing across the room at an inopportune moment. At other times he'd erase the work of a cadet standing next to him at the board if the instructor left the room and the cadet dropped his chalk or momentarily looked away. Nor was Ruderman the only cadet to indulge in such antics, although it does appear he was definitely among the more enthusiastic.

While plebe harassment never really bothered him, a sophomore in his company, who seemed on his case all the time, one day asked if Ruderman wanted to know why. "Yes, sir," Ruderman answered. The yearling replied, "Because you play football, and I can't stand football players." Apparently this guy had been dumped on during his plebe year and felt he'd garnered more than his share, while two classmates in his company who'd played football had gotten off easy. Could Ruderman have confronted his persecutor and said, "Get lost, you miserable jerk, or I'll kick ass"? Ruderman shook his head. "No way I could have done that as a plebe, and he knew it and kept on me all year."

Ruderman played third- and fourth-string. He'd tried out as an end, but before he knew it the coaches made him a guard and cut a kid who'd been a high-school all-American. The big plus of playing plebe football was that it got Ruderman on the football table in the mess hall, where he didn't have to ask permission to eat or talk, and he gobbled down all the chow he could handle. Joe DeFrancisco played plebe football for the same reason. "Guys did whatever they could to cut down on the harassment," Ruderman remembered.

The following year, he found he didn't give plebes as hard a time as he'd endured. "I didn't fully play the game, and as a result pissed off some of my classmates." While Ruderman doesn't consider the plebe system inherently malicious, he does think it allows people the luxury of acting arbitrarily; and while he didn't go the other way by befriending plebes, he just let it alone. "And some people felt I let it alone too much and wasn't doing what the system called for me to do." Later, when he served as a Beast Barracks squad leader, he played it strictly by the book.

There's a system at West Point where, if you're failing a course at term's end, you're what is called "turned out." You have to take a comprehensive test covering the term's work and are thus given a last chance to recoup, saving yourself from expulsion. Although Ruderman was never turned out, he came awfully close a number of times.

Once, it was announced after dinner during exam time, "Will the following second classmen report to the officer in charge upon completion of the meal?" The Mechanics Department, the juniors knew, had just concluded deciding who was still flunking the course in mechanics of solids, so the juniors suddenly sat up as one, their forks dropping like toppled bowling pins as the names of those still flunking were announced alphabetically. "When they got past a name without announcing it, you heard the guy say with a sigh, 'Ahh, ahh,'" Ruderman said. "Guys were literally going bat shit because they weren't turned out." And because Ruderman knew how poorly he'd been doing in the course, when they skipped past his name, he thought "Jesus Christ, thank God." And walking outside, it felt as if he were floating on air. But when he arrived back at the barracks, the CQ said, "Ruderman, you've got a call from Captain So-and-so," who was his teacher in that course. "I thought, 'Oh, shit, they screwed up and mistakenly missed announcing my name.' Turned out, he'd called to let me know that, basically, when they drew the line, separating those who'd made it from those who hadn't, the line went through the bottom third of my name. I came that close."

Ruderman said that most former cadets undoubtedly had similar stories about surviving four years at West Point. "Wes Taylor, Joe DeFrancisco—we all have them." When I mentioned how Taylor sat in the latrine till two, three in the morning trying to unlock the cruel mysteries of calculus, Ruderman nodded as if he'd seen Taylor there. "Wes and I were in the same company for a year or two."

During Ruderman's senior year, word circulated that a senior had flunked out at Annapolis. "Well, that put those of us just getting by on our guard," he said, "because we knew there were

assholes at West Point who just would have loved to show that
Annapolis wasn't tougher on seniors than the Military Academy.''

But despite keeping his guard up during the second semester of
his senior year, Ruderman's name kept appearing dead last on the
printout citing those passing one particular course; Ruderman
thought it was ordnance engineering. This was in April or May,
and for only the third time during his four years at West Point he
sought extra instruction. There he went through a thirteen-step
problem in the textbook that had never been assigned for home-
work. Ruderman dutifully recorded each step of the problem in the
margin of his book.

Now, cadets were allowed to use any notes in their own hand-
writing in their books as reference in the exams, and, miraculously,
it turned out that that thirteen-step problem, with different numbers, constituted the next test. "I'm sure the teacher knew it
would, and it occurred to me that maybe I'd been too pessimistic
about the system,'' Ruderman conceded magnanimously. "Or
maybe the teacher just had a soft spot for me. I'm not sure. But I
remember reading the problem on the exam all the way through—
comma, period, centimeter, whatever—and suddenly realized it
was exactly the same problem, and nobody else had it worked out
because it had never been assigned.

"Well, the maximum grade on that test was 9.0, and when they
posted the scores, if you passed and were 6.0 or above, it was in
the blue. Five-nine and below were in red, and in my section only
about a third of the grades were in blue. Everybody was clustered
around the door, trying to read his grade. I knew mine would be on
the bottom of the last sheet, the last name, because I was just
getting by. So I kind of crawled in on my knees, saying, 'Excuse
me, guys,' and soon I was eye level with my grade, as I knew it
would be down there. 'Eight-nine,'' I said. 'Not bad, Ruderman.'
And everybody said, 'What?' and they looked down. 'Ruderman,
gee, eight point nine,' they said. One guy accused me of cheating.''

The year before, America had begun sending large numbers of
troops over to Vietnam and, Ruderman remembered, they also
started sending guys back—in coffins. He specifically recalled a
fellow cadet from the Class of '65, who'd been killed in February
or March. He'd double-dated with the guy one time, played football and marched to chapel with him, even knew the guy's wife of
seven or eight months. The officer was interred at West Point. "I

was still a cadet," Ruderman said, "a senior, and here I was, helping to bury this guy."

While the funeral brought the Vietnam War home unforgettably, and Ruderman felt terrible seeing the former cadet's young wife, the ceremony did not unnerve him. Like everyone else, he wondered how he'd perform in Vietnam and if he'd survive, and he requested Vietnam for his first assignment. "I'd spent four years to become a second lieutenant, combat arms. 'Let's go,' I thought. 'Let me go do it.' I knew it was inevitable I'd be going, and I felt by going early I could control some of my later assignments, and I was right."

Graduating from West Point, Ruderman experienced "a sense of relief, satisfaction, and accomplishment—all of that and more." His parents came up for graduation. "Although my father had retired four years before, he wore his uniform because he wanted to be able to salute me."

Ruderman said his proudest moment occurred when the graduating class got the order to leave the Corps and march to the far side of the parade field. When they turned around, they were facing the other cadets, who'd be passing in review in front of the graduating class. "Walking across the field, away from the Corps formation, I'll never forget it. The proudest I felt, the best I felt. Even much more than the graduation ceremony. Humphrey spoke, it was a Tuesday, but I couldn't tell you a word he said. Just before walking away, across the parade field, we said, 'Good-bye, guys,' and they said good-bye to us. That walkaway—just head and shoulders above beating Navy one year, tossing my hat in the air, getting the diploma, shaking hands with everybody, all that shit. The walk, the feeling of knowing it was the last ceremony we'd be in as cadets . . ." Ruderman shook his head, savoring the recollection. Then he smiled, a kind of sneaky smile. "Three years before that, after the graduation parade was another ceremony I remembered— getting recognized as a plebe. Another great moment, even though the asshole who didn't like football players was there and I had to shake his hand."

Although Ruderman volunteered for Vietnam immediately upon graduation, the Army wisely sent him first to Fort Hood for six months to learn his job; and prior to Hood, he'd attended Ranger and Airborne schools. Actually, Ranger School was required for a combat arms officer; Airborne was voluntary. But Ruderman thought if he had to attend one, he'd go to both. "If I was going to do it, I was going to go all the way."

He enjoyed Airborne School except for doing pull-ups. "I've never been able to do them. I couldn't do them at West Point, and I can't do them now." His neck problems are several years old, but he believes he probably had them when he was a cadet, although he hadn't realized it then. They affect his strength, and probably explain why he was and is unable to lift himself.

"If you're told to do a hundred pull-ups and you can't do fifty, there's no fucking problem," Ruderman said. "You can't do fifty, and the guy can shout, "Give me fifty more!' till doomsday. You're only going to do the pull-ups you're able to do." Which was exactly what I used to think as a recruit taking basic training at Fort Dix about two hundred years ago; but it was amusing, even endearing, hearing a lieutenant colonel, a field-grade officer, using precisely the same perfectly reasonable language I'd remembered muttering to myself.

The first time Ruderman jumped from a plane, he was so involved in what he was doing, he doesn't remember being afraid. During his second and third jumps, though, he recalled thinking, "Well, shit, maybe I'm stretching my luck." But he was never really scared; apprehensive, yes, frightened, no. "Some guys are afraid, and some guys don't like it. But I had no problems with it."

On the other hand, Ranger School was murder all the way and, Ruderman said, something's wrong with anybody who claimed he loved it. Ruderman never got enough to eat. But what he remembered even more vividly about Ranger School was that he couldn't climb a rope. It extended over a ditch of water, and you had to climb it every morning during the physical conditioning phase at Fort Benning. You had to jump on the rope, which had a big knot at the bottom so you couldn't get a head start. Rope climbing for some people was a cinch. But Ruderman found it impossible, and after a while his pitiful attempts at it seemed to expand into a tired comic routine cribbed from a black humor joke book.

"You used to shout, 'Ranger Ruderman reports he's unable to get to the top of the rope!' " he remembered. "They'd yell at you for it, and then say, 'Let go of the rope!' So you let go of the rope and fell into the ditch. You climbed out and ran to the next obstacle, whatever it was. I could handle the rest of it, but I never kissed the top of that rope. I got close once, about three feet. If you got to the top, you could hang on to a diagonal rope and crawl your way down. There was a friend of mine, a classmate, who'll remain nameless, who couldn't get to the top either. The instructor knew we couldn't climb the fucking rope. Some idiots, they'd fall into the water and beg for another chance. Anyway, this classmate and I would position ourselves to be last in line. We'd report, 'Ranger So-and-so and Ranger Ruderman request permission to hop on the rope.' They knew we couldn't make it, but they'd say, 'Okay, hop on the rope.' So we'd hop on the knot and swing back and forth. We'd fake trying. Then we'd request permission to drop into the water. 'Drop,' they'd say. So we'd drop. Then we'd get out. But we saved our energy."

Ruderman, it seemed unmistakably apparent by now, was a man who took life, the Army, himself, and just about everybody else with a certain measure of proportion. And if something struck him as impossible, crazy, unreasonable, he might try once or twice; but three times probably was once too much.

"I think in some ways I have the proper way of looking at things," he acknowledged modestly. We were talking in a classroom at the Army War College, and plastered on the four walls was a mosaic of organizational charts. "When we first arrived here this August, we were supposed to come up with all the qualities of the perfect War College student. Sense of humor was the first thing I said. If you can't laugh or be laughed at . . ." Ruderman glanced down at his considerably wider than *au courant* necktie. Indiscriminate blotches of lemony yellow competed riotously with those of shocking green and icy blue. "Some people think I'm an asshole because I wear wild ties that sometimes make them do a double take." Garish hardly did the tie justice.

"Why do you wear it?" I asked.

"Why not?" he shot back. "Some guys say they wouldn't be caught dead with a tie of mine. I say, 'Good, don't wear it. You'll live a long time.'"

He had the timing of a natural-born comic, or one who'd learned it as a kid, and I asked if his father had a good sense of timing.

"Tremendous, tremendous," and you could tell from the way Ruderman said it how fond he was of his father. "The best thing about being at the Army War College is that it's two and a half hours from Philadelphia, where my parents now live, and I get up there often. My father just turned seventy-four, and he recently said to me how wonderful it was that we had this chance to see and get to know each other again.''

It struck me about then that Ruderman, with his crazy ties and amusing West Point stories, his Airborne and Ranger schools misadventures, was certainly different, but not because he was Jewish. He was different because he viewed life as amusing, and he approached it with a certain detachment. Though he was Jewish, he could just as well have been Mongolian or an Eskimo. What really mattered was his quirky way of seeing things, as well as his talent for falling against, but not upon, a spike of possible misfortune.

After completing Ranger and Airborne schools and before flying to Vietnam, Ruderman was assigned as an artillery officer to the 3rd Battalion, 19th Field Artillery, 1st Armored Division at Fort Hood, Texas. There he learned the rudiments of soldiering and helped instruct soldiers to become artillerymen. Unfortunately, the battalion commander, like the colonel commanding Paschall's first battalion at Fort Bragg, hated West Pointers and went so far as to tell Ruderman that he'd tried to get him reassigned for that reason. He also said that in his opinion Airborne and Ranger schools were a colossal waste of time. "I'll bet I'm going to have a good time here," Ruderman thought.

During the almost six months he was stationed at Hood, the colonel kept referring to him as "Duty, Honor." It was a joke among other officers of the battalion, and even friends of Ruderman from other battalions would come up to him and say, "I hear you're working for a colonel who really loves West Pointers. Some guys have all the luck."

Bad luck was one thing, but rolling over and playing dead quite another. One Saturday morning, Ruderman was instructing trainees. Other instructors were scheduled to come get the troops, place them on buses, and take them elsewhere for individual training. The colonel had said to Ruderman, "Nobody leaves to take off for the weekend until the last trainee is picked up. Got that, Duty, Honor?" So about fifteen officers were standing around, waiting for the last trainee to be sent on his way. Ruderman was ready to go to Dallas for the weekend. His car, a nifty convertible, was parked nearby, his civilian clothes neatly folded on the backseat, and the officers had gathered around it. When the colonel walked over, he asked whose car it was and if it was okay if he got behind the wheel.

That was the year the government had made hazard flashers mandatory, and the dealers had rigged up some wiring in the car. A little switch was under the dash, obviously out of place; but the colonel asked what the switch was for. Ruderman, thinking the colonel was jerking his chain, said, "That's in case you're ever stuck on a railroad track, for instance, and your car stalls and there's a train coming." The colonel looked quizzically at the others, then said, "I don't understand. Does the switch make the engine start?" Ruderman answered, "No, sir. If you pull it out, it puts a dog tag on your big toe." The colonel looked at him, saying, "A dog tag on your big toe?" Then, realizing he'd been had, he got out of the car and walked away. The other young officers were aghast. "How could you say that to him?" they asked. Ruderman shrugged, replying, "I thought he knew what it was and kidding me."

Later, Ruderman was in charge of his own going-away party. Not that he was without friends, but it seems it was his battery's turn to throw the party and he was the officer in charge when it was his battery's turn. The gift was a drinking mug, which Ruderman had engraved. "Wrap it up, it's a surprise for me," he told the clerk at the PX.

At the party, the colonel got up and made a speech. It was the only time he called Ruderman "Lieutenant Ruderman." Then the guest of honor was called upon for a few parting words. "Well, I guess you all know where I went to school, because it's certainly been a topic of conversation around here. But let me tell you one thing I learned there. When you graduate, they insist that the worst thing you can do is walk out of West Point and think you know it all. 'Go out and get experience,' they tell you." Looking at the colonel, Ruderman said, "Sir, this has certainly been an experience."

When he arrived in Vietnam in July 1967, Ruderman was assigned to the 7th Battalion, 11th Field Artillery, 25th Infantry Division, which was based in Cu Chi, near the Cambodian border in southern III Corps. He served with the unit for a year, during which time he was an executive officer and forward observer. As a forward observer, he was attached to an infantry company. When they were in camp, he was in camp; when they were out patrolling, he was out patrolling. Patrols, often repetitious, were dispatched constantly. Ruderman's job was calling in artillery fire. At night, when he'd camp out in the bush, he'd be plotting targets around him so that artillery would be readily available.

In February 1967, the 25th Infantry was part of an attacking force assigned to crush the enemy dominating War Zone C, which had been controlled by the VC since South Vietnam had been formed. War Zone C was northwest of Saigon, in a flat, marshy area. The closer you got to the Cambodian border, the hillier it became, until the landscape was finally dominated by a single three-thousand-foot mountain, Nui Ba Dinh. By the time Ruderman reported to the 25th, War Zone C hadn't been neutralized, but three VC regiments had been temporarily shattered. The 25th Infantry kept the pressure on the rest of that year. Contacts were insignificant, but the period was marked by considerable jungle-clearing efforts, attracting numerous mortar attacks.

They usually occurred at night, Ruderman remembered. "The VC were able to move around a little better then and set up. They knew where we were, because if the Corps of Engineers with their bulldozers were clearing trees, they realized infantry was providing defense for the engineers. So they couldn't help hearing the engineers and probably even saw us."

When mortar attacks occurred, there wasn't much the troops receiving them could do initially. "You hear mortars coming in at night, you're not sure where they're coming from," Ruderman said. "It's a whomp sound, and if it's close, the earth shakes. You feel the vibrations. You listen to see if there's a patrol out there, or if the perimeter feel they want you to call artillery in anywhere. We have our own mortars, too, so we're able to respond if we can tell the direction from which they're coming." Ruderman said that it was impossible not to realize how helpless you were. "You're out there, and you'll be there next morning or you won't be there next morning, both by the grace of God. Because, if you're being mortared or rocketed and you're walking around when the first rounds land, it's a question of where they land whether you're going to be killed or not. There's absolutely nothing you can do to protect yourself."

Yet Ruderman felt even more helpless as a forward observer when he was aboard a helicopter and his ship was among the first coming in to a landing zone taking enemy fire. Both sides of the helicopter are completely exposed, he said. "When you're a thousand feet up, facing out, you're okay. But when you're coming in at ground level, trying to land, you often see clumps of fire coming from the woods and you don't know who's firing—your guys or the other side's. You're a sitting duck, because there's no way you can really know where the fire's coming from. You want to land and get off the chopper as fast as possible, because a helicopter ten feet off the ground, seventy-five feet from the tree line, is a tremendous target."

If the first rounds didn't get you in a mortar attack, Ruderman noted, you could crawl into a hole or run into a shelter. But coming in on a chopper, the feeling is overwhelmingly, "Shit, I'm a terrific target here and I don't want to be a target anymore." But the pilot can't land before the chopper in front of him takes off. Plus, he's a target himself, because if he's hit, the chopper goes down.

An observant and curious man, Ruderman found himself increasingly watching how other officers reacted in combat situations. He was drawn to those who didn't overreact, officers who realized they were dealing with subordinates obviously less informed than themselves.

One of the operations officers in the 25th Infantry was a man with a reputation as "a screamer." But Ruderman, as he almost always did, withheld judgment. One day he saw the guy blow his stack, pick up a Coke can filled with pencils, and fling it across a room crowded with sergeants and privates. "I'm glad I waited until I formed my own opinion," Ruderman said.

Later, when he was processing out of the unit, that same officer told him over a drink, "I guess you know that when I first got here I tried to have you relieved." The man had actually gone to Ruderman's battery commander his second day with the battalion and said he wanted Ruderman fired. But Ruderman's battery commander said, "What are you talking about?" The operations officer never told the battery commander the real reason; but what he did say was hardly convincing, and the battery commander finally replied that because Ruderman was a good XO he wasn't going to relieve him, and the matter died. Now the operations officer told Ruderman the reason he'd wanted him relieved was because Ruderman wore a mustache. Ruderman replied, "I hope you realized during the last six months that having had me relieved would have been a mistake." The operations officer said, "Yes, but you're the first guy I've ever seen with a mustache I've learned I can trust."

After his one-year tour with the 25th Infantry was up, Ruderman decided to extend for six months, and he's often wondered why. The best explanation he could offer now, he said, was that he was about to make captain then and hoping he'd be given a battery to command in Vietnam. "Don't get me wrong, I had no grandiose plans. I never felt once Ruderman had a command he was going to end this shit."

He was assigned to the 2nd Battalion, 319th Field Artillery, 101st Airborne Division, and ran into a second officer offended by his mustache. In fact, when he reported in, he was told that before the battalion commander would even see him to discuss his assignment, let alone be assigned, he would have to shave off his mustache. "So, not having any fucking choice, I guess, I went and shaved it off."

Ruderman was assigned as an artillery liaison officer. As such, he was responsible for coordinating not just artillery fire, but air strikes and naval gunfire as well. It's a more complicated job than a forward observer's, because a liaison officer has to work with more systems, some of which he can't immediately control. After about a month of orchestrating fire support and flying in a command helicopter with an infantry battalion commander, Ruderman minus his talismanic mustache, was wounded.

The battalion was looking to engage an NVA regiment said by intelligence to be operating in the Cu Chi area. The pilot and battalion commander were in the chopper's front seats. Ruderman and the operations officer sat toward the rear. When the pilot spotted enemy troops, he began circling about two hundred feet above them, and before he realized it the helicopter began taking enemy rounds. Ruderman was talking on his radio, leaning forward. He had a finger in one ear so he could drown out the chopper's noise. Ruderman remembered that the ashtray on the back of the seat in front of him got hit first and splintered. The next thing he knew was a burning pain in the front of his right foot. Although he didn't think he was bleeding heavily, he could feel blood squishing inside his boot.

The colonel had turned around, asking if everyone was okay. Because something was now wrong with the intercom, Ruderman pointed to his foot, giving the cutoff sign. Soon the chopper returned to the battalion's firebase. After the medics sliced away Ruderman's boot, they told him his foot was intact, but a bone had been shattered. They took him to the hospital at Cu Chi, where his foot was X-rayed and he was given pain shots before the doctor began removing bone fragments. Because there was a possibility of amputation, Ruderman was evacuated to a hospital in Japan two days later. Aboard the plane were his battalion commander and operations officer. It seemed that soon after Ruderman had been wounded, their chopper had been shot down and both officers suffered broken backs when the helicopter had slammed into the ground. Because his own wound was only to the front of his foot, Ruderman said he felt awkward talking about it even now.

Fortunately, he didn't lose his foot, although a small part of it remains numb to this day. But Ruderman did have to wear a cast, and the policy was not to return soldiers wearing casts to Vietnam. So he was flown back to the States. The only thing that really scared him about the experience was that the pattern of rounds indicated he'd missed getting hit in the head by inches.

In the fall of 1970 he returned to Vietnam to begin a second tour. This time he was a battery commander with the 7th Battalion, 15th Field Artillery. His battalion headquarters were in Pleiku, about thirty-five minutes from where his battery was actually stationed. "The environment was safe, but the youth that had been creating the turmoil in the States was now in Vietnam," Ruderman said. "Drugs were prevalent, morale terrible. The American Army in Germany was experiencing the same convulsions, and back home the country didn't seem to be doing much better. Frankly, it appeared to me we were falling apart everywhere." Although Ruderman thought he should have been better able to deal with some disciplinary problems he'd encountered, he shied away from citing specifics.

But he couldn't have been a genuine bust, because after four months as a battery commander Ruderman was chosen to be aide to Maj. Gen. Charles P. Brown. "He interviewed a bunch of us and just picked one." General Brown was appointed commander of the 1st Field Force, the equivalent of a corps command, just as Ruderman came to work for him. As aide Ruderman managed the general's schedule and activities.

Brown, an artillery officer, had been a former commander at Fort Sill, and Ruderman had heard some unflattering stories about him. "Not bad stories, but ones that made him come out rough." But, again, Ruderman suspended judgment, and soon he realized that the general's current job was totally different from the one he'd had at Sill. Or perhaps those who'd been critical of Brown at Sill had rather misjudged him. In any case, Ruderman came to think of the general as a superior officer. "He was fair, he would listen to you. He acted upon recommendations rather than set his mind to what he wanted before anyone talked to him. Most important, he was professional, knew what he was responsible for, and how to go about doing it.''

During the time Ruderman was an aide, he could see the Army's role in Vietnam shrinking on a day-by-day basis. Not only was the fighting being turned over to the South Vietnamese, but also American civilians were replacing the U.S. military in advisory positions. In short, the sense of American military withdrawal was quite palpable by the spring of 1971.

As an aide Ruderman learned that a captain, a West Point graduate, had been killed by one of his troops, shot in broad daylight. Ruderman accompanied General Brown when the 1st Field Force commander conducted a preliminary investigation. On the flight back that night, the general asked Ruderman for his thoughts. While the general had received a number of briefings during the day, Ruderman had met a friend from the Class of '67, to whom he'd talked off the record. Ruderman told the general he'd learned that the murdered officer's predecessor had lost control of the company. Consequently, the murdered officer had inherited an unsettled command, one he'd been trying to regain control of. But he kept experiencing a lot of resistance from the troops and had been told by some of his superiors to let sleeping dogs lie.

Naturally, that was hardly the story the general had gotten when he'd spoken to the officers running the battalion. Nor was it the impression the general's inspector general came away with when he conducted a formal investigation. A few weeks later, the IG issued his report. That night, the general asked Ruderman to read it. The next morning, Ruderman told the general he thought the findings did not address the real problems that had led to the officer's death. The general said he had nothing concrete to support Ruderman's conclusion and thought his IG had done a thorough job. But after the general had mailed the report to his boss in Saigon, the general's superior brought up the precise points Ruderman had questioned. Didn't the report, in essence, brush over the chain of command's role in what had happened?

At about this time, too, it occurred to Ruderman that the American effort in Vietnam had become futile. He'd been accompanying the general in a helicopter, and they'd been talking about the frustrations of trying to get the Vietnamese to do certain things. The helicopter was flying west and in the distance loomed the

Cambodian border. "And I thought here was a country that really has it rough," Ruderman remembered. "We'd tried to help them. I couldn't relate to the billions of dollars we'd given them, but I could to the manpower. Yet about two thirds of the Vietnamese officers of high rank my boss was dealing with were semicrooked. And because the border out there was so immense, so vast, it occurred to me that the corrupted Vietnamese Army was never going to be able to defend it. It kind of hit me like a sledgehammer in that helicopter. I said to myself, 'They're not going to win this war, and we're biding our time here.' And then I said to myself, 'Shit, what if we get shot down in this chopper right now? What's it for?'"

It might have helped if the American Army's mission in South Vietnam was ever clearly defined. But neither while Ruderman was there nor when he was stationed back in the States did he believe he knew the Army's mission. "Certainly our role seemed to change more than once, but our overall objective was never made clear," Ruderman insisted. "Shit, I couldn't tell you what it was right now, not even today."

Nor could he affirm with conviction today that a massacre like My Lai would not have occurred had Calley and Medina been West Point graduates. "Boy, I'd sure like to say, 'No, it couldn't have happened if the officers at the scene or near it were West Pointers.' But to say a West Pointer, under the pressures of the body-count syndrome, under the pressures of being constantly told by his superiors that anybody you find is the enemy, wouldn't have committed that atrocity is difficult to assert. I wasn't there when Calley and Medina were briefed, possibly told that the only good Vietnamese was a dead Vietnamese. And I don't know what generated that briefing if, in fact, that's the way they were briefed." Although part of the explanation, Ruderman thought, was that Vietnamese maids and kids kept slipping booby traps in among American officers and troops, and trust became increasingly difficult to extend. "The truth is, it's hard to figure how you'd react shortly after, say, something terrible happened to a close friend."

If Ruderman ends up more sympathetic to officers like Calley and Medina than most, he comes down far tougher than you might expect on Vietnam vets who claim they suffer from poststress syndrome. He finds it difficult to believe American youth of the 1960s and 1970s, who were better educated, probably healthier to start with, and had a higher standard of living, came home after a year more decimated than the youth of the 1940s, who were overseas during World War II for three or four years. Ruderman thinks, in fact, that a considerable number of Vietnam vets claiming poststress syndrome "are going for all the gusto they can get—all the attention, benefits, everything."

Agree or disagree with Ruderman—and it's difficult to accept that many who had served during the Vietnam War were better educated, healthier, or had a higher standard of living than their contemporaries or even than those who'd fought during World War II—it's plain again that Ruderman thinks for himself and is unafraid to spell out his conclusions.

Between his two Vietnam tours, Ruderman was stationed at Fort Bragg and served with the 82nd Airborne Division from December 1968 to September 1970. Although the antiwar movement had become increasingly vocal during this period throughout the country, Ruderman wasn't so sure the country had only recently turned against the war. He got to feeling America hadn't changed so much as that perhaps his initial sense of the country's support for the war had been wrong, inaccurate.

At Bragg, he was assigned as a battery commander. It was the single most stressful job he ever held in the Army. There was intense competition among units in the 82nd Airborne, and the atmosphere was cutthroat, Ruderman said; but, maybe most important of all, Ruderman's boss was not among his favorites.

"Here's a typical example of how he operated," Ruderman said. "We came in from a field problem one time, on a Friday. You always had things to do to clean your equipment up—that was normal, but he sent his staff around to inspect, and they found something wrong with all five batteries. Probably they were told to. The word was, Okay, Saturday morning there'll be a ten o'clock inspection, though the battalion commander had led us to believe in the field we'd be off all Saturday. Well, they came in Saturday for the inspection and checked one thing. In my battery it was binoculars, because the battalion commander heard that binoculars in C Battery were dirty. But he inspected, wearing his golf outfit, because he had tee time coming up."

If this was one of the low points of his career, one of the high points occurred from 1972 to 1976, when Ruderman lived in Gainesville, Florida, where he'd chosen to participate in a four-year program, during the first year and a half of which he earned a masters degree in psychology at the University of Florida. Following that, he taught ROTC for the remainder of the four years. "After two tours in Vietnam, it was time to relax, and let's face it, I did have a good time," Ruderman said. He got the masters because the pervasive feeling in the officer corps then was you had no future in the Army without one. Ruderman now believes he'd picked up the wrong vibes. Proof of that, he said, was he had classmates at the Army War College who hadn't acquired advanced degrees. While it wasn't a mistake to earn the masters, he believes it was a mistake to feel he had to earn one to advance professionally. And it still bothers him that he violated a personal rule by doing something not because he really wanted to but because he felt it was expected of him. Yet, everything considered, his four years in Gainesville were a big plus. "Got my batteries charged," he said.

"Recharged," I amended.

"Whatever." Ruderman grinned broadly. "The best eight years of my life were those four years. Lived like the bachelor I still was, and had a good salary because I was getting my Army pay." Much of the time he wore civilian clothing. His fellow graduate school students couldn't believe he'd been a captain who'd fought in Vietnam. Others who made no effort to learn he was still an Army officer simply didn't know; and when they found out, once he started teaching ROTC, they were stunned. "I remember sitting with people in a bar after they'd discovered I was in the Army, and they said, 'You've got to be kidding.' People who never have any contact with the military have this stereotypical idea of what an Army officer is like—it's not particularly favorable—and I just didn't fit their idea."

He found life in Florida more than pleasant, made a number of friends there, and even his superiors agreed he had better rapport with students teaching ROTC than any other officer. But Ruderman did not do well professionally as an ROTC instructor. It sounds as if he were too popular for his own good. Also, when asked questions, he'd tell his superiors what he really thought, which was not necessarily what they wanted to hear. Thus his efficiency reports suffered.

It was therefore with considerable surprise he learned soon after completing his teaching stint that he was on a list of officers scheduled to attend the Command and General Staff College at Leavenworth. Only the better majors are chosen, and the goal of battalion command is uppermost. Being selected for Leavenworth was therefore a real turning point.

There are many young Army officers who feel they'd be failures if they didn't eventually acquire a battalion commander assignment, but Ruderman had never thought he had a chance at it until he got to Leavenworth. It didn't affect how he continued doing things, Ruderman said; but, no question, Leavenworth gave significantly more substance to his future aspirations, suggesting that it was possible he might prove a success, even the way the Army measures success. Leavenworth, it should be added, was also where he met his wife, Pam Hahn.

"You certainly got a lot out of the place if only for that reason," I said.

Ruderman, however, wouldn't let me get away with that rather pathetic attempt at ingratiation. "Depends on how you look at it," he said, and Robert Mitchum couldn't have delivered the line more laconically. Then he smiled, letting me off the hook. "Well, my checkbook's certainly gotten a lot of activity because of it."

He was back to sporting a mustache at Leavenworth, courted his wife trimming that mustache, and was wearing it when he reported to Fort Bragg in July 1978 as an operations officer with the 1st Battalion, 320th Field Artillery, 82nd Airborne Division. After a couple of months, a new colonel took command of the brigade, and word preceded his arrival that here was yet another honcho who thought mustaches went out of style with Adolf Hitler. But Ruderman walked through the receiving line, his mustache neat and trim, and shook the colonel's hand. The colonel looked at him funny but didn't say a word. Neither did the colonel's wife.

A few days later, Ruderman approached his battalion commander. "I'm a major. I've been around long enough," he said. "I'm past the point where I'm going to stay in or get out. If you think I have to shave off my mustache—"

"Hell, no," the battalion commander said. "I had a mustache for many years myself; I've no problems with mustaches."

But a couple of months later, the battalion commander was at the brigade commander's house, where he found himself saying, "I guess I haven't been as supportive of your policies as I should have been." The colonel agreed that that was, alas, the case. And when Ruderman's name came up, the colonel added that both Ruderman and the battalion commander knew how much he disliked mustaches, yet Ruderman still flourished his.

The day after the battalion commander offered the colonel his version of *mea culpa*, he called Ruderman at home and asked him to drop by; Ruderman had been on leave. When Ruderman showed up, the battalion commander said, "I had a big talk with the colonel last night. Until I decide what I'm going to do, whether I'm going to retire or not, I'm going to play the game. I don't agree with the colonel, that's between us, but I'm going to support him. And I want to ask what is going to be your reaction if I tell you to shave off your mustache?"

"Sure," Ruderman said. "Soon after the colonel got here, I said it was no big deal to me. We talked about it then. I had to do it when I was with the 101st in Vietnam. I've no problems with shaving it."

"Okay," the battalion commander said. "Because when I tell the lieutenants and captains—most of whom, I admit, also wear mustaches—they're going to say to me, 'Well, what about the S-3,' you? And now I can tell them you're shaving yours off."

Ruderman scratched the back of his head now, wondering, it's safe to assume, how this roundelay of his much-maligned mustache was going over. "I was past the point of being a rebel, so it really didn't bother me," he said, before adding, after an exquisite pause, "but it was the first time my wife saw me without a mustache, and *she* almost fainted."

Interestingly enough, a couple of months later, Ruderman's unit went up to West Point to support the Academy's summer training program. Ruderman was in command of the unit's advance party. The colonel had jumped with the rest of the advance party and gotten a little banged around, requiring some patching up. He was flying back to Bragg that night. But before he left, he spent three hours with Ruderman, who was obliged to show him the progress the advance party was making.

That night, Ruderman got a call from his battalion commander, who was still back at Bragg. "Colonel So-and-so came back praising you to the skies," he told Ruderman. "He said he never saw a major so in charge of an operation as he'd seen you at West Point." Ruderman answered, "Jesus, the drugs they gave him when they patched him up really must have been potent." In all honesty, Ruderman didn't feel he'd merited praise quite that high. "Who knows? Maybe shaving off the mustache did it for me with that guy."

When Ruderman found out in the fall of 1982 that he was to

become commander of the 1st Battalion, 29th Field Artillery, 4th Infantry Division at Fort Carson, Colorado, he was excited but also somewhat apprehensive. Most of his experience had been with airborne artillery, which employed towed 105mm howitzers. But the battalion at Carson used 155mm howitzers; and while the principles were the same, the weapons at Carson were self-propelled. In other words, he'd be dealing with a very different, more complicated weapons system, all the problems inherent to a mechanized division, and at a post he'd never been assigned to before. So when he got the word, he was thrilled but leery.

The day before he took command, he called in his officers and told them those things he considered important. "I surprised some of them when I said, 'I'm not here to impress the people above me. I'll be here for two years hopefully, plus or minus six months, but I won't kiss anybody's ass. I'll do what's directed, and if it's a legitimate mission I'll do the best I can. But if I have to do things that I don't feel are right, all the people I answer to can do for me is make up my mind to retire after twenty years.' "

Then he said that if they made mistakes, honest mistakes, he wouldn't crucify them or throw a tantrum. But what he didn't want was to have to hear a lot of excuses or double-talk. The important thing, after all, was to make sure the mistake wasn't repeated and the officer learned from the experience.

When new soldiers were assigned to his battalion, Ruderman also made a point of talking to them. "I said, 'You may never see me face-to-face again, but at least you can say that in your two or three years here you've seen the battalion commander once and heard him talk to you other than in a battery or battalion formation.' " These talks were held in a classroom, and Ruderman tried to conduct them once a month. The chain of command was concerned about taking care of troops, and they worked for the sergeants, he'd tell them, so it was definitely a two-way street. Problems existed in the Army and in the battalion; but most were soluble if everyone cooperated. Finally Ruderman offered an overview, spelling out what the unit would be doing during the next six to eight months. "I felt it was important for them to hear me discussing things like that up-front and personal. Not simply to say, 'You volunteered for the Army. We didn't ask you to join us. Keep your nose clean, period.' That was the old Army's way of doing things." Ruderman brushed an intrusive speck off his rainbow-colored necktie with his nail-chewed thumb. "When I was a lieutenant, lieutenant colonels were old farts. Never saw them. If you were ever talked to by your battalion commander, you were in trouble. Well, times have changed for the better during the past eighteen years."

Although at West Point he'd been taught the importance of following rules and regulations, as battalion commander Ruderman tended to apply them in his own way. For example, while he was at Carson, a sergeant in his battalion, who'd been a passenger in a car, had been killed in an accident. After a few weeks, Ruderman learned that the VA was not going to award the family benefits they'd normally been entitled to because the sergeant allegedly had been drunk. The driver of the car, who'd survived, said they'd been drinking. But that didn't tell Ruderman the sergeant had been drunk. And even after the hospital sent a report citing the sergeant's alleged alcohol blood content, Ruderman couldn't forget that even if the sergeant had been drinking, he hadn't driven the car.

What Ruderman decided to do was help the widow write a long letter to the VA, protesting their decision. "Probably applying the duty, honor, country standard, I did not do the right thing," Ruderman said. "But what was right, I decided, was to try to help the widow, not accept the regulations the VA cited; and it didn't strike me as right their kids weren't going to get money I thought they were entitled to either. Don't misunderstand. It wasn't a crusade on my part, just the way I happened to approach this particular incident."

Not too surprisingly, a number of officers enjoyed working for Ruderman. One member of his staff who'd had a chance to move on to higher headquarters turned the opportunity down. "No, I want to stay right here in the battalion, I want to keep working for you," the officer said. When Ruderman answered, "You know, I won't always be here," the officer shook his head. "I don't care," he said, "I like what I'm doing. There's nothing else I want to do right now."

Lest I be tempted to think Ruderman was a saint in armor, he mentioned in the next breath a major who'd approached him, saying, "I don't think things are going to work out between us, I think I better leave." Ruderman said that after they talked it over, the major decided to stay, and things eventually worked out pretty well. "Not as well as they did with the first guy; but then, in my opinion, the major wasn't as good as the first guy,'' Ruderman said.

He knew he'd probably never have a chance to be more in charge than he was as a battalion commander; and, unquestionably, battalion command was a heady experience for that reason. The job was certainly consuming. Ruderman usually arrived at his office at six in the morning and didn't get back home till six or seven at night.

"I did the best I could. I didn't have the only way to be successful, and I didn't have all the answers. We did some things well. For instance, we went out to Fort Irwin, the National Training Center in the Mohave Desert. Irwin's where we take armored and mechanized infantry troops for about three weeks and they fight a sophisticated, computerized battle with a simulated Soviet force. It's demanding, and there are a lot of injuries, back sprains, heat casualties, a number of burns. That was Irwin, and the battalion performed extremely well, and yes, battalion command was probably the high point of my career till now,'' Ruderman said. "Although I do sometimes wonder how many people who say all the great things about battalion command really feel that way. On the other hand, I think I did appreciate it in a unique way, because until my years as a major I never strove for it, nor did I realize I'd have a competitive chance to attain to that level.''

Attending the Army War College for a year, beginning the summer of 1985, Ruderman has had occasion to reflect that his career has been everything he'd hoped it would be, and, thinking back on how he'd survived some of his earliest assignments, even exceeded his brightest expectations. Has Ruderman, in effect, beaten the system? "Certainly if you sat down and analyzed my career and efficiency reports with 90 percent of the guys who are at the War College this year, you'd wonder what I'm doing here.''

The first really outstanding efficiency report Ruderman received, he said, wasn't until he'd become an aide to General Brown. "He wrote the usual stuff about what a good job I did. But then he added the comment, 'Of the eleven aides I've had, he's equal to the best.' And words to the effect that he found I had excellent judgment and sought my opinion on troop-leading in Vietnam and found my comments to be 100 percent worthy, valid, and so on. That made me feel good to read in a general's rating of me.''

The word among young officers was, Ruderman said, you could screw up as lieutenants but have the slope of your efficiency reports ascending; and once you get up, don't slide back down. "Well, I have a fluctuating graph. I hit a peak as an aide, and then I went down and up. Down in ROTC and didn't get another max again until I was a major. Now I'd venture to say there are guys in this Carlisle class who never got anything but a max efficiency report. I've had guys tell me that. Me, I was always amazed when I got a max."

After completing Carlisle, Ruderman said, he wouldn't mind going back to Leavenworth to teach at the Command and General Staff College, or remain at Carlisle as an instructor, which is what Howie Boone did for two years. Ruderman said Boone's Leadership and Management Department was one he'd like to join, although he didn't believe that Boone, whom he liked, would consider him if a job became available. "I know there are people here who don't take me seriously." It bothers him they don't, he clearly implies, because, knowing his true worth, he believes they should.

When I asked how he explained his success in the Army—success he'd achieved doing it pretty much his way—Ruderman said, "I don't know, I don't know. I've never gone out of my way to attach myself to anybody's coattails, never made a crusade of cultivating people in the know or in powerful positions. I have no sugar daddies. I was an aide only once, and my general retired after Vietnam and I've never called him for a favor. There are War College students here—one guy keeps his Mercedes convertible in the commanding general's garage." Ruderman made a face, cursing below his breath. "Anyway, there are officers who've gotten earlier promotions who are undoubtedly smarter than me, but I doubt they're necessarily better. And, as I said, when I think how I survived my years as a lieutenant and captain, how can I have any complaints about being at Carlisle now?" At Carlisle, by the way, Ruderman sported no mustache, and perhaps that explained the wild ties.

One reason Ruderman's done well is so obvious, it's easy to overlook: He genuinely enjoys being in the military, being part of the group, and even likes the old-fashioned stuff such as drills and ceremonies. "A pain in the ass at times, but I learned I did not dislike it," he said. "I'll never forget when I was teaching ROTC, wondering if I wanted to remain in the Army. One of the officers got promoted and there was a ceremony, and the wife of one of the lieutenant colonels said to me, 'What's this about your considering leaving the Army? I watched you during the ceremony, the way you snapped to and marched. You're not going to get out. It's in you.' I'll never forget her saying that, although it surprised me it was so noticeable.''

Another reason for Ruderman's success is that his units produced because, I think, people working for him put themselves out, took the extra step. He'd probably treated them more decently than most, was certainly less inclined to hang them; and he undoubtedly made their jobs more enjoyable because he's comfortable laughing at life and having a good time—a valuable gift too often unacknowledged, especially in a work situation.

An extension of that is while Ruderman appears ordinary on the surface, in reality he's one of those ''ordinary'' men easy to underestimate. Clearly his understanding has continued to develop when that of cleverer men has dried up, and he's been a better officer at forty-two than he was at thirty-two, though at forty-two his responsibilities were far greater.

''I don't think you will, but don't misunderstand that any levity or sense of humor distracts or interferes with my personal sense of duty or mission accomplishment,'' Ruderman said. ''I've done things in my job with my people that make life a little more tolerable. But I've done the right things when things were important to be done right.''

''I never doubted it,'' I said, although ''never'' might have been stretching matters in the beginning.

Ruderman nodded. Just as long as I understood that, he seemed to be saying.

But then, evidently not wishing to conclude on a grace note so painfully solemn, Ruderman said that when he'd run into Joe DeFrancisco yesterday, he'd asked if DeFrancisco and I were finished talking. ''When Joe said you were, I said, 'Boy, you other guys must really be fucked up, because Ivan told me I'm the only normal guy he's talked to so far.''

Laughing, I clearly understood that in the world according to Ruderman, wearing a dog tag on your big toe hurts only when you can't feel a thing.

NADAL, Ramon A., II (Tony)
COL (Ret.) INF 581-68-6029
BORN: 27 Dec 35, Ft. Benning, GA

Tony Nadal, who'd retired from the Army as a full colonel in 1981, never much cared for the harassment built into the plebe system, neither as a cadet nor, later, as a West Point instructor. He remembered that in the spring of 1955, or during the last two weeks before his plebe year ended and he was recognized, the harassment only seemed to increase. It was the upperclassmen's last opportunity to get their best shots in, and Nadal recalled they used to make plebes jump under the tables in the mess hall, ordering them to do push-ups during the meals. But Nadal would surreptitiously take a pat of butter and slip it on one of the rungs of his chair first. Then, when the upperclassman sitting at the head of the table told Nadal to knock out ten, Nadal hopped under the table, snatched that pat of butter, and vigorously rubbed it into the upperclassman's shoes before complying with the required Mickey Mouse. Of course, there are few things harder than removing butter from a shoe, then spit-shining that shoe and achieving the gleaming shine required of a cadet, yet Nadal twice pulled off his butter act of rebellion.

When he was given the order to do the push-ups in the mess hall a third time, he grabbed for the butter, threw himself forward, and reached for the upperclassman's shoes. But that day, the upperclassman kicked out under the table, catching Nadal flush above the eye. Nadal saw stars and blood began to spurt, requiring his going to the hospital, where they stitched up the cut. Hardly a tragedy, considering he could have lost an eye. "At the time I thought the guy was a horse's ass," Nadal said of the unnamed upperclassman, who's now a major general. "And I'm still not overly fond of him."

218

Nadal, who was born two days after Christmas in 1935, lived in Puerto Rico from 1937 to 1945 and attended school there through the fifth grade. While he speaks English with a charming Desi Arnaz accent, Nadal's daring act in the mess hall underlined two grainier traits than mere charm—physical courage and rebelliousness—and it's hardly an exaggeration to suggest that those traits threaded his more than twenty-year military career.

The ultimate volunteer, Nadal continually sought dangerous assignments, while his rebelliousness gradually assumed a slightly more respectable form—agitating for change in a large, unwieldy organization notorious for resisting change.

His wife characterizes Nadal's carryings-on then as "tilting at windmills and falling on swords." Nadal more prosaically affirms he was often in hot water, especially during the last ten years of his career. An officer who knew him those years said of Nadal, "There were those in the Army who thought he was the greatest thing since chop suey; others considered him the scum of the earth."

Yet Nadal had yearned to be an officer from his earliest days. "I never figured out why I went to West Point, but I remember people asking me what I wanted to be when I was in the first and second grades and saying, 'An Army officer. I'm going to West Point.'" His father, an Academy graduate, would have preferred Nadal's attending school elsewhere.

Nadal's father came from a family of eight, and when his parents died, the children were sprinkled among their relatives. An uncle who'd helped raise him managed to get the young man an appointment to West Point. Though he was poorly educated and spoke fractured English, Nadal's father knew the Academy was his one opportunity for a college education. He had to survive and make a go of the place, and his memories of the Academy are of staying up late at night, a blanket draped overhead and flashlight in hand, forever studying. The harassment his father caught because of language difficulties and prior poor schooling was brutal, and Nadal says his father's nightmares about West Point still disturb his sleep, though he's in his eighties. But it was at West Point, Nadal also said, where he himself had been taught "to go to the sound of the guns," and that phrase became a kind of moral amulet.

Tony Nadal's first permanent assignment was platoon leader and executive officer with the 1st Battalion, 46th Infantry, based in Munich. A mechanized infantry battalion attached to Seventh Army headquarters as a special reserve unit, it was part of a ready reaction force that had first call on the latest equipment and received more field training than other units. Yet Nadal also remembers whole divisions moving en masse across campestral Germany for months at a time, traveling northwest from Munich almost to Stuttgart, a total of perhaps sixty thousand troops playing soldier and tearing up the countryside.

With the 46th Infantry he'd first learned of a Special Forces unit stationed in Germany and tried to join it; but his battalion wouldn't release him. Nadal barely knew Vietnam existed while he was stationed in Europe; rather it was the nature of Special Forces, the nearest thing the Army had to commando units, he found so appealing. "The more gung ho the organization, the more *macho*, the more I wanted to be in it." Although he again requested reassignment to Special Forces upon his return to the States, the Army was preparing to send him to teach ROTC at Loyola College in Baltimore, "which would have been just the pits." But because Nadal had placed "No preference" next to "Protestant" on a form he'd filled out, the college thought that meant he was an atheist or agnostic and requested a replacement. That left his assignment officer with a problem late in the game. Then the guy noted Nadal had twice volunteered for Special Forces. Hell, problem solved, next case.

Sent to the Special Warfare Center at Fort Bragg, Nadal was surprised to learn that the skills he'd acquired the previous three and a half years in Germany as an infantry officer weren't especially valued by Special Forces troops, some of whom had already been to Vietnam and Laos two or three times, performing commando-type operations like setting up ambushes and living off the land behind enemy lines.

"When you arrived at Special Forces, you got your green beret right away," Nadal remembered. "But you only got your patch, what they called a 'flash,' to put on the hat after you qualified." Nadal attended school for six weeks, where he learned demolitions, communications, and first aid. He recalled fashioning a soap dish bomb that blew away a car and learned how to use a silent submachine gun. When he began hearing stories about Vietnam from soldiers who'd already been there, Nadal, smelling gunpowder and glory, immediately put in for Vietnam. But he got sidetracked for a number of months because of subsequent American reaction to the October 1962 Cuban missile crisis.

One day, he was ordered to go home, gather all his gear, and report back. Then he was placed on a bus and sent to Fort Knox,

Kentucky. There he and other officers were told their task was to train a battalion of Cuban soldiers who'd participate in the invasion of Cuba. The plan was for an authentic battalion of Cubans to lead a parade down the streets of Havana, marching just ahead of a massive invading American Army. "Here comes the Cubans who've liberated Cuba from Castro!" Nadal, who spoke fluent Spanish, was slotted to be the battalion's operations officer. He remembered that the Cubans, unused to the cold, came down with sore throats, runny noses, and numerous cases of pneumonia. More important, the American Army never did get to invade Cuba, and so that American-trained Cuban battalion never did get to lead the glorious victory parade down Havana's main drag. Which explains why, after a couple of months, Nadal returned to Fort Bragg and resumed his own training program prior to commanding a twelve-man detachment preparing to leave for Vietnam.

When he arrived there toward the end of 1963, Nadal's unit was sent to Nam Dong, which is south of the A Shau Valley, where the Laotian border cuts in. Nadal's detachment was to run patrols along the border and ambush infiltrators.

The native troops he commanded were typically Vietnamese picked up off the streets of Hue and Da Nang, "brought out there by the press-gang, or something. I really don't know how they got them, but they weren't very good troops," Nadal said. "They weren't accustomed to living in the jungle; they were city boys, and it was a struggle to make soldiers of them."

Nadal had a counterpart South Vietnamese team of Special Forces troops as well as interpreters, and his role was to advise the South Vietnamese Special Forces. "But in my case, in most cases, the Americans came in, super gung ho, the big overpowering Americans, all charged up and ready to go. And the poor Vietnamese, who'd been fighting since 1946, looked at them, and said, 'Oh, shit.' In effect, we took over. We planned ambushes. I was good at that, and my camp had more kills than any other in I Corps during the time I commanded it."

Nadal remembered finding a Viet Cong camp at the base of a ridge separating Vietnam from Laos. The camps were difficult to attack, because only a few, heavily guarded trails led to them. Nadal and his troops ambushed the camp, chasing the VC away. Then Nadal stayed behind for a day or two with maybe a dozen troops, waiting for the VC to come back. "Eventually a VC point or squad would return, and we'd blow them away," Nadal said.

"Those who could, ran like hell. I had an M-2 carbine, fully automatic, not a particularly good weapon, and my own revolver, a .357 Magnum."

His only contact with the outside world was a World War II OSS radio powered by hand-cranked generators. He used Morse code. If there was an emergency, he'd write the message on what was called a "one time" pad. "This was the romantic period of my war days. Here I was, a young kid leading these guys in the jungle. I'd get up in the morning and say, 'Where are we going today? Well, we'll patrol over here, we'll patrol over there.' The war hadn't gotten nasty yet. We were doing a little ambushing and counterambushing." His superiors were headquartered in Da Nang and would check in with Nadal once every two or three weeks.

Nadal was supplied by Army Caribous or Air Force paradrops. They parachuted cows in. "You talk about a sight to behold." A number of cows would break their legs upon landing, so the troops had to shoot them right away. They'd parachute twenty chickens in a wicker basket and live pigs. They fed a pig for a while, slaughtering it when they got sick of C rations.

Toward the end of Nadal's six-month tour, there were increasing indications that more and more VC and NVA troops were using the trails Nadal was patrolling. He remembered briefing a colonel accompanied by a second colonel based in Saigon, telling the first colonel of the increased traffic along the trails. But the second colonel interrupted, saying, "Oh, I think Captain Nadal's probably exaggerating a little bit." To this day, Nadal wishes he'd responded, "Hey, you son of a bitch, you've never been out there, you've never even seen the goddamn trails. Come with me and I'll show you."

Anyway, after six months, Nadal returned to Fort Bragg to train a replacement detachment. At about this time, too, Westmoreland was dispatched to Vietnam as General Harkins' deputy and successor, and because Westmoreland was one of the Army's fair-haired boys, everyone had a sense the Pentagon was beginning to send in the first team.

Less than a year later, as the war became ever more serious, Westmoreland requested use of the 173rd Airborne Brigade, then based in Okinawa. It arrived in May 1965, the first Army combat unit to land in South Vietnam. Hearing of its arrival, Nadal thought, "That's where I want to go," and he requested transfer to the 173rd. The Army, however, insisted he needed experience as a company commander, and he was on orders bound for Korea. But

Korea was too quiet, and Nadal kept phoning his assignment officer, telling him, "Screw Korea, I need to go to the sound of the guns." Finally, while he was home on leave, Nadal got a call ordering him to report to Fort Benning. Nadal didn't know it at the time, but the 1st Cav was filling its ranks to wartime strength at Benning, prior to leaving for Vietnam in thirty days.

When Nadal reported in, he asked to be made a company commander; but no command assignments were available, and he'd been slotted to fill one as a communications officer. Nadal said he didn't want to be a commo officer and asked if he could walk around and try to find himself another job. The major conducting the interview looked at him strangely but finally said, "Well, okay, but come back tomorrow and tell me if you found something."

Although this was hardly standard procedure, Benning was in a frenzy of preparation as the 1st Cav rushed to meet its deployment date. When Nadal got to the 3rd Brigade, he managed to gain an interview with the commander of the 1st Battalion, Lt. Col. Harold Moore. "Sir, I'm looking for a job," he said.

"You're what?" Moore asked, staring at him. Moore saw a solidly built young man who stood at five-eleven, with big brown eyes and square, almost Slavic features.

"I just arrived here yesterday and I'm trying to find a battalion that has a job I want," Nadal said. "I want to be a company commander, and I'd like to know what you have available."

"Well, that's not exactly the way we do it in the Army," Moore said with a cautious smile.

But when Nadal quickly mentioned he'd already served six months in Vietnam with Special Forces, Moore asked him to sit down. And as they continued talking, Moore not only learned details of Nadal's Vietnam experiences but also that Nadal had been a cadet when Moore taught at West Point. Finally Moore said, "Well, you seem to have certain possibilities. Let me call my brigade commander." Then he told the colonel commanding the 3rd Brigade that he wanted Nadal, which required the colonel's calling division headquarters, requesting the transfer. And that, roughly, was how Nadal ended up commander of A Company, 1st Battalion, 7th Cav, which was soon to be absorbed into the 1st Cav.

As for Moore, he was to become, in Nadal's words, "my dear friend, ego model, and everything else. This guy, who later became a three-star general, was one of the great soldiers in the Army, the only colonel I knew in Vietnam who'd leave his helicopter and go out and walk around with one of his platoons. And if contact was made, he was often the *first* officer to join a platoon in combat."

Moore would say, "I want to sniff out what's going on, because it lets me know how big a fight it is and how many people I have to commit." *The New York Times* published a story on him during the early years of the war called "Hal Moore, the Man Who Finds the Viet Cong."

Nadal said that when Moore was his commander, they were always in battle. Other battalions would seek but not find the enemy, yet when Moore's troops patrolled, "we were forever stepping in the middle of shit. And when we found something, Moore wouldn't let go," Nadal continued. "Just tenacious as hell. The troops had sort of ambivalent feelings about him. They couldn't help admiring his personal courage and concern for them; but they also wondered what he was going to get them into next."

At first Moore made him battalion S-2 (intelligence), but he promised Nadal would be given a company to command in a few months. Meanwhile, at Benning, Nadal helped train the battalion in ambush and counterambush tactics he'd picked up in Special Forces. A month later, the battalion was put aboard the U.S.S. *Rose* and spent another four weeks sailing to Vietnam.

The first edition of the 1st Cav, which fought in Vietnam during the first year of heavy American deployment, was one of the very best. In the early 1960s, the Army and Air Force were competing over who would control the use of helicopters, newly perceived as a major deployment tool. It was decided to perform a test, Nadal said. One Army division would use helicopters the Army way; another would use them the Air Force way. Put in charge of the division doing it the Army's way was Maj. Gen. Harry Kinnard, who was told to pick the best Army officers he could find. So he naturally chose brigade and battalion commanders of the caliber of Hal Moore. Not only were the officers choice, but also the privates and sergeants who fleshed out the units were deliberately kept together for longer than normal periods of time. It was a division, then, stacked with talent and cemented with built-in cohesiveness because of the Army's intense desire to beat out the Air Force, which the Army did.

In August 1965, its advance party arrived in Vietnam and was told the 1st Cav's mission would be to safeguard the country's Central Highlands—in effect, prevent the North Vietnamese from cutting the country in two, between Pleiku and Qui Nhon. That being the mission, it was decided to locate the division's headquarters at An Khe, a small town along Highway 19, near Mang Yang Pass.

The division's main body landed at Qui Nhon in September, and Nadal remembered being impressed that the landing seemed to go off so smoothly. The Army, he noted, is an organization that is designed to fight wars but spends most of its time in peacetime garrisons. And that's one of the reasons the peacetime Army seems so awkward and clumsy—the organization doesn't fit the situation.

But arriving in Vietnam, Nadal remembered, suddenly the organization fit the circumstances. "Before we got there, someone said we were going to arrive and the ship would anchor at five-seven, and, by God, the anchor went plink at five-seven. Someone else said that I'd be on the third landing craft, which would heave to at seven-four, and at seven-four I was putting my foot over the side and the landing craft was there. All the pieces fell into place and fit."

The division spent the first couple of weeks in Vietnam trying to build a base camp. In this instance, however, the pieces didn't fit because the troops were grossly underequipped. "You're trying to cut down superhard tropical trees with a dull ax and bayonets," Nadal said with a groan. Nevertheless, on October 1 the division assumed responsibility for An Khe and most of Highway 19, and about a month after he'd arrived in Vietnam Nadal was made a company commander, with about 150 troops under him. The nature of the war, he quickly realized, had changed. "It stopped being a small-patrol kind of fun thing. 'Let's go out patrol and come back for a beer.'" Now big units, battalions, maybe eight hundred troops, would be flown into forbiddingly strange areas, looking to engage not a dozen VC-stragglers but well-trained, well-equipped NVA battalions.

On October 19 the Special Forces camp at Plei Me, south of Pleiku, was attacked by a strong NVA force. First a Special Forces reserve unit was given the mission of breaking through to the encircled Special Forces camp; they did, but were then themselves encircled. When a South Vietnamese armored column sent to try to rescue the Americans asked for help, General Westmoreland told the 1st Cav to move in. On October 23 the division committed a battalion, then a brigade. Ensuing events would be known as the Ia Drang Valley campaign, and the 1st Cav's mission was really to search for the enemy and destroy all they could engage between Plei Me and the Cambodian border.

The brigade, including Nadal's company, spent weeks looking for NVA troops, patrolling areas of twenty square miles at a stretch, but couldn't seem to find them. Then they were about to come out when it was decided to look one last time. This was November 14, and they deplaned at Landing Zone X Ray, which is adjacent to the Chu Pong Range. Less than two hours later, a platoon from B Company, 1st Battalion, moving up a heavily jungled ridge, came under intense fire and was quickly and skillfully cut off.

When Nadal hit the ground, Colonel Moore told him to have his company link up with B Company preparatory to seeking out the engaged platoon. One of Nadal's own platoons had already landed, and they were up forward. There was a creekbed that ran along the edge of the landing zone. Nadal heard firing coming from that direction and thought he'd reconnoiter the tributary. He found his friend and West Point classmate, fellow company commander John Herren, lying on the ground, and nearby was the sergeant of his own platoon. "John, what are you doing here?" Nadal asked.

"You better get your ass down or you'll get shot," Herren said.

So Nadal hunkered down and asked his platoon sergeant, "Where's Lieutenant Taft?" Robert Taft was his lead platoon leader. When the sergeant said that Taft was dead, in the ditch, Nadal said, "Why'd you leave him there?" The sergeant said the troops hadn't been able to extricate him.

But one of the rules Colonel Moore had established before they'd reached Vietnam was that they were never to leave dead Americans on the battlefield. He'd told the troops, "You may die, but you won't be left there. We'll bring you home." Remembering Moore's admonition, Nadal now said, "Shit, we can't leave Lieutenant Taft there." He put down his rifle and took off his pack, and so did his radio operator, Sergeant Gell, and they began heading toward the ditch.

Not only had there been a tough fight in that ditch, but also part of the fight was still going on when Nadal found Lieutenant Taft. Lying next to him was another soldier, Wisnewski, who was still alive but shot in the gut. Nadal and Gell picked Wisnewski up and brought him back as the NVA tossed defective grenades into the ditch. The missiles kept going off, making a whoof sound, but they failed to release shrapnel. After rescuing Wisnewski, Nadal and

Gell returned to the ditch for Lieutenant Taft. By this time another platoon arrived, enabling Herren and his people to pull back. A and B companies now formed a tight perimeter around the landing zone, joined there by C Company, as the intensity of firing kept building up. One artillery battery, six guns, not a lot, was supporting them. Air strikes were called in, but they accomplished little, because the enemy was almost in their face and the air strikes kept landing behind them.

At about five o'clock, A and B companies got word from Colonel Moore to make an assault and try to rescue B Company's platoon, still encircled by the enemy. The troops fixed bayonets and started moving forward. They were walking in waist-high grass punctuated by small trees, and, Nadal remembered, it was almost like traipsing on a Sunday in an uncultivated park. They'd moved forward about fifty feet when all shit broke loose as suddenly they found themselves in the midst of an NVA battalion preparing to attack. The contending troops were maybe five to ten feet apart, still in high grass. The trees seemed to resemble scrub oak, and near the trees were huge termite hills, from behind which the NVA were shooting. You could see the gun flashes, yellow stabs of light. The combat was so close that it was impossible to exercise control.

One of the things Nadal had told his company before the battle was that if someone got shot, not to attempt his rescue immediately. " 'Shoot the son of a bitch who shot him first, then go to his rescue.' But I remember a guy getting shot, and one of my best sergeants, Sergeant Floyd, starting to go for him. I yelled out, 'Floyd, don't go out there, goddamn it!' But he said, 'Sir, that's one of my guys.' I yelled again, 'Don't go out there!' But Floyd went to rescue one of his people, and he got killed."

A little later, during a lull, Nadal was standing up, trying to see what was happening. Next to him was his forward observer. Next to the forward observer was his radio operator. On the other side of Nadal was his own radio operator, Sergeant Gell. Suddenly an enemy machine gun opened up. "I'm standing talking to my forward observer, and I can see bullets as they burrow into his radio operator, then as they burrow into the forward observer. Both men fall. I turned to Sergeant Gell, and he drops shot. The machine gun kills the two guys on my right and the guy on my left, although Sergeant Gell didn't die right away. I roll him over and take off his radio; I have to use it to talk to my troops.

"I call my third platoon, my reserves, telling them to move out and attempt an assault on the left. Then I go over, leading the assault. We advance maybe another fifty feet, but that's it, and people are falling all around. It's getting dark, and we've suffered a lot of casualties. Herren calls Moore and says B Company can't advance either. Moore agrees we should pull back.

"Because my forward observer is dead, I call for artillery support myself. I say, 'I want smoke. I want it almost on top of us. But I don't want any live stuff.' Smoke would provide cover while we withdrew. But the fucking battery doesn't have any smoke. They have white phosphorus, which is very dangerous. When that stuff hits the ground, it explodes in a big white cloud, sending out these tiny particles of white phosphorus that get on your skin and just burn through you."

Yet Nadal decided he had to risk it, because without any kind of cover none of his people would have a chance to get to the ditch. So it was white phosphorus, six rounds, and they landed in front of his troops, making the densest smoke possible. Miraculously, none of his people were hurt. The barrage was so effective that Nadal decided to call back and ask the artillery to do it one more time. Another volley of six rounds and, again, none of his people were hurt. The thick cloud of smoke allowed Nadal to police up his wounded and transport them to the relative safety of the ditch. The smoke also temporarily disconcerted the NVA and helped quiet things down. "From that day on, I tell you," Nadal said, "I was guided by an unseen hand."

That night the ditch was assaulted by the enemy, but they were beaten off, although in the morning they attacked again, and C Company was overrun in hand-to-hand combat. Other troops were ordered to C Company's aid, including a platoon from Nadal's company. The landing zone and battalion headquarters were being threatened. Nadal, leading his platoon, advanced a third of the way and came under intense enemy fire, but the NVA didn't break through, although the fighting lasted all morning. Reinforcements couldn't be flown in to the landing zone; the firing still was too intense, and it wasn't till one o'clock that afternoon that a battalion from the 5th Cav, trekking overland, reached the bruised 7th. By evening, two battalions were defending the landing zone, and the Americans were out of danger. The battle dissipated on the third day, with the enemy leaving over eight hundred dead. The 1st Cav lost between sixty and eighty, Nadal recollected, and suffered maybe more than a hundred wounded.

For recovering the bodies in the ditch, leading the assault when the reserve platoon was committed, calling in the white phosphorus, and for being the last man to withdraw and covering the company with fire as his troops made it back safely, Nadal won the Silver Star.

It meant a lot that he could tell himself he'd performed well in battle. "I was a good company commander. My bosses thought so, and I was given efficiency reports that said I was one of the best company commanders they'd ever seen. But if you're a professional soldier, leading men into battle is what you're about, and that's why I wanted to command a company." Yet he was also proud that during the time he'd commanded, his company suffered less casualties than the other companies in the battalion. "And in the main, I guess I did the right things in the Ia Drang because, after that, I could practically do no wrong as a company commander, and it really solidified my relationship with my troops."

Reaching for a coffee-table book bursting with photographs of the 1st Cav, Nadal said, "One picture's worth a thousand words, right?" And he began thumbing through the pages. "That's Hal Moore," he said after a minute. Moore, who seemed to resemble the impassive Coach Tom Landry of the Dallas Cowboys, was standing bareheaded, talking to Maj. Gen. John Norton, who'd succeeded Kinnard as commander of the 1st Cav. "I could tell you a hundred stories about Moore."

Instead, Nadal began flipping through the book again. "There's Kinnard." Nadal said he was supersmart, a general officer who'd compelled respect without beating up on people. "The military historian S.L.A. Marshall somewhere calls Kinnard 'the gentlest man to ever graduate from West Point.' "

Then Nadal turned ahead to a photo that meant a lot to him. "That's a famous shot of my people patrolling in the Ia Drang." Perhaps twenty troops, spaced apart, were walking through high grass, their weapons extended.

Nadal is not a particularly modest or reticent man. Yet thumbing through the book, his voice seemed to modulate, becoming increasingly softer, almost tender. And pointing to a second picture of Moore and other shots of his troops, it was as if Moore were no longer his former battalion commander but an older brother now, or a cherished uncle, and the soldiers in his company were cousins

Nadal had grown up near, or younger brothers toward whom he still felt protective.

Yet Nadal is the first to acknowledge that all officers over in Vietnam weren't Moore and all units assigned there weren't the 1st Cav. Moore was an extraordinary commander, Nadal said, and there wasn't any question he shared burdens. And not only in terms of physical danger, but also Moore lived unostentatiously, spending his year in Vietnam in a tent. But this was not true of all senior officers. Others had houses built for them.

"One of the things that used to piss me off when I was over there as a company commander was that an engineering battalion took time to build a couple of houses for the generals while we were trying to build a base camp with inadequate tools," Nadal said.

He also remembered spending thirty-seven days in sporadic combat, after which he had two days to shower, clean up, and throw his funky, dirty clothes away before going out on the perimeter. A little time off, naturally, he wanted to get away, walk around the camp, go to the PX. "But there you'd see the Doughnut Dollies, the Red Cross girls, all making out with the lieutenants in the aviation companies and the quartermasters, and all the other rear-area assholes. It kind of pisses you off to come back from operations in the field and see that kind of fat cat living."

In January 1966, the 1st Cav made the first of its many entries into the Bong Son region, and it was during this campaign that Nadal crashed in a helicopter. At the time he was operations officer of the 2nd Battalion, 7th Cav, 1st Cavalry Division, spending four or five hours a day in that helicopter, and, over a rugged mountain area with trees perhaps a hundred feet high, the engine simply quit.

The pilot was a young lieutenant and the copilot an old warrant officer. The moment the engine went out, the copilot took over. The older man just automatically assumed command and the lieutenant was smart enough to let him do it. "I stayed fairly calm," Nadal remembered. "I called battalion headquarters, gave our position, and said we were about to crash. The artillery liaison officer was sitting next to me. It was just us and the pilot and copilot. I considered jumping out before the son of a bitch hit the trees, but I didn't. Instead, I tightened my seat belt."

The warrant officer had mistakenly thought he saw a small clearing, but coming through the trees Nadal could hear the rotor slapping at branches. What the warrant officer had thought was grass turned out to be bamboo, and they landed on a canopy of the stuff, about twenty-five feet off the ground. The bamboo bent over, cushioning the helicopter's impact. Yet Nadal hit his head on the radio and still has a slight scar on his forehead. The warrant officer bit through his lip, and the liaison officer banged his head. But considering what might have happened, they all walked away more than fortunate.

"When I stepped out, I stepped on bamboo that was maybe three feet off the ground," Nadal remembered. He used his portable radio to call his base. "I'll never forget my radio operator back at the base saying, 'Roger, sir, you crashed in the jungle. I'd like to give you a sit-rep,' and he starts giving this long, long report on where the platoons in the battalion were in code. But I'm not interested in that; I'm in trouble and want help." Nadal shook his head in disbelief, as if to say, Jesus, the literal-mindedness of some people. Eventually a platoon came on the ground to lead the men from the helicopter out. That was 1966, his second tour, after which most men would have had enough of Vietnam.

But Nadal volunteered to go back there a third time, in the spring of 1968. He'd been teaching psychology and military leadership at West Point that year. The summer was coming, and the war was still raging. Nadal had approached his boss, the chairman of the Military Psychology and Leadership Department, and asked to be released from his teaching assignment—usually a three-year tour—so he might return to Vietnam. But the department head said that that was quite impossible. Nadal thought, "People are shooting at each other over there, and here I am, stuck teaching at West Point, and they aren't going to let me go. Shit, I've got to get back to that war somehow."

Leave it to Nadal to learn there was a program at West Point providing for a handful of officers to go to another installation during the summer—usually it was to the Pentagon—and assist at a Regular Army activity, so long as that assistance could be viewed in terms of facilitating the teaching process. While such a program existed, no one before had thought of using it to get back to Vietnam. But Nadal came up with the idea of studying how other armies were functioning there—the Australians, the Filipinos, the Koreans, the Thais. His boss agreed to present his proposal to the Academic Board for financial consideration; but they refused to foot the bill. Undiscouraged, Nadal said, "Give me a chance to do a little shopping around, and I'll come up with the financing." Probably thinking nothing would come of it, he was told, "Sure, go ahead, see what you can do."

Nadal went to the Pentagon and, just as at Benning, began knocking on doors. "Cross my heart, this is the way it happened," Nadal said. He'd gone to a couple of offices, made his pitch, and was told nothing doing. About the third or fourth door had a sign that said, "Advanced Research Project Agency." He walked in, said, "Sir, I'm Major Nadal from West Point, and I've a proposal for you. I want to do a study about Vietnam." They talked a little while, and soon the officer in charge expressed some interest. Nadal kept talking. "I said, 'I want to go to Vietnam and use my social psychology and organizational behavior skills to look at the allies over there and see what they're really contributing, and I'll write you a report.'" After a while the officer said, "Hell, nobody's done that before. Okay, we'll pick up the tab." Then he wrote out the appropriate travel orders.

When Nadal returned to West Point, travel orders in hand, the people at the Academy were slightly aghast, their reaction being, "How'd you do it? How'd you get the money?" But because they'd let him seek out a sponsor, they now grudgingly had to let him go for the summer.

"The main thing I learned in Vietnam that third time was that armies are reflections of national experience," Nadal said. "For instance, the most significant impact on the Koreans is their DMZ. As a result, they have the most outrageous bunkers, deep in the ground." He spent two weeks with the Koreans and considered them good troops, although they had a constrained mission. They didn't go out patrolling. They had a perimeter they defended between Nha Trang and Qui Nhon. They had great troop density, and they pacified the hell out of their perimeter. But the whole NVA Army could have swept down a mile or two beyond it, and the Koreans wouldn't have yawned.

The Filipinos' camp was all concrete and whitewashed, and Nadal could have been back in Corregidor in the mid-1930s. "I imagine it was a direct reflection of the American Army, circa 1936. The Filipinos didn't do much fighting. They were there for three years, and I don't think they killed a single VC. But they sure had a nice camp. Everything was lined up; little rosebushes here and there."

Nadal spent a week with the Thais but didn't get a very good feel for them.

He found the Aussies very much like the Americans, slightly irreverent. "I went on a couple of patrols with them. There wasn't a nickel's difference between being with the Aussies and a good American rifle company. Oh, they still had batmen, and they'd stop in the middle of the day and brew up. Here it was, hotter than hell, humid, and yet they'd be making these great canteens of hot tea. They'd sit at noontime, blow on it, and sip up. Slurp. I remember they used Eagle brand condensed milk, and it was real sweet."

While he was with the Aussies Nadal observed, close up, how well their regimental rotation system worked. Unlike the Americans, who went over as individuals, the Australians rotated by battalions. One was being trained to go over to Vietnam, another was just being formed, and the third was serving in Vietnam. At the end of the year, the last would pull out, and each of the other two would move up one.

Their Army was modeled on the British regimental system. Nadal went on to say that studies from World War II showed that the British experienced considerably less battle fatigue, less battle trauma than the American Army, and one reason was the regimental system. If you were in, say, the Gloucester Regiment and you freaked out, you couldn't go home again, you couldn't afford to, because everyone there would know you'd broken down. Nor could you possibly lie about it, because the people you served with, your neighbors, would be among the first to know you weren't telling the truth.

Nadal believes, along with most American officers, that the U.S. rotational system helped undermine cohesion and unit loyalty in Vietnam. Before you got to know someone, the man would be gone. The American Army, Nadal suggested, chose against regimental rotation because Americans historically regard themselves as preeminently egalitarian, and if everyone's the same, how can the unit be so special? More important, *why* should the unit be so special? But units with intense esprit are inspired troops, Nadal insisted, and an essential ingredient of esprit is creating the feeling of *us* as special, of *us* against them, of *us* against the world, if need be.

(On November 8, 1986, or less than a year after Nadal pitched for regimental rotation, *The New York Times* carried a story with the lead, "The Army, in 'a major shift in American Army thinking,' will begin assigning its combat troops by unit rather than as individuals to lift morale, foster loyalty, and improve fighting ability, senior officers said today.")

I wonder how Nadal's wife reacted to his going over to Vietnam a third time. It was not all that common.

"I never asked her," he said. "I guess she knew by that time that that was my way."

Billie Nadal is a slender, naturally gracious woman, whose thick white hair sweeps across her forehead from a side part. She's wearing a red poncho and slacks. When she's called to the phone by her eight-year-old daughter, she stands with a smile, saying, not "Excuse me," but "Will you excuse me?" Her name, the clothes Billie wears, and her energetic but pleasant manner are unmistakably American, and she reminds me of Jean Arthur, someone refreshing and perky.

Her father, an artilleryman, retired as a colonel, Billie said. "I went to twenty-one schools in twelve years, and it became a kind of game after a while." She met Nadal at a party, when her father was stationed in Puerto Rico and she was attending high school there. They began seeing each other while Nadal was a cadet, and married at Fort Leavenworth soon after he'd graduated.

Although Billie thought she knew what to expect as an Army wife because she'd been an "Army brat," she believes she wasn't quite prepared for Vietnam, nor were most Army wives. "The idea of Tony and a few other Americans going off to some little-bitty Special Forces camp in the mountains was kind of scary. People might tell you about all the air support they'd be getting; but it was remote, and there wasn't very many of him."

Yet Nadal had volunteered for Special Forces and Vietnam, and because he'd wanted both so badly, Billie felt there was little she could say to convince him otherwise. "I might as well have been shouting to the wind if I'd asked him not to do it."

Most of the country didn't seem particularly aware of Vietnam then. But approximately two years later, when Nadal returned to Vietnam with the 1st Cav, everyone seemed to know exactly where the place was, and Billie was no exception. She found herself buying more newspapers than she was accustomed to reading, because she wanted to be up on the very latest news, and the 1st Cav was receiving a lot of media exposure.

At the same time, she tried to keep her three-year-old son from viewing snippets of the war on television. "But even as little as he was, he seemed to know what the war was about," Billie said. "He woke up a couple of nights, screaming, 'They killed my daddy, they killed my daddy!' And that sort of thing kind of tears you up at three in the morning." But Billie found that, like Lynne DeFrancisco, she simply couldn't stop watching TV, and occasionally her son would see it by accident. "Certainly if anything about the Vietnam War was on, I was going to watch it, I couldn't get enough of it. TV was so much more graphic, it was right there. A couple of times I caught fleeting glimpses of Tony's friends. They all looked a little skinnier, a little dirtier. But you thought, 'Gee, at least they're in one piece.'"

On the one hand, Billie felt better because Nadal had gone over the second time with American troops, a whole division of them, and just the sheer numbers gave her more confidence. On the other, she had a sense of an expanding war.

When the country turned against the war after Tet, Billie found herself angry. While she sympathized with certain aspects of the protest movement, her reaction was, Don't do this right now, when we need all the support we can get for the people fighting over there. And at one point, Nadal and Billie's father were serving in Vietnam simultaneously. When she got together with friends who were confirmed antiwar protesters, they'd avoid the subject of Vietnam entirely. "I'd think, 'They have their ideas, I have mine. But mine touch a little closer to home right now.'"

Although the Army was often criticized by the media, Billie felt it was the country that had let the Army down, now the other way around. "The country had committed all these people and hadn't followed through," she said. "I thought it was a case of tying the Army's hands behind its back."

Perhaps another part of the explanation was that those in power, America's presidents Kennedy, Johnson, and Nixon, had each inherited a different set of circumstances, and Billie doubted if any of them really understood what he was getting the country involved in. "We all thought Goldwater was raving mad when he ran for president in 1964, and then, really, the others did exactly what he said he'd do in Vietnam if he was elected. But maybe it was too late then. Maybe we should have gone and done it when Goldwater was talking about it. Although I was one of those who'd thought he was raving mad."

Of the posts Billie lived at during Nadal's Army career, one of her favorites, was West Point, where Nadal had taught from 1967 to 1970. He'd received a letter from the Academy while he was still serving with the 1st Cav, asking if he'd consider returning there as an instructor in the Military Psychology and Leadership Department. Nadal had done very well in psychology courses when he was a cadet, and the thought of teaching at West Point after completing his second tour in Vietnam seemed appealing. First, though, he would need to attend graduate school for a year and earn a masters in psych. He chose Oklahoma State University, because Billie's father was teaching ROTC there and she'd moved to Oklahoma to be near her parents while Nadal was completing his Vietnam tour.

"I've told a lot of people that I'd have been better prepared for Vietnam if I'd gone to graduate school first," he remarked. "There was so much written about behavior under stress, and when I was studying social psychology, a lot of the examples they used were similar to what I'd experienced in Vietnam. A lot of stuff on group cohesion, too." In any case, the psychology courses at graduate school proved so interesting to Nadal, he focused on them during the remainder of his military career after getting his degree. "Personnel, behavior, motivation—they became my bag."

Nadal found that living as an instructor at West Point was almost idyllic. You could walk to work, play racquetball in one of the finest gyms in the country, and there was a lot of interesting discourse among the faculty. Besides, Nadal liked being around young people. He'd invite groups of cadets to his house for dinner. "You could never give them enough food. Billie used to say, 'The vultures are coming.' They'd devour everything, fill their plates, tear through the food. Aggh! Then want more. But we enjoyed that, and some of them became guys I kept in touch with. A couple, sons of Army officers, even wound up with advanced degrees in psychology, and I like to think I had something to do with that."

At West Point, Nadal taught both basic psychology and military leadership. Classes were small, twelve to fifteen cadets, and Nadal taught with enthusiasm and intensity. He believed West Point existed to satisfy two aims—provide a college education and impart certain values. "If it doesn't instill duty, honor, country, then close the place."

While the values remained constant, Nadal said, today's cadets have a lot more freedom than cadets enjoyed during his day, and the reason is obviously because society is considerably less authoritarian now. There is a tacitly permissible distance between the values of a society that an organization in that society can deviate from, Nadal suggested. But when society moves quickly, traveling a great distance, that organization also has to move, or it will be a pariah. The need to be tolerated, Nadal said, has a lot to do with the liberalization up at West Point.

During the time he taught there, Tet occurred, and Nadal reacted with anger toward the country's growing lack of support for the Army. "You have to remember I'd come back from leading a rifle company of some really fine young Americans." Yet the longer he was back, the more he kept seeing in the press and hearing on the tube intimations that American troops weren't very good, that the Army had gone down in quality, and that in decline it no longer deserved the country's support.

"But the coin of war *is* armies," Nadal said. "That's what you spend in a war—the quality of your Army. The German Army in 1939 was a hell of a lot better than their Army of 1945; most of the better troops and officers had been killed off. Well, the same thing happened to us in Vietnam."

As a professional soldier, Nadal did not go to Vietnam with the idea that brass bands would be playing to welcome his return. Professional soldiers should not expect huge support when they do their jobs, he said, nor be too surprised, as Nadal was after Tet, when support dwindles. "It's probably different for pfc's, who," Nadal said, "had a right to expect something more from the society that, after all, drafted them to go over to Vietnam."

At the same time, Nadal felt he understood the nature of a democracy, in which people do have the right to speak out, even expressing civil disobedience. "I think civil disobedience is fair in a democracy, as long as you're willing to pay the consequences. But I think it's unfair when the Harvard kids and the Yale kids go through the civil disobedience bit and then catch the first train leaving for Canada."

Tet commenced in January 1968. The My Lai massacre, during which C Company of Task Force Baker, a battalion-size unit of the Americal Division, swept through the hamlet of My Lai and systematically killed between 175 and two hundred people, mostly old men, women, and children, occurred on March 16, 1968. Public exposure came a year later, and Nadal vividly remembers learning about the massacre.

"I opened *Life* magazine, I saw those pictures, and I said, 'Jesus Christ, that can't be the American Army.' Because what I was teaching then was the essence of why something like that shouldn't have happened—leadership. I was personally devastated; and after, I spent a lot of time with cadets, telling them why they can't let that happen again, that it was their job not to let that happen again. I knew from my own experiences that combat quickly washes humanity from people. But you don't let your troops do things that will subsequently cause guilt that will last them the rest of their lives."

Nadal recalled that during a patrol in the Bong Son, his company caught a dozen VC eating rice in a ditch and ambushed them. But after separating the wounded from those dead, he called upon his medic to take care of the wounded. At first, the medic, who'd lost a number of close friends in the Ia Drang, refused. But Nadal grabbed the guy and ordered him to minister to the wounded VC. "To my mind, the rules of war say that when you have control, the war is over. Everything's fair up to the time you're in control of another human being. Then he's your responsibility."

My Lai, in Nadal's view, occurred precisely because the rich and educated kids in America ducked the draft and would not fight in the Vietnam War. That meant the Army was compelled to commission men who, under any other circumstances, would not have made it—people like Calley and Medina. They were "shake 'n' bake" officers, men with minimal training, nor had they absorbed the values the officer corps seeks to inculcate. Nadal noted, too, that the Americal Division had been having disciplinary problems early on, and one reason was that unlike, say, the 1st Cav, it was a hodgepodge unit, carelessly thrown together.

"What happened at My Lai was a disaster," Nadal said. "It was totally, completely, 100 percent inexcusable. If I had my druthers, I'd have castrated Calley and then shot him, because he'd allowed his soldiers to behave like savages."

The division commander of the Americal at the time of My Lai was Maj. Gen. Samuel Koster, who became superintendent of West Point in June 1968. When he was forced to resign in March 1970 because of alleged complicity in the My Lai cover-up, Nadal's reaction at the time was, "If My Lai happened, Koster shouldn't be at West Point, because he's the wrong man at the Academy."

At the noon meal on March 17, Koster stepped onto the balcony overlooking the dining hall and addressed the cadets, saying he was leaving West Point. The ideals of duty, honor, country, he maintained, had always been his guide, and he'd continue to use them for a signpost. His concluding words were, "Don't let the bastards grind you down!" Exactly who Koster meant, and why, were subjects of considerable conjecture. But soon after, the Corps paraded in front of Koster's residence, honoring him before he left West Point. A handful questioned the propriety of Koster's address as well as the parade, and it's interesting to speculate what someone like Nadal, who'd literally been kicked in the face in the mess hall when he rebelled, would have done had he been a cadet then.

As a West Point plebe, Nadal probably had more realistic expectations than most of cadet life. He'd not only heard his father's stories but also attended a military school in Mississippi for two years. "So my West Point years were not terribly traumatic because I had correct expectations." Unlike, say, his roommate of four years, Bruce Hamilton, who'd arrived at West Point with a tennis racquet, a swimming suit, and suntan lotion.

Although Nadal felt prepared, Beast Barracks was still terrible. "As ready as you can be, you can't be ready enough. But I wasn't bewildered, because I knew I was going to catch a lot of crap." He remembered doing exercises on his back at five-thirty the first morning, wearing a T-shirt and shorts. The grass, a soaking green carpet, was a distinct shock to his system. It was meant to be.

Nadal graduated in the top third of the Class of 1958 and did very well in subjects he enjoyed—history, English, social studies, psychology. He knew from the start he wanted to join the infantry branch. "In my value system, other than infantry, only if you were in armor were you okay. Anything else, you were playing at being in the Army."

Commissioned almost exactly thirty years after his father, Nadal said that West Point is a rite of passage intelligent men are willing to undergo, one reason being a psychological concept called "cognitive dissonance," which he explained this way: "The more arduous the thing is, the more you appreciate it once you've finished, because you only had two alternatives: that it was very valuable for me and look what a good man I am for having done it; or, if it was unworthy of my best effort, I sure was a dumb shit for having put up with it." Nadal said cognitive dissonance is also one of the reasons it's so difficult to change the plebe system at West

Point, why, even when the officers want to change it, cadets want to reinstill it: " 'I went through that bullshit nonsense, and it was good for me because it was so bad. Now it'll be good for the current plebes because it's still so bad.' Cognitive dissonance," Nadal repeated, as if it were the favorite refrain of a popular old song.

While he taught, Nadal held a second job at West Point, director of research in the Military Psychology and Leadership Department, and soon he produced a study advocating the abolition of bracing, still then required of plebes, because there was evidence that bracing caused severe nerve damage.

Gen. Bernard Rogers, commandant of cadets, gathered the officers of the Tactical Department together and said he supported Nadal's recommendation. From here on in, no more bracing. Another thing the study discussed was the need for more participation and input from cadets. "Everything's going to be more participatory," Rogers said, "and anyone who doesn't like that in this room can leave."

Because genuine changes were instituted as a result of the study, Nadal became a controversial figure. While some of his peers considered him a bright, progressive officer, others, to whom the plebe system had been sacrosanct, believed he was out to destroy the foundations of the U.S. Army.

But what Nadal advocated was not doing away with difficult, challenging rites of passage. Precisely because such rites are necessary, Nadal advocated making the plebe system more like what soldiers experienced in Ranger School, which Nadal thought was the best training he'd ever received in the Army. "I wanted it to be very difficult in a militarily oriented situation, where upperclassmen would lead plebes, the way a patrol leader leads a patrol in Ranger School." Obviously it was the pettiness, the humiliating nitpicking, doing push-ups under the table in the mess hall that Nadal sought to eliminate or minimize.

In a subsequent assignment after West Point, he was working at the Pentagon, and so was General Rogers. One day Nadal got a call from some friends still teaching at the Academy. Things were starting to regress up there, his callers told Nadal. Gen. Sam Walker, who'd succeeded Rogers as commandant, had said the reform movement had gone too far, the place was becoming namby-pamby, and he was going to change that. A lot of things

Rogers had instituted, supporting Nadal's recommendations, were going to be changed back. "That pissed me off," Nadal said.

Soon after, he got a copy of a memo Walker had put out about the fourth-class system and the need to return to fundamentals. Nadal took the memo over to Rogers, who happened to be working across the hall. "Rogers took the memo and went marching into the chief of staff's office." This was Westmoreland, who, as superintendent from 1960 to 1963, was pretty enlightened, according to Nadal, one who didn't see a lot of sense in some of the Mickey Mouse going on up there.

Westmoreland got on the phone and called Walker. "Sam," he said, "what are you doing up there? I have this memo you've put out." Walker said, "Sir, it's really been misinterpreted." And perhaps it may have been, conceded Nadal. But the next thing he knew, there was a terrific witch-hunt at West Point. Who turned Walker in, and who talked to Nadal? "It really got pretty tight. The guys who called me, man, they didn't want to hear my name. They were afraid they were going to get cashiered. Walker knew I was the instigator and that I'd caused him to get a phone call from the chief of staff of the Army."

A few years later, Nadal and Walker sort of kissed and made up when they both worked for Rogers at Fort McPherson, Georgia. "I think Sam Walker probably views me as a kind of rebel, misguided, but not a bad guy. Well, at least they knew me," Nadal said with a shrug and a smile. "For good or bad, I had an impact."

How he got to the Pentagon tells a lot about Nadal. In the summer of 1970, after having completed his teaching stint at West Point, Nadal had been sent to the Marine Corps Command and General Staff College at Quantico, Virginia, chosen to fill one of the Army's four or five annual slots. He was scheduled to graduate the following June. But early that spring, General Westmoreland came down to visit the school and asked to speak to the Army officers. "I'm Westy," he said, "here's your chance to tell the Army chief of staff whatever's on your mind." Westmoreland went around the table. Nadal was third. When it was his turn, Nadal, who'd anticipated the question upon learning days before of the visit, calmly offered, "Sir, I have a lot to say, but I don't have the time to say it, so I wrote a memo for you." Westmoreland blinked. Then Nadal handed him a six-page memo, the first paragraph of which read: "The major problems of the Army in this decade are going to revolve primarily around people. How does the Army remain an effective, relevant instrument of our changing society? The only discipline which can generate empirical input into the solution of these problems is behavioral science. The Army is not using the available knowledge.''

One of Nadal's major recommendations was to develop instructional teams that would travel to major posts, presenting one-week courses in human relations. He further argued for the need to educate officers about the nature of human behavior in groups and large organizations. Nadal emphasized that treating people with dignity and discipline were not contradictory concepts. ''The focus of our efforts in the people area has to be to develop effective ways to operate within our changing society.'' In a word, Nadal was brimming with ideas as a result of studying and having taught psychology and, leadership, and, surprisingly or otherwise, Westmoreland was receptive. Because, less than a week later, Nadal got a call from Westmoreland's aide, who said, ''The chief of staff of the Army would like to have lunch with you. Can you make it on [such-and-such a day]?''

Nadal thought it was a possibility.

At the lunch were Westmoreland, the deputy chiefs for personnel and research and development, the vice chief of staff, Westmoreland's aide, and a visiting major from Quantico. Or, two four-stars, two three-stars, a full colonel, and Maj. Tony Nadal.

''What I'd said in the paper, basically, was that there was a field of knowledge about human behavior and organizations out there that we can take advantage of,'' Nadal remembered. Now, Westmoreland had been exposed to some of these things when he had attended Harvard Business School in the mid-1950s, and after some roundtable discussion it was decided that Nadal would be pulled out of the Marine Corps school and placed under Lt. Gen. George Forsythe, deputy chief for personnel at the Pentagon. Westmoreland particularly liked Nadal's notion of developing a seminar program teaching Army officers the rudiments of behavioral science and the nature of organizations. But the project required a general in the field to stamp it with his imprimatur. Nadal was told to report to Fort Bragg, to Maj. Gen. Hank Emerson, who was then in charge of Special Forces. Forsythe would call Emerson, telling him about Nadal's project, Westmoreland's support, and how to get the ball rolling.

After some initial resistance at the mere notion of telling Army generals how to operate, twelve teams of three officers each were dispatched from Bragg to preach the new gospel. Nadal and two others circuited the Pacific—Korea, Japan, Okinawa, Hawaii. "I got two medals out of the exercise," he said.

Nadal's seminar pilgrimage occurred during the early 1970s. In 1975 he returned to the United States after spending three years in Germany, and Rogers, now a powerful four-star general, asked that he be assigned to his command at Fort McPherson. Rogers had maintained an interest in Nadal's behavioral science work and wondered what had been happening to it. But because no one pushed while Nadal was stationed in Germany for three years, it had lost its impetus. Rogers said that was a shame but he'd do it in his command, and Nadal was made chief of his human resources staff.

"Rogers is like a puzzle wrapped in an enigma," Nadal said. "Intellectually, he understood all the things I was trying to accomplish, a lot of which is humanistic. But sometimes he personally didn't reflect those values. Rogers can be the most pleasant, charming person you've ever met. Or, issuing a scathing look, he can say, 'You son of a bitch, you're not prepared, get out of here. I don't ever want to see you again.' And turning to his staff, he'd say, 'Don't let that guy in here again.' He's capable of both, and does as he thinks the situation requires. But I liked working for him, and he gave me all the support I could have wanted. And in those days, I was almost messianic in my intention to get an organizational effectiveness concept working for the Army, which was in deep trouble then. The program I created was called, aptly enough, 'The Army's Organizational Effectiveness Program.' I was going out, telling senior officers how to do their jobs, telling them, for instance, to add an OE officer to their staffs."

Nadal again began giving seminars, spelling out his basic thoughts behind organizational effectiveness, one of which was how to use constructively an OE officer attached to a general's staff. He was telling generals that the commander didn't always have the best perspective as to what was happening in a unit, that sometimes it was helpful to have an uninvolved third party talking to both upper and lower levels. Unfortunately, Nadal found some generals took the seminars and his suggestions as affronts to their manhood, although others enthusiastically embraced his ideas. His program thus received mixed reviews, but Nadal found the experience rewarding. "Wheeling and dealing, that's what turns me on," he said. It may also have helped turn him out.

Between the time Rogers had sailed into Westmoreland's office clutching Walker's memo and Nadal worked for Rogers at Fort McPherson, Nadal was commander of the 2nd Battalion, 13th Infantry, Sandhofen, Germany, and the assignment was not among his favorites. "Battalion command should be enjoyable, but I had a shithead of a boss to work for, so my battalion command experience was not very pleasant," Nadal said frankly. "He didn't support me, reassigned some of my best people without telling me, and had a real dislike for West Pointers."

When Nadal reported in, his brigade commander took pains to explain that he'd started out as an enlisted man, and, as a black man, had grown up in a racist Army. Nadal, he added, had spent far too much time at the Pentagon and teaching at West Point; rather than soldiering, Nadal had been wasting his time. Halfway through Nadal's tour, a new brigade commander took over, and Nadal thought the difference between the two men was enormous. "The second guy was just so much better. Yet one of the bizarre things was that the first guy made general and the second didn't."

Because his battalion command hadn't been totally successful, Nadal didn't see the Army making him a brigade commander or a general, and believing he wasn't going to get either, he didn't see a whole lot of other things left to him that he might enjoy in the Army. So, after attending the Army War College as a student and then teaching in its Leadership and Management Department, he began thinking of retiring from the Army. An additional reason to retire early was that his wife gave birth to their daughter in 1977, and he knew he was going to have to work until he was sixty-two if he was to see her through college; and getting a meaningful job at forty-five figured to be a lot easier than landing one at fifty-two.

One day, while he was still teaching at Carlisle and mulling over early retirement, he got a call from a Houston headhunter, who said he was looking for an expert in organizational development who spoke Spanish and would consider working for an oil company based in South America. To make a long story short, Nadal went for a number of interviews and was offered the job, but turned it down, largely because he decided he didn't want to raise his daughter in South America. Yet he was pleasantly surprised at the amount of money he was offered.

He'd had no idea he could command that kind of salary in the private sector, and now he began seriously looking for a job in the United States. He garnered a number of possibilities; one was from

Gulf Oil, another from Mobil. The one place he hadn't sought a job was in the Carlisle area, where the Army War College is located; he wasn't looking for anything there, because what he does best works for large organizations, and he didn't believe there were any around Carlisle. But through a friend, he got to meet the chairman of Carlisle Syntex, who suggested he meet the president of Carlisle Rubber and Tire Company who, it turned out, was looking for a vice president of human resources. Thus Nadal got an offer, decided to take it, and resigned from the Army.

Nadal's company manufactures single-ply, flat rubber sheets used for industrial and commercial roofing. As vice president of human resources, he's in charge of all personnel functions—hiring, firing, training, salary, and administration.

"I think it was the right move for me at the time, although I miss the Army," Nadal said. " 'The military is the modern man's monastery.' That's a line from Janowitz's *The Professional Soldier*, and there's some truth to it. There's a value to selflessness, to dedication, to sacrifice, and though I enjoy my current job a great deal, I sometimes miss those other things. I think it was also Janowitz who wrote that the commitment involved in being a soldier is not unlike the one a priest makes toward his religion. And if you're truly committed, it's like a priest leaving his church: You never get away from it, you never really give it up."

We were talking in Nadal's home. It rests on the side of a mountain, part of the chain linking the Cumberland Valley, which people came down on their way west as the country expanded. To get to Nadal's from Carlisle, which is about fifteen miles away, you drive through flat farm country, coming to the town of Boiling Springs, where there's a handsomely cut stone clock tower, beyond which are the springs. You see the smokelike mist coming off the water, and it looks both magical and eerie. Swans and ducks ply the spring all year round. From there you drive up the mountain along a twisting road. Occasionally Nadal, wearing a three-piece business suit, goes barreling down the mountain to work on a motorcycle. While the motorcycle adds spice to his life, Nadal is the first to acknowledge it's a far cry from crashing aboard a helicopter in the Bong Son or leading an assault in the Ia Drang.

In the fall of 1985, or twenty years after he'd fought there, two soldiers who'd served under Nadal showed up at his door unannounced. Nadal wasn't home, but they spoke to Billie. One was tall, from nearby Harrisburg. The other was short and lived on

Long Island. They'd met in New York when the Vietnam vets marched down Wall Street, renewed their friendship, and decided one afternoon to look up Nadal who, they'd learned from someone else, lived in Boiling Springs.

When they came back another time, Nadal greeted them. It meant a lot to him, not only that they'd sought him out but also that they'd made a second trip up the mountain. Both men kept calling him "Captain Nadal," and said they just wanted to know how he was getting along. The taller man remembered seeing the three troops falling dead near Nadal when the enemy machine gun opened up, and he also remembered seeing Nadal taking the radio from Sergeant Gell. Both still spoke highly of the sergeants in the company, saying how well they knew their jobs and how much everyone in the company seemed to care for each other.

And as Nadal, who'd loved to wheel and deal, sat there, telling about the two soldiers who'd come to visit him, it was difficult not to believe that that visit meant more to him, finally, than having been a mover and a shaker, than wheeling and dealing, than even having had an impact up at West Point and in the Army.

And when he said, "If we got into another war, I'd sign up tomorrow," I thought I knew exactly why. Because who in the wider world Nadal now functions in looks you up twenty years later just to see how you're getting along?

NASH, William L. (Bill)
LTC ARMOR 070-34-9961
BORN: 10 Aug 43, Tucson, AZ

"Understand, I'm a hard guy, I've got very high standards," said Lt. Col. Bill Nash. "I could give you a lecture on the Vietnam Memorial that would burn your ears, because I get incensed, just get incensed by that statue of those three guys." He was referring to the Frederick Hart sculpture of three infantrymen near the chevron-shaped black granite upon which are listed the names of American servicemen killed or missing in Vietnam.

One of the three sculpted figures is a machine gunner, with an M-60 slung over his right shoulder and linked cartridge belts circling his neck and extending down his chest; he's wearing no helmet but a floppy hat. The other two soldiers are bareheaded. One is black and has a towel draped over his neck. The last, standing in the middle, wears an open flak jacket and carries only a .45.

"Understand, I'm very pleased about the memorial itself," Nash said. "It's unique, and putting the names of the dead on it has meaning to me, because I looked up some of those names and I know some of those folks. But it really bothers me that each of the sculpted men is depicted out of uniform. They have ammunition that's being carried improperly, their flak vests aren't on right, they're not wearing helmets, and on and on. What it really is is a condemnation of the United States Army, because had a few more people looked less like those three there wouldn't be as many up on that other part of the memorial."

Nash believes that as the country filled its ranks during the Vietnam War, America's military leadership suffered. A lack of professionalism grew in the Army; officers were too nice to their soldiers to insist they wear their helmets. "But it was a responsibility of an officer to enforce those provisions of discipline, ensuring professional competence, so that you got the job done with the least number of casualties."

Nash, who has receding black hair, brown eyes, and wears gold-framed bifocals, knows that his stance isn't universally shared, because whenever he discusses it with other officers most just stare at him, mutter he's right, and walk away.

This rigorous viewpoint hardly means his troops never relaxed when the time was appropriate. Nor does it mean, Nash hastens to add, that he was himself without fault and hadn't committed tactical errors leading an armored platoon in combat.

Once, he remembered, he tried to consummate a fire maneuver, during which one of his troops pinned down an NVA soldier holding out in a bunker, while another of his troops crawled over and threw in a grenade. But the NVA, crouching toward the rear of the bunker, avoided the grenade and was able to toss out one of his own, which went off in the American soldier's face, wounding him severely. Nash, furious with himself, backed up one of his Sheridan tanks and simply blew the bunker to kingdom come. "So I'm the first to admit I made mistakes; didn't charge another time when I should have, and got that guy hurt unnecessarily when I could have brought the Sheridan over to begin with. But I can also think of a lot of times when I kicked ass to get my guys to keep their stuff real tight, and my platoon suffered less casualties than any other in the squadron while I was in command."

During his first day as a platoon leader, his soldiers cleared jungle for three or four hours; then they were given a ten-minute break to grab a quick lunch and check maintenance on their vehicles, which were staggered to provide coverage. "But first thing, everybody stood up on top of his vehicle, took off his helmet and flak jacket, walked over to the side, unzipped his pants, and took a piss. Everybody's doing this, not just my platoon."

That night, when the platoon set up for dinner, Nash called his vehicle commanders together, acknowledging he was new guy on the block and they were the old-timers. But he asked them if there was a time-out system in the war. Was the war perhaps like a game, where one team could unilaterally request an official respite to catch its breath and take a leak? Nash's vehicle commanders looked at him, puzzled. "Is there a time-out system where, when we're on a break, nobody shoots at us?" he asked. A couple of them muttered, "No, no." Nash circled the nine bewildered faces, trying to make eye contact with each man, before he said, "Well, let me tell you something, guys. From now on, you keep your fucking helmets on and you keep your fucking flak jackets on, from the time we move out to the time I say to take them off."

For a while, his troops referred to him behind his back as "Chickenshit Nash." But gradually, and especially after he began pulling shrapnel out of flak jackets and his troops began to realize that while other platoons were suffering KIA's no one was getting killed in Nash's, the epithet died away. It was partly luck, Nash knew, but he also believed none of his people were killed because he insisted, among other things, on sporadically but abruptly pulling up next to one of his Sheridans so he could jump down its hatch to see if the crew inside were wearing helmets and flak jackets.

"I was an asshole about it. But I learned quickly that if you make them do it right, they'll live. And if they don't, you look them in the eye and you say, 'Go do it right!'"

Nash remembered a phrase in the cadet prayer, "Dear Lord,

help me choose the harder right rather than the easier wrong." That phrase, he said, came vividly back to him in Vietnam. "Being proficient, enforcing discipline, meant choosing the harder right rather than going with the flow. And if what you're doing is trying to draw a link between West Point, Vietnam, and me, maybe that's it—'choosing the harder right.'"

Yet in 1961, or the first time Nash received an appointment to West Point, he turned it down cold. If West Point presumably embodies an Elysian field for those who embrace discipline as wholeheartedly as Nash, why he turned the appointment down and how he wound up at the Academy three years later offer the paradox of a man fighting his fate.

Nash was born in Tucson, Arizona, on August 10, 1943. His great-grandfather on his father's side settled in Arizona Territory shortly after the Civil War. Nash's father was a career Army officer, and though Nash lived his earliest years in the small town of Hayden, Arizona, he later traveled a great deal, following his father from Army post to Army post. In fact, Nash's first memories are of Japan, where his father was stationed during the occupation. Later, his father became military attaché to the American embassy in Jakarta. As a ten-year-old, Nash remembered being aboard a ship en route to Indonesia but spending a week in Saigon Bay hearing French artillery shortly after the fall of Dien Bien Phu. His father had flown ahead, and Nash and his mother ate hamburgers and Cokes in a Saigon restaurant near where the ship docked.

Soon after his father became a full colonel, he was named post commander of Fort Drum, in upstate New York, and it was there he died, the result of a third heart attack. This was two days after Nash's sixteenth birthday. "I still have a baseball glove my father got for me that hadn't arrived until about a week after he died," Nash recalled. "It was a special-ordered, Stan Musial-type mitt, and I still play ball with it."

Following his father's death, Nash and his mother moved from Drum to the nearby town of Carthage so Nash could complete his studies at the same high school where he began them. He always did well academically, and despite his father's sudden death remained top-ranking boy in his class.

His father's boss, the First Army commander, had been Gen. Blackshear Bryan, who'd been superintendent at West Point from 1954 to 1956. Nash would get to see him when Bryan visited his father, and there was talk of West Point. "But Dad took just about the best attitude you could with a son who's the son of an Army officer," Nash thought. "He made the information about West Point available, but there was absolutely no pressure from him on me to go there." Yet, exposed to the Army all his life, Nash did apply to the Military Academy during his senior year in high school, receiving a congressional appointment but turning it down when he decided he really didn't want to become a soldier.

He said his decision had to do with the pervasive beatnik and free spirit mood of the times and his own resistance to regimentation. Besides, he thought he'd found his life's work when he fell in love with chemistry during his junior year in high school, the school year immediately following the summer of his father's death. Although neither of his parents leaned on Nash to attend West Point, the main street at Drum was named after his father, and he did feel pressure from old family friends and the Drum community. "I think I resisted being swept away, and I think maybe that's one of the great things in my life. I didn't feel West Point was right at the time, and I didn't know where I wanted my life to be." Nash's mother, whom he regarded as his closest friend, encouraged him to decide for himself.

He applied to a number of colleges that had strong chemistry departments. And because his sister was married to a professor of accounting at Tulane, he applied there as well, as a courtesy to his brother-in-law, visiting the New Orleans campus that Christmas. He found he not only liked New Orleans a great deal, but also Tulane offered a full-tuition scholarship and was prepared to enter him in an honors chemistry, math, and English program. He was accepted by Union College in Schenectady, New York, as well. West Point made three, but Nash decided on Tulane.

"And there, for the better part of two and a half years, I was in seventh heaven. Fell in love about fourteen hundred times." During his sophomore year he read something in the paper about an American peacekeeping patrol getting fired upon in Korea, and that got him to thinking about the Army and West Point. His grades had slipped, and he considered leaving school. Concluding that would be an unacceptable defeat, he refocused his energies and found he was again able to achieve high grades. Yet the following summer, he read a second item about an American patrol getting fired upon in Korea, and that decided him on the Army at last.

The recruiter thought he'd been kicked out of school, gotten a girl pregnant, or experienced trouble with the law. "I told him none of that was so, I just wanted to be a soldier, and I started taking all the tests. Told my mom. She picked herself off the floor and said, 'Okay, what can I do for you?' And so, on the fourth of December, I enlisted in the United States Army."

Nash was the outstanding trainee in his basic training company at Fort Polk, Louisiana, a leader in his advanced training unit as well as a leader in Airborne School, for which he volunteered. He remembered a live fire exercise in the woods during basic training, with real bullets flying around. "My whole body throbbed. 'This is great, this is what I'm for,'" he recalled thinking. He liked the physical challenges, the camaraderie, the outdoors. He found he was nervous jumping out of a plane, but it was a kind of controlled apprehension. He remembered taking off from Bragg at the beginning of a Memorial Day weekend, arriving in Washington six hours later, partying for three straight days, and just making reveille formation the following Monday morning. "It was all very attractive to me."

Spurred by his mother, he applied to go to West Point through the Army's own prep school program, as Howie Boone had done four years before. Because his father had been a Regular Army officer, Nash was also eligible for a presidential appointment, and that is how he entered the Class of '68.

He recalled processing in at West Point in the old gym, moving from table to table, wearing civilian clothing, and carrying a suitcase. Little old ladies in tennis shoes and soldiers, not cadets, gently shepherded incoming plebes through registration. When Nash walked out the gym door, he vaguely remembers a soldier delivering him to the company to which he'd been assigned. The first cadet he reported to was wearing a red sash, and his career at the Military Academy officially began.

The man in the red sash turned out to be a cadet named Mike Berdy, who was Nash's platoon leader from day one and throughout most of his plebe year. It was a memorable meeting for Nash, because "Mike Berdy was one of the greatest people I've known in my life. The last time I saw him was in Bookbinder's Restaurant in Philadelphia my senior year after the Army-Navy game of 1967. He was killed December 26, 1967, about a month later, in Vietnam, helicopter crash, noncombat death."

Berdy, Nash said, loved the Army, loved being a cadet, loved playing football, and loved life. "A little short shit, stocky guy."

Nash remembered Berdy coming into his room in May 1965, a month before Berdy graduated. He had a habit of poking Nash in the chest when he talked to him. Berdy was holding a box behind his back and asked Nash what was in the box. Nash said he had no idea. Take a guess, Berdy said. Nash said he had no way to guess. Opening the box, Berdy showed him his officer blues, his dress uniform. "He was so proud of those blues," Nash remembered. "A guy who loved being a soldier, could do a job, and had a sense of humor, always so positive, so positive."

Nash found that, compared to Tulane, the classes at West Point were far more structured, but the greatest single academic course he ever took was his year of advanced math there. While most cadets were required to complete two years of math, Nash was one of about fifteen in his class who took advanced math for one year, having already completed two years of calculus at Tulane.

"It was great," Nash remembered, "very demanding. You had to perform six days a week to a very high level of perfection. Differential equations, linear analysis, computer programming." The highlight of his academic career was getting six perfect scores in math for six straight days. He also remembered setting up a computer program "about twenty steps west of the approved solution." The instructor thought he'd done it incorrectly. But Nash argued with him, winning the argument when "I showed him I'd set it up and drove the computer to do it right."

Just about every day was show-and-tell at the board, working out problems and getting graded. Math was disciplined thinking, disciplined regimentation. In the process, it developed a certain habit of thinking. Nash assumed that's why they offered so much math.

The only course he took that gave him a problem was Russian. "It's a very difficult language, and I'm not good at memorizing. I prefer figuring things out, working problems through logically." It was hardly a Marxist plot, but Russian prevented Nash from making it to the top 5 percent of his class until he'd completed two years of language.

During his third summer, he went down to Panama on AOT, Army orientation training, where he helped train a platoon of airborne volunteers, who'd signed up to go to Jump School after finishing advanced individual training. Nash and a platoon sergeant ran thirty to forty of these young soldiers through their paces. This was during the summer of 1966, and Nash asked them the first day what they thought he'd be doing that November. He said that fall he'd be up at West Point going to a football game. Then he asked where they thought they'd be that November. "We're going to Vietnam," a couple of them said. Nash agreed that that, indeed, was the case. "Now let me tell you guys that I'm going to be at that football game with a very clear conscience, because I'm going to work your asses off and I'm going to make you the best possible soldiers I can in the thirty days we've got together."

The platoon never put their weapons in sling arms but carried them at port arms the whole time. Nor did they ever walk down roads. They traveled cross-country, though the jungle. Nash taught them everything he knew, and because they knew he'd enlisted and been through AIT and Airborne School himself, they paid attention. He'd loved training them, and later learned a couple had written the superintendent at West Point, saying how much they'd appreciated Nash's efforts in preparing them for Vietnam. "So," Nash said with a laugh, "I went to that football game with a clean conscience."

As a member of the Class of '68, he found himself deeply aware of Vietnam. Nash specifically remembered writing a letter to his mother back in '65, asking if she could send him information about the Minnesota Twins and Vietnam. That was the year the Twins, his team, made it to the World Series but lost to Sandy Koufax and the Los Angeles Dodgers in the seventh game. Anyway, the clips about the Twins were for Nash's personal use. The news items concerning Vietnam were an indication he'd been thinking about the war as it started heating up. "There were even some in my class scared that the war would be over before we got there," Nash recalled. "I know I wanted to see if I could do it, and I can remember saying, 'I don't want to spend twenty years in this man's Army listening to other people's war stories.' You have to understand, it was oriented on myself, because of a life's work. Can you imagine being a baseball pitcher and never pitching in a game? Just practicing?"

Nash remembered seeing a movie as a kid, *The Red Badge of Courage*, in which Audie Murphy portrayed a character overwhelmed by fear because he's aware of dying soldiers all around him. Was there some mystical cloud that mercifully descends when you face danger, mortal danger in war? Nash recalled wondering. But until you'd actually been to war, he decided, how could you *possibly* know the answer?

In the late 1960s officers like Lt. Col. Alexander Haig were beginning to come back from Vietnam and teach at West Point. Haig had commanded the 1st Battalion, 26th Infantry, and on March 31, 1967, his battalion had participated in the final large engagement of Operation JUNCTION CITY, which occurred in War Zone C. When one of his companies came under intense fire, then found itself low on ammunition and its wounded commander in a state of shock, Haig landed his chopper in its midst and personally took over the battle, averting a disaster and winning the Distinguished Service Cross.

At West Point, Nash was a company commander in Haig's regiment and saw him a great deal. Nash remembered Haig inviting General William DePuy, who'd been commander of the 1st Division, to his office, where both officers answered questions from about fifteen seniors. Although the cadets' queries involved geopolitical considerations, both DePuy and Haig kept emphasizing the importance of being good platoon leaders. Nash respected Haig a great deal and considered him not so much ambitious as a soldier doing his job, a positive influence on cadets. "Yet I had good friends who thought he was a phony and couldn't stand him from day one."

Another officer who spoke to cadets about his Vietnam experiences was John Mason, then a major but later a colonel. "John Mason sat in his living room, talked, and showed slides from his tour in Vietnam as an adviser." Mason, who taught tactics at West Point, was particularly influential in Nash's choice of armor as his branch of service.

"The thing I like about armor compared to infantry is, frankly, you do everything there you do in infantry, but there's more of a technical challenge, there's more of a machine interface as opposed to pure man, although today the infantry's getting more machine interface. But I also became imbued with the spirit of cavalry, and cavalry is a subset of armor, which is a little out front, a little bit different, a little bit reckless." Additionally, Nash's father spent part of his career with the 1st Cav. "Anyway, the idea of armored warfare intrigued me, got me to thinking about tanks and the tradition, the élan, and the elite of the cavalry."

Nash was talking about Lee before Gettysburg, repeatedly asking, "Can you tell me where General Stuart is? Where on earth is my cavalry?" They were Lee's eyes and ears, and without them he felt quite lost. But Nash was also talking about Flemish cuirassiers,

Turkish spahis, Russian hussars, and doomed, mounted Polish officers charging to brave but senseless deaths when they tried to take on Guderian's Panzers during the first months of World War II. When Nash spoke of the tradition, élan, and elite of cavalry, he meant his words to evoke them all.

Graduating thirtieth in a class of slightly more than seven hundred, Nash felt he'd gotten a lot out of West Point. While he'd always believed in telling the truth and in personal honesty, they were not deep-seated beliefs before West Point. But at the Military Academy he was exposed to an institution that as an institution "promoted those values, talked those values, inculcated those values, and they became my values." At the same time, Nash believed the institution should have done better in preparing cadets in basic soldierly skills. "West Point," he remembered a sergeant major once telling him, "makes good field grade officers but lousy lieutenants." Many, the sergeant major insisted, didn't know how to live in the field or how to conduct basic tactics, although that didn't include Nash. "I was number one in my class in tactics and won a Rolex wristwatch," he said. "Now nobody knows that except you, me, and my mother, because that was one of seventy-five awards they gave out at graduation."

Because Nash stood so high in his class, he not only got his choice, armor, but also got to pick his unit assignment, which was the 11th Armored Cavalry Regiment. Although he volunteered to join the 11th ACR in Vietnam, Nash first spent six months as a platoon leader with the 3rd Armored Cavalry Regiment at Fort Lewis, Washington. There he went through tank gunnery, platoon, troop, and squadron training. But perhaps most valuable of all, at Lewis Nash got to know Jim McEliece, his troop commander, a graduate of the Class of '65, the class Nash would have graduated from had he accepted his first West Point appointment. McEliece had served with the 11th ACR in Vietnam and been seriously wounded and evacuated. Aware Nash would soon be serving with that same unit, McEliece seemed to take special care in preparing Nash for what to expect as an armored platoon leader in Vietnam.

When the 3rd ACR went out on field exercises, McEliece put his troop through its paces using European tactics, because the unit's mission was to operate effectively in Europe. But he also made a point of setting aside a day or two each week, during which the troop performed wholly different Vietnam jungle tactics.

Later, McEliece took Nash aside, telling him he considered

Nash a good, aggressive leader, but he wanted to be sure Nash understood that what he'd be facing in Vietnam was vastly different from the most realistic combat simulation he'd experienced at Lewis. So it was important that Nash's aggressiveness be intelligently canalized. And that, combined with something a Ranger instructor had said to Nash about "not being in a hurry to die," made a lasting impression.

"Understand, I was very gung ho, a hard-charger, but they stressed, and not only to me, but to everybody, all the young officers in the platoon, that the bullets in Vietnam were real; and that proficiency, competence, and taking your time to do it right were paramount. The lesson was not to be cautious," Nash said. "The lesson was to be aggressive, but to be aggressive with your stuff together, fused at a professional level, so that you could dominate a battlefield. And maybe I'm alive today because I paid attention to what guys like Jim McEliece said."

Nash reported for duty to the 1st Squadron, 11th ACR during the latter part of June. His squadron commander was a major about to become a lieutenant colonel by the name of John Bahnsen, whom his friends called "Doc."

Doc Bahnsen, Class of '56, was a Military Academy graduate, Nash said, "a hard-nosed son of a bitch, probably the finest combat leader I've ever known. He was fearless, aggressive, and very smart tactically." Bahnsen's headquarters were set up in a track vehicle with a tent attached to it at a firebase called Thunder II, which was just outside of Highway Thirteen, near Lai Khe, in III Corps.

After Nash saluted, Bahnsen took him outside the tent, and they stood together off to themselves. His first question to Nash was, "What was your class standing?" When Nash told him thirtieth, Bahnsen said he was too fucking smart, and he began to chew Nash out, allowing how all Nash wanted was to make it through Vietnam as fast as possible in the easiest way possible, and then go back to the States, attend graduate school, and teach at West Point. When Bahnsen asked Nash what he, Bahnsen, wanted to do, Nash said he didn't know. Bahnsen said, "I want to kill VC and I want to kill NVA, and if you think you're ever going to have that chance to go off and become a teacher at West Point, you better want the same as I want." Although Nash had been warned Bahnsen was flamboyant, he was slightly flabbergasted, not the least reason being teaching at West Point was never something he had seriously considered doing.

Bahnsen stood about an inch taller than Nash's even six feet, was partially bald, in good shape, and appeared to be in his early forties. He talked loud and he talked stern. He swore a great deal. "He's retiring from the Army this June as a brigadier general," Nash said. "A great man, I love him, great man."

After his lecture, Bahnsen called over A Troop's commander, Capt. Fred Palmer, nicknamed Bear. Bahnsen said that Nash was being assigned to A Troop and named the platoon leader Nash would be replacing. Palmer started to argue, because the platoon leader Nash was replacing was the best, not only in the troop but also in the squad. But Bahnsen cut him off with one word, "Decision!" That meant don't argue anymore. "Decision!" Palmer nodded, said, "Come on, Nash, let's go," and soon he was introduced to his platoon.

It consisted of thirty-five to forty-five soldiers and nine vehicles, three M-551 Sheridans and six M-113 armored personnel carriers, which were called armored cavalry assault vehicles, or ACAV's.

ACAV's usually were manned by a crew of five: the driver; a track commander called the "TC," who also fired a .50-caliber machine gun; two M-60 side gunners; and an ammunition bearer, or, in Nash's case, the platoon leader, who stood between his two side gunners for maximum visibility. In the ACAV, the driver, the TC, and Nash would be hooked up to an intercom. Nash and the TC were also hooked up to a radio, so that Nash could talk not only with all his track commanders but also with the troop commander, Captain Palmer.

Nash drew a diagram of an ACAV. Looking down on top of it, there's a hatch up front on the left side for the driver. The soldier manning the .50-caliber machine gun sits behind the driver and in the middle of the vehicle, inside a hatch on a little board, maybe a two-by-eight, with his feet on either side. In the back of the vehicle is an area called the cargo well, which has a cargo hatch that comes back and locks down open. Nash used to take the two-by-eight, about six feet long, and set it up in the back. He'd put some seat cushions on top of it, nailing them down. Nash would ride between the two side gunners, his feet propped, no backrest. His back would kill him at day's end. "I tried to get one of those stadium seats, tried to get my wife to buy me one in the

States. She never could find one. University of Michigan, but she could never find one. Couldn't believe it.'' That was his first wife.

If Nash got tired, he could always stand. To see over the guy directly in front of him, who was firing the .50-caliber, Nash had to stand all the way up by putting his foot on top of the vehicle and grabbing the back of his hatch. Standing, he couldn't see past his track commander, but he could see off diagonally.

"You've got to understand," Nash said, "part of this effort, part of the reason I'm talking to you is that I'm coming to grips with some stuff that I hadn't come to grips with, and get some stuff down that I want to get down; and it would be easier if you write it than if I write it.'' He laughed self-consciously, but then said that it was important to do it right.

The 11th ACR, which consisted of about forty-two hundred troops, was possibly the most powerful ground unit of its size in the Vietnam War, capable of generating enormous firepower. That, combined with its ability to move across difficult jungle terrain, made it so valuable a unit it was often parceled out in squad increments to larger commands.

"Squadron, squadron," Nash corrected me. "That's the second time you said 'squad.' It's squadron.''

His first combat occurred on August 12, 1969, in the Loc Ninh area, near the Cambodian border. The squadron had learned of possible trouble on the night of August 11 and was put on alert midnight of August 12. It was the tenth anniversary of Nash's father's death. "If it had been eight or eleven, it wouldn't have been so bad, but it was ten," Nash remembered. What an irony it would be to die in his first battle, Nash reflected, on the tenth anniversary of his father's death.

On the morning of August 12, Nash's platoon was sent to check out a rubber plantation just north of Loc Ninh. He found nothing. But while he was there, he got a call on his radio from Captain Palmer to return. "Get back here now!''

Nash could tell there was no shooting because he would have heard it in the background. But the urgency in Palmer's voice was unmistakable. Something was expected, something was coming. Nash's vehicles could move at about thirty miles an hour on a road but only ten miles an hour overland.

When he reached Captain Palmer's position, another rubber plantation, the troop commander told Nash to come by him and go up on-line. Nash's platoon positioned their vehicles like offensive linemen. They were, from left to right, two ACAV's; a Sheridan; an ACAV; a Sheridan; an ACAV, which Nash was in; a Sheridan; and two ACAV's. In other words, Nash was in A Troop's sixth vehicle, referred to as "One-six." Another platoon was on Nash's right, still another on his left, echeloned back, so that Nash's platoon was entirely on-line with the other two. Palmer told him they were expecting contact directly in front. Apparently air recon had spotted NVA, which had moved up and dug in.

Nash was familiar with the terrain. His platoon had eaten lunch there two days before, and the NVA had probably moved in from its Cambodian sanctuary the night of August 11, set up hasty positions in jerry-built bunkers, then initiated some contact against American firebases in the area.

A rubber plantation, Nash said, consists of trees, no underbrush. Sheridans and ACAV's do reasonably well in rubber plantations because the trees are spaced about two feet wider than a tank, and you can drive through because the trees, which are about two feet in diameter and grow to between twenty and thirty feet, are planted in lanes.

Five minutes after Nash's platoon lined up, the first enemy rifle-propelled grenade was fired. An RPG can pierce ACAV's and Sheridans, and once it does, stuff inside the vehicle as well as molten aluminium start flying around. It's possible to see the flash when they're fired, but by the time you recognize the firing, they've struck.

No sooner had the first one fired than every gun in Nash's platoon banged off in response. Nash explained that his M-60 gunners were behind their gun shields, finger on the trigger, thumb on the safety, and it's all one motion. When they pulled the trigger, the safety was already off. His .50-caliber gunners had had their pieces cocked twice. Drive down a road, you cock them once, because you don't want the guns going off accidentally. But lined up, everyone was alert, primed, up on his weapon, flak jackets securely zipped, extra ammunition out on the track on top. You've taken away the C ration candy bar you were munching on. Everything is organized. It's no more joke time.

First thing the platoon wanted to do was establish fire superiority. Nash said it took them all of two seconds to grab it. Once you do that, you're in charge. You're putting out more fire than the enemy is putting out at you. "When thou has fire superiority, thou can do anything," Nash said. "You can smoke a cigarette. you can stand up, think, and organize. When you don't you can do very little, and you've got to scratch to get it."

So everyone opens up. You just do it instinctively, and you put out area fire. Because you're not sure where it's coming from, you're putting yours out from near to far. You're shooting trees, you're shooting ground. You want to touch every base, and you'll sort it as you go along. "I can't explain it to you," Nash said, "but after a while you sense where the fire's coming from, and the leaders try to direct their response in that direction."

Meanwhile, the vehicles were starting to move forward, assaulting, and Nash was talking to his track commanders, offering direction and encouragement. "Okay, one-seven, you're doing good," he said to the vehicle on his immediate right. "Now I want you to move up. Come on, one-eight, pick it up, you're falling behind. One-eight, move up two more trees, goddamn it!"

Between times he was encouraging and directing his platoon, Nash was telling his boss, Captain Palmer, "Okay, we're in good shape. No problems yet. First RPG missed. We're moving up."

But the assault wasn't pell-mell, it was done with professional competence: There were no discernible gaps between vehicles, and all fire sectors were covered. Nash could see the other vehicles in his platoon from where he was standing in the back of his ACAV; they were still filling every lane.

At one point when they were assaulting, the soldier standing in front of Nash firing the .50-caliber gun ran out of ammunition. "The guy says to me over the intercom, 'I'm loading, cover me,' and I grab an M-79, a grenade launcher, which is loaded, and fire a 40mm grenade. I come up over and stand partially on top of the track, placing my head and body over the cupola, and I lay that M-79 on his shoulder while he's reloading. I see a bunker a couple of hundred meters away. I can even see the aperture from which the NVA is firing. I just come up over and fire. I don't aim, I point, pulling the trigger. The 40mm goes very slowly, so I can watch it, and I see that sucker go right into the aperture. First round I ever fire in anger in my life. Terrific explosion, logs go flying. The TC turns around, flicks on his intercom, and says, 'I think you're going to work out, LT,' " LT being short for lieutenant. Later, the soldier, Babe Halstead, told the whole platoon what happened. Nash never uttered a word. In fact, it was better that way.

The battle lasted about an hour before the troop commander,

sensing a lack of returning fire, called a cease-fire. So the troop stopped firing and began moving up another hundred or two hundred meters to see what the bad guys were up to. Nash's track was about to pass a rubber tree when all of a sudden there was an explosion. Nash staggered and was thrown back. He felt something gooey all over his face and at first thought he was bleeding. But it was sticky, felt more like gum than blood, and turned out to be white sap from the rubber tree. While Nash's platoon responded to the explosion by firing back, Nash, looking up, could see the fin of the grenade aimed his way extending from the rubber tree adjacent to his track.

Nash's platoon moved up on a ridge. Some helicopters were approaching, and Captain Palmer gave the order for all machine guns to stop firing as the first chopper started pancaking in. Nash suddenly saw a dozen NVA withdrawing, pulling back, one of them on a bicycle about two hundred or three hundred yards in front of him. There was a little valley between them. Nash called Captain Palmer, saying, "I got more NVA, I got more NVA!" But the captain said not to fire because he was afraid of hitting the helicopter.

"To this day, I can see those bastards, and I'm so mad at myself for not shooting them," Nash said. "I should have tried something. I should have gone after and closed with them. I was told not to shoot, and maybe I shouldn't have shot, but I should have charged. I should have done more than sit and talk about it, which is all I did. And to this day I regret the fact I let about a dozen of those bastards get away."

Nash said his platoon fought every day for about a week, from the twelfth on. About the seventeenth, give or take a day, he remembered being part of an assault force that attacked an NVA ambush set up on a road that ran north out of Loc Ninh. Nash's platoon was going to ambush the ambushers. An American tank company moving up the road was bait.

"There was a stream and a road," Nash remembered. "The tanks were on the road, and my platoon ran off the road, about forty to fifty meters to the left of the stream. I crammed every vehicle in my platoon into that space. I mean, we were just tight in there when we hit this ambush on its flank. They were concentrating on the tanks, set up looking across our front, and we rolled them up. Just popped that sucker around the edges, and it was a turkey shoot. But in the turkey shoot, I'll never forget one North

Vietnamese soldier. It seemed there was nothing left in his life. He jumped up, turned, and, carrying an AK-47, ran toward us, as if to charge, then jumped behind a rubber tree maybe thirty, forty meters away. I think every man in my platoon saw that son of a bitch, and every machine gun went to that tree. The tree disintegrated. Then the man came flying out from behind the nonexistent tree and he disintegrated. I can still see it today, I can see it today.''

By the end of 1969, Nash was the veteran platoon leader in 1st Squadron. He went for R&R in Hawaii, where he met his wife for a week. When he returned, his squadron had moved up north of Tay Ninh, into the southern portion of War Zone C, and they were involved in Rome plow operations where engineering companies, using great big plows, go through the jungle, pushing vegetation aside and creating parking lots. A cav troop would be circulating behind them for protection. Nash's platoon was working with engineers from the 1st Cav. ''By this time, A Troop had gotten a new troop commander,'' Nash said, ''kind of an asshole, really didn't know, didn't understand that the bullets were real. He was trying to play John Wayne. Once he got wounded, he left the troop and got out of the Army. But I'll tell you more about him as we go along.''

On the night of February 5, Nash's platoon was ordered to pick up a platoon of infantry placed in the middle of the jungle to set up an ambush. ''We used to put snipers out, and then go pick them up,'' Nash said. ''I had to do that a couple of times, make a night march in the jungle.'' There are no lights on the vehicles, and you're riding in the dark in moonlight, trying not to think about mines. Scary.

Two days later, on February 7, Nash was fortunate not to meet his Maker. A Troop was on a jungle-clearing operation, accompanying four or five Rome plows and an infantry company. ''Clearing jungle,'' Nash remembered, ''in what we used to call 'a tactical cut.' We were not cutting the sides of the road, clearing off the road, we were just marching through the jungle looking for a fight.''

They were working an area near the Cambodian border, and Nash was still tired from the night march of two days before. He was on the right flank. A Rome plow was leading his column, followed by one of Nash's Sheridans, followed by Nash, then the rest of his platoon. Nash's right gunner was a soldier by the name of Carroll Thatcher, nicknamed Twiggy. Twiggy suddenly said,

"There's a dink!" and he pointed down. Nash said over the radio, "Action right!" The whole platoon abruptly shifted toward Nash's right, but Nash couldn't see the NVA. He handed Twiggy his M-16 rifle and told him to shoot the son of a bitch. Twiggy fired one round.

The next thing Nash remembered was seeing a sparkle caused by a ricochet and being knocked down by shrapnel bouncing off the top of his track and slamming against his flak vest. While this was happening, his troop commander was saying over the radio that nobody was out there. "The fuck they're not!" Nash replied. "I just got shot at!"

What happened was they'd missed an enemy bunker complex by ten meters and didn't know if the NVA were waiting to open up or just hoping the Americans would wheel on by. But when Twiggy fired that one round, it was like tipping a hornets' nest.

Just as soon as the enemy began firing, Nash's platoon opened up. "Fire superiority, okay, fire superiority," Nash said. The infantry they'd been carrying immediately dismounted. Lucky for them they did, because the fight turned into a four-hour battle.

Nash's platoon started assaulting in heavy vegetation. But the fighting was so intense that they were able to move forward no more than five hundred yards during the four hours. Midway in the battle, Nash's troop commander ordered a cease-fire, but Nash tried to argue him out of it, saying there were more NVA out there.

"Some guys get really shook up with all this noise going on," Nash said by way of explanation. "They can't think and operate with the noise, so it's easier to stop firing and then think." Nash, on the other hand, wore the thickest possible pads, double pads on the earcups of his earphones so that he could hear as well as possible. "Every afternoon I'd finish the day with a horrible headache. But when I got in a fight, I could hear because it was very, very snug. But it was very, very loud, too."

The sequence was hazy, because shrapnel tore the side of one of his legs, stunning him. But at some point, the troop commander pulled up alongside Nash's ACAV and started tossing riot control gas. "To this day, I don't know why the son of a bitch did that." In any case, in the midst of the fight, his platoon had to put on gas masks. The troop commander's crew, in the meantime, evacuated their vehicle, and Nash saw his troop commander jumping off his track and running to the rear. "It gets better, it gets better," Nash promised.

Eventually the troop commander returned, and he was shooting his .45. Nash, who was still somewhat dazed because of the pain in his leg, jumped to the conclusion that he was about to be overrun. He found his own .45 and strapped it on, expecting to discover NVA climbing over the top of his track. "For a second I thought this was the Little Big Horn all over again."

While they were still wearing their gas masks, Twiggy got wounded from shrapnel and fell down, bleeding from the neck. Nash thought he was dying, but he took his hand and swiped away the blood. There was a nick about an inch or two on top of bone, but Twiggy was okay.

"Get up, goddamn it, you're okay!" Nash yelled at him.

Twiggy, grateful his wound only appeared serious, jumped up and started shooting. Nash was firing as well. "It used to calm me to shoot."

"Cease fire!" Nash heard his troop commander ordering over the radio.

"No, goddamn it, they're still out there!" Nash responded.

"Cease fire, I'm telling you!" the troop commander said. "This is a direct order. Cease fire! One-six, cease fire!"

About a minute later, the platoon completely stopped firing. Ten seconds later, boom! An RPG hit Nash's track from about ten meters. It literally sheared the front—Nash didn't remember which one—of TC Mike Styles's foot. Styles hobbled off the track, limped away, and was gone, and Nash hasn't seen the Chicagoan since. "Mike Styles, bless his heart, nicknamed Mama, was, I later learned, evacuated by helicopter." Nash didn't see him limping away because when the RPG hit, he was knocked back down, and the inside of the track began filling with smoke. The electrical cord to his radio was disconnected by the violence of his fall. Nash didn't hear anything. There was shooting going on, but he was only aware of smoke. "This must be what it's like to die—black smoke, no sound, no feeling," Nash thought. Then he started hearing sound and realized he was lying flat on his back inside his track. He got up, but it was impossible to see anybody.

Nash grabbed his M-16, leaned over the side, and fired it in the direction from which he thought the RPG had come. He noticed a half-filled belt hanging down the M-60 side gun on the right side and emptied it in the same direction. Then he grabbed an M-79 grenade launcher and squeezed the trigger. But what he hit was too close, so it was like throwing a rock really hard, because the grenade had to go a certain distance before it would explode. He remembered to plug back into his radio, and he heard his platoon sergeant saying from a nearby vehicle, "One-six is dead, I'm taking over."

It was a logical conclusion, because the sergeant had seen the antitank round piercing the side of Nash's track. It had penetrated the engine, the oil pan, and the crew compartment, and while the oil wasn't burning, it was vaporizing. Nor had he seen Nash because of the smoke, or heard him over the radio because Nash had been disconnected for a number of minutes. But now, reconnected, Nash came back on, saying, "The fuck I'm dead, I'm still in charge."

And, in charge, Nash began pushing again, rallying his platoon, and, eventually, the other two platoons in the troop as well, because the troop commander was God only knows where.

That night, Nash was the squadron's hero of the day, but he was so stiff and tired the following morning he could hardly stand as the commanding general of the 1st Cav came down and pinned a Silver Star on his chest.

As a platoon leader commanding men in combat, Nash said, he went through four distant stages, stages analogous to what a pilot flying a plane experiences. The first two hundred hours of his flying life, the pilot is nervous but thorough. This is followed by a dangerous period when he begins to acquire confidence, although he thinks he really knows more than he actually does know. That's followed by a healthier period, during which you know you don't know it all, but you do know a quite a lot, and you can distinguish between the two. The fourth period is when you start to believe you're invincible. "You get the attitude that you've met the enemy and he's yours, you've met yourself and you're you. You know the bullets are real, but you've gotten an A in the course, maxed the whole nine yards." And that's when foolishness succeeds wisdom, and you can get yourself and others who've learned to trust you killed out of recklessness. When this last begins to appear, hopefully, the officer's boss will spot the first signs and realize it's time for the man who thinks he's immortal to move on to another job.

Nash clearly remembers going through each stage, but he particularly recalled when he thought he knew it all but really didn't and got into an argument with Captain Palmer, who'd been after him to improve a certain procedure. When Nash stood up to Palmer, telling him to quit picking on his platoon, Palmer chewed him out in the jungle. "He got my heels and the cheeks of my ass pressed together real tight, and he ripped me," Nash remembered. "Ripped me, and all my guys are standing there, trying not to watch, but they're seeing me standing at full attention, which is something you hardly ever did out in the jungle. But it was well deserved. Needed it, and I knew I needed it."

On the other hand, once Bahnsen, playing a scene and testing mettle, chewed Nash out undeservedly, telling him his platoon was screwed up. Nash responded that it was Bahnsen's maintenance people who were screwed up, the argument being over maintenance problems involving Nash's vehicles. "I stood nose-to-nose with the man, yelling at him," Nash remembered. "And he started shaking, saying, 'Nash, you're learning. This is the wrong goddamn place, but you're learning.'"

In fact, Nash said, he's adopted some of Bahnsen's style over the years. He meant the part about testing people, testing their mettle. He tested me. You smile.

"That day you first talked to a group of us and got thrown a few hard questions," Nash reminded me. "I wanted to make sure when you wrote about a Sheridan, you wouldn't say it had a 150 but a 152mm gun. People like me are very sensitive about that nitty-gritty stuff. You had to convince me you could get the facts right, because the story I want to tell is the importance of professional competence."

When Nash returned from Vietnam to the United States in July 1970, he found he experienced no decompression problems, perhaps because he was guardedly optimistic about the war. When he'd left Vietnam, American forces were still in Cambodia, and he thought that meant that although we were withdrawing, we were withdrawing correctly. Also, he'd observed a number of South Vietnamese units and considered them capable of holding their own against the enemy. In addition, he believed that during the wind-down years of 1970–72, American forces would train other Vietnamese units so they'd all have the capacity to perform reasonably well.

Then there was the fact that he'd participated in combat and knew that when the bullets were real, he'd acquitted himself well. "I'd found my life's work. I don't like killing, and I don't like holding people who are shot. But after Vietnam, I knew I could perform the acts of a professional soldier."

Nash's adjustment was also easy because he'd been assigned to the crack 82nd Airborne Division, first as an operations officer, later as a troop commander.

Finally, he and his wife, whom he'd married three days after graduating from West Point, would be living together, really, for the first time since they were married.

Because of those reasons, Nash said, external events such as the country's turmoil in the early 1970s had little impact on him. "I guess like Americans sometimes do, I opted for isolation. Kind of went into myself and went into my Army cocoon."

He came out of it beginning in 1973, when he attended Flight School, where he learned to fly a helicopter. It was, Nash thought, a natural extension of his decision years earlier to be associated with cavalry units, the same who'd used helicopters so effectively in Vietnam. After graduating from Flight School and completing the advanced course in helicopter flying, he was assigned to the 11th ACR, which was now stationed in Germany, serving with them for almost two years as a scout platoon commander and an operations officer. He found the work exciting for two reasons: First, helicopters were evolving from primarily troop carriers to attack choppers, with the ability to destroy tanks; and second, his platoon often found itself playing tag with Russian helicopters along the edgy East-West dividing line.

Nash believes he was lucky, because the American Army was starting to rebuild its European-based forces during the time he was stationed there. "The push was to get the U.S. Army, Europe, back up to standards, and that made it an exciting time, a good time to be there. A lot of work. Lots of field time. A lot of hard soldiering. A lot of time away from the family. But there was a purpose."

Consciously broadening himself in those years, Nash seemed to learn from a variety of commanders a number of useful lessons he would later apply when he became a squadron commander in 1983.

During the time he served with the 82nd Airborne, for example, the division commander was Maj. Gen. George Blanchard, who worked people hard. Blanchard, later a four-star general, was the first general officer Nash knew who made a serious and concerted effort to take care of soldiers' families. It was Blanchard who, when there was a huge snafu during the time the 82nd converted to a computer payment system, insisted that company commanders put in time over at the finance office, personally ensuring that their soldiers' pay records were straightened out. In doing that, Nash said, Blanchard was sending a message to every trooper in the 82nd, the message being, Your superiors throughout the chain of command give a damn.

His last year at Bragg, Nash's squadron commander was Joe Lutz, then a colonel and now a major general. Lutz was the first officer who taught Nash to manage by circulating. "It's amazing how much an old colonel can learn just by walking around, talking to soldiers."

In Europe, when Nash was an operations officer with the 11th ACR, his boss was John Tilelli, then a major and now a colonel. "Tilelli was a leader much smarter than he let himself on to be, which was sneaky of him," Nash said. "But he was a guy who always made you think you were working with rather than for him. He had this incredibly light touch, and though he was clearly in charge, he made everyone working for him think they were all in charge. 'All of us are smarter than any of us'—that kind of thing. But he certainly knew how to channel people's energies, and a fellow named Eisenhower became president of the United States doing that, as I recall. I could go on and on about guys I learned from, and the best is yet to come."

He meant the time he worked in the Pentagon as an aide to Gen. John Vessey, when Vessey was vice chief of staff of the Army and later chairman of the Joint Chiefs of Staff.

Nash had begun working in the Pentagon in July 1978, in the operations readiness directorate, concerned with the ability of the United States to reinforce rapidly American forces already based in Europe. "This is an exaggeration, but when you're a staff officer in the Pentagon, you get your little area of expertise, and it's a very narrow slice of the Army," Nash said, "but you're in charge. As a troop commander, you're boss of 150 soldiers, you've got the whole bag, but it's only 150 guys."

During the year he was in the readiness directorate, Nash made a number of trips to Europe, prepared his bosses for congressional appearances, and wrote a long report that went to the secretary of Defense on Army issues concerned with reinforcing NATO. Heady and exciting, Nash's Pentagon years were capped by becoming an aide to Vessey in 1979.

A couple of months before the job became available, Nash had been asked if he wanted to compete to become an aide to another four-star general; turning the bid down because he didn't like the guy, Nash figured that was the last chance he'd be afforded the opportunity to become an aide. Then, less than two months later, he got a call from a personnel officer asking if he'd want to compete to become an aide to Vessey, the new, recently appointed vice chief. Nash asked for a day to think about it. That afternoon, he went up to an office in the Pentagon where records of all general officers were kept.

He'd remembered being impressed by hearing Vessey speak at the Command and General Staff College at Leavenworth. At the time, Vessey was commander of American forces in Korea. But reading the general's biographical sketch, Nash thought it was the usual stuff—until, that is, he turned the page and noted Vessey's source of commission: battlefield. "So I said to myself, 'Self, any guy who goes from battlefield to four-star general has got to have a story that would be interesting to know.'"

The day after Nash checked Vessey out, he called the personnel officer back, saying he'd like to compete for the job.

Personnel sent the records and pictures of the eligible officers over to Korea, where the general's staff reviewed the candidates and made their recommendations to Vessey. He then notified personnel, saying all the officers were qualified, but he chose Nash.

Why Bill Nash?

"He picked me because A, I was an aviator and he was an aviator and liked aviators. B, I was working in the directorate he was in charge of when he was a one-star. His exec was armor and had served with the 11th ACR, and Vessey probably felt comfortable with him and figured he'd be comfortable with me. There has to be a bond between a general and his staff, and I just had some things in common with him."

The first couple of weeks Nash worked for Vessey, the general was very subdued. "He was testing me, as, you know, everybody does." Nash remembered scheduling some orientation trips for Vessey; but then Vessey wanted to tack on an additional trip, which greatly complicated matters. Nash was compelled to rework the schedule, and when Vessey began reviewing it, he challenged Nash's product and logic, saying, finally, "These arrangements don't make sense."

"Goddamn it, General, the only reason we're going it this way is cause you said so," Nash exclaimed, slamming the table.

Nash was assistant exec at the time, and the exec, a colonel, almost fainted. But Vessey never batted an eye. "Let's go ahead and change it back," he said, meaning change it back to how Nash had arranged the trip in the first place.

"He's one of the great men of our era," Nash said, "and he put up with wise-ass majors and taught them a whole lot, too."

Vessey was a quiet man who worked through channels. He was humorous. He liked to talk about the Redskins every Monday morning, Nash said, as well as about soldiering and Vietnam. He was very smart, but even wiser than he was smart. "Yet you interview him in front of shining lights, and get Dan Rather, Sam Donaldson, and other slick-tongued devils together, and Vessey might not come across looking really good. That wasn't his strength.

"First of all, when you describe General Vessey, you begin with the fact he's a Christian, who believes in the sanctity and importance of man," Nash said. "He believes in consideration, in charity, and in the religious tenets of Christianity. Probably the most religious man I ever worked with. But also a very basic soldier. He enlisted as a private with the Minnesota National Guard. Rose to the rank of first sergeant before receiving a battlefield commission at Anzio. Then went up through the ranks, though he'd often been slighted, not promoted when he should have been. But his first duty was to his nation and to his Army, and he hung in there. He's not a fast mover, not a burner, but a dedicated, quality man."

Much of the Army chief of staff's time is absorbed by his responsibilities as a member of the Joint Chiefs of Staff. Consequently, the vice chief runs the Army on a daily basis, heading all the committees, and managing the staff.

As aide to Vessey when Vessey was vice chief, Nash sat in on everything he wanted to sit in on, save for private conversations between Vessey and the chief of staff. The experience was invaluable. "I learned how the Army works," Nash said.

Vessey expected to retire in 1981. Instead, he got picked to become chairman of the Joint Chiefs. In other words, he went, not from chief, but vice chief to chairman, which was unusual. Vessey took Nash along with him. His exec would be a brigadier general, but Nash would be his deputy exec, and Nash's duties focused on the transition. Transition, because Nash was soon due to command a battalion. In cavalry, that meant commanding, not a squad, Bill, but a squadron, and after five years in the Pentagon Nash was anxious to move on, becoming commander of the 3rd Squadron, 8th Cavalry, based in Mannheim, Germany. "My life's dream—to do a command. Loved it." He was in charge of seven hundred soldiers. "By that time I'd forgotten how much fun being a soldier was. I knew it was great, but I was surprised just how great it was."

He found that being a squadron commander was even more enjoyable than being a troop commander, because he could influence more, bring more resources to bear, solve more problems, affect more training. *"I was the colonel."*

The gratification came from seeing one of his people go down to Officers School and come back number one graduate, solving soldiers' problems, and watching his troop commanders performing well.

"If you really want a heady experience, I just had one this weekend," Nash said. "I had a former platoon leader in my squadron in Germany visit me, Tom Balish. Tom's a mature officer now; he's grown and can face problems, in part, because you helped develop him. There's a teaching aspect to command. Popular word in the Army today is 'mentor.' "

Nash attempted to allow his troop commanders as much freedom as possible, often proffering hints rather than issuing orders, and sometimes even saying, "Well, you do whatever you think is right." At other times he'd say, "Well, why don't you consider this possibility?" He tried to develop a relationship with subordinates based on the Tilelli-inspired notion "All of us are smarter than any of us," and if they discussed things together, maybe they could help each other.

"But every day wasn't sunshine." Nash had an accidental death of a soldier, he had a murder, he had a disciplinary problem with a senior member of the squadron he didn't want to talk about. "So there are many sad moments, but there are so many thrills. Good people out there, Ivan, good people, but not too many from New York."

"Hey, there are a couple of good ones from New York," I said.

"I can't think of any. Sam Huff, who used to play middle linebacker for the Giants in the 1950s, only good guy I associate with New York City." Nash smiled.

He said that when he was squadron commander he would try to remember how little he thought his squadron commanders knew about what was going on in the ranks when Nash, a subordinate, was working for them as a platoon leader. Yet he's frank to acknowledge he was guilty of never believing his troop commanders and platoon leaders knew their jobs as well as he knew his job when he was in their shoes. "But I tried very hard to fight that." They were different men, of different backgrounds, dealing with different situations and different people, and he always tried to remember that. "I understand all of that better now than I did in Mannheim six months ago, because you get some distance.

"Did I have the best unit in the U.S. Army?" Nash wondered out loud. "I don't know, but it was a pretty damn good outfit, and we did a lot more things than most folks." He remembered marching his squadron more than a hundred miles, tanks and everything, and 98 percent of the vehicles made it on their own power. Nash said he was the only commander in the division in the two years he was there who practiced his war plan, moving everybody out to the border and back.

"What have you got against guys from New York, Bill?" I've lived there all my life, save for the two years I'd spent in the service.

"I graduated from high school in New York," Nash said. He was talking about the town near Fort Drum, Carthage.

"You know what I mean, New York City."

"I don't like it because it's arrogant," he said.

"Am I arrogant?"

"Huh? No, but New York's arrogant. New York City is a very arrogant place. Goddamn Yankees, for one thing."

"You man George Steinbrenner?" I reminded Nash that the principal owner of the Yankees was born in Cleveland and lives in Florida.

"The arrogance of New York in general—'The Big Apple.' The night General Bradley died there, I remember driving through downtown at one in the morning near the armory where he'd been staying and saying, 'This city doesn't need a mayor, it needs a first sergeant.'" Nash shook his head. "'The Big Apple.'" The way he said it made everyone who lived in New York sound like a slob.

"That's like my saying all officers in the Army are jerks," I said.

Nash smiled. "I didn't realize you were so sensitive about coming from New York or I wouldn't have said anything."

"There are seven, eight million people in New York."

"There's got to be some assholes, right?"

"That's right, but there's got to be a couple of good ones, too."

"There are. I've a dentist friend who lives there, but, of course, he's a coke freak. But, all right, I've had some good times in New York."

Until recently, Nash had avoided discussing Vietnam, because America hadn't accomplished its purpose or imposed its will there. "The nation had lost and my Army had not won, and my association with my Army is very, very tight." But the war, he said, wasn't the Army's idea. "We were hit with a paternity rap for an illegitimate child of the nation. But we weren't the fathers of that war. Maybe we failed to articulate to our political masters things that needed to be done. But the war wasn't our idea."

Although soldiers who'd served honorably in Vietnam suffered the greatest consequences, Nash believes that those who'd served submitted their consciences to the same scrutiny as those who'd searched their hearts and minds and decided to live in Canada. Surprisingly, his feelings toward those who'd opted to go north were ambivalent. While he didn't respect them, he also said he does respect people who, right or wrong, stand up for what they believe and have the courage to face the consequences. His problem with many who went to Canada were the consequences they chose to avoid.

"In the long term, Vietnam means to me that you can think you're right, but you can also not necessarily be right," Nash said, another surprisingly tempered response. "I believe in being strong-willed and dedicated, but at the same time, in the nature of things, man does not know everything."

He said that during the time he was fighting in Vietnam he'd vigorously supported American policy, but those "things don't seem quite as solid today." And that was why he was somewhat hesitant in commenting about the people who'd gone off to Canada. "I'd like to feel very strongly about them, speak my mind, and strike my fist. But I just may not know." While he believes some who went to Canada were cowards and others were simply fleeing a societal obligation, there was a third group "that had honest beliefs and sincere doubts and a true questioning of right and wrong. They searched their souls and went in a certain direction. 'Walk a mile in my shoes.'"

In the fifteen years since he'd returned from Vietnam, Nash said a lot of things have impinged upon his values—a rebuilt Army, divorce, his mother's recent death six months ago, being exposed to people like Vessey and Tilelli, Bahnsen and Jim McEliece, the last two of whom he's kept in touch with, remarriage—all have contributed toward an outlook on life he's taken to call one of "informed humility."

A particular regret Nash experienced was that his father wasn't living when he returned from Vietnam so they could have shared experiences, told each other war stories, compared Vietnam to what his father went through during World War II in the Philippines. "My father served his time in combat and conquered that. And living up to him and to my mother's expectations had an impact on me. Pleasing my mother has been a big motivator in my life."

Nash stood and brought over a double picture frame. One photo showed Nash being awarded the Silver Star the February day after he came closest to dying in Vietnam. He was thinner then, but had the same eager, intense expression that's characteristic of him today. The other showed his father as a young soldier in the Philippines also being awarded the Silver Star.

When you folded the frames together, father and son were practically facing each other, and if you attempted an imaginative leap through time, and another through space, they were even close enough, I thought, to reach out and connect. But maybe Nash does that each time he goes to play ball, putting on that specially ordered twenty-five-year-old Stan Musial mitt.

NYE, Roger H.
COL (Ret.) ARMOR 483-16-8269
BORN: 10 Jun 24, Ida Grove, IA

Col. Roger Nye, of the Class of '46, taught for seventeen years at West Point, first during the mid-1950s, then from 1961 until 1975, when he retired. Apropos of the Vietnam War, it seemed to Nye he was attending a memorial service a week. "You're affected by the few you knew best," he recalled, "and you wonder when you get back in the classroom if the next cadet you're talking to is someone whose funeral you'll be attending next year. But this is tempered by the understanding that the men knew exactly what they were getting into, and they were often killed doing something foolish. You really felt sorry more for the parents or the wife.''

We were sitting in Nye's study, in a three-story house on a bluff overlooking the Hudson, within walking distance of West Point. A number of birch and Colorado blue spruce trees were casually soaking up the springlike sun. There's a white flagpole pitched farther down the slope, perhaps forty to fifty feet from Nye's many-paned study windows, and in front of the flagpole rests a low stone fence. You can see, roughly, for a mile up and down the river. On this cloudless March afternoon, stone buildings with terra-cotta roofs appear quite splendid in their relative isolation, dappling hills across the river.

Nye's study is really an enclosed plant-filled porch. There's a rectangular-shaped picture frame crowded with photos of Nye in uniform hanging on the far wall. Close by is an autographed photograph of Don Holleder, an all-American who played for West Point in the 1950s and was later killed in Vietnam trying to rejoin his unit surrounded in the jungle, Nye said, cut down by machine-gun fire.

A trio of bells start going ding-dong in my head. Holleder, I seemed to remember, was left-handed. So am I. He graduated in June 1956. So did I. A great athlete, he played end. I was no great athlete, but I loved to crisscross twenty yards downfield with a second wide receiver, reaching for a perfectly thrown spiral with outstretched fingertips. So, I presume, did Holleder.

Nye said he'd usually maintained close contact with a few athletes from each class. They were the ones with the tough mental approach to life, who thought in terms of ''I will win, I will prevail, or I will bump someone to win who's not as tough.'' Sports generally, Nye said, had been a useful barometer, suggesting whether a kid would make it through West Point. ''It's this drive to win, especially when everything is going bad. Just the other day I was reading a book about Rommel that said the true test of a commander is when he's getting pounded, still losing, and then turns around and wins. You really shouldn't judge a commander until he's lost and see if he recovers. And sports teaches that.'' Nye is echoing, in a sense, the George Marshall quote on a plaque near the West Point football stadium that reads, "I have a secret and dangerous mission. Send me a West Point football player."

Holleder wasn't a particularly good student, Nye remembered; but he had a roommate, Perry McCoy Smith, who helped nurse him through the academic program. During Holleder's senior year, Coach Red Blaik, hurting for a passer, decided he'd make a quarterback of him. Nye recalled that Blaik put an assistant who later became head coach at West Point, Paul Dietzel, in charge of Holleder's conversion, and Dietzel an Nye even talked later of writing an article for *Sports Illustrated* on how you produce a quarterback in twenty-two days.

Although Holleder threw spirals, they were bullets, and none of his less gifted teammates seemed able to hang on to them. He was a tall kid, and when he'd take a step to hand the ball off to one of his running backs, he almost invariably took too large a step, distorting the rhythm of the play. It got to the point where Dietzel tied a measured cord around Holleder's ankles in practice, so that Holleder was compelled to step off no more than the proper distance, or lose his footing.

Despite his conversion to quarterback, when West Point played Michigan that year, they got murdered, something like 56–0. "It was, I think, the worst defeat we ever had," Nye remembered. "And Holley came over Sunday afternoon, went through a pot of coffee, and kept saying it was his fault, it was only his fault. 'It's my fault, all my fault. I've got to work harder, practice more.' Fifty-six to nothing could hardly have been all his fault. But everything was forgiven when we won the Army-Navy game that year, although I don't think Holley passed once that game. We won it on the ground."

In his senior year, Holleder was a company commander who might be known to have maltreated another cadet if he thought that cadet had stepped out of line, something strictly illegal. "But the executive officer was his roommate, Perry McCoy Smith, and they made a great team," Nye said. Smith is an Air Force major general now, commandant of the National War College, and Nye had received a letter from him just the other day.

College instructors often talk of the most visceral pleasure they derive from dealing with young, maturing minds that haven't been corrupted by cant. But that refers to the enduring satisfaction of all teaching, and mentoring, which is closer to what Nye did, is quite another, far from engaging matter. Mentors, for one thing, seem to take a lifelong interest in certain protégés, an interest that finds expression in correspondence, like Smith's letter, and visits parceled out over decades. Mentors also seem to possess a rare disinterestedness, one that encourages an unusual degree of trust. Or, as Noah Webster would say,

> **men ♦ tor** 'men-,to(ə)r, 'ment-ər   *n* [L, fr. Gk *Mentōr*] **1**
> *cap*: a friend of Odysseus entrusted with the education of
> Odysseus' son Telemachus **2 a:** a trusted counselor or
> guide **b:** TUTOR, COACH **men ♦ tor ♦ ship**   -,ship   *n*

Nye was certainly aware of his own mentors. His first, Gen. Arthur Trudeau, gave him "two mind-expanding books": Balthazar Gracian's *The Art of Worldly Wisdom*, the maxims of an eighteenth-century Spanish Jesuit, and Peter B. Kyne's *The Go-Getter: A Story That Tells You How to Be One*. Trudeau, who'd graduated from West Point in 1924, was in the Corps of Engineers and a well-read man, Nye said. Later Trudeau commanded the 7th Division in Korea and was in charge of research and development for the department of the Army, retiring in 1962 as a lieutenant general. When Nye worked for him as an aide, from 1948 to 1950, Trudeau was commanding general of a constabulary brigade headquartered in Wiesbaden, Germany.

"When we went on an inspection, he would ask me afterward as we drove back, 'Do you think I should relieve that man?' " Nye remembered having to give his reasons. Then Trudeau would tell him what he decided and why. Trudeau wasn't using Nye so much as a sounding board as he was educating him. "He saw himself as a trainer, a teacher, and it was a continuing school. That was the old way of doing things."

While it was a terrific experience, Nye decided early in his career that becoming a general officer was not something he particularly coveted. "The kinds of things General Trudeau had to do all day didn't interest me very much. You have to respond to everything that comes up. If you're in charge, you're really at the receiving end. General Trudeau thrived on it, and I thought you *had* to thrive on it in that kind of job."

Germany was still quite devastated when Nye was first stationed there, so devastated he found it difficult to see how the country was ever going to recover; and until the Marshall Plan got going, it really didn't. Nor were Army officers very competent at the time.

The victorious American Army wanted to return to the States at the conclusion of the war, and the question was who'd be going back to Europe and Japan to perform occupation duty. "It tended to be drunks and misfits," Nye said. "We had a lot of ex-sailors." They'd left the military but came back in, one reason being it took a while for the American economy to regain its stride after the war. Not only had there been a number of crippling strikes, but also industry needed time to retool. "It was very hard, for example, to buy a car, because we hadn't manufactured many civilian cars for five years."

Before becoming an aide to General Trudeau, Nye had been stationed at Schweinfurt, which is a hundred-odd miles from the Czech border. It was near the end of the line, and convoys had to be sent to ensure the troops received adequate supplies of food and gasoline. The heating systems were chancy, which made living there miserable for much of the year. Americans were part of the Allied constabulary body, manning the border posts. It was a difficult mission, especially picking up border crossers and having to send them back. "Of course, we didn't agree with that, but it was policy, an agreement with the Russians, and there wasn't much you could do about it," Nye said.

His second mentor was Col. George Lincoln, who'd headed the Social Sciences Department at West Point from 1954 to 1969. Lincoln, of the Class of '29, had been a Rhodes scholar and a member of General Marshall's planning group during World War II. A brigadier general at war's end, he'd decided to teach at West Point, which meant reverting to the rank of colonel. But he'd had enormous impact, more than most generals, Nye said, and when West Pointers talk of "Lincoln's Brigade," they're not referring to Americans who'd fought for the Loyalists during the Spanish Civil War but to members of the Social Sciences Department during Lincoln's tenure.

Lincoln strongly believed in the idea of interdisciplinary education for an Army officer, and when he hired people to come teach, it was not with the idea of immediately studying something you were going to teach tomorrow. For instance, to handle modern historical analysis, Lincoln believed you had to know economics, Keynes and Marx, as well as technology, nuclear weapons, and communication. The contemporary world meant complicated connections, and it was impossible to offer an historian's view if you couldn't convincingly and knowledgeably make the connections.

When it came time in the early 1950s for Nye to get a graduate degree, if that was what he wished, and then teach at West Point, Lincoln suggested he attend the Woodrow Wilson School for International Relations at Princeton, specifically because it offered an interdisciplinary program. West Point was just beginning to encourage its instructors to obtain advanced degrees; and colleges like Harvard and Princeton, giving more national security courses because the Cold War had settled in, were interested in counting military people among their graduate students.

At Princeton, Nye found himself attending seminars with fourteen other graduate students, who had degrees in history, economics, political science, and sociology. You were expected to view problems across a spectrum and write weekly papers on subjects as varied as "Did the Banking Act of 1863 promote sectionalism in the United States?" or "Is the Joint Chiefs of Staff presently formed as it should be?" A third was, "Is it fair to tax people in New York to send children to school in Mississippi?"

Lincoln had told Nye to take as much history as possible at Princeton, but not American history, because West Point was not teaching American history then. But Nye found himself immersed in political science and international relations. Lincoln had also told him to think about where he might want to get a Ph.D. and on what subject if he concluded he'd want to make a career of teaching at West Point. Probably it was at Princeton that Nye decided he definitely wanted to teach in college, even if he wasn't sure about remaining in the military, although he gradually came to believe that was, indeed, the logical thing for him to do.

Lincoln's influence is readily apparent in *Military Men*, by Ward Just, written during the Vietnam War, in which Just quotes Nye to the effect that a professional officer had to understand " 'the social framework in which he practices his profession,' " meaning Martin Luther King was perhaps as important as Clausewitz. " 'If the military man wants to have his advice taken, he must be an all-purpose man. He must understand the context of the thing. The core of his advice must be military. But he must be sensitized. He must understand the sense of his advice in the total situation.' " The words are Nye's, but they might just as well have been Lincoln's.

The ways Trudeau and Lincoln influenced him were arresting, Nye suggested, but not all that uncommon in the Army. Take Eisenhower's brigade commander in Panama, Gen. Fox Conner, who lent Eisenhower military books to read. "Life with General Conner was a sort of graduate school in military affairs and humanities," Eisenhower later wrote, "leavened by the comments and discourses of a man who was experienced in his knowledge of men and their conduct."

Nye did not commence his military career with the idea of becoming a mentor. He'd chosen armor because his imagination had been captured during World War II by Patton's slashing tank columns racing across the continent of Europe. Riding horses was also an integral part of cadet training, and Nye's class was the last to enjoy that pleasure. "You see, technically I really started out in the cavalry, then it became the armored cavalry, and finally armor."

Cav officers of Nye's generation aspired to imitating people like Patton, Rommel, and for those who knew him, Col. Creighton Abrams. "We rode about the training grounds in our tanks and armored cars, with cigars and yellow scarves and tanker boots with straps—boots that would not let us walk more than a few miles." And back in their footlockers were dog-eared copies of books by or about Patton, Rommel, and Guderian.

The first time Nye got to know Abrams, who'd become famous as a battalion commander in Patton's 4th Armored Division, was when Nye took the advanced course for armored officers in 1952 at Fort Knox. "Abrams was an instructor on tactics, and that's where he became our ideal," Nye recalled. Abrams' personality was hardly easygoing, but he was enormously competent and experienced, and, Nye remembered, he wouldn't put up with bureaucratic interference.

The next time he ran into Abrams was when Nye was secretary to the General Staff of the U.S. Army, Europe, headquartered in Heidelberg. Abrams was a brigadier general then, an operations officer. This was during the last years of Eisenhower's second administration, and Europe was clearly on the rebound. American aid has been pouring in for perhaps a decade. Construction was ubiquitous, and the West German economy, in particular, was booming.

There were eighteen generals assigned to Heidelberg, and Nye found it fascinating to observe how power was distributed, how the four-star in command decided what to do, finally, after listening to a disjointed chorus of advice from seventeen other generals. "Mostly, he did what Abrams suggested," Nye said.

Picture a big conference room, a large table, around which are seated eighteen generals. Nye is taking notes. He knows in advance Abrams' position on the particular matter the generals are debating. The argument skips about the table like sheep gamboling in a field. Everybody else is talking, yet Abrams doesn't seem to be saying much of anything. But as the clock gets to, say, about eleven-forty, Abrams breaks in, "That reminds me of a story." Then he tells a somewhat off-color anecdote, which not only is an attention-grabber but also gets most of the generals laughing. Then Abrams says, "You're suggesting this, you're suggesting that. Why don't we put those two suggestions together this way?" A resolution almost identical to what Nye knows Abrams wants in the first place. Everybody looks around, gazes up at the clock, and two or three say, "Why, sure, that's fine. Why don't we do that?"

"It was an interesting two years," Nye said. "But, again, I really didn't think I wanted to play those games. There are so many problems that are intractable, you don't do much about them, although you hear them over and over again. Yet by the time you reach fifteen years' service, you wonder why they can't be solved."

It was during this period that Nye met and married his wife, Nan Lake, who was working for the University of Maryland, which sponsored an educational program for Army personnel stationed in Europe. George and Joanne Patton were the couple's best man and matron of honor. Patton, son of the World War II hero, wanted Nan to ride in a tank from the church to the reception—an old armored tradition. But since the journey consisted of a single street, Nan was just able to talk Patton out of it.

Nye was looking forward to returning to the States the following year to resume teaching at West Point. He'd first taught there in the fall of 1954, after having acquired his masters from Princeton, and soon found Middle East history becoming his main interest. Nye also taught a course in modern European history, which was required of all cadets, but it was the Middle East course that really absorbed him, and the question was how to tool up in order to be able to teach it intelligently.

After having spent two years at Princeton, Nye had a pretty solid theoretical background on how to approach historical problems, but he knew neither Hebrew nor Arabic. Luckily, the State Department had become growingly aware of the lack of expertise about the Middle East in the federal service and commenced a series of courses on the subject. As a result, Nye spent seven weeks attending the American University at Beirut in 1955. Then he traveled with a State Department group of about twenty, visiting Teheran, Damascus, Amman, Cairo, and winding up in Israel. The group was given high-level briefings in each country, and Nye particularly remembered being driven up to Nablus one morning with four others, where they were taken to lunch with a short man wearing an eye-patch. Among other things, Moshe Dayan described the problems of taking a revolutionary force like the Irgun and transforming it into a professional and legal army. "He was fascinating, charismatic, even more interesting than the character Yul Brynner portrayed in the movie." That summer, Israel and the Arab world came wonderfully alive for Nye, and when he returned to West Point in the fall, he felt well prepared to deal with the problems of teaching Middle East history.

Tony Nadal remembered taking a course with Nye, then seeking him out after class. "I thought he was a neat guy," Nadal, a not uncritical man, said. "Smart, articulate, empathetic."

When Colonel Lincoln suggested that Nye come back and rejoin the department in 1961, West Point was starting to build the idea of a more permanent faculty, and upon his return Nye took over the history courses for the Social Sciences Department. At the same time, he began attending Columbia University, earning a doctorate five years later. His thesis was "The United States Military Academy in an Era of Educational Reform, 1900–1925."

By 1963, Nye not only became West Point's first associate professor but also firmly decided he'd complete his military career teaching at West Point. The old system was still fairly intact then, and Nye hardly noticed any changes from the mid-1950s. By the late 1960s, though, the Academy was starting to tear down old buildings and construct new, larger ones to accommodate a considerably expanded Corps of Cadets. At the same time, Vietnam was starting to impact, and Nye went out to the Far East to see for himself.

His trip was courtesy of the National War College, which took its students to various places in the world during the summers, to acquaint them with current geopolitical problems. Colonel Lincoln had convinced his friend Gen. Andrew Goodpaster, who was then commandant, to include Nye with the group that went to Asia in 1968. Nye flew over the Pacific in a C-141 and sat next to a Navy captain who wore a baseball cap and knitted to pass the time. The group received briefings in Taiwan, Tokyo, Seoul, and Thailand. Nye remained in Bangkok for about three months. There he worked on a study of Communist insurgency in northern Thailand for the Defense Department. Occasionally he'd catch a plane ride down to Saigon. Trying to get a feel for the war, he'd contact old friends. He flew up to Dalat and saw George Patton. He remembered visiting Hank Emerson, Class of '47, who retired in 1977 as a three-star general, near Route One, in a building Emerson called the "pink palace." When a call came in that the enemy was engaging units Emerson commanded, Emerson hurried out of the pink palace, boarded his helicopter, and went after them, inviting his friend and visitor Roger Nye to come along.

In the chopper, Nye marveled how Emerson used the console of radios at his command. "I watched Hank work that helicopter as a commander, a real master at pushing all those switches on this big console, talking to whom he wanted, saying, 'What do you have out there? How large a force? All right, you move this unit over there. Start bringing artillery out at this point, but don't fire.'" Everything seemed to fall in place and come alive—terrain, doctrine, weaponry, manpower—allowing for a series of quick decisions on how and where to deploy forces.

For what it's worth, Nye had initially opposed sending American troops to Vietnam. He remembered discussing American involvement at a cocktail party in 1965 with the wives of the dean and superintendent. He'd been teaching a course in the history of foreign relations that term and said he didn't favor U.S. involvement because he didn't see Vietnam as a vital American interest. It was just a small country over in the corner of Asia, and American foreign policy experts were sensitive to the historical risks of landing an American army on the Asian continent. "I'm sure I said it at the time, because I believed it then—'Vietnam maybe wasn't an important issue, but certainly we'd win.'"

The conversation was an indelible memory, because his view, crystallized at the cocktail party, presented a dilemma of sorts. On the one hand, Nye was opposed to sending American troops to Vietnam. On the other, he was teaching cadets who were certainly going to fight soon in that war. What was Nye's obligation as a teacher? "I assumed it was my duty not to burden cadets with my views," he said. "I would raise the question in my teaching, though—Was it wise to send American troops to Vietnam? In class I said, 'Probably not, but we'll win anyway.'"

The History Department, Nye said, was formed in 1969. History courses from the Social Sciences Department were merged with military history courses that had been administered under the aegis of the Military Art and Engineering Department. That was certainly a change, though hardly a sweeping one.

But even the truly important changes, Nye insisted, didn't transform the objective, which was producing an army, only how you got there. "Yet these changes became so important that by the mid-1970s you'd reached the point where the traditional Academy that had produced the MacArthurs and Eisenhowers was not really operating anymore. Other things had taken over. A new way of doing business was in effect, it's continuing to evolve, and the outcome remains in doubt because the institution is still adapting to the changes." And it's this conflict between the old and the somewhat unknown future that still concerns everyone, Nye added. Much of it has to do with the role of the individual in an institutional setting.

The traditional Academy, Nye said, had been based on a small Corps of Cadets and on a small officer corps. West Point had correctly assumed that Americans as a people weren't really interested in serving in the armed forces for a number of years. Unlike, say, the English nobility, of whose second sons military service was an expectation honored for centuries. It was, therefore, extremely important for West Point to act as a lightning rod, attracting good people, training them well, and having guaranteed jobs for them. You joined a small fraternity in which everyone knew everyone else, a band of brothers. After graduating, the Army then offered recently minted officers military training.

For a number of years, as a function of the budget and in response to economic conditions such as the Depression, the primary means of obtaining a commission was to have gone to West Point. But by the end of World War II, America had become the world's preeminent power, and the question of just how large its standing Army should be was an important consideration. By the time of NATO and the Korean War, this question became absolutely urgent, because America had to commission a couple of thousand people a year.

"But three quarters of the officer corps at any one time are lieutenants and captains," Nye said. "So not only do you have to acquire a lot of lieutenants to man your programs, but you also have to get rid of a lot of them because you only need so many majors and lieutenant colonels. I think 50 percent of those currently captains are never going to be lieutenant colonels. They'll disappear somewhere along the line."

Traditionally, you had a vertical officer corps, not a pyramidal one, in which the Army commissioned lieutenants and retained them, because there were always available jobs. But, say, by 1960, the question was, If America needs three thousand lieutenants a year, should 50 percent of them be coming from the Academy? That would be fifteen hundred, but the Academy was graduating only four hundred a year. (Today ten thousand officers are commissioned annually, and a thousand come from West Point. They're available because the Corps was expanded in 1964 so that it now has a total of approximately forty-four hundred.) But in expanding the Corps, you're not only losing compactness but also raising the question, What is the purpose of the Academy? Does it prepare people for a lifetime career, or for the pyramid, down which many will slide?

And, that's just expansion, Nye said. Another part of the revolution at the Academy involved obligations and commitment. Before World War II, the Academy said, "Come here and study. We'll give you a college education and some training. In return, you give us four years of military service." But in 1946, Superintendent Maxwell Taylor thought the Army could no longer recruit on the basis of the four-year obligation, because people wanted to forget about the war. So the obligation was reduced to three years, and there was a return to the old notion of attracting people to the military by acting as a lightning rod. With the Vietnam War the obligation jumped back to four, then five years, and the regulations now stipulated that if you finished your work and graduated, you *had* to accept a commission. And even if you resigned after two years, you would *have* to enlist for two years to make up for the training you'd received before resigning. "From the mid-1960s on," Nye stated, "we wanted to make sure."

A third profound change in the Academy's method of operation occurred in military instruction, especially if you include leadership training, Nye said. Before World War II and shortly after, you didn't specifically train people for leadership, you didn't have courses organized for that purpose. But Eisenhower, chief of staff from 1945 to 1948, sent a letter soon after the war saying he thought it was time for West Point to start teaching courses in psychology and leadership, and he cited gains made in those areas during World War II. So it was finally decided that somewhere along the line a cadet should get leadership instruction as well as leadership experience while he was still a cadet.

But a whole set of problems occurs when you're consciously trying to develop leaders. Although the attrition rate among cadets is about a third, and it's remained fairly constant, the content has changed, Nye explained. Generally, people were *forced* to leave as a result of academic failure. Because West Point today is much more academically rigorous in its admissions, cadets now *choose* to leave for other reasons. Why? One of the answers may be that if you have leadership systems telling them they're not going to make good leaders, then you have built-in incentives compelling intelligent people to say, "Hey, there's another field for me of greater interest elsewhere."

Certainly one effect of the leadership concern was that the Academy began to maintain large folders filled with observations about every cadet. All that had to be compiled, handled, then fed back to the cadet in terms of counseling, and one consequence was an increased number of officers supervising cadets.

The officers believed, or were encouraged to believe, that they were responsible, not the cadets, for the cadets' development. Therefore they were morally obliged to inspect, counsel, and test more, not less.

"There's an ex-cadet coming for dinner tonight, he's a lieutenant now," Nye said. "He was an outstanding athlete for West Point and a good student. But I used to hear him say more than once when he was a cadet, 'I'm so tired of being treated like a little boy.' "

Very few officers supervising the traditional Academy were interested in constantly looking at and judging a cadet, Nye continued. True, cadets were locked in and couldn't get out, and they had to provide their own entertainment; but there was little concern how they managed their time off. In the late 1930s there were only seven tactical officers for a Corps of Cadets of about nineteen hundred. Since that time, and Nye cautioned his figures might be a little off, the Corps had been increased two and a half times, but administrative personnel jumped five times and the Tactical Department about seven times, although when Nye says Tactical Department he's including Phys Ed, MI, and Leadership. Still, the numbers do add up to markedly increased supervision.

Shifting away from leadership, Nye said it was impossible for

West Point not to have been affected by the civil rights movement. Consider another set of numbers. In 1968, nine blacks were admitted to West Point. But from 1969 to 1974, about fifty blacks were admitted to each plebe class, and blacks now constitute about 10 percent of the corps. "That didn't come from the Vietnam War, although there was some argument the Army did need more black officers in view of the events in Vietnam," Nye said. "I don't know where instructions came to increase the number of blacks at West Point." Probably from Congress, so the Academy might more accurately reflect civil rights legislation passed during the early and mid-1960s. "But by 1968, we were in the mood to admit more blacks, and did so, although this created a few problems."

For instance, black cadets soon argued that the haircut regulation didn't take into account the different texture and shape of a black man's hair. They also noted there were few black women at the dances arranged by West Point authorities. When some white cadets complained that black cadets were dancing with white women, Academy officials decided to let black cadets schedule a dance of their own. Nye said that the problems were pretty well resolved by 1976, in part because the Academy granted many of the black cadets' requests, and in part because of racial seminars conducted with the idea of increasing communication between blacks and whites. Yet the cohesiveness of the Corps, in which all cadets were once viewed as the same, seemed not quite as it once was. And what bothered some people at West Point was that in this instance a measure of control Academy officials were accustomed to exercising over West Point's internal affairs had been diluted.

Nor were Academy officials particularly enthusiastic when three cadets who'd been dismissed from West Point in 1972 got a federal court to reinstate them on the ground that their due process rights had been violated. Following their reinstatement, the Academic Board met for six weeks in an attempt to work out a new understanding bridging the gap between individual rights and the notion that certain of those rights were surrendered when plebes entered the Academy. One Academic Board member called the process an attempt to "crank due process into the system."

A third loss of control became apparent when a cadet challenged mandatory chapel and a federal court ruled in 1973 that none of the service academies could require attendance at church, because such requirement violated a cadet's right to religious freedom guaranteed by the First Amendment.

Don't misunderstand, Nye cautioned, the traditional Academy believed a great deal in fairness and justice. But the presumption was that the military were the experts on what rights military people should have. And they *could* toss cadets out of West Point and have it accepted. But this was no longer a certainty once, say, due process found its way into the system. The mechanics of recognizing due process, incidentally, bulged with legal trappings: certain pieces of paper had to be signed; lawyers were involved; cadets confronted their accusers; federal judges, civilians, told military officers, "You will, you must."

Nye removed his horn-rimmed bifocals. He wore an ascot rather than a tie, and it gave him a sporting, jaunty air, the look of an English country gentleman. Standing up, he stretched. He looked about six feet, had white hair, and a ruddy face. A civilized man, I thought, kind with his time and generous, like most mentors, with his knowledge.

When he sat down and put his glasses back on, he said three other major changes occurred at West Point during this period: curriculum changes, faculty upgrading, and the introduction of women into the Corps.

The West Point curriculum, it could be argued, had been out of date since World War II. The institution still required a great deal of math; physics; chemistry; and mechanical, civil, and ordnance engineering. In a number of ways it was good training, and it was taught quite well. Though many cadets complained it was dull, it was demanding and rigorous. Then the Korean War came along and the Army performed badly, validating the need for change sensed by many since the end of World War II. By 1953, committees had been formed to see if cadets might be allowed some electives in what up to that time had been an almost totally required curriculum.

The question was, basically, a philosophical one, Nye said. There was a strong argument that West Point shouldn't offer electives because, unlike liberal arts colleges preparing students for many careers, West Point was preparing all cadets for one career; and wasn't it, therefore, logical to offer them all one curriculum? Since its inception, the argument continued, the Academy had relied on the unity of the Corps of Cadets to achieve its purpose, and once you began fragmenting that unity by offering electives, weren't you then blurring, if not distorting, the focus of the institution?

This argument was so pervasive that when the Corps expanded, a quite serious debate grew over what the institution was to do about the size of its mess hall. The Corps had always eaten all its meals together, at one sitting. But given the Corps' approved expansion, this was quite impossible, and the obvious, efficient solution was to have two sittings. But no, it was argued, the Corps had to be held together in all possible ways. All cadets are the same. All cadets are one group. All cadets have one objective. So the same mess hall, which had three wings, was doubled in size, and the Corps continues to eat as one.

At the time, Nye thought the solution silly, and he remembered one of his friends saying that if it was so important for all cadets to eat together, why not take the mess hall, with its enormous ceilings, and put in a glass floor? In that way they'd not only eat together, but also, sweet God, they'd be able to see each other eating.

Not too surprisingly, Washington became involved in deciding on the changes projected for West Point. It was generally the chief of staff of the Army, through his chief of personnel. But as budget considerations became more important, government comptrollers made their influence felt. And soon you got operations people into it from the military training standpoint. Then, because of the appointment system, where each cadet has to have a congressional or presidential appointment, you got continuing but increased congressional oversight. "Is that new program they're suggesting for West Point good?" congressmen asked each other. "More important, will my appointments be taken care of by these new changes?"

One deeply involved in the changes was Gen. Gar Davidson, superintendent in the late 1950s, who ordered a massive number of questionnaires, committees, and studies, the upshot of which was that by, say, 1962, a cadet was authorized two electives. Then by 1964, four. By 1968, Nye thought, it was six. Not too long after, the Academy understood it needed some way of making sense of the electives. Were they going to be chosen haphazardly, or with some degree of purpose by being grouped into areas of concentration?

By 1970, the Vietnam War was still raging, the Corps had been increased, new buildings were sprouting up, and this curriculum change was also proceeding along. Nye believes that in a ten-year period, two hundred new courses were created. "So West Point changed considerably during this period, and what cadets did all day long changed considerably. And when people say it hasn't changed, they're looking at the uniforms to a large degree and they're considering the mental set of the cadets.''

At the same time many new courses were created, the demand quickly set in for a more highly trained faculty. Previously, some faculty members had not even earned a masters degree, but now it was compulsory. Department heads scurried, making contacts in the academic world, ensuring that their people would have graduate schools to attend so they might be properly prepared to teach at West Point.

''From the standpoint of expertise in the academic subjects they taught, the level had definitely been raised,'' Nye said of the faculty he remembered in the 1970s compared to the one he knew in the 1950s. ''Those newer instructors had sat around listening to professors in good graduate schools; they'd simply heard and read a lot more.''

They were also better equipped to deal with a more sophisticated student body. In the first place, most post-Vietnam War graduates entered West Point far better prepared in terms of their high-school education, which was almost invariably more advanced than their predecessors'. Then there was the fact that plebes in the late 1960s and 1970s had probably owned cars and done some traveling. ''Chances are they worked for money, not on their fathers' farms, but for themselves, and had saved a couple of thousand bucks,'' Nye said. ''Which probably meant they handled their own bank accounts.'' So you've got a considerably more savvy student body to convince on both a social and intellectual level when you're standing before them lecturing.

Bill Holley made another interesting point about this upgraded faculty, Nye added. ''Holley, a history professor from Duke who taught at the Academy for a while, said he believed the most important reason for West Point is the training of the faculty, which will go out into the Army after completing its three-year teaching assignment and carry those skills with them into other assignments.'' Injected into the mainstream of the Army will thus be a group of Army officers who'd completed two years of graduate school and three years of teaching cadets; and this continual transfusion of educated personnel is bound to change the tone of the officer corps.

As for the impact women have made on West Point, Nye said that while it was genuine, he doubted he could define it yet. But the way it happened was, in a sense, unfortunate. They'd first arrived at West Point during the summer of 1976, after the Academy got the order to admit them the previous year. Before then, the superintendent and the institution were under specific instructions from Washington to say nothing in favor of admitting women. Thus the institution had done little or nothing to prepare for women. The superintendent at the time, Maj. Gen. Sidney Berry, had to make a sudden transition at a time when no other military institution in the world had tried anything remotely like it. All the green-covered manuals, after all, had been written for and about men.

For openers, what women would be sought out and admitted? Then, once women arrived at the Academy, where would they be housed? Separately, or with the men? And if you placed them in the same barracks as the men, would you divide them among each company or try to keep a certain number clustered together so they might support each other? After they're settled in, how do you make sure they'll receive a fair shot at the better leadership jobs parceled among the cadets? Meanwhile, do you reduce the rigor of the men's physical training to put it on the same level as the women's?

And even after you solve those fundamental problems, Nye said, there was still the question of their career opportunities if women can't serve as commanders in combat. Aren't such opportunities limited and a woman thus has to consider after the graduates if she has the chance of a serious Army career? Nye believes that to be successful in the military, women probably will have to adopt what he refers to as a "masculine outlook," which he characterizes as aggressive, competitive, and one that takes some pride in miserable living. Men have to, also. "As you can see, I'm interested in this," Nye said, "but I didn't have the answers, I'm just speculating."

He'd inherited his curiosity from his mother, who'd taught Greek and Roman history. His father was a dentist. Nye was born on June 10, 1924, in Ida Grove, Iowa, a small farming community of twenty-two hundred in the western part of the state. Nearby towns had German names like Holstein and Schaller. A work ethic based on agriculture, on the farm and being productive, was pervasive.

The Depression had a major impact, Nye remembered. About 90 percent of the farms in the area were taken over by the banks and insurance companies. But the farmers remained on the land, hired by the financial institutions that now owned the farms. President Roosevelt was no hero to the citizens of Ida Grove. "My father, a Republican county chairman, was pretty mild in his comments about Roosevelt compared to many of the townsmen," Nye said. "Floyd Maxwell, who ran the local shoestore, threatened to march on Washington many times with a gun to personally shoot him." It was federal interference with local laws and customs that people like Maxwell bitterly resented. That, and handing out relief money to people whom they believed had no right to it. Self-sufficiency was the byword, and the New Deal offended such farming communities' sense of independence.

"Although many historians tend to regard the twenties and thirties as antimilitary," Nye said, "Merle Curti, one of our best historians, wrote a book in 1936 about what he called 'the permanent arming of America,' in which he described patriotic movements, veterans' organizations, and war movies that seemed to stamp that era with a very prominent military theme." Certainly the American Legion played a very important role in the town's activities. All the leading businessmen seemed to be members, and they conducted the summer baseball program for kids. July Fourth was a big holiday, Nye remembered, and sporadic fireworks commenced three or four days before the concerted main event.

He was already attending the University of Iowa in 1943, a member of the Navy Officers Training Program, when his father called, asking if he'd like to go to West Point. "I may have said, 'What's that?' " Nye joked. His father said there was a vacant appointment in Iowa and Nye could have it if he chose. Nye said, "Should I?" His father said, "Yes." And that's the way he wound up at the Academy.

He was four or five weeks late, arriving at West Point by train in August 1943. After walking up the hill, he was taken into headquarters and sworn in. Poor guy, he'd missed half of Beast Barracks. The plebe system was operating full tilt, but it was much more personalized in those days, a "sort of college boys' fun and games." Upperclassmen really didn't pay all that much attention to plebes. The institution was generally geared for people who might not have been very good academic candidates, and because of the war, cadets attended the Academy for three years rather than four. Yet the program was slower-paced than it is today, Nye said. The military faculty had gone off to fight; in their place were reserve officers who'd been college professors in civilian life, and many were superb.

During his second summer, Nye was sent to Oklahoma, where he took basic flight training, piloting a biplane. "It was great fun, except I kept getting sick," Nye said, shaking his head. Then he graduated to the single-wing AT-6. The thought was he might not get sick in the faster plane; but after five hours, that didn't work out either, and it was mutually agreed Nye wasn't fated to fly in combat.

After the war ended in 1945, the problem was what to do with newly commissioned second lieutenants. "We didn't talk in terms of a career," Nye said, "but the assumption was that you'd be in the Army for a long time." While an enormous Army was going through a disbanding process, the military would be required to meet occupation commitments in Germany and Japan. Nye was assigned to the Armored School at Fort Knox, where he took the basic branch course, then served in Germany. When the Korean War broke out in June 1950, he was still up to date on armored equipment and didn't have to return to school before being sent to Korea, where he commanded a tank platoon in the 2nd Infantry Division that October.

On October 1st, American troops had crossed the Thirty-eighth Parallel and begun an offensive. They'd captured the North Korean capital of Pyongyang and were driving toward the Manchurian border. It was cold, Nye remembered, and the topography consisted of narrow roads and hills about as high as those rising above the Hudson Valley around West Point.

Intelligence reports of Chinese Communists troops entering the war persisted through November, and when the Chinese struck en masse toward the end of the month, what seemed like rolling waves of arms and legs sent American forces reeling back down the Korean peninsula. Chaos reigned as the Chinese broke through, circling behind much of the 2nd Division and surrounding them. Nye's squadron, fortunately, had been diverted and avoided being trapped. But the organization broke down, in the sense that the commander fled south with the maintenance. Nye's platoon of five tanks traveled with a regiment performing rearguard duties, and he remembered his unheated tank manning a river line that bitter November.

Retreating, Nye's platoon would hold an intersection until the last of the scrambling infantry got safely away. Then the tanks would move to another assigned intersection, leapfrogging among descending squares of an imaginary checkerboard. Nye's instructions were not to get engaged to the point where he'd have to be extricated. Knowing when to move out was therefore critical, and it was usually at night.

"We ran into first-class Chinese troops," Nye recalled, "and what you noticed were their mortar gunners. They were using old, beat-up equipment, but they were excellent. If we sat there on a line, by the third shot they'd get you. So you learned not to remain stationary. Luckily for us, those people were killed off early in the game, and the Chinese Army that existed months later was entirely different."

Nye remembered sitting in a tank on November 26, ranged along the Changchun River near Kunu-ri. The bank to his front was strewn with hundreds of Chinese bodies, troops who'd tried to cross the river during the night and were cut down. When a group of civilians walked down the opposite bank to the river's edge, one of Nye's sergeants began firing at them, but Nye countermanded him, calling for a cease-fire. They got into an argument, which was resolved only when the sergeant was wounded by a mortar round from across the river and had to be evacuated. But Nye couldn't be sure he hadn't endangered his troops by not firing on the civilians, some of whom were known to have been forced to hide mortar rounds under their clothing. The following day, Nye remembered firing his .50-caliber machine gun at a group of shadowy figures running across a field and dropping one. Would he have fired as quickly the second day, one imagines Nye reflecting later, if not for the contentious, wounded sergeant?

The 2nd Division, suffering almost 80 percent casualties, was badly beaten and overhauled in December and January. At about that time, Nye was assigned to IX Corps headquarters as a staff officer. There he got to observe Lt. Gen. William Hoge, the corps commander.

Told that the Chinese had broken through the center of the peninsula and were pouring down roads and valleys threatening his command, Hoge said he'd take no action. His dismayed and anxious briefers encouraged Hoge to move his headquarters that evening. But that evening, Hoge again refused to take action. The following morning, he told his staff that the Chinese offensive would soon run out of food and supplies before achieving their objective, Seoul, far to the west; nor did they have the flexibility or

doctrine to change direction in an offensive of this size. Hoge
thought a recon company would be able to inform him when the
time was ripe to counterattack their flanks as they retreated, and he
proved entirely correct. Nye never forgot seeing a general up close
"who believed so strongly in his insights about the enemy he could
predict and take tactical risks that seemed contrary to all the
collected wisdom around him."

That experience is among many Nye touched upon when he
wrote a book called *The Challenge of Command* after retiring from
the Army in 1975. His peers were surprised Nye retired then,
because he was deputy chairman of the History Department and
would have taken over when the chairman retired. But Nye decided
he'd rather write. The department, too, had jelled, becoming more
specialized and less interdisciplinary than Nye would have preferred. All in all, the timing to leave seemed right to Nye.

"This book of commentaries about military command," he
writes, "was conceived to answer, at least in part, the question that
shadowed me through four decades of work with military students:
'Sir, what should I read?' There is, of course, no general answer to
this very individual question. I have, however, encouraged all to
keep asking that question, remembering George S. Patton, who,
according to the movie *Patton*, watched the Afrika Korps wither
before his defense and shouted, 'Rommel, you magnificent bastard, I read your book!'"

The first thing to say about Nye's is that he writes with a sense
of style, and, after reading a number of books by colonels and
generals, that is no small compliment. The next is to note that it's
a book neither about the Middle East nor modern Europe, subjects
a history professor like Nye might be expected to write. Rather,
it's an instructive book, suggesting other books young officers
might profitably read to increase their understanding of an aspect
of their profession, or the kind of book a mentor would particularly
feel comfortable composing.

As for Nye's future writing plans, he mentioned that in completing his thesis, "The United States Military Academy in an Era of
Educational Reform, 1900–1925," he'd tracked West Point as an
educational institution that, unlike most American colleges, experienced few changes during the early 1900s. That story needs to be
carried up to World War II, Nye said, and he expects to write it.
But before he does, he plans to compose a number of essays about
what's happened to the Military Academy since World War II, in

the belief that will make the earlier, transitional period easier to deal with.

In addition to his own writing, Nye works as a military editor engaged in publishing a series of out-of-print classics, like *Morale: A Study of Men and Courage* by John Baynes and *Defence of Duffer's Drift* by E. D. Swinton, books that have to do with command, management, and leadership. Many were written by Englishmen who, for one reason or another, seemed to have the particularly felicitous knack for combining theory, biography, and good story-telling Nye finds so appealing.

When he retired in 1975, Nye did so with the feeling he'd been spoiled by having been surrounded in his everyday dealings with people of high quality for the thirty years he'd spent in the military. Where was he to find such people again? He thought he'd solved that problem by moving to Highland Falls, the town immediately adjacent to West Point. "By high caliber, I mean pretty well academically trained, talented people—Rhodes scholars, athletes, and so forth. But also people very much concerned about the nation, about political life, and about taking care of soldiers. I really have been very fortunate being here at West Point, with the Social Sciences Department, where there was a very high concentration of talented people, then dealing with civilian faculties across the country, and with the government people who come here to speak. It's a group that doesn't spend its evenings discussing if they're going to buy a new living room rug.

"The other part of that good fortune is that I started out from high school in Ida Grove, Iowa, in 1942, and the Army carried me through an undergraduate degree, through a masters degree, through a Ph.D., studying at the American University at Beirut, traveling to the Far East, living in Germany for six years—all of that experience. I don't know whether it could be duplicated today. In some ways it was hinged to World War II, an Army scattered around the world, and a rather generous educational program which is now too expensive for us, I think. But maybe we're tending to spend too much on equipment and too little on people at this stage." Certainly it's the people who've always fascinated Nye.

In his book, Nye tells of a picture given to him by a former cadet, Paul Bucha, who was among those who'd once asked, "What should I read, sir?" Bucha later commanded a company with the 101st Airborne in Vietnam, and the picture shows him "in the jungle, kneeling by his radiotelephone operator, microphone in hand. His company was surrounded, casualties were heavy. For his bravery in this action he later received the Congressional Medal of Honor. But in this picture there were tears in his eyes. He wrote on it: 'This picture was taken at the moment I realized the high price we pay for the pursuit of undefined goals.' "

When Nye earlier said it seemed he'd attended a memorial service a week in the late 1960s for former cadets killed in Vietnam and felt sorrier for the parents and wives than for the officers killed, it sounded worldly, the kind of reply you offer to a relative stranger who'd asked a probably more pointed question than he'd had a right to pose. But actually cared more for wives and parents Nyc didn't really know than for the young men he'd mentored, who were sleeping their last sleep?

Surely the picture and inscription Bucha sent Nye suggest otherwise. So does the picture of Don Holleder. And why wouldn't someone like Tony Nadal single out Nye as an instructor who was "empathetic"? Finally, would the young lieutenant coming for dinner have told Nye how tired he was of West Point "treating him like a little boy" if he'd thought Nye unworthy of his confidence? You hardly generate that kind of loyalty over a period of years without paying for it with one form of heartbreak or another. But why suggest something that intimate to a prying stranger?

TIMBOE, Harold L. (Hal)
COL MC 569-58-9807
BORN: 23 Mar 46, Long Beach, CA

Col. Harold Timboe of West Point's Class of 1968 is five-ten and weighs about 155. He has blue eyes, and a dimple indents his chin. His hair, which started out brown, is turning a sandy gray and thinning on top. Yet his face remains boyish and so does his voice.

He was born March 23, 1946, in Long Beach, California, which is southeast of Los Angeles and home port to a flotilla of U.S.

Navy ships. Timboe's mother's family moved out to Long Beach from the Texas panhandle during the dust bowl days. His grandfather, looking for work, landed a temporary job at Procter & Gamble and ended up staying with them for about forty years. Timboe's father's family came from Norway and originally settled in North Dakota. But they, too, moved to Long Beach during the 1930s. When Timboe's parents married in high school, between their sophomore and junior years, his father got a job as a gas station attendant. Later he served in the Army and went to Japan, a member of the occupation force during the late 1940s. Timboe lived with his mother's parents while his father was stationed overseas, and he's always felt close to his grandparents. His brother, Richard, was born in 1949.

Did Timboe have any other brothers or sisters?

"No, just one brother, who went to West Point and graduated in the '72 Class," Timboe said. "He played football and was offered something like a hundred scholarships. My father also played football in high school, and his father was an all-American high-school basketball player back in North Dakota." Timboe himself played and still plays basketball, although his best sport probably was baseball. A left-hander, he covered first and pitched. He could throw hard and didn't walk many, and his high school won the state championship during his senior year.

It was toward the end of his sophomore year that Timboe had first thought of attending West Point, when a senior at his school received an appointment to the Naval Academy. "There was also a show I used to watch on TV those years called something like *Men of West Point*, and I not only enjoyed watching it but it probably planted a seed or two."

During his junior year, Timboe's father became a lobbyist for the Northrop Corporation and took his family to Washington, D.C. There Timboe saw a dozen classmates actively trying to gain West Point appointments. One of his father's coworkers was Bill Clark, Gen. Mark Clark's son, who'd said early on he'd try to help Timboe enter West Point.

But Timboe's family moved back to California during his senior year, and he received the appointment through his California congressman. He'd also gotten a partial scholarship to USC and probably could have played some basketball on the freshman team. Yet it was West Point he finally decided to enter. That spring, his mother asked him, "Is this really what you want?" Although he answered he thought so, he probably sounded surer than he felt. Before traveling East, he went up to Mammoth Lake in the High Sierra, where he'd been taken on vacations since he was two or three. "We still occasionally go back there, my brother and I. They stock the lake, so you can always catch a trout or two. It's beautiful country."

Timboe's father accompanied him and another West Point appointee East that June. They stopped in Washington and thanked the congressmen who'd appointed them, flew up to New York, where they caught a bus to West Point, stayed at the Thayer Hotel the night before having to report in, and got up the following morning, excited but nervous.

"I need to go back a little bit," Timboe said. "We didn't talk about my sister." When he was in the ninth grade, his parents decided to adopt a baby girl. At the time, Timboe's grandmother was working for a lawyer who'd arranged for the adoption. His parents, who'd had marital difficulties throughout his childhood, possibly saw adopting a child as a way of stabilizing their marriage. "And it did for a while, because when they ended up getting a divorce, it was about the time my sister graduated from high school," Timboe said.

He recalled that the first guy he met at the bus station in New York was captain of the baseball team, and his first West Point roommate was a high-school all-American pitcher. Others were number one graduates in their high-school class, still others were from famous military schools like Fork Union. "Gee, I'm going to be a nobody up there," Timboe remembered thinking.

After settling in that first day, he went out in the hallway, looking to take a shower. He found a guy brushing his teeth and asked where the showers were. The guy said, "Hit the wall!" Having not the slightest notion what that meant, Timboe went over to the door and slammed it twice with his fist. *Wham! Wham!* Incensed at Timboe's literal-minded response, the guy screamed for him to hit the wall again. Shrugging, Timboe slammed the door with his fist twice more. *Wham! Wham!* Finally, in an utterly exasperated tone of voice, the guy explained that "hit the wall" meant for Timboe to brace against the wall, you moron, stand aside, make way for an upperclassman to pass by.

Despite this inauspicious debut, Timboe quickly learned the value of maintaining a low profile. He saw who kept getting picked on and why, and figured out how to avoid drawing special attention. His major problem that first summer was improperly shining his shoes, although he proved a whiz at quickly changing his uniform, an exercise upperclassmen seemed to enjoy making plebes perform ceaselessly in Beast Barracks.

Those running Beast also made sure plebes took showers at the end of the day. But before being allowed into the showers, plebes had to show sweat. "So what you had to do was brace against the wall and stand there, until you sweated through your bathrobe," Timboe explained. "Basically, you're doing isometrics. Some of the guys would do a bunch of push-ups, run in place in their rooms before they'd come out to shower formations. Well, I just didn't pick up on that one. I could brace real hard, but I just couldn't generate a sweat. So I was always one of the last guys to do that and it got me into a little bit of trouble."

Asked if he ever considered leaving West Point during Beast Barracks, Timboe said that about three or four days after arriving at the Academy, he had, in fact, made up his mind the place wasn't for him and thought he ought to resign. He went through the chain of command, finally telling his tactical officer, and it sounded as if West Point were perfectly willing to let him go. The tac phoned his parents, telling them Timboe was in his office and wanted to resign.

"But my parents said, 'No, we're not going to give our permission,' or that sort of thing." It was a short conversation. Timboe wasn't sure why his parents objected but guessed they thought he was just going through a spell of homesickness. "Anyway, when they said no and the tac relayed that information to me, it was kind of like, 'Oh, okay. Well, I guess I'm here. And I'll just proceed along.' I never tried to argue the point. It was kind of like seeing what my parents would say, and if I could get out. I'm glad they forced me to stay, in a sense."

Was it possible the tac might have called his parents before the call Timboe heard, suggesting if they said no without talking to Timboe, who wasn't allowed to phone them, he'd probably acquiesce? Timboe doubted it. "I think when he called, they were kind of surprised, almost shocked, and probably a little bit angry."

Came September, Timboe not only had learned to shine his shoes but also performed well on an intramural team, contributing to his company's success. As a result, the upperclassmen to whom he answered began treating him with relative civility. He'd also settled in academically and did well above average in math and most everything else. He'd hoped to make the freshman basketball team but didn't, yet managed to stay with the varsity as a manager. That meant he helped out during practice. During the games he'd sit on the bench, but he never suited up. More important, being a manager enabled him to sit with the athletes in the mess hall, away from the regular tables and harassment. Then, in the spring, he made the freshman baseball team as the number four pitcher, which also kept him from being harassed in the mess hall.

But being a basketball manager turned out to be far more important for another reason: it was how Timboe met his wife, Donna Murray. Donna's brother, Dick Murray, was captain of the basketball team. During a game against St. John's, Timboe noticed a couple of girls sitting in the section reserved for relatives, and he asked one of the other managers, who'd happened to live near Murray in Ramsey, New Jersey, if he knew who the girls were. "Oh, that's Dick Murray's family." After the game, Timboe approached Murray in the locker room, saying, "Hey, Dick, how about if I take your sister to the plebe dance?" Murray looked at him strangely. "Are you serious?" The sister Timboe had in mind was fifteen and a half. "It was kind of a blind date I'd arranged," Timboe said. Although he saw Donna a couple of times that spring, they didn't get together during the summer or fall. But near the end of his sophomore year, he asked Murray, "Hey, how's your sister doing?" One thing led to another, and when Murray married days after he graduated, both Donna and Timboe attended the wedding.

Murray and most of the Class of '66 knew they'd soon be going over to Vietnam. As for Timboe, he was certainly aware the war was heating up. Reading *The New York Times* every day, it was impossible not to be aware. "Besides, a lot of guys at West Point were really gung ho about Vietnam," Timboe remembered. "They said, 'Hey, I came to join the military, to be a military professional, this is part of our profession,' and they viewed it as an opportunity."

When it came time to decide on his branch, Timboe chose Air Defense. It was a highly technical branch, and Timboe had done well in subjects like operations research and nuclear physics. Another reason was that Air Defense installations were usually located near or around major urban areas; and after four years of being sequestered at West Point, Timboe felt he needed to integrate himself back into American society and being stationed near a city would help do that. "I really didn't consider Vietnam and I really didn't know if I was going to make the Army a career; and maybe if I thought I was going to do twenty, thirty years, I might have chosen another branch."

During his third summer, Timboe was slated to become a platoon leader at Camp Buckner, where he was fortunate to lead an exceptionally talented group of yearlings, with four or five of the very top men in their class as members of his platoon. The various platoons were in constant competition at Buckner, and because Timboe's came out on top he was selected as an outstanding leader and given a watch. He thought that might translate into a high leadership position—perhaps he'd be made a captain during his senior year. Unfortunately that didn't materialize, but he was appointed an executive officer.

Academically, he seemed to do better each year, graduating 109th out of 706, or in the top 15 percent of his class. It was during his senior year, too, that his brother became a member of the plebe class. "We had a good time being together up there."

It sounded as if Timboe were close to his brother?

"Oh, yeah." Timboe's brother played quarterback for the freshman team but injured his shoulder. Although he was a very good passer, Army was not a passing team in those years, and his brother often ran the other team's offense in practice.

Timboe remembered coming in from chapel one Sunday morning and going to the mess hall; breakfast was optional Sundays, and cadets sat at tables on a random basis. Timboe was concentrating on his food when his brother sat at the other end of the table, neither noticing the other. But when the first classman sitting at the head of the table began giving Timboe's brother a hard time, Timboe, recognizing his brother's voice, suddenly looked up. "Hey, today's Sunday and that's my brother," he told the guy.

From the beginning, Timboe had fully supported the honor code. One time during his plebe year, an upperclassman questioned him about his inadequately polished belt buckle, came away dissatisfied with Timboe's response that, indeed, he'd polished his belt buckle, and reported him to the honor rep of their company, who interrogated Timboe but determined he'd been telling the truth. A couple of years later, Timboe was himself nominated to serve on the honor committee but didn't get selected.

"During my senior year, my brother had a situation where he—and it was when he was learning what constituted an honor violation—may have committed an honor violation, and so I reported that to the honor system," Timboe said. "Turned out he hadn't. That was shortly after I'd gotten that commandant's award for leadership out at Buckner, and the commandant, or superintendent, with whom we were having breakfast, said to me, 'Gee, I heard there was something about your brother, and it took a lot of courage, that sort of thing. He wanted to console me, or just say it took a lot, or whatever. So he expressed his feelings.

"The incident was something like my brother was on guard duty and supposed to come off duty at a certain time," Timboe said. "Either he looked at his clock or changed the time on his clock to indicate it was time to go, or something like that. And so another guy took his place, that sort of thing. Somehow it came to my attention. Now, the honor code says that a cadet will not lie, cheat, or steal, or tolerate anyone who does. And so, by having some sort of vague knowledge of a potential violation, I was really under an obligation.

"My own class had had a big honor scandal during our plebe year. I think they were giving answers to tests. Some people did it, and some knew their roommates were doing it. And so with some it was an act of commission, and with some it was they tolerated it. I forget how many had to leave—twenty-five, fifty, seventy-five?"

Had Timboe's brother said anything to him about it after?

"No, I don't think he knows about it," Timboe said. "Obviously, he was approached by his honor rep, who said, 'Hey, we heard you did this.' And the way he was talking, telling people about it, it could have come from a number of sources. So, no, he's never asked me. In a way, I'm sure that first summer he had some ideas, too, about why he was there. Because, as I'd said, he'd had over a hundred offers to play college football. Tommy Prothro, the UCLA coach, thought he had the best arm he'd ever seen. And, in fact, the guy who'd played second string to my brother in high school went to UCLA and ended up fifth in the Heisman Trophy balloting one year. My brother was that good and, for a while, he regretted going to West Point. But now he doesn't. He can see it was a quality institution and that it left you with things later on."

Timboe graduated on a Wednesday and married Donna two days later, in the West Point chapel. His parents were living in Plainfield, New Jersey, that year, and a lot of relatives flew in from California to attend both ceremonies. The night before his marriage, he remembered sleeping on a cot in his parents' bedroom. Timboe's sister was sleeping in the next cot. The other rooms were filled with visiting relatives. The following morning, his grandfather helped him wash his car. It seemed a pleasantly familial note to end on. . . .

Timboe handed me a gold-covered chapbook called *Bugle Notes* the next time we got together. The book, given to all entering cadets, contained among other things, "The Military Code of Conduct," "Schofield's Definition of Discipline," "Fourth Class Customs and Traditions," and two pages of facts and figures about West Point that plebes were expected to memorize. "You might want to take a look through it at your leisure and return it to me. It'll give you an idea what plebes face during Beast Barracks."

Timboe also thought a book about Vietnam I'd find useful was *On Strategy* by Col. Harry Summers. We were scheduled to discuss *Timboe's* Vietnam experiences that afternoon, but before we started, Timboe wanted to mention two or three matters he'd been reflecting on, and Summers' book was one of them. "I think Harry Summers really put a lot of what the officer corps had come to feel in examining themselves in the years after Vietnam," he said. But I cut him short because I'd read the book. Applying Clausewitz's principles of war, Summers basically concluded America suffered a major failure in strategic military doctrine because the country had failed to concentrate on the political aim to be achieved, containing North Vietnamese expansion.

Timboe next pointed out that during his senior year the football team was so successful, losing only one game, it had earned two bowl bids. West Point had never received a bowl bid before, and the team eagerly accepted the one from the Sugar Bowl. But the secretary of the Army refused to let the Academy go, and the reason given was that the country would perceive an emphasis on football and athletics inconsistent with the mission of the Military Academy.

That decision so upset the senior class, Timboe continued, that the commandant felt obliged to speak to them in the auditorium, saying the decision has been made, you have to live with it, there is no use discussing it further. But that veto left a number of cadets with the sinking feeling, "Gee, if these are the decisions made by our senior civilian leadership, what kinds of decisions are they making in Vietnam? Also, what was the real political reason for not letting West Point play in the Sugar Bowl?"

One night, a number of seniors, not including Timboe, sneaked back into the mess hall and removed all the sterling sugar bowls, about three hundred of them, dumping the sugar out in the middle of the tables. Eventually, of course, they got returned, but even at West Point, Timboe said with a smile, protests of one sort or another were going on. Then he nodded, as if to say, Okay, on to my Vietnam.

But before we proceeded, there was one subject from the previous week that, I thought, required a reprise. "Tell me again about your brother and the honor system."

"I was a senior and he was a freshman," Timboe said. "I was out at Camp Buckner during my senior summer, and he was going through Beast Barracks. I guess on one of their camp-outs he was supposed to be on guard duty, and he related a story to me and my parents on some sort of picnic in the afternoon. He kind of told a little bit how he got out of guard duty an hour or so early because of something. In thinking about that, it sounded a little bit like a potential honor violation, and I was kind of saddled: What do I do with this? He was also kind of unhappy, as many plebes were, during that period. I guess in a way, I said, 'Gee, I've got an obligation here. But maybe this is also an opportunity. If I report it, he really has a choice to make.'

"'Either I did that on purpose, it was an honor violation, and I'm out tomorrow, or else I'm confronted with do I want to stay?' And I guess he really said, 'Gee, I do want to stay here.' Sometimes cadets would commit an honor violation because that's an easy though maybe not very honorable way to get out."

Adopting Nash's vivid phrase, I walked a mile in Timboe's shoes, yet felt compelled to ask, "Did you ever say to yourself, 'Maybe I should talk to my brother first and tell him perhaps he should report himself'? Wasn't that a possibility? Or did you immediately feel obliged to report him? Do you know what I'm saying?"

"Yeah, you're right, that would have been one of the options—to go to him," Timboe said. "But to me it was easiest to do it anonymously, I guess, rather than confront my brother. And maybe that's not a very strong moral position. It never really occurred to me, because the easiest way to tell my honor rep, who'd then go to my brother's honor rep, who'd then decide if he needed to go to my brother."

"But what would have happened if they'd kicked your brother

out? How do you think you'd have dealt with that? Wouldn't you have felt lousy? Wouldn't you have felt, 'Jesus, what did I do?'?"

"I guess that's what everybody, or not everybody, would think because very few know or knew about it. I think I told you the general knew, because it got to him from the honor committee. But I don't think my brother knows, or my family, and I'm not sure my wife knows. I might have told her last week. But I think it would have depended on how he reacted. In other words, at that point he was wishy-washy. 'Do I want to finish the summer here, or do I want to go enroll in UCLA and get my football scholarship?' If he would have been very happy and upbeat about leaving at that point, I would have said, 'Gee, I helped him along to come to a conclusion.' "

"But what if it had been the other way—what if he'd felt lousy? It's a shitty but natural question."

"No, you're right," Timboe said. "Fortunately, it didn't come to that, and it really could have had some long-term effects. The family tells it that my grandfather on my father's side, his brother was going to enroll him in the reserves or in the Army. But somehow he didn't enroll my grandfather. And that older brother ended up a colonel in the Army and had a very successful adulthood; and, basically, my grandfather ended up a policeman for a while in Long Beach and then a teamster driving a truck delivering bananas and produce, and had a somewhat less satisfying social status-type adulthood. And I think there was a little animosity there. But if you look back on their younger years, my grandfather had had much more potential for leadership and doing well in the military. So I guess there was the potential that we could almost repeat this; and if my brother would have ended up not doing well, I would have had to live with that, and it might even have inhibited my development. But, I guess, consciously, the long-term consequences never really came up."

We moved on to the time Timboe served in Vietnam. In 1971 he was told by his personnel officer that he was about to be assigned either to Vietnam or Korea, and Timboe chose Vietnam. He was going there to put in his time as the United States was getting out, he said. He didn't sense a great commitment to the American war effort, which was barely in existence then; this was just another military assignment. It would be a short tour away from his family, and he'd learn some professional things as a military officer.

Timboe had hoped to get an Air Defense assignment, but when

he arrived in Vietnam in December, Air Defense units were being withdrawn. Nor did it appear that the branch back in the States had much of a future, because an increasing number of its programs were being canceled.

Yet Americans were still being sent to Vietnam as advisers to the South Vietnamese or assigned to support units of the U.S. Army, Vietnam. The support units during Timboe's year were stationed in Pleiku or Nha Trang. Assigned to Pleiku, Timboe was told by its commander he'd be the staff's recreation officer, and his first task was to set up a volleyball tournament. Timboe felt slighted. That wasn't what he came to Vietnam for. He went back to the assignment people and renegotiated, landing a different job in Nha Trang. There his duties would include dealing with plans and security.

The permanent party in Nha Trang totaled about two thousand. They were tenant units, living on the installation and had specific jobs—say, communications, or sending out food or ammunition to combat units. The commander and his staff, acting as city managers, basically provided a safe home, food to eat, recreation, and various service facilities.

As America kept drawing down its forces, support units became increasingly involved in turning over their facilities to the Vietnamese. "For instance, we had to plan for consolidating and closing down mess halls, and I was the mess hall officer," Timboe said. "If the cease-fire came, we had to be out in sixty or ninety days, and how would we do it? And to facilitate the drawdown generally, I kept taking on an increasing number of staff jobs that weren't being done, as people kept leaving without being replaced."

Nha Trang was a relatively safe town. It had been a resort favored by the French, with a lovely seacoast and a number of strikingly attractive Buddhist temples. Special Forces had one of its headquarters there. The city was defended by Korean troops, and the VC seemed to go out of their way to avoid them. "Looking at the Koreans, the ROK's, and what a good reputation they had twenty years after their war, when they'd had a terrible reputation, I was hoping the South Vietnamese would soon be producing units as good as the Koreans'," Timboe said.

Immediate security was provided by a tribe from the Central Highlands. They sat up in towers and patrolled to make sure the claymore mines were in place and barbed wire surrounding the installation was intact. Timboe was in charge of overseeing and paying them. He'd have preferred serving with an American division, as his father had served with the 1st Cav during the occupation in Japan, but it just wasn't in the cards.

A number of American troops, Timboe said, actually enjoyed being in Vietnam and particularly enjoyed living in Nha Trang. They really didn't want the war to end. Maybe they didn't have families back home; a few had come back to Vietnam for a third time. Other American troops, who didn't want to be in Vietnam at all, were also glad to be stationed in Nha Trang, away from the risks of war generally. These men didn't suffer from bad morale. They were putting in their time, doing their jobs. A third group, for perhaps lack of a meaningful job, would get into trouble using drugs. Fortunately, there was a drug treatment center on the installation. A number of desertions occurred while Timboe was there, and he suspects that some of the MIA's one continues to hear about are guys still over in Southeast Asia who've set up new lives for themselves.

From the day he left for Vietnam, Timboe was looking forward to returning home. Yet he also returned with a sense of satisfaction. He'd done his duty, he said. The government had sent him to do that, it was behind him, and in many ways it had prepared him as a military professional to go on. While Vietnam didn't contribute to his professional technical development as an Air Defense officer, he knew Air Defense was not something he was going to be in for the long term. "But I guess I liked the person that came out of Vietnam, and I recognized it was a different person than went in," Timboe said. More mature, more capable of doing his job within the military, regardless of his branch. He wasn't challenged nearly as much as other people. But he'd made some decisions while he was in Vietnam. First, he was going to try to get into medical school. Second, he became a Born Again Christian.

Timboe said that although his parents believed in God and had attended church sporadically, they weren't particularly religious. So while he'd probably heard all the right things the Sundays he'd gone to church, nothing had really clicked. Nor had it before he'd left for Vietnam and his wife had given him a Bible, "as though somehow that might protect me while I was over there." Yet he decided he'd read the book from cover to cover, so many pages each day, as a way of getting through the year.

Arriving in Vietnam, Timboe began looking for things to do at night and during the weekends. Some people occupied their spare time drinking at the club; others spent it in favorite purlieus downtown, still others in athletics, while a fourth group wrapped themselves in their jobs. "For me," Timboe said, "it was reaching out to some wholesome activities, because that's what I was used to." There were missionary people from the Christian and Missionary Alliance and the Wycliffe Bible Translators, who were part of the military chapel program; they'd hold services throughout the week, and Timboe got to know them. They were Americans, both men and women, and had families over there. They'd been in Vietnam a long time, since the 1920s and 1930s, and because they were able to explain Christian doctrine to him lucidly, everything seemed to come into focus. In addition, they had challenged him: Do you believe or don't you? No one had really ever done that before, and over their testimony and their witness he accepted Christ.

During the time Timboe courted his wife, they'd talked about religious matters because each felt it was important couples share common value systems. He'd learned that his wife had had a similar religious past, in that her family had also only occasionally attended church. But his wife basically believed in God and believed that God had an influence in people's affairs, and before their marriage she was rebaptized. "I'm not sure what significance I attached to it at the time, but she felt she needed that to be ready for marriage. And then, as I said, when I went to Vietnam, she gave me the Bible, and I was touched by that."

A number of Army officers, former West Pointers, went through a similar Born Again experience over in Vietnam, Timboe said. "The phrase, by the way, comes from the New Testament. 'Except a man be born again, he cannot see the Kingdom of God.' It refers to a spiritual rebirth, or a spiritual reawakening."

At the same time this spiritual conversation was taking place, Timboe realized that once he returned from Vietnam he'd have less than a year to fulfill his five-year obligation. So he had to start thinking whether he wanted to remain in the Army, and if so, the direction he wished to pursue. A number of former West Pointers at this stage in their careers go back to the Academy—teaching on the faculty or becoming tactical officers. And Timboe, too, had thought in terms of obtaining a graduate degree and returning to West Point to teach. He'd wanted to get the degree in operations research. But no teaching vacancies would have been available in that subject during the time he'd have had to return to West Point.

On the other hand, the Physics Department had offered to send Timboe to graduate school so he might teach nuclear physics, but he turned them down.

He'd never considered the possibility of becoming a doctor, Timboe said, until a West Point classmate stationed on the installation at Nha Trang found out about an Army-funded program that sent a college graduate to medical school while he remained on active duty. Timboe, who'd been very good in math and science, got to wondering if perhaps medicine might satisfy his inclinations and talents. It meant working with people, but the work would be heavily science-oriented. That seemed to fit. Medicine and his spiritual conversion seemed to fit as well. "In fact, you might call my becoming a doctor a result of a religious calling; or you might conjecture it was merely a matter of timing. But who's to say?"

At any rate, he soon wrote his wife, asking her to send him whatever information she could find about entering medical school, then arranged to take his medical entrance boards over in Vietnam. He did very well, which was the first solid indication medical school was something he'd probably be able to handle. And from 1974 to 1978, he attended the University of Texas Medical School in San Antonio.

Although he hadn't been to school for five years, he found the classroom routine and reading assignments relatively easy. During the time he attended medical school, Timboe said, a number of them were going through a pass-fail system. "That meant you basically failed a test if you were two standard deviations below the class mean on that particular test. So all it really meant was that you had to beat five or six students out of a hundred, and you'd get a pass. And after a few exams, you got a sense of, 'Hey, as long as I put in my routine effort I'm never going to be in that bottom five or six in the class.' So there was never really pressure. Besides, I found the work enjoyable and looked forward to satisfying a social need, helping others."

Deciding to specialize in family practice, Timboe took his residency at Tripler Army Medical Center in Hawaii. "I've always been a generalist, wanting to know about a lot of different things, maybe not deeply, and to a certain extent family practice is like that. You learn about most of the common illnesses. In a sense, family practice is the gatekeeper of medicine."

When you graduate from medical school, Timboe said, you've got a lot of basic foundation knowledge but not a whole lot of experience. But during your residency years, when you specialize, you're taking on the actual responsibility for medical care, the practical aspects of medicine, and you're learning what's important and what's not. Also in the military, residents are given more responsibility early, so it's a period of rapid growth. Timboe thought the reason for the early responsibility might be the amount of staff the military devotes to its teaching hospitals compared to what's traditionally found in civilian hospitals.

During his last year at medical school in San Antonio, he'd taken a course in public health, which is understanding diseases in terms of population rather than in terms of individuals. He thought a knowledge of public health would be particularly useful if he chose to remain in the military. And because Timboe had an opportunity to attend a school offering other public health courses in Hawaii, he wound up getting a masters in public health service, planning, and administration. His thesis was on theater evacuation policy—that is, how to design a medical force that would go to war in terms of its size, and whether you were going to treat casualties in-country, or when and how you were going to evacuate them.

Upon completing his residency in 1981, Timboe thought he'd like the opportunity of getting back with a military unit. So he volunteered to become a division surgeon, or the officer who is the division commander's principal adviser on medical planning and preventive medicine. A number of divisions were available, Timboe was told. Where do you want to go? Among those offered was the 82nd Airborne Division, at Fort Bragg. Timboe knew there was a family practice residency at Bragg he could perhaps join and be in charge of after his division surgeon's assignment was completed; and because he wanted to locate his family in the same geographical area for five or six years, the Bragg possibility sounded particularly promising. As it turned out, the residency job wasn't available when it was Timboe's time to negotiate another assignment. But when Bragg had been offered, he'd said, "Shoot, no choice, I'll take the 82nd."

In addition to his other duties, Timboe was in charge of the division's sick calls. Five medical clinics were scattered throughout the post, servicing seventeen thousand troops. He had eight doctors and about sixteen physician assistants working for him. Sick calls for the soldiers were held in the morning. The clinics would reopen in the afternoon for family care. The kids would come in and get their well-baby checkups. Wives would come in for Pap smears, birth control pills, and any other medical problems. Timboe would do some sick calls; he'd also be out on the drop zones when the division conducted jumps, for there was sure to be a busted ankle or a fractured arm or two as a result of the jump. Incidentally, as a member of the 82nd, doctor or otherwise, Timboe had to jump once a quarter, though he hadn't jumped since completing Airborne School ten years before.

The 82nd was part of the Rapid Deployment Force, the RDF, created to offer speedy support to friendly nations in the Persian Gulf area, Timboe said. A joint exercise, Gallant Eagle '82, involving Army, Navy, and Air Force units, was held in the Mohave Desert in California, to see if the United States could transport a considerable force and all its supplies into a Middle East- or Persian Gulf-type area. About eighteen hundred paratroopers made a transcontinental flight from Bragg and jumped onto five drop zones. Tragically, a higher than normal wind wasn't detected in one of the drop zones, affecting 350 troopers. When they landed, they hit harder than usual and were dragged for longer distances, suffering 150 injuries and four fatalities. Usually one of every hundred jumpers required some kind of medical evaluation, and maybe one in a thousand resulted in a hospitalization. But here the casualty rate was close to an unusually high 10 percent.

Timboe, who'd happened to be on the drop zone where the casualties occurred, remembered seeing one trooper whose chute didn't open plummeting to the ground. His immediate reaction was to have his driver take him to where the soldier had landed, so he could determine if anything could be done or make a quick pronouncement. On the way, he hadn't really expected to find other problems. But once there, he started hearing a number of troopers calling for help and one of them performing CPR. When it quickly became apparent an unusually high number of soldiers had been hurt, Timboe started going from place to place, trying to get an accurate sense of the overall situation.

"Of course, we were right in the middle of the very worst of it, and we wanted to get radio reports about what had happened on the other drop zones," Timboe said. "Fortunately, it didn't turn out as bad anywhere else. After a while I went to the main collecting area of that drop zone, a kind of first aid station, to see that everything was running smoothly. That was our casualty procedure, to collect everyone in one area. We had helicopters standing by, and a lot of medical troops who'd walk the ground to see if anyone needed help; and we had a hospital set up to receive our patients. In other words, we knew beforehand where to evacuate patients and how to evacuate them. And once I saw that that was going reasonably well and the helicopters were taking patients to the hospital, I decided I'd better get to the hospital, too, which was ten miles away.''

At the hospital, he checked with the hospital commander to determine how their procedures were running and what kind of volume they anticipated and were receiving. Although most procedures were running smoothly, in part because the hospital had practiced a few days before for just such a contingency, patients requiring X-rays were backed up. At about that time a couple of the senior generals arrived, and Timboe briefed them.

He then began to concern himself with those patients who couldn't be swiftly taken care of in the hospital. Was the intelligent move to evacuate them to Army and Air Force hospitals in the area? Or was it wiser to fly them back to Bragg? Believing the latter made more sense, Timboe presented that recommendation to the generals, saying he might need their help in getting an Air Force C-141 to transfer about fifty or sixty of these patients that afternoon or night.

Then Timboe talked to the hospital commander back at Bragg. "I won't send you anybody complicated, because they won't be ready to travel," he said. "We've gotten all the difficult patients to local hospitals; these are your broken ankles and sprained wrists. A few of them may require hospitalization and may even need orthopedic surgery. But basically we're putting some splints or casts on them. We won't be able to X-ray them. But I think they want to get home, and I think it's a good idea to fly them out as a group." Timboe encountered a little resistance because that wasn't standard procedure, but he did prevail.

Gallant Eagle '82 generated both congressional and Pentagon investigations. Did everyone follow the correct procedures? Were they adequate? Were any corrective actions necessary? Timboe said Congress quickly got the sense it was an unfortunate incident but that the Army had taken reasonable action, both in handling the situation and in initiating some corrective future actions.

His next assignment was as commander of the Army hospital at Fort Irwin, California, the same hospital where the injured jumpers of Gallant Eagle '82 were first taken. Timboe had been completing his tour as division surgeon with the 82nd when the Army surgeon general, a three-star, came to visit Fort Bragg. The general had served in an airborne unit as a medical officer and seemed to show an especial interest in a number of the programs Timboe had instituted at Bragg, and before he left he asked what Timboe would like to do next. "Command a hospital someday and be chief of the family practice residency."

It happened that the doctor who'd trained Timboe in family practice was now on the staff of the Army's health services command headquarters; and, pushing to get a family practice doctor into the suddenly vacated commander's slot at Irwin, he'd penciled in Timboe's name. When that recommendation came to the surgeon general's attention days after his visit to Bragg, the three-star still had Timboe freshly in mind, and the fortuitous marriage of timing and circumstance took care of the rest.

About three thousand soldiers and officers are stationed at Irwin, and another three thousand come there for training against a simulated Soviet force. Though it's a relatively small hospital, the commander's job calls for a colonel's rank. In many respects, Timboe found running that hospital more difficult than running a larger one. Because the staff was relatively inexperienced and small, he had little flexibility, and everyone counted.

Timboe had an executive officer, similar to the hospital administrator in a civilian hospital, and a medical staff chief in charge of all doctors. In civilian hospitals, doctors apply for privileges. In the military, doctors are assigned to hospitals, and one of Timboe's jobs was to ensure that no tyros performed services they weren't qualified to practice. Timboe had a company commander in charge of disciplining and satisfying the needs of the soldiers staffing the hospital. He also had a chief of nursing. But it was Timboe who oversaw all of them. "There's really not a comparable position in a civilian hospital, unless you'd say it was kind of the chairman of the board."

In the Medical Corps, there aren't many officers or doctors either inclined or prepared to perform as chairman of the board; but Timboe, who'd always wanted to command, finally got his opportunity when he was assigned to Irwin. "My name 'Harold' means Army commander," he said, "and I knew that even as a kid and suspect that's part of the reason I went to West Point and decided to remain in the Army."

Like any doctor in his command, Timboe made rounds at Irwin and kept up his medical skills. Conversely, Timboe's credibility with combat arms officers derives from his having gone to West

Point and served in prior military assignments. "They know I've experienced a lot of what they experienced, and so they can accept me. They listen to my advice. Plus, I can feel for that military family, because my family used to go to the Army hospital in the middle of the night when my kids became sick and I was still in Air Defense."

Timboe would like to command a larger hospital as well as be in the medical planning and operation process, guaranteeing the Army is medically ready to fight anywhere in the world. He believes West Point prepared him for this, in the sense it provided an intellectual foundation upon which he could build.

"It's funny, but that perspective doesn't come until you've been out for a while," he said. "My brother left the Army after fulfilling his five-year obligation following his graduation. He's doing very well. Fully enjoys his life as a vice president for administration at our local state college, has a good income, and is very happy. But he said, 'Is there some way you could get me a job at West Point? To be associated with an institution like that on a long-term basis, to have some influence over the lives of a lot of young men in our country who are going to go out and do a lot of different things, you could feel a real sense of accomplishment.' I looked at him and said, 'Rick, you—' He said, 'I know that sounds funny coming from me, because I was kind of a goof-off cadet and got out of the military right away.' "

In 1986, Hal Timboe was attending the Army War College and lived off post, a mile or two from the installation, and before we parted he said he wanted me to meet his wife and children, inviting me for dinner the following Thursday. He said the support he'd received from his wife had meant a lot to him, and that year he'd spent in Vietnam, a time during which they might have drifted apart, allowed them to examine the commitment they'd made to each other. "I experienced a lot of different emotions in Vietnam," he remembered, "and I kind of gave myself permission to exhibit those emotions. I may have been somewhat cold and perhaps not very interesting before that. But after, I felt I could express myself a little bit better and it was okay to do that. Before, little things would upset me. Now I know they, too, will pass."

Donna Timboe is a tall, strikingly attractive woman, with a model's high cheekbones, who looked more like her two daughters' sister than she did their mother. The Timboes have four children altogether, ranging from eighteen to eight years.

The family, including the children, said a prayer before sitting down to dinner. There were flickering blue candles on the table, blue plates, and the tablecloth was white trimmed with blue. I'd brought along a bottle of red wine and gave it to Timboe, who had asked if he ought to chill it. We drank from glasses rimmed with gold that, Donna said, they'd inherited, and ate broccoli with hollandaise sauce and chicken curry with all the side dishes. Dessert was pumpkin or lemon meringue pie and coffee.

Donna remembered meeting Timboe after the basketball game. "Army had just beaten St. John's," she said, "and my brother, who was captain of the team, came out and asked if Harold could take me to a dance. Harold, who was one of the managers, had seen me. My brother had said, 'That little girl?' I'm six and a half years younger than my brother. So he said, 'I'll ask my father.' He said to my father, 'This cadet wants to take Donna to this dance. I wouldn't push anybody, but he's the type of guy you'd like to have for a brother-in-law.' I'm only fifteen and a half, mind you, and he's saying this. So my brother came and said, 'This cadet would like to take you,' and I said, 'Sure, I'll go.' But I didn't think right away I was going to marry him. I went out with other people after."

When they married two days after Timboe had graduated, Donna was particularly happy her father attended the ceremony; he'd been unable to when her brother had graduated and married two years before because he'd been recovering from a heart attack.

"I never felt like I was madly in love with Harold, like maybe I'd been with some other boyfriends," Donna said. "But I always felt that he was so strong and he loved me, and I felt so wonderful, like a real lady around him, and I liked that. And so I thought I'd work out all these things. I'd even gotten mad at him, but I'd gotten through it."

Timboe's first assignment subsequent to graduating was as a platoon leader and executive officer of an Air Defense battery at Homestead Air Force Base, Florida. He and Donna had considered requesting an assignment with a Hawk missile battalion in Germany near Garmisch, but because of her father's heart condition they'd decided to remain closer to home.

Then, in the spring of 1969, or about nine months later, when a personnel officer called one night, asking if Timboe was interested in going to Saudi Arabia as an aide to a one-star general, he said,

"Sure, I'll throw my hat in the ring." A number of people were nominated, but the general chose Timboe.

Donna accompanied him and lived in the Middle East for two years, save for the three months she'd returned to the States to have their first child. Timboe was often away from home, traveling with the general on something like seventy-five trips throughout the region.

Donna was all of twenty, and there were only six other American women living in their compound, with the next youngest a woman of thirty-two, who had four children. Donna wasn't allowed to drive in Arabia, and that made her feel somewhat isolated. "Harold would leave the house at seven to go to work and get home by seven," she remembered. "We could drive to this town about ten minutes away and get some vegetables. But sometimes Harold would say, 'No.' And I'd say, 'Thanks a lot. What do you mean, no? You can't say no.' I remember one time, and this is terrible to say, but we had a big fight. We knew by then he was on his way to Vietnam, and I said that maybe it would be the best thing that ever happened for him to go. Not because he was off fighting, but because it would make both of us look into ourselves."

Donna remembered gigantic Arabian roaches. They were about three inches long and had antlers. "We called them 747s." But they were a mere bagatelle compared to the mice, who'd jump out of her toaster when she'd walk into the kitchen. "Agggh! It was awful. I started knocking on my way, saying, 'Okay, mice, I'm coming,' and I'd hear, *Thump, thump, thump.* So I didn't have to look at them. One time I had meat thawing out on the counter, and I came back in and it had been chewed on by the mice. I said, 'We're going to the club tonight.'" But Donna also recalled delicious shrimp, huge and cleaned, she could buy for four rials, or eighty-eight cents a pound.

They went to Iran a couple of times and once to India, where they saw the Taj Mahal, taking their little girl, who was four months old. Timboe got food poisoning there, and Donna remembered rushing him to the hospital in the middle of the night. "He was going both ends, high fever, it was scary. I got him to the hospital, and the doctor said, 'He might have hepatitis, but you can go home.' Then, on the way out, I saw a rat the size of a cat running down the hallway."

They were both a little mad, Donna said, when they found out

Timboe had to go to Vietnam, because Saudi Arabia had been a somewhat difficult tour. During their two years there, Timboe had had six months' TDY (temporary duty) time, which meant considerable traveling away from his family. In addition to the TDY time, he'd been required to make those weekly regional trips of one or two days. So they felt they'd been separated a lot already. And although the war was winding down, Donna didn't want her husband to be the last man killed. She'd also learned she was pregnant with their second child shortly before Timboe found out he was going to Vietnam.

When he'd left before Christmas in 1971, Donna went to live with her parents in New Jersey. She was only twenty-two, and there were few people her age nearby. Sometimes her mother would baby-sit, and she'd walk to the nearby shops. She remembered shopping with her younger sister once, wearing a tentlike trench coat that came down to her ankles and wedgie shoes she'd worn while she was pregnant. They'd run into a couple of boys she'd known in high school who'd been a year behind her. Good-looking twenty-one-year-old men who, they'd once looked up to Donna, the former cheerleader. "I'd always imagined in my life, fifteen, twenty years down the road, they'd say, 'Boy, you changed, you're really something.' I said, 'Hi, I'm Donna Timboe, used to be Murray.' One guy whispered, 'She's changed.' But the way he said it, I wanted to vomit. When I went home, I was sick. Next day, I bought myself a hot pants outfit and high boots. I just couldn't stand the thought of being old." A has-been at twenty-two!

Donna laughed. She laughed a lot that night, a girlishly engaging, unaffected woman. No wonder Timboe was so proud of his wife, and I thought I understood why he'd wanted me to meet her.

She was bored the year Timboe served in Vietnam. They wrote each other long letters. Although Donna usually went to bed early, that year she'd stay up late, past twelve, composing page after page. Her only real friend then was a young woman Timboe's brother, who was still attending West Point, had been dating.

During the first years of their marriage, Donna considered divorce. "I thought of it as a real option. I know that hurts Harold to hear. I don't think of it now, but I did then." She also had a recurring dream in those years. In the dream, Timboe and Donna married, had a son, and Timboe went off to Vietnam, where he was killed. Donna believed the source of the dream was Timboe's cousin, Timmy Timboe, a Marine who'd been killed in Vietnam a couple of months before they'd gotten married. But because of the dream she didn't want to give birth to a boy and was relieved that her first two children were girls.

A second recurring dream revolved around her former boy-friends, and she wondered who among them would accept Timboe's children if she ever got together with one or another. "A lot of times I took that to mean maybe I was thinking about other men, and I didn't like that thought and would try to suppress it. And that's one reason I never told Harold about it until just last week. Because I was afraid he might get hurt I was even thinking it."

Donna became aware of a change in Timboe when they spent a week together on R&R in Hawaii three months after he'd left for Vietnam. He seemed different right away. He told Donna about the missionaries and wanted to pray with her. "We'd never prayed together before," she said, "and that made me feel calm."

Timboe, his wife continued, had never been exposed back in the States to people like the missionaries he'd met in Vietnam. They believed so intensely and were so articulate about their faith, he started attending church with them. "In most churches, they don't really teach," Donna said. "Mostly, it's a do-good sort of thing. Be a good person, instead of understanding that Christ did it for us. He paid the debt. It's like a gift-giving. Anyway, for once in his life Harold accepted it. He believed it." Perhaps the reason he accepted and believed it then, Donna added, was that for the first time in his life Timboe didn't feel he was in control. That wasn't the case before being sent to Vietnam, when he'd always felt confident and in charge. "But this time he was definitely different, changed," Donna said. That was in the spring.

Then in July, Donna received the letter asking her to send Timboe information about entering medical school. She'd thought after having spent the week with him in Hawaii he might be leaning toward the ministry, so the letter came as a huge surprise. "But he really felt it fit in with his Christian conversion, like God opening his eyes, saying to him, 'Your math and science back-ground plus your military background can be combined into military and family medicine.'"

Later that year, they spent a week together in Vietnam. Timboe said he never would have thought of bringing her to Vietnam had it not been for Saudi Arabia. He had two motives. One was just to be together. The other was that if Donna spent a week with him in

Vietnam, they'd share the experience, just as they'd shared being together in Arabia, and it would help cement their relationship.

Timboe had been aware of advisers' wives coming over on official programs of one sort or another, and, after determining that Nha Trang, an in-country R&R spot even during the height of the war, was still fairly secure, talked Donna into joining him there. The missionaries had guest quarters and were agreeable, and Donna got a visa listing their address.

Leaving her two young daughters with her parents, she flew to Saigon. Timboe met her at the airport. He told her they'd take a plane to Nha Trang. But when Donna saw the plane, a small ten-seater, she told him, "I've never been in a plane that small before, and I'm not going to get into one in Vietnam," and they had to wait around a couple of hours for a larger plane. "I think only because Harold missed me so much he put up with that. Any other time, he'd really have gotten mad at me for making a fuss."

Nha Trang reminded Donna of Hawaii. The same type of weather and lush green mountains that seemed to stretch down to the South China Sea. The time was September 1972. Timboe wasn't on leave, and he'd go to work each morning, returning home for lunch and dinner. But one morning, they were lying in bed and heard a loud noise. Donna got scared and said, "What's that?" Timboe thought it was just guys on a garbage truck banging some cans around. But Donna said it didn't sound like any garbage truck to her. "All of a sudden, his beeper sounded and he sat up and said, 'Oh, my God, we're on red alert! We've never had a red alert before!'" Donna asked him what that meant. Timboe said, "It means we're under attack!"

"You mean I've left my babies, came over here, and we're being attacked!" she exclaimed. She jumped up and began getting dressed. Timboe was already lacing his boots. "I started brushing my hair," Donna remembered, "and Harold looked up at me and said, "I don't believe it. We're on red alert, and she's brushing her hair!'"

Finding his wife a flak jacket and helmet, Timboe hurried her to a nearby bunker. They could hear other explosions, but it was hard to determine whether they were caused by outgoing rockets or those slamming in, and Donna began to think, "Why am I here?" Sandbags were omnipresent, and she wondered what would happen if they landed on her, or what she'd do if Timboe were killed. The noise outside lasted less than thirty minutes. After a while, Timboe began checking around. Eventually he learned that it was a Vietnamese holiday and the North Vietnamese had sent in a single stray rocket. But after that morning, Donna, who'd been staying with Timboe in his BOQ, resided in the guest quarters of the missionaries. There she got to meet a number of Vietnamese, saw the military everywhere, but didn't spot any other army wives. All in all, it proved a fascinating week.

Back home, Donna was aware of the war, generally speaking, because she rarely missed the nightly news. She said seeing the war on the tube made her mad. "It was like the war was right in your living room, and that only made you feel worse. But I was even angrier about the antiwar people. I felt they really didn't understand. They acted as if the military had created the war. But who more than the military wanted it over? We didn't want our husbands being killed, and Harold didn't want to be away from us. The reason we have the military is to prevent wars, not to have them. It's to keep strong so that they don't happen. That's the philosophy of most military people. Sure, there are a few who really enjoy playing war games. But most of them don't really like to be in war, and they don't like to kill anybody."

Donna felt that the antiwar movement, given great TV exposure, jeopardized American soldiers' lives. She'd doubted the movement was as prevalent as its exposure seemed to suggest; but that exposure must have given the North Vietnamese the impression America was deeply divided, more divided than Donna believed, which couldn't help but bolster their morale and confidence.

Because it was almost time to leave and both her husband and brother were West Point graduates, it seemed only natural to ask about the effects Donna thought the Academy had on cadets.

"Not only Harold and my brother, but Harold's brother graduated from West Point," she reminded me. "And although each is a different personality, they share a camaraderie because they've gone through the West Point experience. It was a certain amount of discipline they were willing to let themselves undergo when everybody else was off experimenting with drugs. And I also think they respect their country perhaps more than most people. The 'duty, honor, country' is ground into their heads from the day they go there. I certainly don't have the same sense of priorities. To me it should be family first."

It was after ten when I stood up to say good night and thanked them for dinner. Timboe drove me back to my motel. It had been warm for December, and that morning I'd walked around the town of Carlisle wearing only a sweater. The old courthouse near the intersection of High and Hanover streets still bore scars caused by Confederate shelling in the summer of 1863, a day or two before the Battle of Gettysburg. Touching those nicks, it was both pleasant and sad to think of Lee and Meade, Longstreet and Hancock, a band of brothers, attending West Point together something like 150 years ago.

A quarter moon, shaped like a teenager's glitzy earring and silvery in the distance, lit up the highway leading to the motel. When Timboe mentioned the upcoming Army-Navy game he and his family were planning to attend that weekend, I thought about how he'd "hit the wall" his first day at West Point, wanted to resign less than a week later, and wound up twenty-odd years after, commanding an Army hospital. Then I thought about his brother, receiving a hundred football offers but living back in his hometown of Long Beach, who now wanted to return to West Point.

"Would you be interested in going to the Army-Navy game?" Timboe asked.

But that wasn't a good idea even if I'd wanted to go.

The following week, I made a point of sending the Timboes a dozen long-stemmed roses. Considering the trouble they'd gone to having me for dinner, it seemed the least I could do.

ANDERSON, James L. (Jim)
COL INF 291-28-1993
BORN: 3 Apr 33, New Lexington, OH

New Lexington is a farming community of about fifty-five hundred in southeastern Ohio. When Col. Jim Anderson, West Point '56, was growing up, the town orphanage was a two-story red brick building with an attic and a basement, and it was run by a couple whose forbidding titles of "superintendent" and "matron" belied their good natures.

— About forty boys lived on the first floor, something like thirty-five girls resided on the second. The children slept in open bay dormitories, their beds lined up in rows, head to foot. Everyone had chores, and Anderson's as a boy was to make a row of beds and mop the floor around the beds before breakfast. Because the orphanage was part of a working farm, Anderson as he got older assumed some of the hardier chores, such as slopping hogs and milking cows. While he remained in the orphanage until he enlisted in the Air Force upon graduating from high school in 1951, his father continued living twenty miles away, in Zanesville.

Anderson had two slightly older sisters and a considerably older brother. His mother had died shortly after he was born, and his father remarried a woman who had a number of children of her own. This was during the Depression and there was not enough to go around. Anderson and his sisters first entered the orphanage when he was about three, left it for a few months when he was four, but returned with his sisters when he was five. Because there was little interaction in the orphanage between the boys and girls, Anderson hardly got to know his sisters.

"If there are saints, Mr. and Mrs. Dornbirer are two of them," he said of the couple who ran the orphanage. Mrs. Dornbirer's first husband was a Lutheran minister who'd died early on. Rufus Dornbirer, her second husband, stood about six-one and owned a nearby farm, but had others running it while he remained superintendent of the orphanage. Yet, Anderson said, it would be a mistake to think of either Mr. or Mrs. Dornbirer as ever sitting in an office, supervising.

Mrs. Dornbirer's friends called her Josie, short for Josephine. An outgoing woman who'd been a teacher before taking over the orphanage, she was about five-three, matronly, and had thinning gray hair, which she wore in a bun. She loved flowers, and the orphanage seemed enveloped by them. Her workday was endless, and Anderson remembered accompanying her at eleven or twelve at night, carrying buckets of water and holding a ship's lantern so that Mrs. Dornbirer could see to plant vegetables in the orphanage's garden. "She just worked like the devil," Anderson said, "yet she was the kind of person who baked a cake if somebody died in the town. Literally anybody." Her hobby was collecting salt and pepper shakers from all over the world, and everyone who remembered took pleasure in sending her an unusual pair. "She must have owned a thousand of them when she died."

Anderson recalled going into restaurants with her, where she'd carry on conversations with strangers, learning their life's history and telling them hers. "As a kid, it was terribly embarrassing. You'd hear her begin talking to these strangers, and you'd say to yourself, 'Oh, my God, not again,' and you felt terribly self-conscious. But she was a wonderful person," Anderson said, "and I consider myself very fortunate, because in the long run the Dornbirers had a much greater positive impact on me than would have been the case had I been reared by my father and stepmother."

Anderson soon developed the reputation of being the smart kid in the orphanage, did very well in school, and invariably stood out as the boy with the highest marks in his class. He also played quarterback on the high school football team, and a number of townspeople seemed to take an interest in his future. The man who'd been his Sunday school teacher, for example, offered to pay his college expenses if Anderson agreed to become a Methodist minister, and he'd have seriously considered the offer had he not received others. But he'd made third-team all-state quarterback and was recruited by Woody Hayes to play for Ohio State. He was doubtful, however, because the scholarship was contingent on his making the team, and Anderson didn't think he was that good a passer.

One day during his senior year in high school, Mrs. Dornbirer asked him, "Jim, what would you think about going to West Point?" She had a powerful contact, Robert Taft, one of the Senate's grandees, who'd been her classmate at Ohio University. The possibility of attending West Point seemed intriguing to Anderson, and soon after they talked, Mrs. Dornbirer contacted Senator Taft, who said he'd be glad to help but didn't have any nominations left. What he did was call Congressman Walter Brehm, from the nearby town of Logan. Later, during his senior class trip to Washington, Anderson was taken to lunch by Brehm, who said he could offer an immediate appointment to Annapolis but Anderson would have to wait till the following year if he had his heart set on West Point. Not sure why, except perhaps because he rooted for Army when they played Navy, Anderson said he'd be willing to wait.

It was during his senior year, too, that he met his wife, Joyce Folden, who was two years behind him in school. Anderson was in charge of an honor study hall, and Joyce's mother said the person who'd be able to help her with geometry problems was Jim

Anderson. Fortuitously, Joyce's mother had been the schoolteacher who'd taught Anderson math in the seventh grade.

After graduating from high school, Anderson, waiting to enter West Point the following year, might have attended Ohio State. But he'd talked to Senator Taft, who told him, "I think what you ought to do is go into the service as an enlisted man for a year and see how the other half lives."

Anderson thought he might eventually want to become a pilot and decided to enlist in the Air Force. This was during the Korean War, and he was sent to Lackland Air Force Base in San Antonio. Because of the war and a shortage of personnel, and because he did well passing a battery of tests, the Air Force made him an instructor. He taught math, took no basic training, and was promoted to sergeant after less than three weeks. In those days the Air Force not only seemed disorganized but also Anderson found himself repeatedly underwhelmed by the people he met at Lackland.

To ensure he'd do well on West Point's entrance exams, he was scheduled to attend the Army's prep school, which, at the time, was located at Stewart Air Force Base in Newburgh, New York. Yet it took a tortuous series of phone calls from Anderson to Brehm's office to the Air Force to get his bungling company commander to release him finally.

"That was the kind of stuff that went on," Anderson recalled, "and I decided then I didn't want to get messed up in that kind of setup. So when I graduated from West Point, rather than join the Air Force, which you could do those days, I'd stick with the Army. I was really more interested in working with people than machines."

At the prep school he studied college-level algebra, English, some history, and also played a little football. He took the exams in February, learned in the spring he'd passed, and looked forward to entering West Point that July.

Anderson believes that Beast Barracks wasn't as terrible for him as it probably was for most because he was used to close-in living. "As a matter of fact, West Point was the first time I had a room with only three people in it—that was pretty plush for me." He was also a year older than most of his classmates, and West Point was not getting him right out of high school. In addition, he'd been in the Air Force for a couple of months. "It all seemed to help, and I never really thought of Beast Barracks as being so terribly difficult. Not that it was ever enjoyable," Anderson said in a rich baritone, straightening his parted, pepper-and-salt-colored hair, which, combed across his forehead, gave him a decidedly collegiate look even at fifty-two.

One of Anderson's classmates and a friend he made during Beast was Jack Egnor, who later flunked out of West Point. "He's a lawyer today, practicing in Kansas City," Anderson said. His sister was a famous TV personality in the 1950s, a buxom blonde who went by the name of Dagmar. Once, Anderson remembered, Egnor received a package from home when an upperclassman stopped him. "Dumb smack Egnor, halt!"

Egnor slammed against the wall.

"Is that a package you're carrying?"

"Yes, sir."

"Is that your package?"

"Yes, sir."

"Do you have something to eat in there?"

Egnore grinned. "Well, sir, you might say that."

But what was inside the package, the upperclassman soon discovered, were autographed cheesecake pictures of Dagmar for every upperclassman in the company.

Laughing, Anderson said he had a hundred Egnor stories. There were seven plebes sitting at the table in the mess hall when Anderson was in Beast. The table commandant was an upperclassman, Ray Colvin, and he was assisted by two other upperclassmen. One of the plebes, Egnor, was "the gunner," and it was his responsibility to announce the food as it came to the table. Another plebe poured the cold beverages and was called "the cold beverage corporal." Still another plebe was "the hot beverage corporal," and that was Anderson, who sat next to Egnor. When any of the upperclassmen spoke to any of the plebes, all the other plebes had to drop their forks and stop eating. Consequently, whenever there was a lull, all the plebes would concentrate on ingesting their food. Yet if you took too big a bite, you were reprimanded. Ditto if you gazed around the mess hall. "Dumb smack Anderson, what do you want to do, buy this place?"

On this occasion blessed silence reigned; but as the other plebes wolfed down their chow, the temporary peace and quiet proved too much to Egnor: "Mr. Colvin, sir, may I ask a question?"

Colvin indulged him, saying, "Yeah, dumb smack Egnor, what is it?"

"Sir, would you tell Cadet Anderson to take his hand off my thigh?"

Anderson reported what followed resembled an eruption from Vesuvius. Upperclassmen seemed to descend upon their table, and, needless to say, not a plebe there got another bite to eat that meal. "But Egnor was always pulling stunts like that and became the darling of the upperclassmen, because he had the nerve to do that kind of thing and was clever about it."

Academically, Anderson found the first year very tough. He'd come to the Academy thinking that because he'd always been top boy in his class back in New Lexington he'd wind up close to the top at West Point. "But that was when I learned I was not another Einstein, and that was a good lesson for me."

The first day, the instructor in French started speaking French, a language Anderson had never taken in high school, and he thought, "Oh, my God, I don't understand a word he's saying." He struggled with French that semester, sure he'd fail the final exam, but just managed to pass.

At no time did Anderson remotely consider quitting. Although he had supporters in his hometown, a number of people in New Lexington, not so much the kids as their parents, always seemed to look down on the children from the orphanage.

The only black around was a young girl in the orphanage, and in that part of Ohio during the late 1930s, Anderson said, there was a "sunshine law," which meant any blacks in town to shop had to be out by sundown. "We're talking about small-town rural America, and I suppose because there were no blacks for them to look down on and they needed to feel superior to someone, they looked down on the kids at the orphanage. Which was why there was no way in hell I'd ever give them the satisfaction of quitting at West Point so they'd be able to say, 'What did you expect? He's from the orphanage.'" Anderson paused, looking away, and his expressive blue eyes seemed to turn inward. "That's one of the things about being raised in an orphanage—it did the opposite for me of what you'd expect. Because I said, 'I'm better than they think I am. I know that. They may not.'"

He found his yearling year easier, but the third year was tough, mainly because of the engineering courses, one of which cadets nicknamed "The Mystery Hour."

When Anderson returned to Ohio each summer during the school break, he stayed with the Dornbirers at their farm because they no longer ran the orphanage. "They were really my mother and father, and I never had much to do with my real father after he put me back in the orphanage the second time."

Anderson recalled Mrs. Dornbirer's Sunday dinners with great pleasure. "When I say 'dinner,' there you ate breakfast, dinner, and supper, not breakfast, lunch, and dinner." For Sunday dinner Mrs. Dornbirer would make southern fried chicken, pot roast, and probably a ham. That was for six people. Always mashed potatoes and about three different vegetables. Salad was normally cut up fresh fruit, which Mrs. Dornbirer would freeze. Dessert would probably be angel food cake, or what Mrs. Dornbirer called "an old-fashioned cream pie," which Anderson considered nonpareil. "My wife tried to get the recipe from Mrs. Dornbirer, but she never had it written down. It was all in her head. My wife would say, 'How much of this?' And Mrs. Dornbirer would say, 'You just take a handful.' She never used a measuring cup. It was always, 'A dash of this, a dab of that.' But that pie was absolutely delicious."

Meanwhile, Anderson and Joyce had corresponded throughout his four years at West Point, becoming engaged during the beginning of his senior year, Labor Day weekend, 1955. Like most cadets, Anderson enjoyed his senior year. He knew he was going to graduate, looked forward to the Army, and anticipated marrying his childhood sweetheart in the West Point chapel the day following his graduation, June 5, 1956.

Anderson remembered having something like $320 to his name. He'd taken out a loan and bought a two-door, two-tone '56 Chevrolet. It cost almost $2,000. He and Joyce drove it to New York City, stopping at the Barclay Hotel. There he suavely asked the doorman to put his new car in the hotel's garage. Not too long after, his hotel room phone rang. The doorman told him the car wouldn't start. "That's impossible," Anderson said. But it turned out something had gone wrong with the voltage regulator, and his $320 began looking smaller and smaller. Still, the newlyweds went to an expensive restaurant that night, where coffee cost $1.75. "You don't want any coffee, do you, Joyce?"

That summer, Anderson was fortunate to get a job as an ironworker in Cleveland, because his oldest stepbrother had a journeyman's union card he wasn't using. Anderson worked around the clock, making $3.50 an hour, or more money in seven weeks as an ironworker than he did in seven months as a second lieutenant. He was installing monorails in factories, and it was dirty work; but Anderson would sit there with a wrench, saying to himself, "That's a dollar, that's two, that's three." He was used to hard work and hot places from having worked on the farm in the orphanage, and by summer's end he was able to pay off the loan on his car and commence being a professional soldier.

Anderson's military career is dominated by an almost twenty-year teaching stint at West Point and two tours in Vietnam. The first began in 1963 as an adviser to the South Vietnamese 2nd Battalion, 14th Regiment, 9th Infantry Division. He remembered hearing about Vietnam initially in 1961, when he was an instructor in Ranger School. Then in 1963, learning he was going to be sent either to Korea or Vietnam, he chose Vietnam, arriving in-country wearing civilian clothing and not really knowing what to expect.

He'd asked a friend who'd returned from Vietnam for some tips about getting along with the Vietnamese, and the guy told him to learn how to use chopsticks. Anderson said the Vietnamese loved it when their big, gung ho American advisers looked silly and got some of their biggest laughs from watching Americans using chopsticks ineptly. Anderson, practicing with peas at home before he left for Vietnam, learned to eat like the Vietnamese, holding a bowl near his mouth and shoveling the food in.

Another way advisers were humiliated was when they got drunk on cognac as they tried to keep up, drink for drink, with the encouraging Vietnamese, who'd learned to imbibe it from the French. Anderson would obligingly drink a shot or two with them. But before the third round, he'd say, "I've a new game." He'd pour out a shot, then take a match and light the top of the cognac, and drink it down. "The trick is you don't stop. You just take it and throw it back." He'd learned the gimmick at a bachelor party for a classmate. "Because I knew I wasn't going to be able to keep up with them when they kept passing that bottle around, I started flaming the brandy; and because they wanted no part of that, they quit trying to get me drunk."

Anderson found being a battalion adviser an interesting but frustrating challenge. "It was not unlike being a schoolteacher, discovering what educators call 'teachable moments.'" The South Vietnamese battalion commander had been involved in fighting the Viet Minh as an NCO for years, so he was not about to take advice from a relatively inexperienced American officer.

At first, the battalion had been stationed in II Corps, in the mountains. But after about four months, the unit got transferred to IV Corps in the Mekong Delta, which is flat land sprinkled with rice paddies; and because the battalion commander was frightened in the Delta, never having been out of the mountains before, he began listening to Anderson for the first time.

"The point I made was that it was dumb to move during daylight in the Delta because you had so little cover; you've got to move at night," Anderson said. During daylight, the battalion hid and rested. Soon it began conducting a series of night operations, a lot of patrols, a lot of Ranger-type operations. The problem was that the South Vietnamese were not confident about sending out platoons or trusting platoon leaders to conduct operations. The battalion commander would lose face if he dispatched a platoon and it got creamed; probably he'd have been relieved. "So it was difficult getting their young leaders trained to the point where they'd show initiative, and I felt that was the biggest problem between the Vietnamese and the Americans."

Anderson was finally accepted by the battalion commander during an operation in the fall of 1963, when the battalion was given the mission of taking a supply column to another South Vietnamese unit purportedly surrounded in the Delta. The mission sounded fishy to Anderson, a setup. Plus he reasoned that the people who'd had the South Vietnamese surrounded weren't just going to let the rescuing battalion come waltzing in with supplies. But that seemed to be precisely what the battalion commander proposed doing next morning. When Anderson offered objections, the battalion commander told him with a smile that he worried too much.

But early that night, the regimental commander had arrived at the scene and asked the battalion commander what his plan was. Then he asked if Anderson agreed, and for the first time Anderson said he disagreed with the battalion commander in front of his superior. Asked what he'd do differently, Anderson mentioned a midnight river crossing by one reconnoitering company, dispatching a second flanking company for security, and moving the third company with the supplies out under cover of darkness that night to a location some distance from their final destination, where it would set up a command post. The regimental commander thought a minute, then told the battalion commander to follow Anderson's plan.

The next morning, the flanking security force encountered an enemy battalion, surprising them. But outnumbered, the flanking force had to pull back, until it reached the command post.

Anderson remembered seeing VC about twenty-five yards away, trying to overrun the command post. "There was a young South Vietnamese soldier near me, and we were both firing over a parapet. All of a sudden, I turned and looked at him just as his head kind of exploded like a watermelon. He got hit in the face, killing him instantly and splashing blood all over me."

As the defending force kept contracting around the command post, the battalion commander asked Anderson what they should do. When Anderson said they needed to counterattack, the battalion commander immediately got out his .45, turned around, and yelled at his troops to follow him. Then he bravely climbed over the parapet and began walking toward the VC. His troops looked at him for a stunned second, then started moving out after him, and the startled VC broke and ran. It was one of the first times, Anderson said, that a South Vietnamese battalion had beaten a major ambush attack, and next day the corps commander, a general, came out and asked how they did it.

Not too long after, Anderson left the battalion, becoming a G-3 adviser, a staff job. It was in a province south of Saigon, mostly desk work, and Anderson found it deadly boring, a letdown after the night patrols and fighting in the Delta. At the same time, he was fortunate, because he'd had a number of close calls and even remembered showing his "turtle," the new guy coming in to succeed him as G-3, some hot spots around the countryside when an enemy machine gun opened up, slamming through the helicopter and shattering the aluminum pipes supporting their nylon seat straps. The shrapnel from the pipes missed Anderson but tore into his successor's thigh, and the wound proved so severe the guy had to be evacuated and a new G-3 was brought in.

Anderson himself had been slightly wounded when shrapnel pierced his boot during the time he was a battalion adviser out on patrol. He hadn't realized he'd been hit until he was sitting down to supper that night and the South Vietnamese captain pointed to a blood stain on his jungle boot. Anderson had the South Vietnamese medic treat it, but an infection set in the next morning. He tried to walk on it, but finally called for a medivac helicopter. Lucky Anderson, because had he waited another day, he was told, he'd have lost his foot.

He'd left a message in his records that his family was not to be notified for minor wounds, not realizing during that early stage of American involvement that Madam Nhu personally wrote letters to relatives of any American wounded; the result was that Joyce soon received a handwritten note from the sister-in-law of the president of South Vietnam telling of Anderson's wound.

Mixups like that, snafus, were typical, and Joyce was more than lucky she was spared an even more unfortunate mistake. When Anderson first left for Vietnam, he flew over with a classmate, Mike Conrad, and another officer, named Tom McGregor. The same day Anderson was wounded, McGregor was killed, and somehow the message got back to the United States in unofficial channels that Anderson was the one killed. Some of his friends even held a memorial service for him. Then, a couple of months later, when he happened to run into Conrad, his classmate turned ashen, saying, "Jim?" When Anderson responded, Conrad said, "My God, there's been a terrible mistake. I heard you were killed and they held a memorial service for you back at Bragg."

At the conclusion of his tour in 1964, Anderson said it was obvious to him it was going to take a huge effort on America's part if we were going to win in Vietnam. Little surprise, then, when he heard people back in the States saying we ought to send a division over there to straighten out the mess, mop the place up, he invariably replied, "But you don't understand. We could send a division over there and it could go out in the middle of the jungle, get lost, and we'd never see them again. You just don't grasp the magnitude of the problem. It's not going to take a division; it's going to require considerably more than that, a major effort, and it's going to be a long, drawn-out affair."

Later Anderson realized that the enemy didn't even have to win; it just could not let itself be defeated. And, considering typical American impatience and the other side's endurance, Anderson finally concluded that the United States never had much of a chance over there from the start.

While he was in Vietnam, Anderson had been asked by the chairmen of the English, Social Sciences, Military Art and Engineering, and Phys Ed departments to return to West Point as an instructor. Because he loves sports and is something of a sports nut, he chose Phys Ed, got a masters in the subject from Indiana University, and taught at the Academy from 1965 to 1968. He lectured on the fundamentals of physical fitness, teaching swimming, golf, tennis, and squash, and also talked to cadets about leadership, describing his Vietnam experiences. American soldiers were going over to Vietnam in large numbers during those years, and a considerable number of cadets wondered whether they were ready to perform in a combat role. Anderson told them the one school in the Army that would best prepare them for combat was Ranger School.

He was aware of no institutional changes taking place at the Academy during the late 1960s as a direct result of Vietnam. Cadets were trained to be leaders before Vietnam, which meant placing a high priority on professional competence, concern for soldiers, and personal integrity, and those same priorities were of course emphasized during and after the Vietnam War.

But cadets' perceptions of what to expect in Vietnam probably were altered as a result of talking to instructors like Anderson. "Cadets had to understand that the South Vietnamese had a very different culture from ours—for example, they believed age was synonymous with wisdom and therefore they didn't encourage initiative on the part of young officers; and the frustration of not getting them to follow our suggestions was a real problem, yet the result of two cultures clashing."

At the end of his three years at West Point, Anderson was anxious to move on. He was a major, on a command select list, which meant he'd soon be a lieutenant colonel, slated for battalion command. Then one day he received a call from a classmate who was in personnel, asking how Anderson would feel about going to Korea for a year. Anderson said he thought if the Army was planning to send him to Asia it would be back to Vietnam again. But his friend said the Army was not sending major promotables to Vietnam unless they volunteered, because they didn't want people selected for battalion command there who, fearful of ruining their careers, refused to assume command; and a lot of that had been going on.

Nonetheless, Anderson volunteered to go to Vietnam rather than be sent to Korea, and shortly after he'd arrived he received a letter from Gen. Creighton Abrams, who'd succeeded Westmoreland as commander of the U.S. Military Assistance Command Vietnam, COMUSMACV, asking if Anderson would like to become his aide. Anderson had had a friend who was Abrams' aide at the time. Also, Anderson had worked with Abrams during his first tour as a brigade staff officer with the 3rd Armored Division stationed in Germany in the late 1950s. Anderson wrote back saying he'd love to become Abrams' aide, but he also wanted to command a battalion and didn't want to extend to do that, which meant he'd be

Abrams' aide for only about six months. Abrams responded that the only person he'd want as an aide was someone who'd aspire to command a battalion. Nor did he believe in soldiers' volunteering to be away from their families, which is what an extension would have entailed.

"What a person he was!" Anderson said of Abrams. "He awed people."

Abrams, standing close to five-eight and weighing about 190, was built like a pulling guard. Though he could be gruff at times, Anderson found him extremely sensitive. He loved classical music and would have records shipped to him, which he'd put on tapes. He'd play the tapes but store the records, taking them out only when someone else who loved classical music would listen to them with him. He was also fond of photography and sent pictures he'd taken as Christmas cards. "As an example, he loved to take close-up pictures of flowers," Anderson said. "He'd sprinkle a little water on the flower to make it glisten."

The only times Anderson saw Abrams lose his temper were when people wouldn't give him straight answers or tried to mislead him. Anderson remembered a major, an S-4, a supply officer, who'd fallen asleep during an exercise in Germany and didn't get his briefing charts up to date. When he briefed Abrams, he erased the date and quoted from the same briefing charts he'd used the day before. Abrams immediately realized what was happening. Yet the major kept trying to string Abrams along. With every answer his cover-up became more obvious, and finally he broke down and started to weep. Abrams stood up, saying, "I just want you to know I don't appreciate being lied to or having someone trying to make a fool of me." Then he turned and walked away.

A complex man, Abrams could always get to the core of the matter. Once he went out to a firebase after an intense attack had been beaten back the night before. A young farm boy was sitting there with his machine gun. The attack had, occurred in a rubber plantation, which was filled with red dirt resembling rust, some of which had gotten on the soldier's weapon.

"I understand it was pretty rough out here. How'd it go last night?" Abrams asked the soldier.

"Oh, yes, sir, but Betsy here never let me down."

"How'd it fire?" Abrams asked.

"Oh, sir, Betsy never missed a beat."

"Had any problems with it?"

"No, sir, never had any problems."

"That the weapon fired," Abrams later told Anderson, "*that's* the important thing. It certainly looked like it was dirty, and maybe it was even dirty. But he'd kept the important parts clean. It was functioning, and *that's* what counts, not the spit-and-polish. A lot of things look good that don't work worth a damn."

If Abrams was perfectly comfortable talking with young pfc's, he was equally at ease conversing with a William Buckley or an Allard Lowenstein, naturally voluble men from opposite ends of the political spectrum, both of whom came to Vietnam and remained virtually silent during long interview sessions with Abrams. Indeed, Lowenstein sat listening to Abrams discussing the war for so long he missed his curfew, and Anderson had to accompany him back to his hotel. "*That's* who they ought to have in Washington defending this operation," Lowenstein said.

But Anderson thought the congressman had it only partly right. Because with Abrams it was telling the truth that counted, not advocating a particular political position.

When it came time for Anderson to seek out a battalion to command, he asked if the general had any recommendations.

Earlier that day, they'd been discussing a fragging incident that had occurred in the 1st Battalion, 5th Cav, 1st Cavalry Division. The executive officer, a major, had been experiencing friction with a number of black soldiers in the rear, and he became so afraid of being fragged he began setting traps of his own. He'd also appealed for help to his battalion commander, who told him he would have to solve his own problems. When the major was later found dead, shot by his own pistol, the battalion commander was relieved.

"Why don't you take the battalion that had the fragging?" Abrams suddenly suggested.

"I'd love that battalion," Anderson said.

"Do you want some help?" Abrams asked.

"If I need it, I'll let you know."

Anderson then called personnel and said if they were still looking for a battalion commander for the 1st of the 5th he'd like to be considered. What complicated matters was that the brigade commander, Bob Kingston, then a colonel and later a four-star general, had already promised the battalion to someone else. But Anderson was, after all, the fair-haired boy of COMUSMACV;

and in asking for the 1st of the 5th he'd undoubtedly had Abrams' blessing. Case closed.

Or, human nature being human nature, hardly. Because about six months later, or a few days before Anderson was to leave the battalion, he and Kingston had a beer one night. "Jim, I just want you to know, when you came into this brigade you had two strikes against you," Kingston said. "I was just looking for an excuse to get rid of you. The smartest thing you did during the time you were here was not saying to me 'Creighton Abrams' or 'General Abrams.' "

"I didn't know I needed to," Anderson replied. "I wasn't working for him, I was working for you."

Anderson had had close to a thousand men under his command. Knowing that he faced an explosive racial situation, he'd immediately collected his officers to discuss the problem with them. When he said he'd next get all the NCO's together for a similar discussion, several of the officers told him that was a bad idea because of the enmity between the white and black NCO's. Anderson replied that while people seemed to be talking within chosen groups, the groups were hardly communicating with each other. And how could the battalion possibly fight as a unit, a brutally obvious military necessity, if the NCO's remained isolated in their various cliques?

The white NCO's resented black soldiers using the black power salute and wanted those who did court-martialed for insubordination. Anderson agreed that was one approach. But then he said that the black power salute hadn't come into existence the last day or two, and for that reason struck him as a deeply rooted problem requiring a more subtle solution. Asked what he'd do confronted by a black power salute, Anderson said he'd return it. Asked what about the regular hand salute, Anderson said the hand salute originally came from days of chivalry; it signified that the man offering it wasn't carrying a weapon. Putting the hand near the forehead, he continued, came from lifting the visor, showing a further unwillingness to fight. "So that's what the hand salute is about. But right now, we have a segment of our population to whom the black power salute is important. And forbidding them to do that isn't going to win any battles for us. And winning battles is what we need to deal with right now."

Anderson's solution was, yes, to return the black power salute, then salute the regular way. And what he soon found was that black soldiers began returning his salute, and the issue of saluting in general seemed to lose its angry importance.

"The idea was to get our black soldiers to the point where they no longer felt threatened, and to accomplish that I'd sit with them and had a lot of talks about racism."

Once, when some black soldiers complained that a white soldier was displaying a Confederate flag near his bunker, Anderson talked to the white soldier, who said it was his state flag and he'd meant no disrespect to the black soldiers. Anderson believed the white soldier and decided to get him and the protesting black troops together. When the black soldiers again voiced their objections, Anderson drew on his credit. "Did I say the black power salute was threatening to me? Did I demand you stop that? Why don't you let this man prove through some overt action he is, in fact, threatening you? The truth is he has as much right to display the flag as you do to give the black power salute."

On May 1, 1970, the 1st Cav was sent into Cambodia. Anderson had received a call at one o'clock that morning, during which the officer on the other end asked, "How soon can you have your battalion make an airmobile operation into Cambodia?" Anderson reflected a minute before saying, "If you can give me the helicopters by first light, I can start landing tomorrow morning at eleven." Unopposed when they landed, the battalion spread out into the enveloping jungle and before long captured a huge cache of weapons soon termed "The City."

One night later that month, Anderson's unit got hit by NVA sappers. Anderson said his firebase, unlike others, wasn't an oval but rather designed in the shape of a five-point star. Bunkers would be placed in the points of the star as well as where the lines joined, toward the star's center. The advantage was that any bunker under attack had fire support from at least four other bunkers. Between the points, Anderson had set up claymore mines. Beyond them, at hand-grenade distance, he'd put in concertina wire.

The night the base got hit, the sappers had worked their way through the wires. Anderson said the NVA were very good at that, as well as at removing the blasting caps of the claymore mines and thus disarming them. But one of the sappers had inadvertently tripped a flare, lighting up the firebase and alerting the Americans. Still, attacking in force and using grenades, the NVA managed to gain control of two of the battalion's bunkers, imperiling the whole firebase.

Anderson's standing order that troops wear helmets at night helped save the unit, since bareheaded enemy could easily be picked out and were blown away. Others attempted to withstand a counterattack consisting of a reserve force of cooks and bakers, which retook the two bunkers after a hard fight that lasted much of the night.

The next day, the stench was overpowering because of enemy dead, about 150 of them, and Anderson had his troops place them in body bags before a 'dozer was brought in to dig a hole large enough to bury them in a mass grave coated with lime.

He said there'd been no lack of fear on his part that night. "I don't know exactly how it works, the psychological mechanism that allows you to perform; but something seems to take over, and the effects of the fear don't seem to register until after the battle's over. Then you start looking out and seeing the bodies—and those claymore mines really rip people up—and you think, 'My God, my God . . .'"

Upon completing his second Vietnam tour, in 1970, Anderson returned to the States and was assigned to the Pentagon, working out of an office known as SAMVA (special assistant, Modern Volunteer Army). President Nixon had let it be known soon after he'd assumed office in January 1969 that he favored an all-volunteer Army. A phasedown was instituted, and from mid-1969 on, draft calls were steadily pared. Then on January 27, 1973, Secretary of Defense Melvin Laird stated that "a zero draft" condition had been achieved.

In 1970 the Pentagon had placed Lt. Gen. George Forsythe in charge of the SAMVA office, and it was his task to start up the all-volunteer Army. Forsythe's people, Anderson among them, were told they were going to run into all kinds of problems, the most prominent of which would be bureaucratic inertia. But Forsythe, Anderson feels, was exactly the right man for the job. "He told us, 'You guys go out and get things done; that's your job. You're going to piss off some people along the way, but don't worry about that. I'll come along after you and police up the battlefield.'"

Anderson, in charge of concepts and plans, had a $2.5 million research budget. The British, he'd learned, had completed a series of studies that found that only 1 percent of their draft-age population wanted to become soldiers. The Army, Anderson decided, needed to run a survey, learning if that figure was valid for

America's draft-age population as well. Anderson particularly wanted to find out how to attract high-school graduates, because those who could barely write their names, he thought, would only cause the volunteer Army unnecessary problems.

His section developed a plan so that if a man volunteered to join the Army for from three to six years, the government would pay for his college education—a semester of college for each year served. A bonus was proposed for those who'd stay in the Army six years: Their fourth year of college would be thrown in. The minimal three-year parameter was established, because at three the government begins to break even in terms of training costs; anything less is a loss, anything more pure gravy. Anderson's section also developed an intricate system whereby some college work could even be started in the Army, and a consortium of colleges around the country agreed to accept each other's credits.

Working out of SAMVA, Anderson was somewhat surprised to learn about the quality of life experienced by many in the military. He discovered, for example, that the Springfield, Virginia, area, which was a bedroom community for the Pentagon, was among the runaway-children capitals of the world, and he even visited some of the houses for runaways in the D.C. area. "I tell you this, because when you think of the Army, you think of going out and shooting guns. But who thinks of the numbers of children of Army officers who are runaways? Yet I could cite case after case."

Fortunately, the assignment also had its less serious aspects. For instance, Anderson learned at the last minute that the survey of young men he wanted to run required permission from the White House. "A piece of cake," Anderson thought, considering that the all-volunteer Army was the president's idea, and he asked who in the White House to contact. Given a name, he was told permission usually took six months. "You've got to be kidding," Anderson said.

He sat down and wrote a memo describing the purpose of the survey and said he realized the man to whom he'd addressed the memo was very busy. To avoid unnecessary paperwork, Anderson continued, he would assume that if he didn't hear from the man after two weeks, permission had been granted. Two weeks seemed to unreel faster than a day, and, hearing not a word, Anderson commissioned the survey. "Run it."

About six months later, Anderson was getting ready to leave the Pentagon, moving on to another assignment, when he finally got a call from the White House. The guy to whom he'd addressed the memo asked if the Army was still interested in running the survey. Anderson said, "I don't understand." The guy casually repeated the question. "I don't understand," Anderson said, "because we've run it, got the data back, and are moving on." The guy asked, "By whose authority?" Anderson said, "Didn't you read the last paragraph in the memo? I didn't hear anything and assumed it was approved, and we've already run the survey." There was a pregnant silence of perhaps a minute before Anderson heard the guy exclaim, "That's a bloody outrage! Colonel, you're going to hear about this!"

And within minutes, it seemed the phones started ringing. The calls had gone from the White House to Defense to Army to Anderson, who decided this day might be a propitious one for General Forsytle to make good his pledge. "So I went into his office and told him what I'd done. Then I said, 'I think it's probably time for you to start policing up the area.' He laughed like hell."

In all, Anderson worked on the volunteer Army project for about eight months, and during that period he received a call from the head of the Phys Ed Department at West Point, Col. Frank Kobes, who said he was planning to retire in two years and asked if Anderson was interested in applying to replace him. Succeeding Kobes meant that Anderson, like Roy Flint, would take himself out of the mainstream of the Army. Kobes told him that if he got the job—director of the department and full professor—he'd first be required to return to graduate school and get a Ph.D.

"I really don't know if I want the job," Anderson said coolly. "But I'll put in my application and I'll make up my mind as we go through the process."

West Point's Academic Board appointed a committee, consisting of the commandant of cadets, the head of the Engineering Department, two or three others, and Colonel Kobes. About seventy people applied for the job. The committee narrowed the choice down to four or five candidates. Anderson, as one of the remaining four or five, went up to West Point for an interview. "At that point I came in in the greatest position possible," he said. "I didn't come in with my hat in my hand. Basically I was saying I hadn't made up my mind whether I really wanted the job yet. But I'm here to talk about it."

Physical education professionals from other universities were asked to evaluate the finalists; then there was a committee vote, after which Anderson got a call informing him he'd been selected for the job. Would he accept it? He said he wanted to talk to his wife, and he'd give his final answer within the week.

While Joyce liked the idea because it offered the family a certain stability, she was concerned about whether West Point was really what Anderson wanted. He said that after carefully measuring all the pluses and minuses, it was.

His decision to accept had its roots in the orphanage. One day in the mid-1940s, Mr. Dornbirer had called Anderson and his sisters into his office. There he told them that their brother, Lester, had been killed in action in Italy. Anderson remembered going into the boys' bathroom and weeping uncontrollably. Being alone and having no one to share his grief, though he hadn't really known Lester that well, was unforgettable. He still remembered, forty-odd years later, sitting on a shelf near a window in the bathroom as the pain seemed to radiate from the center of his heart. And that, combined with his growing sensitivity to the tragedy of runaway military children whose fathers worked in the Pentagon, only increased his awareness of what might happen to his own son and daughter if he spent many more years working long hours in the D.C. area. "It made me different from a lot of other people, who in my position might have and probably would have decided differently."

In truth, Anderson was close to making general. When he informed his superiors he would accept the West Point offer and so take himself out of the running for promotion to general, Westmoreland, who was chief of staff then, asked to speak to him. There was concern in the military about the attitudes of officers, and Westmoreland was worried that Anderson, so close to becoming a general officer, was leaving the Army's mainstream as a kind of protest, perhaps one against the volunteer Army concept.

But Anderson said that was hardly the case. "Then I told him when I'd graduated from West Point, my goal was to be a general officer, and I knew that it was within my reach. But now I heard a different drummer. Now it was no longer that important to me."

Anderson had liked his job at the Pentagon, thought it better than most brigadier generals' jobs. But it was unlikely he'd get as good a job if he returned to the Pentagon as a one-star general. Besides, what he'd wanted to do most was command troops. But even if he got to command a brigade for a year or two and a division for another year or two, that still meant he'd probably spend another ten to fifteen years in the Pentagon. And he'd observed other generals in the Pentagon working weekends, toiling long hours far into the night and often traveling away from home.

"So I'm not trying to make a statement or anything like that," he told Westmoreland. "This is strictly a personal thing."

Anderson returned to Indiana University for his Ph.D. in 1972. His dissertation was "A Comparison of the Effects of Physical Education Classes in Boxing and Gymnastics on the Self-Concepts of College Freshmen." Winners probably feel great, but what happens to the guys in boxing classes who get their clocks cleaned ten times out of ten? Anderson wondered. He chose the topic because he was hoping to come up with answers that would prove beneficial to cadets taking the mandatory boxing program at the Academy. What he found was that even people who lost ten matches in ten still came away with increased self-confidence, just from having participated. But you couldn't say that about the self-confidence of those who flunked gymnastics.

"I think the reason was that in gymnastics only you know what's going on inside your head. If you're afraid to try a stunt, you think less of yourself," Anderson said. "But in boxing, you don't get the opportunity not to throw punches in a ring. You can be afraid, but you have to do something, or else you're going to get your block knocked off. So you're forced to confront fear. In gymnastics you're not forced to confront fear. Anyway, that's my view."

Interestingly enough, 90 percent of today's cadets say they never had to box before attending West Point, much less been in a fight. One reason for the latter, Anderson thought, is that so many sports activities for kids today are supervised. When Anderson was playing ball in playgrounds during the 1940s, there were no adults around, and if spats occurred they'd be settled between the boys, with a bloody nose usually resolving the issue. But kids don't experience that today. As a result, some cadets come to their first boxing lesson so afraid they wet their pants; others defecate. Anderson quickly gets them away to avoid any public embarrassment, then tells them they'll be able to handle anything they're asked to do. "They all go through it," Anderson said, "and not very many of them like it. And if you made it voluntary, damn few would do it, and that's why it's mandatory. But what we want, what I want, is for them to face fear and overcome it. I know from having been in combat that facing fear is inevitable. I did a number of times, and anybody who says he's not afraid in combat is lying to you.''

A conservative by instinct, Anderson is also profoundly practical as he demonstrated when the admission of women began to be debated. Initially he'd opposed it, because women would not be allowed into combat arms branches. At the same time, Anderson began having PT tests administered to high school women and those in ROTC programs, collecting data as early as 1973.

One day he got a call from a public-affairs officer at West Point, who said that some media guy in Washington had just phoned, claiming West Point was collecting data preparing for the admission of women to the Academy. The PA officer had responded that the idea was absurd, but he'd check to make sure.

"Sorry, but we are collecting data, because I'm anticipating the possibility," Anderson informed him.

But that was terrible, the PA officer responded, because the secretary of the Army had recently said he'd resign before letting women enter West Point. "My God, what am I going to tell the media?''

"Listen," Anderson said in his most disarming manner, "why don't you tell the guy that the policy of the secretary of the Army is that women will come to West Point over his dead body. However, there's some nut up at the Academy who thinks he ought to be prepared for the contingency, in case Congress does mandate the admission of women. He's out collecting data, but that has nothing to do with the secretary of the Army. And if they want to talk to someone, rather than bother the secretary, have them call the nut and give them my number.''

Now, Anderson said, he's a big supporter of women at West Point, although he still believes they're not capable of serving in combat because the majority cannot physically live up to its rigors in terms of stamina, strength, and agility. "But I'm a tremendous supporter of what we ask women to do at West Point and I've insisted we let them prove what they're capable or not capable of doing. Nor do I assume they'll never be capable of combat, which means we have to constantly check where they stand. But compared to when they first arrived, there have been no significant changes.'' The reason Anderson supports the admission of women to West Point is that men aren't required to enter into combat arms branches upon graduation either.

During the years he's been a member of the Academic Board, Anderson has been consistent in maintaining that the honor code be upheld. When the honor violations involving the Class of 1977 occurred, a number of congressmen suggested that if so great a number of cadets were involved—forty-seven were separated and 105 were suspended, then offered readmission with the Class of 1978—then perhaps the fault resided in the institution rather than with most individuals; and perhaps even the toleration clause, given today's prevailing values, was unrealistic.

Anderson disagreed, believing that what those cadets did was the result of no institution shortcoming but a severe violation of personal integrity; and letting any of them back in amounted "to our saying we don't think this is as important today as it used to be." Some congressmen didn't want those cadets even suspended, Anderson continued, but West Point insisted on at least that much punishment. "We made concessions, we had to, in order to keep from having to make even greater ones."

The day the secretary of the Army came up to the Academy to announce his decision, Anderson was sitting as the president of a board of officers hearing another case involving a cadet charged with using marijuana. Testimony had been heard and the cadet had already been found guilty; the board was in the process of deciding on a sentence. "In our deliberations we'd gotten along far enough so that the indication was we were going to recommend separation," Anderson remembered. The recommendation would then go to the superintendent, who had the final say. But before the board's vote could be taken, it received word that the secretary of the Army was there to announce his decision, and they trooped over to the auditorium. Soon they heard the secretary describe the number to be separated and those to be suspended. The board then returned to its deliberation room. "If we can't kick people out for violating the honor code, how can we kick someone out for substance violation?" the majority now argued, before voting, not for separation but for suspension.

Yet Anderson continued to insist the honor code had as much application then as it ever possessed. And he continues to believe that, noting there are still no locks on the doors to the rooms at West Point. "I suppose that's difficult for people to understand," he said with a shrug.

I said I could easily understand the part of the honor code that referred to not lying, stealing, or cheating. But what would always have been difficult, if not impossible, was the toleration clause, or reporting someone, which seemed to me twin to informing.

"I think it's probably difficult for everybody," Anderson said, "and that's one of the reasons what you first do is confront the guy, giving him an opportunity to do the honorable thing, which is to report himself, saying, 'I did wrong, I screwed up.' That's the key to it."

Nonetheless, if a cadet made a mistake involving the honor code, Anderson continued, as a member of the Academic Board he almost invariably voted for separation. "You may think of me as being very tough in that area. But if it's a question of a character flaw, a failure of character, my view is that the chances of turning him around are so slim you're better off as an institution getting rid of him—at least when that institution is one that stresses high character."

But even more compelling than those reasons in accounting for Anderson's position, I think, is his intense identification with institutions. It began back at the orphanage, and how could it not? When Anderson was abandoned by his father, it was the orphanage in New Lexington that provided him food, shelter, and Mr. and Mrs. Dornbirer, who made him feel safe and perhaps even happy. Then, when it was uncertain he'd be afforded the opportunity to attend college, it was again an institution, West Point, that offered him free room and board. None of the other fourteen siblings, children or stepchildren of his father, ever attended college. Then it was still another institution, the Army, that not only presented him with a series of interesting and challenging jobs but also exposed him to a general like Creighton Abrams, a man who compelled enormous affection and respect. Finally, it was again West Point that invited Anderson back, to live within the comforting green shadows of its arching trees at about the same time he'd decided that family disruptions caused by his possibly becoming a general officer were not worth the price he'd be required to pay.

It would be sweet to say that a child who found himself emotionally saved in an orphanage was so moved by the experience that he later felt only forgiveness toward cadets who transgressed. But life is, alas, more complicated. Certainly it's cold comfort to those cadets made to leave West Point partly as a result of votes cast by Anderson to know this, but in voting to separate them Anderson was also voting to honor those institutions that had given him his life in the most physically fundamental and emotional sense.

When I mentioned Westmoreland's speech to the Class of 1964 before he left for Vietnam, during which Westmoreland said West Point was a special place and West Pointers a special breed, Anderson replied he wasn't aware of that speech. But then he added, "I think the institution is special, and what makes it so are the requirements cadets must satisfy in order to graduate. And that's why a certain amount of attrition is a healthy sign. If the program doesn't produce any, the program probably isn't rigorous enough."

Not too long ago, Anderson continued, his son, who was currently a cadet, asked him why he wore his West Point ring on his left hand. Anderson replied that when he was a cadet, it was the appropriate gesture, although he noted many cadets today wore the ring on their right hand.

"The design of the ring is such that when you wear it on your left hand and you're wearing it properly before you graduate, your class crest is worn on the left side, closest to your heart," Anderson explained. "When you turn it around, after you graduate, the Academy crest is the one closest to your heart. Yet somehow cadets today don't understand that kind of thing. It's been lost, and I'm not sure how important that loss is. But, you know, I have great loyalty to this institution, and I have great loyalty to our country. And I feel that the only value of my loyalty to this institution is because of the loyalty to my country. And I'd like to think we could get that kind of attitude through to today's cadets. While I don't believe there's a place in American society for 'ringknockers,' those who consider themselves special just because they've graduated from West Point, I make no apologies if what I'm talking about, loyalty to this institution because of loyalty to the country, represents a kind of elitism."

Another way of seeing things, though, is that when Anderson emerged from the orphanage at the age of eighteen, whole and sane, despite the fact his father lived twenty miles away, it was a triumph about which even a man as profoundly democratic as General Abrams might have said, "*That's* when he was really elite."

Epilogue

"I have been informed by my superiors that action has been instituted against me in connection with my performance of duty in the spring of 1968 while serving as commanding general, Americal Division, in Vietnam," Maj. Gen. Samuel Koster told the Corps of Cadets at their noonday meal on March 17, 1970, standing on the balcony overlooking the cavernous dining hall.

"I have, therefore, requested reassignment in order to separate the Military Academy and you of the Corps from the continuing flow of public announcements or any other connection with the alleged events which took place in Vietnam involving elements of my former command," Koster said, announcing his resignation as superintendent.

A member of the Class of '42 and a strikingly handsome officer, Koster had won a Silver Star serving with the 104th Infantry in Europe during World War II. Later he returned to the Academy as a tactical officer, and still later directed the Eighth Army's guerrilla campaign against North Korea. He'd assumed the superintendency of West Point on June 26, 1968, or a little more than three months after the My Lai massacre, which represented for most Americans the moral nadir of the Vietnam War.

On May 19, 1971, Koster received a letter of censure, his Distinguished Service Medal was withdrawn, and he was reduced in rank to brigadier general. The fact that Koster, a former cadet, tactical officer, and West Point superintendent, was considered by the department of the Army to have been derelict in his duty for failing to investigate thoroughly the My Lai incident despite his knowledge that troops under his command might have been guilty of serious misconduct, cast in a particularly brutal way Ernest Hemingway's notion that everybody behaves badly, given the proper chance.

A month after Koster stood before the Corps and told them he was leaving West Point, General Westmoreland, then Army chief of staff, wrote a letter to the Army War College commandant saying that a number "of unfavorable events occurring within the Army during the past few years have been a matter of grave concern to me." He was particularly anxious about the integrity and professionalism in the Army, and no doubt My Lai and Koster's reassignment fueled Westmoreland's concern. Although Westmoreland did not believe "that the Army as an institution is in a moral crisis," he thought an Army War College study of the officer corps would be useful. If we have problems, what precisely are they, Westmoreland wondered, and how can they be corrected? He specifically said he wanted the views of junior officers as well as their seniors'. "Junior officers" then meant most of the twelve men in this book and their peers.

In assessing the Army's existing climate, emphasis was to be placed on standards of professional competence and moral behavior. Five basic questions were to be answered. First, what are the ideal values of the Army officer? What are the actual standards? Third, of the differences between the ideal and the actual, which have major significance for the Army? What's causing the variances? And last, what are the answers, the solutions, or how can the ideal and actual be made to join hands?

Four hundred fifteen officers responded to a questionnaire, and 250 among them participated in group discussions. First, the bad news. The traditional professional standards of the Army officer— duty, honor, country—did not characterize the existing 1970 climate, the study plainly concluded. Nor was the Army perceived to be taking actions to ensure that high ideals were not only articulated but also practiced. In fact, institutionalized pressures were seen to be gnawing at traditional values. "A scenario that was repeatedly described in seminar sessions and narrative responses includes an ambitious, transitory commander—marginally skilled in the complexities of his duties—engulfed in producing statistical results, fearful of personal failure, too busy to talk or listen to his subordinates, and determined to submit acceptably optimistic reports that reflect faultless completion of a variety of tasks at the expense of the sweat and frustration of his subordinates.''

While the authors of the study found a striking consensus in viewpoint, one that sketched an Army obviously out of step with the image it wished to project, they also noted with relief that the younger officers who'd participated in the study still articulated a deep commitment to the ideals reflected in the duty, honor, country trinity. These men were intolerant of brother officers who transgressed, and thought the inept, dishonest, or immoral among them should be quickly separated from the service. But they were frustrated by pressures produced by the system, discouraged by selfish senior officers, and found a preoccupation with insignificant statistics uninspiring and wrongheaded.

Although it was difficult to isolate prime causes, the widespread feeling was ''that the Army had generated an environment that rewards relatively insignificant, short-term indicators of success, and disregards or discourages the growth of long-term qualities of moral and ethical strength on which the future of the Army depends.''

Yet three institutional factors probably contributed to the climate of unethical behavior: an unrealistic demand for perfection, which made truth-telling more difficult than it needed to be; an officer-rating system that stressed ''efficiency'' rather than ''efficiency plus the quality of the man,'' which suggested that only getting the job done mattered, means were irrelevant; and an emphasis on the acquisition of certain preferred assignments rather than the development of genuine expertise, which meant that real substance counted for far less than mere ''ticket-punching.''

The study went on to state that external factors such as the Vietnam War, rapid expansion of the Army, and the then current antimilitary feeling fretting the country did not contribute in a major way to the pervasively poor climate existing in the Army. ''There is no externally imposed rationale for the seemingly prevalent uninhibited quest for personal success at almost any price. There was no outside force that directly caused the isolation of senior officers; no obvious excuse for the seeming penchant for rewarding those who don't 'rock the boat.' "

Given the breadth of this less than ideal climate, corrective measures were obviously in order. Not only did they have to come from the top, but also the system of rewards, including promotion, selection for advanced education, and desirable and challenging assignments, had to be seen as specifically supporting traditional ethical behavior.

Among the recommendations suggested for prompt implementation were honest communications between junior and senior officers, increased assignment stability, a new emphasis on the development of real expertise, reducing the competitive edge adhering to promotions, and revising the officer efficiency reporting system.

While none of the colonels in this book participated in the study, it undoubtedly reflected much of what they were thinking at the time. And if My Lai and Koster's resignation at the Academy represented a tragic aspect of their sojourn in Vietnam, the Westmoreland-commissioned study suggested a second, more mundane one: Young officers like DeFrancisco and Taylor, Ruderman and Nash were going to have to make their way during the early 1970s and after Vietnam in an Army that had acknowledged its standards were being severely compromised internally.

Yet it would be fair to say that both before the plague years of the late 1960s and early 1970s and after, the twelve in this book performed successfully as officers. Eight—Paschall, Taylor, Turner, DeFrancisco, Flint, Nadal, Nash, and Anderson—are Silver Star winners. Three—Flint, Nye, and Anderson—are Ph.D.'s. One—Flint—is a dean; another—Timboe—is a doctor. Anderson and Turner head departments at West Point. Paschall runs the Army's Military History Institute, and Howie Boone is the Army's chief engineer in Korea. All have masters degrees, save Nash, who'd graduated thirtieth in a class of slightly more than seven hundred and obviously could have earned one had he chosen to. Nash was an aide to Vessey when Vessey was chairman of the Joint Chiefs of Staff, Anderson was an aide to Abrams when Abrams was COMUSMACV, Paschall was an aide to Weyand when that three-star general headed II Field Force, and both Taylor and Ruderman were aides to CG's, I Field Force. Two or three of the younger men probably will make general officer themselves, and, God help us, but this probably is beginning to read like a beaming mother's speech extolling her son, the colonel.

Nevertheless, it is interesting to speculate if the twelve in this book are representative of the officer corps. Many of them seemed to think so, but I suspect they're being modest. I got to know six of the twelve at the Army War College, and admission there is a weeder. Four were suggested by Col. Jack Yeagley, the public-affairs officer at West Point, and it hardly figured he'd be offering inarticulate, unattractive candidates. I'd come across the names of the two who'd retired, Nadal and Nye, in the book *Military Men* by Ward Just, and they'd sounded interesting. While other officers were approached, these twelve agreed to be interviewed, in part, because they believed they had something to say. For what it's worth, I think they were correct. In any case, the twelve in this book are the only twelve I interviewed, and I think I was lucky in the group I landed.

The oldest, Nye, was born in 1924; the youngest, Timboe, in 1946. DeFrancisco was raised in Albany, New York, but none was really a big-city boy. West Point has traditionally attracted most of its cadets from small towns and farms, or those less populated areas where the opportunities of the city are not readily apparent. Six of the men in this book had fathers who'd made a career of the Army—another source West Point has historically drawn from.

In seeking to attend the Academy and becoming officers, what these men chose was a life-style unconcerned with profits they might have earned in an economically competitive marketplace. To DeFrancisco, West Point and the Army meant "serving an ideal." Flint likened the Academy to a "cell of monks," although Nye cut a more secular figure performing there as a mentor. But implicit in each characterization is a profound lack of selfishness. In acting selflessly and perpetuating their calling, Army officers trained at West Point sought to display courage and honor above all other qualities.

Courage, according to a bosun's mate in Nye's *The Challenge of Command*, meant not running away. Nye goes on to say courage had been the first requirement of the warrior since Adam. Wes Taylor approached courage by talking of its opposite, fear, which he'd come to regard as "an old friend." Not something to deny or crush so much as something he grew to know so well, it helped him function by making him more alert, sharper, more aware. Because Nash did not wish for twenty years to hear other men's war stories, he sought combat; and because he wished to tell others truthfully that he'd committed only shameless acts when he fought, he drove himself to do well, yet wondered even as a platoon leader if a mystical cloud mercifully descended when a man truly faced mortality in battle.

Honor, the late critic and essayist Robert Warshow once suggested, was more inclusive than courage, virtue, or duty. "It is a style," he wrote, "concerned with harmonious appearances as much as desirable consequences. . . ."

Flint kicked three instructors out of West Point's History Department, relieving them because, in acting like alley cats rather than gentlemen, they'd offended his sense of propriety. Anderson still insists cadets measure up to high ethical standards, though many would suggest Anderson's notion of honor is out of touch with the changes American society has undergone since at least the inception of the Vietnam War. Yet honor was also what compelled Nadal to insist that his medic treat wounded VC in the Bong Son, though his medic had lost close friends in the battle of the Ia Drang. "Everything's fair up to the time you're in control of another human being," Nadal spelled out his faith. "Then he's your responsibility."

Ideally, one third of an officer's career is spent in command, another third in staff work, and a final third in attending various schools. The men in this book all loved command; some hinted they were even willing to put up with the other two thirds precisely for the chance to command. Most seemed to have tolerated staff work, as long as it wasn't in the Pentagon, which most of them hated. The civilian schools they'd attended to earn advanced degrees broadened them as officers and citizens, as well as helped make them more effective in a more sophisticated and technical Army than was the case before Vietnam. And the Army schools, such as the Command and General Staff College and the Army War College, prepared them for higher command. It was there, too, that an officer intimately learned of his peers' weaknesses and strengths. "These schools are valuable, but the main thing is not what's coming off the platform," said one of them who asked not to be quoted by name. "The important thing is you learn who you do and don't want on your flank in a shooting situation. For instance, you learn who can handle his liquor and who can handle his wife. And you don't want a guy on your flank who needs a drink all hours of the day or who's going to be so concerned by woman troubles he's going to forget there's an enemy out there looking to do us all in."

It was Vietnam, a war America lost, that particularly tested these men. No surprise Vietnam was for many of them a demoralizing experience. Yet they were able to persevere, sustaining more than twenty-year military careers.

The crucial historical reason explaining their perseverance, I think, is that America was still perceived as a power to reckon with after Vietnam, despite those who said the country then fielded a hollow Army. Had the defeat in Vietnam been generally seen as irredeemably damaging, there's little doubt a number of younger officers would have resigned their commissions soon after 1975.

A second reason accounting for their success and perseverance is an undiluted ambition just about all of them clearly demonstrated. Walk in the corridors of Root Hall, the hub of the Army War College, and you can practically feel the electrical impulses emitted by its students. These are light colonels who'd recently succeeded in battalion command. They wouldn't be at Carlisle if the opposite were true. Almost all will soon be promoted to colonel. Plus a third will go on to make general. You'd have to be plastic not to be able to taste further advancement, and you'd have to be plastic to be able to conceal the fact that you dream about it every other night.

A third reason is that before, during, and after the war, but especially during the war, these men performed bravely and effectively. When the bullets were real, *their* platoons, *their* companies, *their* battalions won, not lost their battles. Concomitantly, Lyndon Johnson may have shot his wad for strictly political purposes to ensure, say, that Khe Sanh didn't turn into a Dien Bien Phu; but because it didn't, officers like Taylor and DeFrancisco, sent to Khe Sanh to relieve the besieged Marines, could later tell themselves for a reason they might not have been aware of at the time. It wasn't our fault America was unable to impose its will. Our units didn't blow it.

Nor was the fact they didn't blow it ignored later on. Consider that when American troops were dispatched to Grenada, the first group of Rangers to jump in was led by Wes Taylor. At the same time, Tex Turner was head man at the Army's toughest training school. And less than a year before, Rod Paschall was commander of DELTA, the elite unit stationed at Fort Bragg that is trained to rescue hostages. Hardly the kind of command given to an officer who hadn't operated successfully in the past. " 'Make the other son of a bitch die, but you be careful' " were Paschall's watchwords throughout his years in Southeast Asia. And I think they would be again, given the appropriate circumstances, both for Paschall and for a number of the others found in these pages.

While history, ambition, and prior success accounted for part of their resiliency, what counted for most, I believe, was a receptivity from the beginning to what the Army offered, a receptivity cultivated at West Point. The colonels in this book found life in the military unique and meaningful. And handed a new cup containing a different assignment every two or three years, most drank deeply of it. It was the Army that kept offering those vessels, and that's why most of them love the Army. And while most suffered anguish because of the country's defeat in Vietnam, the intense satisfactions they've experienced performing as officers over the years seem to have outstripped by far that anguish. The undramatic truth is, life did not stop for these men, as it seems to have done for others, with Vietnam.

Not too long ago, I walked to the nearest bus stop up at the Academy and waited for an Army bus that would drop me off in front of the Thayer Hotel, where I'd reserved a room for the night. It was late afternoon, early February, and dusk was descending on West Point. Snow covered the ground and the air was sharp, penetrating. Not another soul seemed to be around, nor did I see a single car, and the enveloping silence had the strange, poetic quality of an immense stillness.

To my immediate front stretched a vast field, two, three, maybe four football fields in length—it was impossible to gauge with precision in the darkening afternoon. I guessed it was "The Plain," that huge parade ground upon which the Corps had always marched so impressively.

Standing in the cold, I tried to keep warm by thinking the first thing that came to mind as I pictured the face of each of the twelve I'd gotten to know.

First, I thought of the two no longer in the Army. Nadal, a controversial officer, admired by some, despised by others, who, opening a coffee-table book of the 1st Cav, spoke about the officers and soldiers he'd served with in the Ia Drang, articulating an intensity and tenderness most men reserve for members of their family. As for Nye, the farthest he wished to move, upon resigning his commission, was, in the end, to a bluff within easy walking distance of the Academy's beckoning gates.

I thought next of those still at West Point—Flint, Turner, and Anderson.

Flint, the adopted son who, though not an Academy graduate, was appointed its dean and now sits at one end of the long table in the hushed Academic Board room, opposite the superintendent.

I saw a black and gold Ranger tab when I thought of Tex Turner, remembering how cold it was during the winter of 1959 when he'd attended Ranger School, but how warm he felt twenty-odd years later upon learning he'd been appointed its honcho.

Mrs. Dornbirer *was* a saint, and the foods she'd made but never kept the recipes of were transcendent forms of nourishment, ennobling Anderson's unusually saddened boyhood.

Who else but Nash would drop by my apartment when he was visiting New York to check me out as he'd checked out Vessey's personnel records at the Pentagon? We went to the Russian Tea Room, where you outdrank me that Sunday afternoon, Bill, absolutely took me to the cleaners. But maybe there'll be another afternoon, and we'll just have to wait and see how New York fares next time.

I thought of Timboe and his brother spending a year together at the Academy, and I remembered the squeaky sound the Diet Pepsi can made pressed between Boone's hands as he spoke of Cassandra, the light of his life.

Five minutes after being in Paschall's humongous office, I said to myself, "My God, I've landed a gold mine." The stories flowed, one richer than the next. But what I recall most vividly was Paschall's reclusive attempt to burn Southeast Asia out of his system by running marathons and studying Chinese at forty-four.

I couldn't help smiling when I pictured Wes Taylor joyously leaping to his feet upon learning he'd soon be sprung from the frustrations of toiling in the Pentagon.

When Ruderman said the best part of being assigned to the War College was that Carlisle was within driving distance of his parents' and how wonderful it was getting to know his seventy-four-year-old father again, I remembered thinking, "Screw his crazy ties, there's a dude who's got his priorities straight."

Is that twelve? Let's see, no, I seem to be missing one. Boone, Paschall, Taylor, Tex, Joe . . . Joe! Joe DeFrancisco, who'd wanted to teach at the Academy, one reason being he'd had problems talking to people growing up and thought teaching might help him overcome his difficulty. Why do I find that so engaging? Because I, too, had had problems talking to people growing up? Nor will I again fail to consider the military wives left behind. Only why hadn't their isolation and particular anguish ever occurred to me before?

Jesus, but it was cold that afternoon at West Point. When the wind picked up, I lifted my collar and tried to shrink within the protective confines of my slightly tattered trench coat. Air resembling smoke kept venting from my mouth, as if in mute protest. After a while, God must have taken pity, because I could see in the distance to my left a lumbering bus circling the roadway bordering the farthest rim of "The Plain." My feet were hurting as the temperature kept sinking, and I watched the bus with greedy eyes. When it came to a full stop still two football fields away, my heart nearly dropped. For a brief moment the bus seemed as frozen in silence as each of the scattered monuments gazing out upon the vast, blue parade ground. Then, shuddering to life, it started again. A bugle call, martial yet forlorn, rose across the field, sounding what, retreat? I no longer remembered. Turning, the bus's two yellow headlights swung my way.

Acknowledgments

I would like to thank my dear friend and agent, Candida Donadio, who thought combining West Point and Vietnam was a winning idea from the first day, and persisted in her belief though a good number of editors disagreed.

The one who didn't, Alan Williams, improved upon my original notion, suggesting I not only write about the effects West Point had upon its graduates who fought in Vietnam but also describe the changes that took place at the Academy as a result of that war.

I'm grateful, too, to Arbor House's Andy Dutter. He never failed to return my calls, and his informed responses invariably proved helpful.

Also to be thanked is Col. Jack Yeagley, West Point's public-affairs officer when I first started researching this book, who offered his immediate patronage. Besides opening doors at West Point, Yeagley suggested I visit the Army War College.

There I dealt with Col. Nick Hawthorne, the public-affairs officer at Carlisle. He and his assistant, Mrs. Virginia Giordano, could not have been kinder or more amusing, a wonderful combination.

The people who let me interview them were far more generous

than I would have been in their place, and it is a pleasure to thank them formally by name: Col. Howie Boone, Col. Rod Paschall, Col. Wes Taylor, Col. Tex Turner, Lynne and Col. Joe DeFrancisco, Brig. Gen. Roy Flint, Lt. Col. Gill Ruderman, Billie and Col. (Ret.) Tony Nadal, Lt. Col. Bill Nash, Col. (Ret.) Roger Nye, Donna and Col. Hal Timboe, and Col. Jim Anderson.

My buddies Mario Puzo, Jack Leiser, and Mel Shestack have been so unswervingly loyal and encouraging over the years, it may seem I take their friendship for granted. But I know, even if they might not, that their fraternal support never meant more to me than when I was working on this book.

Moody, compulsive husbands are not the easiest to put up with under the best of circumstances. Not only was my wife Crede almost always cheerful and patient during the past two years, but she also was first reader and critic of innumerable drafts, hardly the most enviable of jobs. No wonder the book is dedicated to her, and to the memory of my parents and a cherished uncle who died in 1947. He was forty, I was eleven. I thought the world had come to an end.